# A Tempest of Iron and Lead

## Spotsylvania Court House, May 8–21, 1864

Chris Mackowski

SB

Savas Beatie
California

First edition, first printing

Library of Congress Cataloging-in-Publication Data

Names: Mackowski, Chris, author.
Title: A Tempest of Iron and Lead : Spotsylvania Court House, May 8-21, 1864 / by Chris Mackowski.
Other titles: Season of Slaughter | Spotsylvania Court House, May 8-21, 1864
Description: El Dorado Hills, CA : Savas Beatie, [2024] | Original title "A season of slaughter: the battle of Spotsylvania Court House, May 8-21, 1864" published by Savas Beatie in 2013. | Includes bibliographical references. | Summary: "May 1864. The Army of the Potomac and the Army of Northern Virginia spent three days in brutal close-quarter combat in the Wilderness that left the tangled thickets aflame. No one could imagine a more infernal battlefield. Then they marched down the road to Spotsylvania Court House. The author has crafted a meticulous and comprehensible study of this endlessly fascinating campaign. With nearly two decades of insight the author has created a readable and satisfying single-volume account of this campaign"-- Provided by publisher.
Identifiers: LCCN 2024026473 | ISBN 9781611217179 (hardcover) | ISBN 9781611217186 (ebook)
Subjects: LCSH: Spotsylvania Court House, Battle of, Va., 1864.
Classification: LCC E476.52 .M34 2024 | DDC 973.7/36--dc23/eng/20240613
LC record available at https://lccn.loc.gov/2024026473

SB

Savas Beatie
989 Governor Drive, Suite 102
El Dorado Hills, CA 95762
916-941-6896 / sales@savasbeatie.com / www.savasbeatie.com

All of our titles are available at special discount rates for bulk purchases in the United States. Contact us for information.

Printed and bound in the United Kingdom

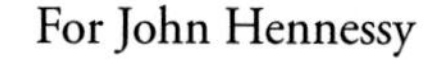

For John Hennessy

*The Bloody Angle* by N. C. Wyeth, from Mary Johnston's novel *The Long Roll.* Author's Collection

# Table of Contents

# Table of Contents

*continued*



*Photos have been added throughout the text for the convenience of the reader.*

# List of Maps

*Maps by Edward Alexander*

# List of Maps

*continued*

# A Note About the Language

Soldier spelling was wildly inconsistent when it came to locations. The correct spelling of "Spotsylvania" has only one "t," but soldiers frequently used two: "Spottsylvania." I have left spellings as they originally appeared. Similarly, soldiers wrote "Court House," "Court-house," and "Courthouse." If referring to the county seat, the correct spelling is "Court House" (the village that houses the court), although soldiers hyphenated the spelling, as well, which I have left uncorrected. "Courthouse," as one word, refers to the building where court is held.

In a few instances, I have directly quoted language from soldiers that may sound offensive to modern ears. I have tried to convey these men as they spoke, thought, and acted in and of their time.

Dialogue that appears in quotation marks has been quoted directly from a source. On occasion, where a source indirectly quotes a person's speech, I have opted to put that dialogue in *italics* rather than in quotation marks. That has allowed me to convey the sense of what a person said without misrepresenting their words as exact quotations.

This report, written in the midst of active operations, is scarcely more than a general sketch, and must necessarily be very defective from the absence of so many sub-reports and the loss of so many commanders whose information would have served as a guide in awarding credit by special mention to many gallant officers and men, both of those who fell and those who have survived through this eventful and unexampled campaign.

— John Gibbon, official report
*O.R.* Vol. 36, Pt. 1, Pg. 452

I never expect to be fully believed when I tell what I saw of the horrors of Spottsylvania, because I should be loth to believe it myself, were the case reversed.

— Thomas Worcester Hyde
*Following the Greek Cross*

# Foreword

*Gordon C. Rhea*

By the spring of 1864, Federal forces had won a string of victories in the Civil War's Western Theater. In the East, however, Maj. Gen. George G. Meade's Army of the Potomac had achieved little since defeating Gen. Robert E. Lee's Army of Northern Virginia at Gettysburg in July 1863. Desperate for military success in the East, President Abraham Lincoln placed newly promoted Lt. Gen. Ulysses S. Grant, architect of the Union's western triumphs, in charge of the nation's military.

The new general in chief planned for Federal forces in both theaters to move in tandem, fighting without quarter to destroy the Rebel armies. Grant determined to defeat Lee in Virginia by employing the same principles that governed his national strategy. Meade's army, marshalling some 119,000 soldiers against Lee's 66,000, was to cross the Rapidan River and attack Lee; the Army of the James, commanded by Maj. Gen. Benjamin F. Butler, was to advance up the James River, capture the Confederate capital of Richmond, and continue into Lee's rear; and a third Federal body, under Maj. Gen. Franz Sigel, was to threaten Lee's left flank and disrupt his supply lines by marching south through the Shenandoah Valley. In sum, Grant meant to crush Lee in a three-pronged vice.

The campaign opened the night of May 3 as the Potomac army moved across the Rapidan downriver from Lee, circumventing strong Confederate defenses. Meade intended to swing below the river toward Lee, passing through a forbidding forest of tangled second growth known as the Wilderness. However, he chose to halt for a day in the Wilderness to enable his supply wagons to catch up, a grave mistake that afforded Lee an opportunity to seize the initiative.

An 1887 illustration by Thure De Thulstrup, widely reproduced as a chromolithograph by Boston publisher L. Prang & Co., stands as the most famous depiction of the battle of Spotsylvania Court House. *Library of Congress*

---

Lee recognized the Army of the Potomac as his chief threat but was uncertain when and where it would cross the Rapidan. He also worried that he might have to dispatch part of his army to help protect Richmond. Accordingly, he posted cavalry along the Rapidan past each end of his fortified river line and awaited Grant's advance, keeping almost a third of his infantry several miles in the rear where it could rush to Richmond by rail if necessary. Above all, Lee determined to hold his position below the Rapidan. "If I am obliged to retire from this line," he cautioned the Richmond authorities, "either by flank movement of the enemy or want of supplies, great injury will befall us."

The resulting campaign involved 43 days of constant fighting and maneuvering that took the armies from the Rapidan to the James. Dubbed the Overland Campaign, the battles generated some 90,000 casualties and rank among the Civil War's bloodiest six consecutive weeks. Almost a third of the casualties occurred during the fighting near Spotsylvania Court House, one of the campaign's major battles and the topic of this book.

In the late 1970s, I became interested in the Overland Campaign and began visiting the battlefields. To my disappointment, I could find only one book-length treatment of the campaign's opening confrontation in the Wilderness and nothing at all covering in detail the subsequent fighting at Spotsylvania Court House, the North Anna River, Cold Harbor, or the maneuvers to Petersburg. Since then, several historians have labored to fill that void. The first book dedicated to Spotsylvania Court House was William D. Matter's *If It Takes All Summer: The Battle of Spotsylvania*, published in 1988. My *Battles of Spotsylvania Court House and the Road to Yellow Tavern, May 7–12, 1864* appeared in 1997, and Chris Mackowski and Kristopher D. White's *A Season of Slaughter: The Battle of Spotsylvania Court House, May 8–22, 1864* appeared in 2013. Jeffry D. Wert's *The Heart of Hell: The Soldiers' Struggle for Spotsylvania's Bloody Angle* came out in 2022.

Chris Mackowski's *A Tempest of Iron and Lead: Spotsylvania Court House, May 8-21, 1864* is the latest book to grapple with the horror and complexity of the fighting around Spotsylvania Court House. He brings fresh insight to the topic, having conducted numerous tours of the pertinent sites, written scores of articles and a previous book about the battle, and delivered a multitude of talks interpreting the campaign. He has not only uncovered new sources, but his sparkling prose brings the participants to life, be they generals or the commonest of soldiers. He also introduces us to local residents, such as Sarah Spindle and her family, who found themselves caught in an open field between the two contending armies and fled for their lives as their home burst into flames.

*A Tempest of Iron and Lead* is an engaging and entertaining read that adds to our knowledge of this fascinating battle.

# Prologue

John D. Starbird stood with his face to the provost guard, his back to his grave. His yet-empty coffin sat next to the yet-empty hole in the earth. Several yards in front of him, a captain was passing out rifles—seven loaded with ball cartridges and one with just a flash of gunpowder. Each man in the firing squad could ease his conscience, if he needed to, by telling himself that *his* was rifle loaded with the blank. *He* had not gunned down a fellow soldier in cold blood, even as an act of duty, even if the man was guilty.

But deception was perhaps the order of the day. The men of the 19th Massachusetts Infantry's Company K knew the man standing in front of his own grave as John D. Starbird, but he'd gone by Lawrence J. Hoyt, too. A Boston native, he was only 21 when he enlisted in the regiment back in September 1861. Sometime in the spring of 1862, he had slipped away and later joined another regiment, getting a bounty for doing so—and "in a short time joined still another getting another bounty." Someone finally rounded him up, though. A court-martial tried and sentenced him, but "upon the urgent solicitation of his mother, he was pardoned by the President." In the years ahead, as the story of his death was told and retold, that detail always survived the telling, even if other details went missing or changed: John D. Starbird was pardoned by President Lincoln. And Starbird squandered it.[1]

1 Gordon Rhea, *The Battles for Spotsylvania Court House and the Road to Yellow Tavern, May 7–12, 1864* (Baton Rouge, LA: LSU Press, 1997), 421n65. Rhea credits work done by National Park Service historian Eric Mink; Earnest Linden Waitt, *History of the Nineteenth Regiment, Massachusetts Volunteer Infantry, 1861–1865* (Salem, MA: Salem Press, 1906), 316; John Day Smith, *The History of the Nineteenth Regiment of Maine Volunteer Infantry, 1862–1865* (Minneapolis, Great Western printing company, 1909), 172.

In February and March 1864, the 19th Massachusetts returned to its native Salem for a 30-day furlough. During the regiment's time home, Starbird and two other deserters were reunited with their original unit and shipped with them back to the front. "The charges against him had been placed on file on condition that he serve faithfully to the end of the war," regimental historian John Adams later noted.[2]

Starbird's faithful service lasted until the battle of the Wilderness. There, on May 7, in the heat of the battle and the burning forest, Starbird "desert[ed] his post and the colors of his regiment while engaged with the enemy."[3]

He slunk his way back, though, and was with his regiment as it marched to Spotsylvania Court House on May 8, as it crossed the Po River on May 9, and it faced enemy fire on May 10—and Starbird fled again. "[T]he soldier's courage failed him and . . . he did not advance with his regiment," one witness said.[4]

Another court-martial. No intervention from mother this time. No presidential pardon. Instead, on May 17, General Order 127 from Army of the Potomac headquarters: "Corps and division commanders will bring to immediate trial the deserters from the battle-field now being returned to the army. . . ." Commanders were to forward trial results, without delay, for the commanding general's endorsement so that "no time may be lost in inflicting summary punishment for this disgraceful crime."[5]

The hunt was on for "skulks and stragglers."[6]

"At that time," said a man from Starbird's regiment, "there were in the ranks of every regiment, men who had no interest in the cause. They had enlisted for the bounty, and did not intend to render any service. They not only shirked duty, but their acts and conversation were demoralizing good men."

The problem had become "so serious an evil as to excite the attention of everyone," said II Corps division commander Brig. Gen. John Gibbon. The problem, as Gibbon saw it, was that no one did anything about it, and so "the evil continued and even increased." He painted a picture of the "more faithful" men

2 John Gregory Bishop Adams, *Reminiscences of the Nineteenth Massachusetts Regiment* (Boston, Wright & Potter printing company, 1899), 94.

3 Charles H. Banes, *History of the Philadelphia Brigade: Sixty-Ninth, Seventy-First, Seventy-Second, and One Hundred and Sixth Pennsylvania Volunteers* (Philadelphia: J. B. Lippincott & Co., 1876), 258.

4 Smith, 172.

5 General Orders No. 127, *The War of the Rebellion: A Compilation of the Official Records of the Union and Confederate Armies*, Robert N. Scott, ed. (Wilmington, NC: Broadfoot Publishing Company, 1985), Vol. 36, Pt. 2, 843. Hereafter, the *Official Records* shall be abbreviated as *O.R.*, with volume, part, and page listed thus: *O.R.*, 36:2:843.

6 Birney, circular, *O.R.*, 36:2:912.

doing the hard work in combat while shirkers, slinking away from battle, "literally filled" the roads behind the lines.[7]

Major General David Bell Birney, another II Corps division commander, agreed with Gibbon. "Summary punishment should at once be inflicted on all such men," he ordered. A "pale, Puritanical figure, with a demeanor of unmoveable coldness," Birney predicted "a beneficial effect" from such punishments, carried out in front of each guilty man's regiment to make an example of him. In addition to a loss of month's pay, Birney suggested other "punishments sanctioned by usage, such as tying up, placarding, riding wooden horses, &c. . . ."[8]

Starbird served in Gibbon's division, and he was being served up as just such an example as Birney had suggested—although Gibbon, for his part, had an even harsher example in mind: he recommended that courts-martial "inflict in every clear case the penalty of death, in order to save life and maintain the efficiency of the army." Gibbon saw Starbird's case as especially flagrant, all the more so because Starbird came from "one of the best regiments in my division."[9]

Starbird's court convened on May 19 on the edge of the woods near division headquarters. Proceedings were of "the most summary character, the main point being to establish the guilt of the accused." Gibbon, of grizzled face and long moustache, reminded the court: "The fact that a man is sent back under guard to his regiment after a battle, and is unable to show any authority for his absence, ought to be sufficient for his conviction."[10]

Witnesses swore in. The court took testimony, though kept no record. It reached a verdict and handed down a sentence. Everything was duly noted and signed.

The court acquitted Starbird of the charge of cowardice in the Wilderness, but found him guilty of the charge on the Po River. "[T]he man was *in the habit of running away* every time the regiment went into action," wrote an incredulous Gibbon.[11]

Army of the Potomac commander George Gordon Meade returned his approval. "The major-general commanding is determined to exercise the utmost rigor of the law in punishing those cowards who disgrace their colors by basely deserting them in the presence of the enemy," his adjutant wrote.[12]

7 John Gibbon, *Recollections of the Civil War* (New York: G. P Putnam & Sons, 1928), 223.

8 Theodore Lyman, *Meade's Headquarters, 1863–1865: Letters of Colonel Theodore Lyman from the Wilderness to Appomattox*, George R. Agassiz, ed. (Freeport, NY: Books for Libraries Press, 1922), 266.

9 Banes, 257; Gibbon, 223.

10 Banes, 256–7.

11 Gibbon, 224.

12 Banes, 258.

The execution of John Starbird would have looked much like the depiction of this execution in January 1862 in Alexandria, Virginia. Starbird's was particularly remarkable in that it took place during active field operations—an unprecedented event. *The Illustrated London News*

---

At 7:00 a.m. on May 20, a provost guard marched the blindfolded Starbird to his waiting grave. Starbird appeared stoic. "The behavior of this prisoner at his death-scene seemed to give a denial to the specifications against him," noted Col. Charles H. Banes, assistant adjutant-general of the brigade. "He walked unsupported in front of the firing party to the place appointed for the execution."

The entire brigade assembled in formation to watch the example being made on their behalf. Eight men from the 19th Massachusetts comprised the firing squad. Captain Dudley C. Mumford loaded their rifles and distributed them.

*Sit,* someone told Starbird. He lowered himself onto the edge of his coffin, next to the open grave.

Mumford readied his men. Then "Aim!" Then "Fire!"

"Oh, my poor mother!" Starbird cried.

Six shots struck him near the heart; the seventh musket "hung fire," and the ball entered his leg. The eighth musket eased consciences.

Starbird died at once.

"May 20th, 7:08 a.m.," Gibbon noted in his journal. "He is just shot."[13]

Colonel Banes described the execution as "an example of military severity"—but one that achieved its desired effect. "Men who had straggled and kept out of battle now were in the ranks," said a man from the brigade, "and the result to our corps alone was as good as if we had been re-enforced by a full regiment."[14]

"[T]hose who witnessed it," he added, "will never forget."[15]

* * *

By the morning of Starbird's execution, May 20, the Federal II Corps had reported 12,839 casualties in the spring campaign thus far—and that number may have been underreported. Another of the army's commanders, Maj. Gen. Gouverneur K. Warren of the V Corps, had fudged casualty reports just two weeks earlier in the Wilderness, worried that no one would be able to handle the truth. "It will never do . . ." Warren said, "to make a showing of such heavy losses." Under a similar shroud, it's possible the II Corps may have lost as many as 16,000 men. The entire Army of the Potomac had, by that point, lost as many as 36,065 men.[16]

In the statistical context of such calamity, what was one more man?

Instead, perhaps better to ask: *Why* one more man?

The Army of the Potomac had undergone metamorphosis during the previous winter. Where seven army corps had combined for victory at Gettysburg in July 1863, four began the 1864 spring campaign—and one of those corps didn't even belong to the army. Commanded by Maj. Gen. Ambrose Burnside, the IX Corps formally operated as an independent force working in conjunction with, but not subservient to, the Army of the Potomac. Of the corps from Gettysburg, two had been reassigned to the Western Theater and two, chewed up by casualties, had to be consolidated into the remaining three as part of an army reorganization in late winter. Only two of the victorious corps commanders still retained their positions.

On the regimental level, Pvt. Wilbur Fisk of the 2nd Vermont noted the changing character of the army. "We have five distinct classes of recruits," he wrote. Historian Carol Reardon summarized them: "the initial volunteers of 1861; new recruits in the spring of 1862; additional men from Lincoln's call for 300,000 more volunteers in the late summer of 1862; drafted men and substitutes of late

13 Gibbon, 224.

14 Adams, 94.

15 Smith, 172.

16 Morris Schaff, *The Battle of the Wilderness* (Boston: Houghton Mifflin Co., 1910), 210.

1863; and newly arrived recruits for the 1864 campaign." That last class, noted Fisk, "are those that have come here under the last call of the President."[17]

The enlistments of the army's initial recruits—by now battle-wizened veterans—would expire over the coming summer, draining much-needed experience from the army. The newer men, by contrast—often drafted against their will—represented a less-reliable class of soldier, both in experience and in willingness to be there at all. On paper, Federal forces would begin the spring campaign with 119,000 men, but the quality of those men varied wildly.

Confederates, on the other hand, would begin the campaign with 66,000 men, nearly all of them hardened by battle and the Confederacy's chronic lack of food and clothing. The Army of Northern Virginia needed every single one of those veterans. "I hope that few of the soldiers of this army will find it necessary at any time in the coming campaign to surrender themselves prisoners of war. We cannot spare brave men to fill Federal prisons," army commander Gen. Robert E. Lee told his men in an April circular.[18]

Like the North, the South had resorted to a draft to fill depleted ranks. A February 1864 Conscription Act made any male aged 17–50 eligible to serve through the end of the war—an age range widened from an earlier conscription window of 18–35, reflecting the Confederacy's growing desperation for men. Lee also tried to help the numbers crunch by offering a furlough to any soldier who could get a man to enlist.

To keep veterans in the ranks when their enlistments expired, the Confederate government offered a mix of carrots and sticks—sometimes successful, often coercive. A surgeon with the 19th Mississippi, Robert H. Peel, watched "whole Brigades" step forward to reenlist: "Men who have undergone all the hardships of a three years war, many of whom have wives and children at home and have not seen them since they enlisted, barefooted while the snow covers the earth, and with just sufficient food to keep them from actual starvation."[19]

Lee had focused much of his attention over the winter on supply issues. In his genteel but firm way, he worked the political levers of the Confederate president, the secretary of war, and the War Department, urging them to shake loose whatever

17 Wilbur Fisk, *Hard Marching Every Day: The Civil War Letters of Private Wilbur Fisk, 1861–1865*, Emil and Ruth Rosenblatt, eds. (Lawrence, KS: University of Kansas Press, 1992), 209; Carol Reardon, "A Hard Road to Travel: The Impact of Continuous Operations on the Army of the Potomac and the Army of Northern Virginia in May 1864," *The Spotsylvania Campaign*, Gary W. Gallagher, ed. (Chapel Hill, NC: University of North Carolina Press, 1998), 175.

18 Robert E. Lee, circular, *The Wartime Papers of Robert E. Lee*, Clifford Dowdey and Louis H. Manarin, eds. (New York: Da Capo, 1961), 693.

19 Robert H. Peel, letter, 17 February 1864; FSNMP BV.

they could from the Confederacy's dwindling stockpiles. "If I am obliged to retire from this line, either by a flank movement of the enemy or the want of supplies, great injury will befall us," he warned in mid-April.[20]

This 1865 portrait of Gen. Robert E. Lee invites examination. Is that determination in his eyes? A subtle challenge? Danger? Crankiness? Sorrow? Known as "the Marble Man," Lee's eyes are as expressive as they are inscrutable. All these things tugged within him as the spring 1864 campaign built to its open. *Library of Congress*

Lee even turned to his wife, in ill health, for assistance, urging her and her acquaintances to knit socks for the troops. "I am anxious to get as many socks now as possible, before active operations commence," he told her on April 9, 1864, at the tail end of a winter-long series of footwear-focused letters. That the commander of the South's most important army had to employ his sick wife to make socks for the troops suggests a remarkable if pitiful state of affairs for the Confederacy.[21]

Hopes across the South began to turn toward the fall election in the North. "Every bullet we can send against the Yankees is the best ballot that can be deposited against Abraham Lincoln's reelection," the *Augusta Constitutionalist* declared in January 1864, framing an intertwined political/military strategy for the coming year. "The battlefields of 1864 will hold the polls of the momentous decision." Southern leaders reasoned that if Lee and other army commanders could just hold on through the spring and summer, Northerners, stuck in stalemate and tired of war, would turn Lincoln out of office and elect a new president willing to sue for peace on the basis of Southern independence.[22]

20 Lee to Jefferson Davis, letter, 15 April 1864, *Wartime Papers of Robert E. Lee*, 700.

21 One year later to the day, he would be asking for surrender terms rather than socks.

22 *Augusta Constitutionalist*, 22 January 1864.

Lee's army hunkered down on the southern bank of the Rapidan River near Orange Court House, blocking a Federal advance along the Orange and Alexandria Railroad, which Federals depended on for their supplies. Lee had three army corps at his disposal, including the recently returned First Corps under Lt. Gen. James Longstreet, which had spent the winter on detached duty in East Tennessee. Lee was relieved to have his "Old Warhorse" back with him, particularly since his other two commanders, Lt. Gens. Richard Ewell and A. P. Hill, had proved lackluster.

North of the Rapidan, the Federal army occupied camps around Culpeper and Brandy Station. Meade's Army of the Potomac shook off its winter dust on May 3, but instead of going straight at Lee along the axis of the railroad, the Federals swung around the Confederate right. Their path took them into a 70-square-mile area of second-growth forest known as the Wilderness. Meade was under orders to be alert and be aggressive: "If any opportunity presents itself to pitching into a part of Lee's army, do so without giving time for dispositions."[23]

Opportunity presented itself on the morning of May 5. An advantageous lookout station atop Clark's Mountain allowed Lee to spot the Federal move and respond almost immediately. As Meade's army advanced into the Wilderness, lead elements of Lee's army materialized near the head of their column. As ordered—albeit with some delay—the Federals pitched in. Lee, not fully ready for the fight, held on while the rest of his army rushed to the battlefield.

Fighting raged through the Wilderness on May 5, intensified on May 6, and devolved into skirmishes and potshots on May 7. "And who can describe the fighting that was done there . . ." asked the regimental historian of the 150th Pennsylvania volunteers.

> [N]ot on the open field, face to face with the enemy . . . but amid the densely tangled brushwood and in the ravines and glens of the Wilderness the conflict raged, and the thunders of the artillery, the fierce shrieking of the shells, and the sharp rattle of musketry, all combined, echoed and re-echoed, making the scene one horrid saturnalia of sound, that might well have been copied from Dante's Inferno; while the smoke of battle, unlimned by one ray of sunlight, settled down like a dark funereal pall upon the scene, and all through this horrid, ensanguined ground the dead and dying lay. . . . Like the leaves of autumn they covered the crimsoned ground. . . .[24]

23 Grant to Meade, 5 May 1864, *O.R.* 36:2:403.

24 Kate M. Scott, *History of the One Hundred and Fifth Regiment of Pennsylvania Volunteers: A Complete History of the Organization, Marches, Battles, Toils, and Dangers participated in by the regiment from the beginning to the close of the war, 1861–1865* (Philadelphia: NewWorld Publishing Company, 1877).

Men stacked the bodies of dead comrades around them as makeshift fortifications to protect themselves as they blazed away at each other through the foliage and powder smoke. Wounded men, roused by the "hot breath" of forest fires, "dragged themselves along, with their torn and mangled limbs, in the mad energy of despair, to escape the ravages of the flames . . ." said one Federal officer. "Christian men had turned to fiends, and hell itself had usurped the place of earth."[25]

During three days of fighting in the Wilderness, Federal forces lost 17,666 men. Confederates lost 11,033. In terms of percentages, that was nearly 15 percent for Federals and nearly 17 percent for Confederates.[26]

In the wake of such a bloodletting, the armies typically disengaged and fell back to lick their wounds. They took time to reinforce, reequip, and reload. But for the Army of the Potomac, there would be no turning back. The Wilderness would become one of the turning points of the Civil War because the very nature of the war, and how the armies fought it, was about to change significantly. There would be no pause.

In the midst of this unfolding catastrophe, it bears asking why Private Starbird would run from the battlefield, not once but twice in a four-day span, knowing he was on probation. Starbird had a history of jumping, so perhaps we need look no further than that for an explanation. But the nature of the fighting, once it erupted, was unlike anything men in either army had experienced before. Yes, they had seen brutal combat and dense, dark woods and raging forest fires and nighttime fighting and field fortifications, but they had never seen all of it together, sustained for days and days that would blur into exhausted weeks.

In that sense, Starbird's tendency to slip away from the fight when he could no longer hold up did not fit, metaphorically speaking, with the Army of the Potomac's new way of operating.

This campaign was turning into something else entirely.

25 Horace Porter, *Campaigning with Grant* (New York: Mallard Press, 1991), 73.

26 Thomas L. Livermore, *Numbers and Losses in the Civil War in America, 1861–1865* (Boston: Houghton, Mifflin, and Company, 1900), 110–11.

May 4

May 5

May 6

May 7

# May 8

As the late-night hours of May 7, 1864, ticked past midnight into the early hours of May 8, Maj. Gen. George Gordon Meade headed into new territory. For three days, his Federal Army of the Potomac had grappled with the Confederate Army of Northern Virginia in the dense tangle of second-growth brush known as the Wilderness. "Forbidding," "simply infernal," "a region of gloom and a shadow of death," "one of the waste places of nature"—such were the descriptions soldiers gave to "the dark, close wood."[1]

Meade's infantry had struggled to move with alacrity through the thick foliage. His artillery had few open platforms to effectively deploy. His cavalry had limited roads on which to maneuver. "It is impossible to conceive a field worse adapted to the movements of a grand army," wrote a Federal officer.[2]

Indeed, the wily Gen. Robert E. Lee had utilized the terrain to his advantage, nullifying the superior numbers of the Federals. Thus unable leverage any advantage against them, Meade's army disengaged. But instead of withdrawing to resupply and reinforce—a process that often led to months of delay before another engagement—the Federal army did something it had never done before: it marched around the Confederates, intent on outflanking them to draw them out of the protection of the Wilderness.

1 For these and additional descriptions of the Wilderness, see chapter two of Chris Mackowski, *Hell Itself: The Battle of the Wilderness, May 5-7, 1864* (El Dorado Hills, CA: Savas Beatie, 2016).

2 William Swinton, *Campaigns of the Army of the Potomac; a critical history of operations in Virginia, Maryland and Pennsylvania, from the commencement to the close of the war, 1861–5* (New York: C. B. Richardson,1882), 428.

The Brock Road/Plank Road intersection in the Wilderness became the site of one of the Civil War's major turning points on the evening of May 7, 1864. Rather than disengage to end the battle, the Army of the Potomac would shift positions and continue fighting. Artist Edwin Forbes captured the scene. *Library of Congress*

---

With swaths of the forest ablaze around them, Meade rode among a small gaggle of officers and staffers to the Brock Road/Plank Road intersection, the scene of the Wilderness's most intense combat. A turn northeast up the Plank Road meant a retreat to the safety of Fredericksburg or, perhaps, a return to Culpeper on the far side of the Rapidan River. Instead, the group pointed southeast, down the Brock Road.

The Federal Army was not ending its offensive: it was continuing to take the fight to the enemy.

"Soldiers weary and sleepy after their long battle, with stiffened limbs and smarting wounds, now sprang to their feet, forgetful of their pains, and rushed forward to the roadside," recalled Horace Porter, a Federal staff officer. "Wild cheers echoed through the forest, and glad shouts of triumph rent the air." Men swung their hats, tossed up their arms, and clapped their hands.[3] No matter how brutal the fight had been, there was no turning back.

Speed and secrecy were the keys to the next stage of the offensive. The Brock Road ran roughly north/south, and the Federal II Corps manned the earthworks

3 Porter, 79.

that lined the road. Behind their protective screen, the V Corps marched southward along the road. Once the column passed beyond the end of the works, the V Corps threw out flankers to protect its Confederate-facing right flank. "Plunging into the mysterious gloom of a deep cut and washed out road, men occasionally tumbled into rocky furrows, or stumbled over carcasses," wrote a Marylander. "At intervals, darkness would be made visible on the right by blazing brands dropping from some distant tree trunk, still aglow in the depth of the Wilderness, like a signal-light of goblins. The low, damp air, reeked with the pungent, acrid snuff of horse and human slaughter."[4]

The Brock Road twisted through the dark countryside toward the heart of Spotsylvania County. "[T]he road was narrow, and the trees made it very dark," wrote Maj. Abner Small of the 16th Maine. "[I]t was a desolate and dismal track." From the head of the column, men whispered down the line to "jump the run" and "look out for the log," recalled Charles Davis of the 13th Massachusetts, noting they had cautionary orders not to lose connection with each other, or to step out of the path. The men looked like shadows walking through deeper shadows, Davis wrote, with "every lighted pipe being distinctly seen in the darkness."[5]

As the column marched away from the Wilderness, the country became more open, but Porter noticed "it still presented obstacles of a most formidable nature. . . . The country was undulating, and was at that time broken by alternations of cleared spaces and dense forests."[6]

Twelve miles away waited Spotsylvania Court House, the quiet county seat. "The village itself consisted of perhaps a dozen buildings, partially concealed behind a grove of pine woods," wrote Col. Byron Cutcheon of the 20th Michigan. "A weather-beaten court house, a typical Virginia country tavern, a couple of small churches, and a few weather-stained dwellings made up this world-famous hamlet." Near the courthouse building itself, the Brock Road intersected with the Fredericksburg Road before meandering past Sanford's Hotel on its way south toward the Confederate capital. Meade intended to be in the village by 8:00 a.m. to capture control of the road network that flowed in and out, thus giving him the

4 L. A. Wolmer, *History and Roster of Maryland Volunteers, War 1861-1865* (Baltimore: Guggenheimer, Weil and Col, 1880), 269-270.

5 Abner Small, *The Road to Richmond: The Civil War Letters of Major Abner Small of the 16th Maine Volunteers*, Harold Adams Small, ed. (New York: Fordham University Press, 2000), 135; Charles Davis, *Three years in the army. The story of the Thirteenth Massachusetts Volunteers from July 16, 1861, to August 1, 1864* (Boston: Estes and Lauriat, 1894), 332; Charles Wainwright, *A Diary of Battle*, Allan Nevins, ed. (New York: Da Capo, 1998), 355.

6 Porter, 88.

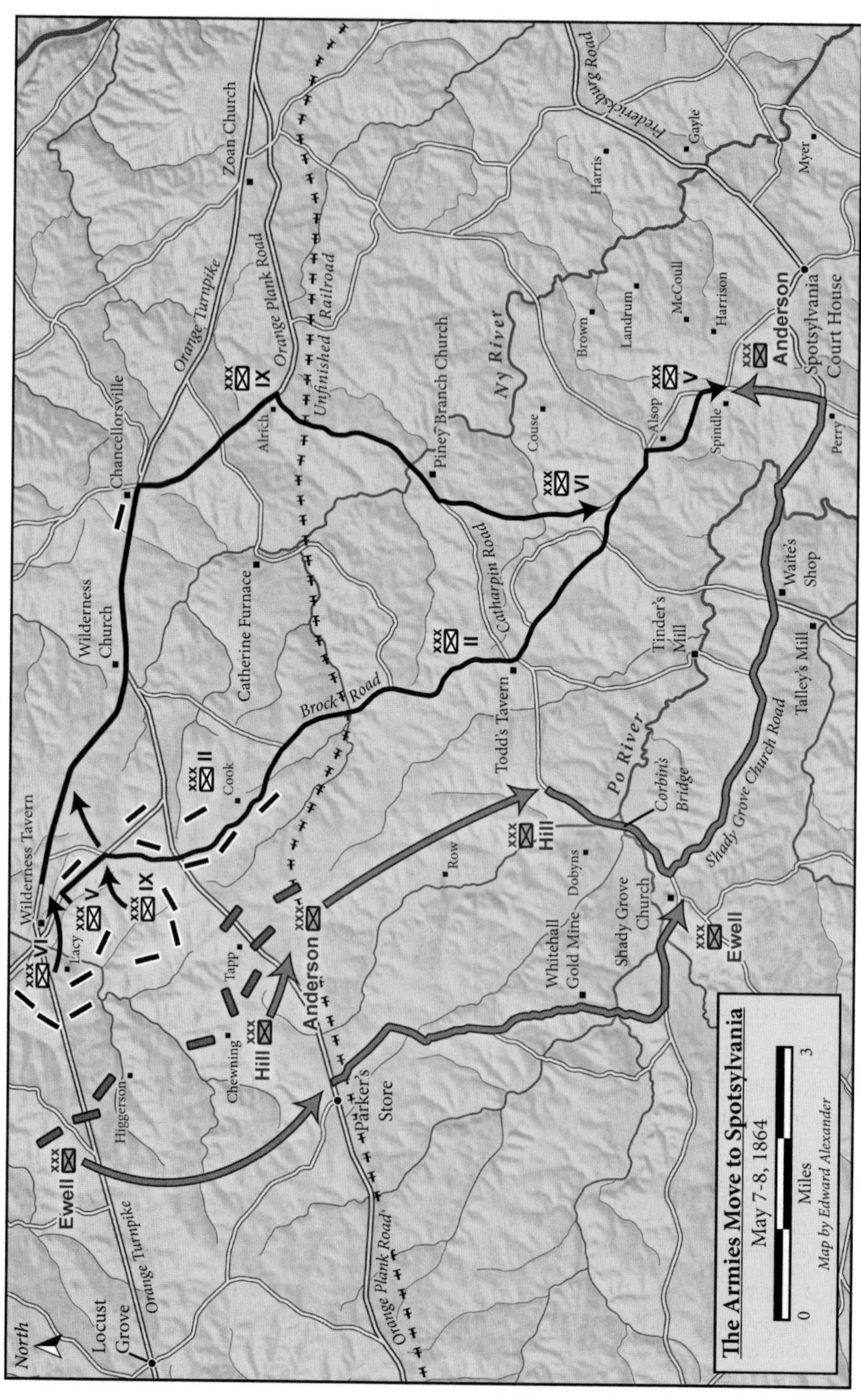
The Armies Move to Spotsylvania
May 7-8, 1864
0 Miles 3
Map by Edward Alexander
North
Locust Grove
Orange Turnpike
Orange Plank Road
Ewell
Higgerson
Chewning
Hill
Parker's Store
Anderson
Tapp
Lacy
Wilderness Tavern
VI
V
IX
II
Cook
Wilderness Church
Catherine Furnace
Chancellorsville
Orange Turnpike
Orange Plank Road
Zoan Church
Unfinished Railroad
Alrich
Brock Road
Row
Dobyns
Whitehall Gold Mine
Shady Grove Church
Todd's Tavern
Corbin's Bridge
Po River
Shady Grove Church Road
Catharpin Road
Piney Branch Church
Tinder's Mill
Talley's Mill
Waite's Shop
Couse
Ny River
Alsop
Spindle
Perry
Spotsylvania Court House
Brown
Landrum
McCoull
Harrison
Harris
Gayle
Myer
Fredericksburg Road

**The Armies Move to Spotsylvania**—On the night of May 7–8, 1864, the Army of Northern Virginia had twice as far to march as the Army of the Potomac, in some cases along roads the Confederates had to create from scratch. Effective delaying tactics by the Confederate cavalry bought the necessary time for their infantry to make the march in time, blocking the Federal advance into Spotsylvania Court House.

---

inside track to Richmond and a number of options for prosecuting the next phase of the campaign against the Confederate army.[7]

To ensure swift passage, Meade had sent his cavalry—under the command of Maj. Gen. Phillip Sheridan—to clear the Brock Road in advance of the infantry column now coming down the road with Meade. Sheridan sent back a rosy update. "I have the honor to report that I attacked the rebel cavalry at Todd's Tavern . . ." he gloated, "[and] drove them in confusion toward Spotsylvania Court-House." Todd's Tavern, a one-and-a-half story wayside inn, sat at the Brock Road's intersection with Catharpin Road, which ran along a northeast/southwest axis. The roads met on the southeast fringe of the Wilderness about halfway between the Brock Road/Plank Road intersection and the county seat.[8]

Events at Todd's Tavern had not gone smoothly for the Federal cavalry, and Sheridan either intentionally misled Meade or possessed little grasp of the tactical situation. Hours of fighting had failed to dislodge their Confederate counterparts from the road. Instead, Confederate merely fell back along the Catharpin Road and blocked the road near Corbin's Bridge over the Po River. A push by Federals in that direction would have taken them to the right flank of the Confederate army. Unbeknownst to Sheridan, Lee had ordered a road cut south from the Wilderness to the vicinity of Corbin's Bridge as a makeshift escape hatch.

Another portion of the Confederate cavalry fell back along Brock Road, blocking it roughly one mile south of Todd's Tavern, some four miles north of the courthouse intersection. "Our Brigade dismounted and went in on Foot . . ." recalled John Inglis of the 9th New York Cavalry. "[Q]uite a number of dead Rebs lying along the road [and] a good many of our officers wounded." A Pennsylvania trooper declared the day was filled with "[v]ery heavy skirmishing."[9]

7 Byron M. Cutcheon, *The Story of the Twentieth Michigan infantry, July 15th, 1862, to May 30th, 1865* (Lansing, MI: R. Smith Printing Co., 1904). According to the 1860 census, the county had a population of 16,076: 8,290 free residents and 7,786 enslaved.

8 Philip H. Sheridan to George G. Meade, *O.R.* 36:2:515.

9 Inglis, diary, 7 May 1864, Fredericksburg and Spotsylvania National Military Park Bound Manuscript Volume 394. Hereafter, the park's collection will be abbreviated as FSNMP BV394; Capt. Isaac H. Ressler, diary, FSNMP BV 42.

Sheridan's exhausted troopers gave up the fight as darkness set in, consolidating defensive positions at or near Todd's Tavern. Sheridan, apparently content with their work, rode off.

The way to Spotsylvania remained closed.

* * *

Meade rode into the Todd's Tavern intersection around midnight. Theodore Lyman, one of the general's staff members, made note of the tavern, which sat amid a complex of other, smaller structures. "It is an ordinary old building, of moderate size," he noted. One of Sheridan's division commanders, Brig. Gen. David McMurtrie Gregg, came out to meet his boss's boss. Gregg was one of the finest cavalry officers in Meade's army, but the clear-eyed appraisal he shared with the "very crabbed and crusty old customer" was anything but positive.[10]

Time was of the essence. The Army of the Potomac had the jump on the Army of Northern Virginia, but Meade had no idea how long he might retain the advantage. For all he knew, Lee had already mobilized his men, doing just as Meade feared. Meade needed to get Spotsylvania first.

Sheridan, as head of the cavalry, should have been present to snap his troopers into line, but Meade could not find him anywhere. Under such pressure as he was, the army commander instead issued orders directly to Sheridan's division commanders. "I find General Gregg and Torbert without orders," Meade wrote to Sheridan after the fact. "They are in the way of the infantry and there is no time to refer to you." Meade invited his cavalry chief to modify the orders "after the infantry corps are in position."[11]

The troopers scrambled into formation and soon pushed southward down the Brock Road to face whatever resistance waited in the wee-hour darkness and clear the way as Meade had intended. The army commander, meanwhile, fumed. At times a genial man, and always the consummate professional soldier, Meade possesed a legendary temper. His men had taken to calling him "a goddamn goggle-eyed snapping turtle," and even the sympathetic Lyman referred to him as "Old Peppery."

Meade had reason to be concerned. For three days, the Army of the Potomac had been brutalized in the Wilderness in a way it had not suffered since the three-day clash at Gettysburg some 10 months earlier. "[I]n fact the sudden transition from a long winter's rest to hard marching, sleepless nights, and protracted fighting,

10 Lyman, *Meade's Army*, 143; Charles Henry Veil, "An Old Boy's Personal Recollections and Reminiscences of the Civil War," FSNMP BV 43.

11 Meade to Sheridan, *O.R.* 36:2:551.

with no prospect of cessation, produced a powerful effect on the nervous system of the whole army," warned Lyman.[12]

Now, exhausted and strung out for miles along Brock Road, the Army of the Potomac held the initiative but also found itself vulnerable.

* * *

Another reason Meade was so acutely aware of the high stakes was that his boss was traveling with him. Lieutenant General Ulysses S. Grant, commander of all U. S. forces, had chosen to accompany Meade's army in the field.

Meade stood tall and courtly, said one observer, and "his trim gray hair, and neat regulation cap, gave him a martial look." In contrast, the shorter, slighter Grant dressed plainly. If not for the shoulder straps with his three stars, nothing would have distinguished him as an officer of note. He looked "clear and steady, calm and confident" with a closely cropped beard, square chin, and firm mouth, often with a cigar clamped between his teeth.[13]

Not all impressions were favorable. One Rhode Islander described Grant as "a short thick set man [who] rode his horse like a bag of meal," while a Pennsylvanian likened him to "small potatoes." "There is no enthusiasm in the army for Gen. Grant," said a colonel from Maine; "and, on the other hand, there is no prejudice against him. We are prepared to throw up our hats for him when he shows himself the great soldier here in Virginia against Lee and the best troops of the rebels."[14]

Such was the yardstick by which they all measured him: "Well, Grant has never met Bobby Lee yet."[15]

Grant had come to the east after a string of victories in the war's Western Theater: Forts Henry and Donelson, on the banks of the Tennessee and Cumberland Rivers, in February, 1862; Shiloh, Tennessee, in April of that same year; Vicksburg, Mississippi, on July 4, 1863; and Chattanooga, Tennessee in November, 1863.

Those months between July and November had proven an interesting study in contrast between Meade and Grant. Meade had been appointed to command of the Army of the Potomac on June 28, 1863, and just three days later found himself embroiled in what would be the war's bloodiest battle, Gettysburg. Meade scored a

12 Lyman, *Meade's Army*, 145.

13 George F. Williams, *Bullet and Shell* (New York: Forbes, Howard & Hulbert, 1884), 328; Ibid.

14 Elisha H. Rhodes, *All for the Union* (New York: Orion Books, 1985), 142; Elisha Bracken, letter, 17 April 1864, FSNMP BV 322; Selden Connor, letter, 16 May 1864, FSNMP BV 54.

15 Ulysses S. Grant, *The Personal Memoirs of Ulysses S. Grant,* Vol. 2 (Hartford, CT: Charles Webster & Co., 1885), 292. Hereafter, cited as *Memoirs* with volume and page listed thus: *Memoirs*, 2:292.

LEFT: "[M]y Chief . . . is a thorough soldier, and a mighty clear-headed man," Theodore Lyman said of Maj. Gen. George Gordon Meade. "I never saw a man in my life who was so characterized by straightforward truthfulness as he is." *Library of Congress*

RIGHT: A West Point classmate remembered Ulysses S. Grant as "a plain, commonsense, straightforward youth; quiet, rather of the old-head-on-the-young-shoulder order; shunning notoriety; quite contented while others were grumbling; taking to his military duties in a very business-like manner; not a prominent man in the corps, but respected by all and very popular with his friends." *Library of Congress*

---

much-needed victory there on July 3—a day before Grant's victory at Vicksburg—but afterwards, his battered army could not prevent Confederates from slipping away to safety south of the Potomac River. Lincoln wrote a scolding missive to his new army commander, which he ultimately did not send, but the writing for Meade was already on the wall—or at least tucked into Lincoln's writing desk. Meade's first operation as commander of the Army of the Potomac had unfairly pigeonholed him as too cautious.

Meade followed up in the fall with a series of back-and-forth maneuvers along the Orange and Alexandria Railroad, largely dictated by Lee's attempts to regain the initiative. Outmaneuvered and outgeneraled by his Confederate counterpart,

Meade nonetheless scored small victories at Bristoe and Rappahannock stations—enough to keep him in the game but never enough to score the knockout punch Lincoln needed. Expecting a hero's welcome in the capital after his victory at Rappahannock Station, Meade was instead rebuffed by Lincoln and Secretary of War Edwin M. Stanton.[16]

Meade's final nail came in the days after Thanksgiving. An aggressive stab at Lee's army went awry because of poor communications and lackluster leadership from his corps commanders. Tipped off, Lee went to ground on the west side of Mine Run, a small tributary of the Rapidan River, and constructed the most formidable defensive position yet created in the war. Seeing the strength of the works, Meade refused to throw away the lives of his men, and despite immense political pressure for a big win, he called off his attack. "I would rather be ignominiously dismissed, and suffer anything, than knowingly and wilfully [sic] have thousands of brave men slaughtered for nothing," he told his wife. Incessant rain forced the army back into camp 25 miles to the north around Brandy Station and Culpeper, where they remained for the winter.[17]

While Meade was reeling from Stanton's rebuff and then the rebuff in front of Mine Run, 520 miles to the southwest, Grant was rescuing the beleaguered Army of the Cumberland, trapped in Chattanooga since its drubbing at the battle of Chickamauga in mid-September.

Grant's knack for finding a way to win even in the worst circumstances made him the ideal candidate for Lincoln. "I need this man," Lincoln had reportedly once said of him. "He fights."[18] With the 1864 presidential election now only a year away and the Army of the Potomac languishing under Meade—and perhaps the entire Northern war effort languishing all across the map—Lincoln turned to Grant to shake things up. In March 1864, with congressional approval, Lincoln promoted Grant to lieutenant general, a permanent rank that had only ever been held before by George Washington, and placed him in overall command of all U.S. forces. "I wish to express, in this way, my entire satisfaction with what you have done up to this time . . ." Lincoln had told him. "You are vigilant and self-

16 The Bristoe and Rappahannock Station Campaigns played out in October and November of 1863 respectively.

17 George Gordon Meade, *The Life and Letters of George Gordon Meade*, vol. 2 (New York: Charles Scribner's Sons, 1913), 158.

18 The widely quoted comment "He fights" is actually suspect and may be apocryphal. Historian Brooks Simpson, who has done excellent detective work on this, contends that "Lincoln probably never uttered the phrase. . . ." Brooks Simpson, "Lincoln and Grant," *Abraham Lincoln: His Speeches and Writings*, Roy Basler and Carl Sandburg, eds., (New York: Da Capo Press, 2008), 149

reliant; and, pleased with this, I wish not to obtrude any constraints or restraints upon you."[19]

Upon assuming command, Grant changed the war at once. As he later wrote:

> From the first I was in the conviction that no peace could be had . . . until the military power of the rebellion was entirely broken. I therefore determined, first, to use the greatest number of troops practicable against the armed force of the enemy, preventing him from using the same force at different seasons against first one and then another of our armies, and . . . second, to hammer continuously against the armed force of the enemy and his resources until, by mere attrition, if in no other way, there should be nothing left to him. . . .[20]

This reflected a significant shift in strategy. Formerly, Federal armies had tried to capture Richmond and force the Southern government to capitulate. Grant now wanted to use the Northern army's numerical superiority to tie down Confederate forces and then hammer them into submission. At the same time, Federal armies across the South would destroy the Confederacy's socioeconomic base through the destruction of crops and factories and the emancipation of the enslaved population. Grant would, in short, take the fight to the Confederacy's armies even as he undercut the South's ability to wage war—a strategy of both annihilation and exhaustion.

Attrition and exhaustion might take more time than Grant had, though. A presidential election loomed in the fall of 1864. If Federal armies could not somehow break the stalemate, Lincoln's prospects seemed dim. An election loss would open the door to a Democratic president apt to sue for peace predicated on the recognition of Southern independence. Lincoln needed Grant to somehow engineer a knock-out blow. This injected the spring campaign with an urgency the Army of the Potomac had not yet felt.

Rather than oversee his strategy from Washington, D.C., Grant chose to make his headquarters in the field. Confident that his Western protégé, Maj. Gen. William T. Sherman, could successfully manage events in the military theater between the Appalachian Mountains and the Mississippi River, Grant decided to travel with the Army of the Potomac. His presence, he reasoned, might motivate it as it had not been motivated in the past. He also hoped to act as a shield between

19 Lincoln to Grant, 30 April 1864, *Collected Works of Abraham Lincoln, Volume 7* [Nov. 5, 1863-Sept. 12, 1864] (New Brunswick, N.J.: Rutgers University Press, 1953), 234.

20 Grant, "Report of Lieut. Gen. Ulysses S. Grant," 22 July 1865, *O.R.*, 36:1:12–3.

the political machinations of Washington and the headquarters of the Army of the Potomac, situated less than 50 miles from the nation's capital.

Meade fully expected the new general in chief to replace him. "You might want an officer who had served with you in the west," he conceded in a private meeting on March 10 during Grant's first visit to the army. "Do not hesitate about making the change. The work before us is of such vast importance to the whole nation that the feeling or wishes of no one person should stand in the way of selecting the right men for all positions." Meade then offered his resignation, for the good of the service.

"This incident gave me even a more favorable opinion of Meade than did his great victory at Gettysburg the July before," Grant later admitted. "I assured him that I had no thought of substituting any one for him."[21]

Ironically, some in Washington had thought of substituting Grant for Meade the previous summer. Frustrated by Lee's post-Gettysburg escape, politicians began privately floating Grant's name as a possible commander for the Army of the Potomac. Grant demurred, saying such an assignment would bring him "more sadness than satisfaction." Among the reasons he cited were army politics: "more or less dissatisfaction would necessarily be produced by importing a General to command an Army already well supplied with those who have grown up, and been promoted, with it."[22]

Those politics still held true and served as another reason for keeping Meade in his post. As a "western" general, Grant knew he wouldn't be any better received now than he would have been the previous summer, even if he was now in his more elevated position as general in chief. Should he relieve one of only two generals who had managed to best Robert E. Lee, animosity would soar. Grant also needed to look no further than the example Lincoln set the previous year with Maj. Gen. John Pope. A westerner, Pope replaced the other general who had bested Lee, Maj. Gen. George B. McClellan. During the disastrous Second Manassas campaign that followed, Pope managed to alienate everyone from the common soldier to Lincoln to Lee himself.

Grant and Meade seemed quite different if not opposite. Meade, the older of the two, was born on December 31, 1815, in Cadiz, Spain, while his father—a well-connected Philadelphia merchant—served there as an agent for the United State Navy. Grant was born seven years later on April 27, 1822, in Point Pleasant,

21 Grant, *Memoirs*, 2:117.

22 Ulysses S. Grant to Charles Dana, letter, 5 August 1863, *The Papers of Ulysses S. Grant, Volume 09: July 7, December 31, 1863*, John Y. Simon, ed. (Carbondale, Illinois: Southern Illinois University Press, 1982), 146.

Horace Porter (left) and Theodore Lyman (right) serve as literary alter egos for their bosses, Ulysses S. Grant and George Gordon Meade, respectively. Lyman's journals, written contemporaneously, show a bulldog-tough loyalty to Meade. Porter's memoir, published in 1897, paints a respectful but adoring picture of Grant. Together, Porter and Lyman offer a valuable look into the Federal army command during the 1864 Overland Campaign. *Library of Congress/National Park Service*

---

Ohio, the son of a tanner. Both men attended the U.S. Military Academy at West Point, Meade graduating in 1835, ranking 19th out of 56, and Grant in 1843, ranking 21st out of 39. Both served in 1846–48 during the war with Mexico, where they each earned brevet promotions for battlefield bravery.

When civil war erupted in 1861, both worked their way up to army command through excellent service at the brigade and division levels, earning the respect of their peers and subordinates, if not always their superiors.

"[Grant] is so much more active than his predecessor, and agrees so well with me in his views, I cannot but be rejoiced at his arrival, because I believe success to be the more probable," Meade later wrote to his wife. "My duty is plain, to continue quietly to discharge my duties, heartily co-operating with him and under him."[23]

Initially, Grant intended to give Meade a free hand commanding the army while Grant would stick to larger overall strategic issues. "My instructions for that

23 Meade, *Life and Letters*, 189.

army were all through him [Meade], and were all general in their nature, leaving all the details and the execution to him," Grant later explained. He gave Meade one mission: "Lee's army is your objective point. Wherever Lee goes, there you will go also." Richmond, in other words, would no longer be the strategic objective—although by moving against the capital, the Federals could force Confederates out into the open for battle.[24]

That's why Spotsylvania Court House became so important to Meade on the night of May 7–8: The roads there offered him the inside track to Richmond. Lee, forced to protect the capital, would have to withdraw from the safety of the Wilderness and try to stop him. If Lee abandoned the defense of Richmond, Federal cavalry could swoop in and capture the prize, depriving the Rebels of the political and economic engine of the Confederacy.

It was a lose-lose situation for Lee and a pivotal moment for Meade.

During the battle in the Wilderness, Grant had begun to take a heavier hand commanding the army than he had originally suggested. If Meade were to regain some of that operational control, he needed to seize Spotsylvania Court House and the road network of opportunity and initiative it offered.

Unfortunately, before he could direct his push in that direction, Meade faced an obstacle more explosive than the Confederates.

* * *

In the midst of the spring-green forest, Piney Branch Church stood out for its yellow exterior. Known as "the little yellow church," the Episcopal congregation dated to 1768. But on May 8, 1864, few seemed to recall it was the sabbath as Meade and Grant established their headquarters there. "[T]he overrunning of the country by the contending armies had scattered the little church's congregation," noted Horace Porter. "The temple of prayer was voiceless, the tolling of its peaceful bell had given place to the echo of hostile guns. . . ."[25]

Shortly before noon, Maj. Gen. Philip Sheridan rode into headquarters. He was, by his own admission, "very much irritated." Meade had bypassed the chain of command and given orders directly to Sheridan's division commanders, throwing Sheridan's planned cavalry dispositions into disorder. It didn't matter to Sheridan that his horsemen hadn't cleared the Brock Road as ordered. Nor did it matter that Sheridan hadn't been on hand so Meade could have directed orders through him.

24 Grant, report, *O.R.,* 36:1:18; Grant to Meade, 9 April 1864, *O.R.,* 36:1:828.

25 "History of Piney Branch Baptist Church." https://pineybranchbc.org/about/ (accessed 12 November 2023); Porter, 83.

"Little Phil" Sheridan was "a small, broad-shouldered, squat man, with black hair and a square head," said Theodore Lyman, who added, "Sheridan makes everywhere a favorable impression." *Library of Congress*

It didn't even matter to Sheridan that Meade was his superior officer.

Standing only 5-foot-5, "Little Phil" cut a queer figure that drew attention wherever he went. President Lincoln had once described him as a "brown, chunky little chap, with a long body, short legs, not enough neck to hang him, and such long arms that if his ankles itch he can scratch them without stooping."[26]

Only 33 years old, Sheridan had enjoyed a meteoric if surprising ascent. He had graduated in the bottom third of his West Point Class of 1853. When civil war broke out, he started as a quartermaster on the staff of Maj. Gen. Henry Halleck, but he eventually worked his way up to division command where he served ably if obscurely, said one historian. That all changed during the battle of Missionary Ridge at Chattanooga in November 1863, where Ulysses S. Grant watched Sheridan lead his division up the sheer mountainside and drive the ensconced Confederates from the crest. Grant liked Sheridan's spunk and tapped him for greater responsibilities.[27]

When Grant came east, he brought Sheridan with him and placed him in command of the Army of the Potomac's cavalry. Sheridan saw the cavalry as a mobile strike force: give troopers repeating rifles, get them to a far-off spot quickly, and let them shoot it out with their superior firepower. This stood in contract to Meade's traditional view of cavalry as a force to screen movements, gather intelligence, and protect flanks and supplies. Sheridan wanted to unleash the

26 Roy Morris Jr. *Sheridan: The Life and Wars of General Phil Sheridan* (New York: Crown Publishing, 1992), 1.

27 Sheridan's tutor at West Point was future Maj. Gen. Henry W. Slocum. Sheridan was to graduate with the class of 1852, but he was expelled for one year after he assaulted future Union general William Terrill with a bayonet.

cavalry's offensive potential and this, unsurprisingly, put him on a collision course with his direct superior.

Whether Meade harbored an inner "I told you so," he did not record, but he had every right to throw one in Sheridan's face: The cavalry's offensive potential had gone unrealized along the Brock Road on May 7. Sheridan, meanwhile, blamed Maj. Gen. Gouverneur K. Warren's V Corps for the army's difficult advance. The "behavior of the infantry was disgraceful," he groused, taking no responsibility for failing to clear the road to the court house or for failing to make that failure clear to army headquarters. Meade, for his part, "had worked himself into a towering passion regarding the delays encountered in the forward movement," said Horace Porter, a member of Grant's staff.

Arriving at headquarters, all thunder and hooves, Sheridan was "plainly full of suppressed anger," said another witness. Meade was, too, and when Sheridan appeared, the army commander "went at him hammer and tongs." Sheridan had blundered. He was absent from the battlefield when his commander had needed him. His men had failed to do the one thing Meade had ordered them to accomplish.

Sheridan, "equally fiery," felt unjustly treated. "[A]ll the hotspur in his nature was aroused," Porter wrote. "His language throughout was highly spiced and conspicuously italicized with expletives."

"I will not command the cavalry any longer under such conditions!" Sheridan protested. "If I could have it my way, I would concentrate all the cavalry, move out in force against Stuart's command, and whip it!"

Meade, for all his volcanic temper, tried to deescalate the argument. *I didn't mean that,* he told Sheridan, placing his hand on Sherman's arm. *I didn't mean that.*

Sheridan, who believed Meade's "peppery temper had got the better of his good judgement," didn't want to hear it and stormed off. It was, Porter summarized, "a very acrimonious dispute. . . ."

It was insubordination, is what it was. But Sheridan was Grant's hand-picked cavalryman, so there wasn't much Meade could do. Disgusted, Meade stalked over to Grant's nearby command tent to recount the conversation. When Meade got to the part of Sheridan riding off to whip Stuart, Grant interrupted him. "Did Sheridan say that?" he asked. "Well, he generally knows what he is talking about. Let him start right out and do it."[28]

28 Accounts from the dispute come from Lyman, Meade's Army, 144; Porter, 83–4; Sheridan, 368, 370. Sheridan boldly claimed on pg. 153 in his own memoir that "Had Gregg and Merritt been permitted to proceed as they were originally instructed, it is doubtful whether the battles fought at Spottsylvania [sic] would have occurred. . . ." Had Sheridan cleared the road as ordered on May 7, it is just as doubtful that the battle of Spotsylvania would have occurred!

Imagine Meade's reaction in this moment. His immediate superior, who had already been undercutting Meade's authority by taking a more direct hand in the army's operations, just undercut him further. Grant had supported his crony instead of his army commander. That Sheridan had blown up about a breach in the chain of command—and now benefitted from that very same kind of breach—must have seemed bitterly sardonic.

Imagine Grant's rationale, which he did not record for posterity. He knew first-hand from experiences inflicted on him by Nathan Bedford Forrest and Earl Van Dorn in December 1862 how disruptive enemy cavalry could be in an army's rear. He had encouraged Col. Benjamin Grierson, in April 1863, to inflict that same kind of disruption through Mississippi's interior. Now here was Sheridan, thinking disruptively and aggressively—in an army that did not, in Grant's mind, think aggressively enough.[29]

By 1:00 p.m., army Chief of Staff Andrew Humphreys cut the orders to cut Sheridan loose. The bandy-legged little Irishmen was delighted.[30] "We are going out to fight Stuart's cavalry in consequence of a suggestion from me," he crowed; "we will give him a fair, square fight. . . ."

On the morning of May 10, Sheridan galloped off at the head of a column of 11,000 troopers with a plan to draw out the Confederate cavalry and engage with them in open battle. The result would be the May 11 battle of Yellow Tavern on the northern outskirts of Richmond where a Federal cavalryman would shoot Maj. Gen. James Ewell Brown "Jeb" Stuart in the gut, mortally wounding him. Stuart would die the next day, even as Sheridan and his men found themselves in deepening jeopardy that would take days to escape from.

Had cooler heads prevailed, Sheridan would not have been allowed to ride off into the distance with nearly all the Federal cavalry. He left behind only one of his regiments, plus one regiment and one squadron of the provost guard, and four regiments of the IX Corps cavalry that fell outside his sphere of command. This left Meade's entire army with little better than six regiments of cavalry—roughly a brigade—to scout, act as flank guards, protect the supply train, and

29 Forrest hit Grant's supply line in Jackson, Tennessee, on December 19, 1862, and Van Dorn hit Grant's forward supply base in Holly Springs, Mississippi, on December 20, 1862. The raids forced Grant to abandon his first overland attempt on Vicksburg.

30 One of my favorite Shelby Foote-isms—so good that the term gets used widely now without attribution. See *The Civil War: A Narrative, Vol. 1: Fort Sumter to Perryville*, 732 (where Foote also says Sheridan has "a head as round as a pot").

guard prisoners—nearly the identical situation the army found itself in 53 weeks earlier during the 1863 Chancellorsville Campaign.[31]

Sheridan essentially left the Army of the Potomac with no eyes and ears. Leaving the army blind and deaf would cost thousands of lives.

In retrospect, authorizing the raid was one of Grant's worst decisions of the war.

* * *

The action that led to the dispute—and the eventual departure of the Federal cavalry—unfolded along the Brock Road.

Confederate cavalry under Maj. Gen. Fitzhugh Lee blocked the way south while a second division under Maj. Gen. Wade Hampton blocked the Catharpin Road leading west. Had Federal troopers pushed in that direction, they would have intercepted lead elements of the Army of Northern Virginia making their own hasty march out of the Wilderness as Hampton's men screened their movement. Instead, Federals concentrated on pushing down the Brock Road in the direction of Spotsylvania Court House, as Meade intended.

Brigadier General Wesley Merritt, just weeks away from his twenty-eighth birthday, was tasked with spearheading the southward effort. Never one to shrink from a fight, he nonetheless couldn't make headway against the barricades of felled trees and fence rails his Southern counterparts were throwing up across the road. "All we had to shoot at was the flashes of the enemy's guns," one Federal cavalryman lamented. Even Sheridan's sudden appearance on the scene—barking, "Quick! Quick!"—couldn't leverage Merritt's men forward. "The enemy were felling trees and placing other obstacles in the way, in order to impede the movement," Porter later wrote, "and the cavalry afterwards was withdrawn and the infantry directed to open the way."[32]

General Warren's V Corps led the Federal column, with Brig. Gen. John C. Robinson's division in front. "Oh, get your God damned cavalry out of the way," Robinson barked. "There is nothing ahead but a little cavalry. We will soon clean them out." Robinson, one of the hairiest men in an army of hairy men, sent Col. Peter Lyle's brigade forward with orders to use the bayonet. The men from

31 The 5th New York Cavalry was detached from Sheridan's corps. This assessment does not include the handful of cavalry companies and couriers scattered through the army and attached to various corps and divisional headquarters.

32 Veil, 55; Porter, 83.

"An especial favorite of General J. E. B. Stuart, [Fitz] Lee (above) played a gallant part in all of the operations of the Cavalry Corps," wrote historian Ezra Warner, "particularly distinguishing himself at Spotsylvania Court House, where the stand of his division made it possible for the [First] Corps to secure the strategic crossroads in advance of Grant's arrival with the main Federal column." *Library of Congress*

Maine, Massachusetts, New York, and Pennsylvania shook out from column of march into line of battle and advanced.[33]

"[The enemy] advanced heavy forces and attacked me at daybreak," reported Lt. Col. William R. Carter of the 3rd Virginia Cavalry. "We fought them [and] we raced them back from the barricade until outflanked . . . we then wheeled back the left flank and fell back into the works, fighting every step."[34]

In the face of the Federal push, Fitz Lee divided his cavalry. The lead elements would block the road and resist the advance while the rest of the horsemen rode rearward to the next ridge to create the next set of obstructions. In this way, Confederates leap-frogged their way backwards down the Brock Road, using the rolling terrain to provide cover and amplify their efforts. Harassing ambushes, pockets of stiff resistance bolstered by barricades, and cat-and-mouse dismounting-and-remounting tactics all thwarted the Federals, whom the Confederates could slow but could not stop.

"The strategic importance of Spottsylvania C.H. was well understood, and in the race that ensued for its occupancy, we were successful," Fitz later boasted in his handwritten report.

Fitz watched part of the action from a ridge where his horse artillery had deployed. As Federals pressed in, he ordered the artillerists to withdraw. Coolly,

33 Veil, 55.

34 Lt. Col. William R. Carter, diary, 8 May 1864, of, FSNMP BV 18; Robert K. Krick, *Lee's Colonels: A Biographical Roster of the Field Officers of the Army of Northern Virginia* (Dayton, OH: Morningside, 1992), 86.

Maj. James Breathed retired one gun while "the other continued to fire." Lee was shaken to see "the enemy . . . rapidly advancing a heavy line of skirmishers supported by a line of battle towards the piece, the former firing as they advanced." In the face of this threat, Lee's mounted skirmishers withdrew, leaving Breathed and his gun isolated. Captain Preston Johnston, commander of the piece, went down, as did many of the battery's officers. "The enemy were now so close that their shouts for surrender of the gun could be distinctly heard," Lee wrote.[35]

As Breathed ordered the remaining men to limber the gun, his horse was killed. Extracting himself from beneath his dead mount, Breathed leapt upon the lead horse of the team pulling the gun from the field. That horse, too, was killed under him. Not missing a beat, Breathed cut the dead horse loose and leapt upon one of the middle horses. When that horse was struck down, too, he finally leapt upon one of the wheel horses, "turned the gun around when the enemy were almost near enough to touch it, and galloped off with it down the pike, miraculously escaping unharmed."[36]

In the meantime, Rebel couriers raced rearward with word for their own infantry to come to the front as quickly as possible. The messengers had a circuitous route to follow: southeast along the Brock Road to the Block House Road to the Shady Grove Church Road where, somewhere along the way, they hoped to find the lead elements of the Army of Northern Virginia.

As their luck would have it, those infantrymen—the First Corps under Maj. Gen. Richard H. Anderson—had progressed further along on their route than they were originally supposed to be. Lee had ordered Anderson to move his men out of the Wilderness at 2:00 a.m. on May 8, but the area where they departed from along the Plank Road was ablaze, so Anderson marched his men away from the inferno beginning around 10:00 p.m. The four-hour head start would make all the difference.

Forty-two-year-old "Fighting Dick" Anderson was just hours into his tenure as the First Corps' commander. Lee had promoted him on May 7 following the accidental wounding of Lee's second in command, his "Old Warhorse," James Longstreet. Arriving on the Wilderness battlefield at exactly the right spot during a moment of crisis, Longstreet had saved the Army of Northern Virginia from annihilation, but in the course of his powerful counter-attack, he was accidentally shot by his own men. That they were executing an attack through the Wilderness against the Federal flank, just a few miles away from where Lt. Gen. Thomas Jonathan "Stonewall" Jackson had been accidentally shot by his own men while

35 Report of Major General Fitzhugh Lee of the Operations of His Cavalry Division, A.N.V. From 4 May 1864 to 19 September 1864 (both inclusive), Museum of the Confederacy Collection, FSNMP BV 178.

36 Ibid.

"Gen. [Richard] Dick Anderson was as pleasant a commander to serve under as could be wished," said artillerist E. Porter Alexander, "& was a sturdy & reliable fighter." *Emerging Civil War*

executing a flank attack through the Wilderness against the Federal flank just a year earlier, was not lost on anyone. "The evil genius of the south is still hovering over those desolate woods, [where] we almost seem to be struggling with destiny itself," Alabamian Edward Perry said afterwards.[37]

At the time, Anderson was commanding a division in Lt. Gen. A. P. Hill's Third Corps. However, Anderson had once commanded a division in the First Corps prior to the army's reorganization in the wake of Stonewall Jackson's death. Lee tapped Anderson for the job because, in the words of Longstreet's adjutant Moxley Sorrel, "We know him and shall be satisfied with him." Lee had been leaning toward Jubal Early or Edward "Alleghany" Johnson but could not argue with Sorrel's logic; he believed the First Corps would respond well to Anderson, and in an army where personal magnetism and leadership effectiveness were often intertwined, such things mattered.[38]

Not that Anderson possessed all that much magnetism. Southern historian Douglas Southall Freeman described "that modest gentleman, the easy-going, generous 'Dick' Anderson" as "Tall, strong, and of fine background" and "beloved in the Army for his kindness, his amiability, and his unselfishness." A South Carolinian by birth, Anderson had graduated 40 out 52 in the West Point Class of 1842. His subsequent career in the U.S. Army included service at Carlisle Barracks in Pennsylvania, frontier duty in the American West, and combat in the Mexican-American War. He also helped quell unrest in Kansas in 1856–7 and Utah in 1858–9.[39]

37 Edward Perry, "Reminiscences of the Campaign of 1864 in Virginia," *Southern Historical Society Papers*, Vol. 7, No. 2 (Feb. 1879), 59. Hereafter, cited as *S.H.S.P.* with volume and page listed thus: 7:2:59.

38 G. Moxley Sorrel, *Recollections of a Confederate Staff Officer* (New York: Neale Publishing Company, 1917), 243.

39 Douglas Southall Freeman, *Lee's Lieutenants, Vol. 1: Manassas to Malvern Hill* (New York: Scribners and Sons, 1970), xix, 158.

When civil war broke out, he commanded forces in Charleston, South Carolina, and then Pensacola, Florida, before finally transferring to Virginia, where he began serving under James Longstreet. Unassuming and unimpressive, Anderson received promotion to major general on July 14, 1862. He commanded troops in major action at Second Manassas, Antietam, and Chancellorsville, but at Gettysburg, he underperformed, sapping much-needed momentum from Longstreet's July 2 assault and drawing the ire of brigade commander Cadmus Wilcox.

Now here was the vanilla Anderson, trying to fill Longstreet's considerable boots, leading the First Corps out of the burning Wilderness. "I found the woods on fire and burning furiously in every direction, and there was no suitable place for a rest," Anderson recounted. He kept his men on their feet until, finally, as dawn began to streak the eastern horizon, Anderson let his men fall out for rest. They were, he estimated, three miles outside Spotsylvania Court House and "within easy reach of that place."[40]

The lead division of Anderson's column, under the command of fellow South Carolinian Joseph B. Kershaw, snatched about two hours of rest before the first courier from Fitz Lee came blazing up the road. "Come to my support with all the speed," Lee pleaded, "for my cavalry was hard pressed and could not hold the place much longer." Anderson roused Kershaw's men and put them back on the road immediately and at the double-quick. Major General Charles Field's division, the next in line, had barely rested at all before they, too, were back marching. For the second time in three days, the stalwart First Corps was called upon to stem a Federal offensive.[41]

"Soon we see an old Virginia gentleman, bareheaded and without shoes, riding in haste towards us," wrote Augustus Dickert, a member of Kershaw's Brigade, marching at the vanguard. More frantic news. More grim tidings. More panicked pleas to hurry.[42]

The race to Spotsylvania Court House had begun before Anderson had even realized it, and already it looked like the Federals might win.

Four days into the campaign, Robert E. Lee was already running on fumes. One staffer noted the commander of the Army of Northern Virginia was sleeping three or four hours a night, and those nights had been fraught.

40 R. H. Anderson to Cpt. Edward B. Robins, letter, 14 May 1879, Mass. Mil. Hist. Soc. Coll., Boston Univ., FSNMP BV245.

41 Ibid.

42 D. Augustus Dickert, *Kershaw's Brigade, with complete roll of companies, biographical sketches, incidents, anecdotes, etc.* (Newberry, S.C.: E. H. Aull Company, 1899), 358-9.

On the morning of May 4, Lee had overseen the mobilization of his army toward the Wilderness, shaking off five months of winter cobwebs as it marched. On May 5, Lee divided his attention between the unfolding battle on two fronts and nearly got captured in the process. In the early morning hours of May 6, Federals launched a massive assault that brought the Army of Northern Virginia to the brink of annihilation, and only the timely arrival of Longstreet's First Corps at the point of crisis staved off disaster. Longstreet had paid a grievous personal price for his heroics, suffering an accidental gunshot through the shoulder and throat from his own men. In the wake of Longstreet's wounding, Lee could not regain the lost momentum, despite personally directing events in that sector of the battlefield, nor could he recapture it with a late-day attack on the north end of the battlefield. He spent his shortened night mulling over options for Longstreet's replacement.

Many had believed Maj. Gen. Jubal Early, an irascible, hard-fighting division commander in the Second Corps would get that call. At 47 years old, the former lawyer from Lynchburg, Virginia, was as profane as he was talented—reportedly the only man in the entire army willing to swear in front of Lee, who seemed amused and called him "my Bad Old Man." Lee had been giving Early ever-increasing responsibilities since the battle of Fredericksburg in December 1862. There, Early had showed initiative, marching to the sound of the guns, throwing back a Federal breakthrough that threatened the entire right flank of the Confederate army. That he did so in violation of orders from his superior, Stonewall Jackson, made the decision even more remarkable—but success forgave the transgression.

The following May, Lee charged Early with protecting the army's rear during the Chancellorsville campaign. In the late fall of 1863, Lee placed Early in temporary command of the Second Corps while its commander, Lt. Gen. Richard Ewell, took a brief medical leave.

Early seemed ready for permanent corps command, but Lee promoted Anderson instead—although another leadership opportunity presented itself for Early almost immediately. On the morning of May 8, Third Corps commander A. P. Hill reported ill—an unfortunate flare-up of an ongoing "social disease" contracted years earlier while a cadet at West Point. "General Hill has reported to me that he is so much indisposed that he fears he must relinquish the command of his corps. In that case, I shall be obliged to put General Early in command of it," Lee wrote to Ewell, his ersatz second in command.[43]

And so it was that Lee's army left the Wilderness with two new commanders at the head of three of its corps. Of the triumvirate of subordinates who'd served at the

43 Lee to Ewell, letter, 8 May 1864, Lee, Robert E., *The Wartime Papers of Robert E. Lee*, Clifford Dowdey and Louis H. Manarin, eds. (New York: Da Capo, 1961), 725.

peak of Lee's successes in 1862–63—Longstreet, Jackson, and Stuart—only Stuart remained.

As events were about to play out, the loss of Longstreet at this particular moment would prove especially problematic. In the midst of all this early May turmoil, Lee continued to try and wrap his head around his new adversary, Grant. Lee did not know him at all—they'd met only once, in passing, when they both fought for the U.S. Army in Mexico years earlier. No one else in Lee's army seemed to know him, either, with the exception of Longstreet and Maj. Gen. Cadmus Wilcox. Wilcox, Longstreet, and Grant had served together years earlier in St. Louis, where Wilcox and Longstreet had attended Grant's wedding.

Maj. Gen. James Ewell Brown "Jeb" Stuart's "fearlessness, buoyant manner, and reassuring words inspired [Joseph] Kershaw's veterans and earned their admiration," says Stuart biographer Jeffry Wert. "War suited him." *Library of Congress*

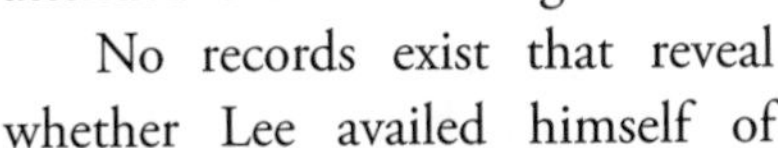

No records exist that reveal whether Lee availed himself of Wilcox's opinions about Grant, or that he even knew the two knew each other. As a division commander, Wilcox did not have close, frequent interactions with Lee. Longstreet did, however, and Lee almost certainly picked Longstreet's brain about this new foe from the West. "We must make up our minds to get into line of battle and to stay there," Longstreet had warned when he heard of Grant's promotion to general in chief of the U.S. Army; "for that man will fight us every day and every hour until the end of the war." Longstreet advised Lee to "outmaneuver him, and husband our strength as best we can."[44]

Now, following Longstreet's horrific wounding, the one person who could best give Lee insight into Grant was out of reach and would be for months.

Yet the Old Warhorse's prophecy had already begun to come true. Lee had marched into the Wilderness with 66,000 men; after three days of fighting, he was marching out

44 Porter, 47.

of the Wilderness with only 55,000 men. The Army of Northern Virginia had suffered more than 11,000 killed, wounded, and missing—nearly 17% of Lee's army.

Unbeknownst yet to Lee, his First Corps was now enmeshed in more fighting, this time on the outskirts of Spotsylvania Court House. He knew, though, that Grant was on the move and that some sort of collision with Anderson was likely. After sending Stuart ahead to personally "ascertain what is going on," Lee began to mobilize the remainder of his army.[45]

"I desire you to move with your corps as rapidly as you can, without injuring the men, to Shady Grove Church," Lee ordered Ewell. "Anderson by this time is at Spotsylvania Court House and may need your support."

With the Third Corps holding the Confederate position in front of the Federal II Corps at the Brock Road/Plank Road intersection, Ewell was to shift position from the north end of the battlefield, march behind the Third Corps' screen, and out of the Wilderness along a road "through the pines" newly cut by the Confederate artillery battalion. Once Ewell passed, the Third Corps could follow.

Grant and Meade had side-stepped, and now Lee matched them, shifting the central axis of both armies from an east-west orientation to north-south. With the forests still burning behind him, Lee set off toward Spotsylvania Court House. It was Sunday, May 8, just before 10:00 a.m.

* * *

By the time Ewell's corps stepped off, the front end of Lee's column had been on the field for more than two hours. The lead regiments of Kershaw's Brigade—the 2nd and 3rd South Carolina—had appeared first, double-timing to the answer of Fitz Lee's call for help. The brigade commander, Col. John W. Henagan, was officially starting his second full day on the job. A 41-year-old antebellum politician and sheriff of Marlboro County, South Carolina, Henagan had marched off to war with the 8th South Carolina and had led the regiment in every major engagement from the Peninsula to the Wilderness. He advanced to brigade command as part of the domino chain of openings triggered by Longstreet's wounding.

Now on the morning of May 8, Henagan urged his brigade to the front. Cresting the southern slope of Laurel Hill, the Palmetto soldiers found cavalry commander Jeb Stuart awaiting them, mounted on his dark dapple-gray horse.[46]

45 Lee, *Wartime Papers*, 724.

46 Krick, *Lee's Colonels*, 189; Joseph H. Crute, Jr., *Lee's Intrepid Army: A Guide to the Units of the Army of Northern Virginia* (Madison, Georgia: Southern Lion Books, Inc., 2005), 129.

John Coxe, among the first South Carolinians onto the field, called the 31-year-old Stuart "a towering presence" who "sat his horse to perfection":

> In every way Stuart was a grand man and every inch a true soldier. In the early morning of that day we privates though him more than the equal of any other living man in cool bravery, dashing heroism, manly beauty, and all that went to make up our ideal of a military chieftain.[47]

Stuart had, upon his own arrival on the field, immediately grasped the importance of the ground: it was the last defensible position before the Court House and its nexus of roads. His troopers needed to hold out until the infantry arrived. The South Carolinians arrived shortly thereafter. Stuart cheered them on even as he directed them into position. "Run for our rail piles," he instructed; "the Federal infantry will reach them first, if you don't run."[48]

As the Brock Road approached Spotsylvania from the northwest, it split into two paths at a place called the Alsop farm, then reunited on the north edge of Sarah Spindle's field. There, the road cut due south across the field for a little more than 500 yards before intersecting with Block House Road, which came up from the south, at the field's southern edge. At the intersection, Brock Road took a left turn and wound onward toward the Court House, just a mile-and-a-half away. Stuart's cavalrymen had piled fence rails along that dog-leg section of the road and had begun to fortify the position further. This was the position to which Stuart directed the 2nd South Carolina. The 3rd, meanwhile, took up a position on the west side of the road along a ridge hidden in a tree line. This also put them slightly to the rear of the 2nd. "Our men sprang forward as if by magic," one South Carolinian said—"rushing pell-mell at full speed around there just as the enemy came up," said another.[49]

On the far side of the field, Col. Peter Lyle had deployed his five Federal regiments in a column along the east side of the road. Joining them was the 4th Maryland, the lead regiment of Col. Andrew Denison's Maryland Brigade, which had gotten mixed up with Lyle's men during the morning's harried advance. The cat-and-mouse exertions with the Confederate cavalry had left them "stupefied by sleepless overwork." Austin Stearns of the 13th Massachusetts noted, "The *zyps, zyps* of the bullets were coming thick [warning of] the prospect of warm work ahead."[50]

47 John Coxe, "Last Struggles and Successes of Lee," *Confederate Veteran*, Vol. 22, 358.

48 Dickert, 357.

49 Ibid., 358–9; Cpt. John W. Wofford of the 3rd South Carolina, recounted by Jane W. Wait, History of the Wofford Family (Spartanburg, SC: Band & White Printers, 1928), 207–8, FSNMP BV 236.

50 Wolmer, 271; Austin C. Stearns, *Three Years with Company K*, Arthur A. Kent, ed. (Cranbury, NJ: Associated University Presses, 1976), 263.

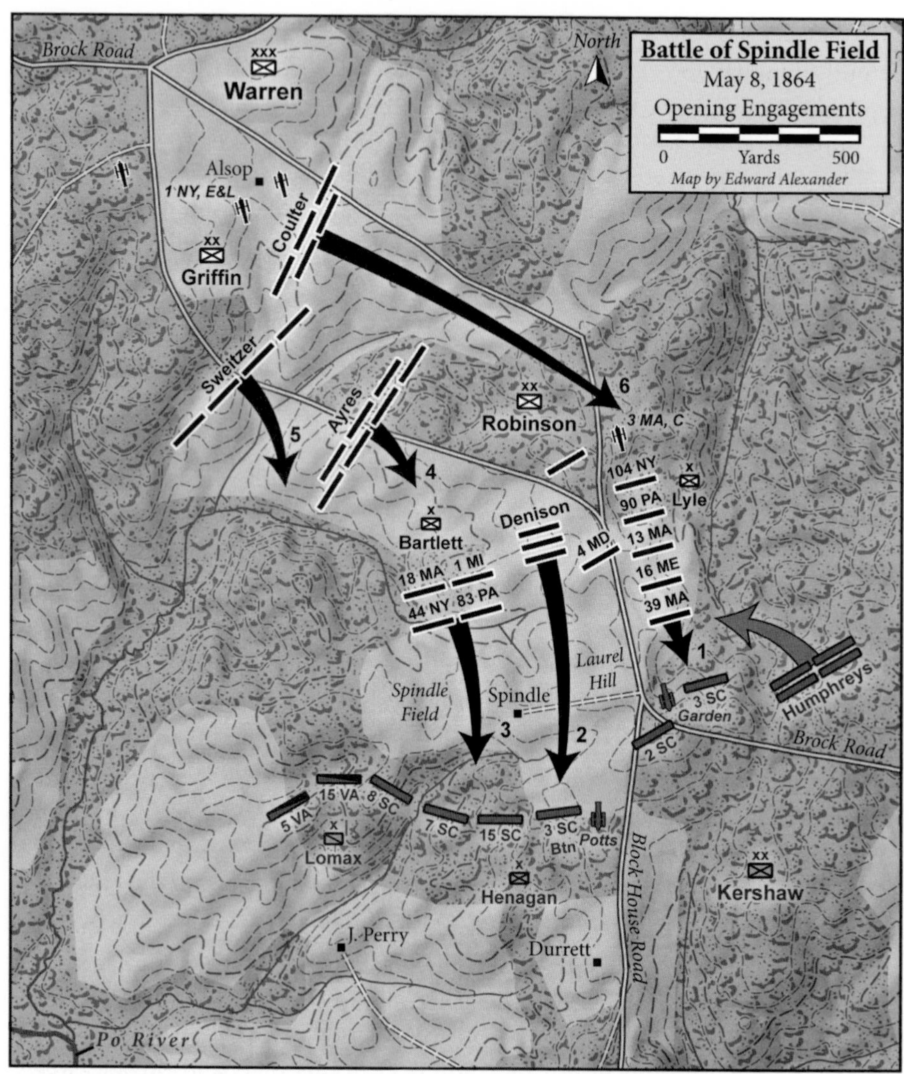


**Battle of Spindle Field, Opening Engagements**—In the Wilderness, Federal V Corps commander Gouverneur K. Warren opened the battle by organizing his divisions before attacking, which earned him criticism from his superiors because the delay gave Confederates time to consolidate their own position. Warren tried a different tack at Spotsylvania, throwing his brigades in as soon as they became available in the hope that he could catch the Confederates off guard. Confederates hung on because of timely reinforcements, repulsing six separate waves: 1) Lyle, 2) Denison, 3) Bartlett, 4) Ayres, 5) Sweitzer, and 6) Coulter, who arrived just in time to blunt a Confederate counterattack.

The 500-plus yards of open ground ahead of Lyle's men rolled downward slightly before rolling up to create a small knoll, then dropped into a large punchbowl depression before rising again. The Brock Road coursed along the uphill edge of the punchbowl as it made its leftward bend toward the Court House. Lyle's men could see Confederates along that ridge "working like beavers to finish the work," downing small pine trees to act as obstructions in front of their rail-pile position.[51]

Once situated, those Confederate infantrymen could deliver significantly more firepower than the Stuart's troopers. Although the units bore a mix of firearms that included U.S. Model 1855 and Enfield rifled muskets, on average, those guns possessed at least twice the effective range as the cavalry's firearms, with plenty of open ground to extend their reach even farther.[52]

Not that Lyle's men quite realized yet what they were up against. "Out into the open we went, over rough ground, under fire," recalled Abner Small of the 16th Maine. As the brigade advanced, the men found the field "badly gullied," which broke up their formation. Yet "nothing could abate our zeal," claimed Charles H. Porter of the 39th Massachusetts, which led the way. They swept over the small knoll, then plunged into the punchbowl. "[T]o the right a battery which was sending shot after shot at us," wrote Austin Stearns of the 13th Massachusetts. "One struck the colors, breaking the staff without any injury to the bearer."[53]

On the far side of the punchbowl, the brigade swept up all the way to the rail pile just in front of the Confederate line. "We were in the most perfect cover," Porter said, "so close to the enemy that when they fired it was in the most hurried manner & with no aim."[54]

The Federals could not exploit the purchase they had gained, though, and after several hard minutes, they gave ground. Rather than retreat back across the field, though, they retreated into the punchbowl and flattened themselves to its uphill face. The rail pile above them suddenly served as protection, keeping the South Carolinians far enough back from the lip of the bowl that they could not depress the barrels of their guns enough to fire at the men pinned down in the punchbowl. Lyle's men soon found themselves protected from artillery fire, as well: a piece from Stuart's horse artillery unlimbered near the bend in the road but, like the infantry, it could not depress its barrel enough to shoot down into punchbowl. Instead, it aimed straight down Brock Road at the next Federal column.

51 Charles H. Porter to C. L. Pierson, letter, 18 April 1879, FSNMP BV 55.

52 Some of the Confederate guns could reach distances of 1,000 yards but were rarely called upon to do so.

53 Austin C. Stearns, *Three Years with Company K*, Arthur A. Kent, ed. (Cranbury, NJ: Associated University Presses, 1976), 263.

54 Small, 135–6; C. Porter to Pierson, letter.

That column was the balance of Denison's brigade of Marylanders, advancing along the west side of Brock Road. Denison had only three of his four regiments with him, the fourth having already gone forward with Lyle. The Marylanders had open ground in front of them that did not roll like the ground Lyle's men had crossed. Instead, the field sloped gently up to a ridge. Where the Brock Road made its eastward turn, a dirt lane branched off and ran in the opposite direction along the crest of the ridge to the Spindle farm—"a large two-story farmhouse and outbuildings"—a couple hundred yards to the west. What Federals could not see from their perspective was a dip in the ground behind the ridge, which hid another quarter of the field. The result was a kind of optical illusion that made the far tree line seem closer than it was.[55]

In that tree line, Stuart had deployed the rest of Henagan's Brigade, with another artillery piece anchoring their right. "Hold your fire until the Federals are well within range and then give it to them," the cavalryman told the South Carolinians, "and hold this position to the last man. Plenty of help is near at hand." Stuart was "just as cool as a piece of ice, though all the time laughing." One witness heard him cheerfully singing verses of the otherwise-doleful song "Lorena." The Palmetto infantry lay down behind the improvised defensive works and waited.[56]

Later, a V Corps staff officer would recall somewhat ominously that they had believed, up to this point, that only cavalry opposed them. V Corps commander Maj. Gen. Gouverneur K. Warren wanted to drive that cavalry off before they could get artillery into position. "Never mind cannon! Never mind bullets!" he snapped at the Marylanders as they began their assault. "Press on and clear this road. It's the only way to your rations." Following Warren's cue, Robinson and Denison rode forward with the attack.[57]

Confederates opened fire. "Kershaw's veterans, behind the works, lost no time in proceeding to business," a fatalistic Marylander later recalled. The topography offered some protection to the Federals as they advanced, but when they crested the ridge, they suddenly stood silhouetted for the Confederates even as they discovered that they had more open field to cross. Shocked, the Marylanders stopped momentarily and, "Naturally enough, the front rank was goaded into a return fire," said their brigade historian, while "men from the rear pressed impatiently forward to repeat the process." The pause in their momentum proved disastrous. "[T]he time of exposure was fatally prolonged," the historian, L. A.

55 Coxe, 357. The ridge would lead some soldiers to mistakenly refer to Spindle field as Laurel Hill, an actual local topographical feature, but about a mile away.

56 Ibid; William Porcher DuBose, *Reminiscences,* Southern Historical Collection, 132; Wert, *Cavalryman*, 344.

57 Wolmer, 271.

LEFT: This rare image of John C. Robinson shows him in his older years, posing with his crutches, missing the leg he lost in Spindle Field. *Congressional Medal of Honor Society*

RIGHT: Charles E. Phelps had his horse shot out from under him in the Wilderness. Following his capture at Spotsylvania, he would be rescued by Sheridan's horsemen. *Library of Congress*

Robinson and Phelps both received the Medal of Honor for their actions on May 8, 1864.

Wolmer, wrote. "[T]he situation, at that moment, was very plainly that of a forlorn hope, calling for nothing but quick and reckless work."[58]

Robinson, on horseback, tried to urge the men onward. *Use the bayonet!* he growled. Soldiers could barely hear him over the dim. "[T]he drone of bullets blended into a throbbing wall," one noted. One of those bullets whizzed in and shattered Robinson's left kneecap, knocking him from his saddle and out of the fight. Dennison, also on horseback, took a bullet in his right arm. Command thus devolved to the senior colonel in the brigade, Col. Charles Phelps of the 7th Maryland. Phelps rode to the front of the Marylanders and, in vain, tried to rally the Old Line State brigade. A hail of gun fire flew in the Harvard graduate's direction, striking his "$90 overcoat," which he wryly deemed "good as new, barring five or six unimportant bullet holes." Phelps fell wounded.[59]

58 Ibid., 272, 273.

59 Ibid., 273.

"In falling to the ground there was a vivid flash of acute pain, as if a thousand crazy-bones had been struck in one," Phelps related after the war. "The violent passage of the ball scoring its way through the breast clothing delivered the reactionary effect of a smart blow upon the region of the heart, followed by the complete severance of the large nerve and fracture of the crazy-bone." Phelps, pinned beneath his horse, passed out, although Capt. Ephraim F. Anderson of the 7th Maryland sprang to his aid.

The two men found themselves just a couple dozen yard in front of the Rebel lines, although Confederates seemed reluctant to sally out into the open field to capture them. Instead, from inside their works, Confederates shouted out to the men, imploring them to surrender, even as the remains of Maryland Brigade tumbled to the rear. Wounded, hatless, sword lost on the field, and with bullets tearing the ground around them, Phelps and Armstrong gave themselves up. Days later, Sheridan's cavalry would free them on its raid toward Richmond. For his actions at Spindle Field, Charles Phelps would eventually be presented with the Medal of Honor.[60]

Confederates had no time to rest. Brigadier General Joseph Bartlett's brigade advanced against them next. Bartlett's brigade represented the lead unit of Warren's next division, that of the crusty "Old Army" Indian fighter, Brig. Gen. Charles Griffin. Griffin and Robinson had taken different branches of the Brock Road at the Alsop farm—Robinson took the eastern leg, while Griffin took the western leg—allowing their divisions to both come nearly simultaneously to the spot where the branches reunited at nearly the same time. This allowed them to support one another, but it also meant they began getting mixed up. Robinson's brigades already suffered problems with unit cohesion because of the running fight down the Brock Road in the early morning hours; now Robinson's brigades began to get mixed up with Griffin's. Blistering heat and dry, dusty roads added to the misery, even though it was now only 9:15 a.m.

The road configuration presented another challenge for Warren, as well. At the front, Brock Road spewed Federal units onto the field like a firehose, but in the rear, units began to bottleneck once forward units made contact with the enemy. In his hurried attempt to clear the bottleneck, Warren began throwing in V Corps brigades and divisions piecemeal. "[T]he trouble lies in the fact that the enemy reached the line of ridge to be occupied, and commanding the situation only a

60 Phelps obituary and 1906 article summary in the FSNMP BV 117; *Baltimore Sun*, 27 December 1908.; *Baltimore Sun*, 28 December 1908.; Kevin Conley Ruffner, *Maryland's Blue & Gray: A Border State's Union and Confederate Junior Officer Corps* (Baton Rouge: Louisiana State University Press, 1997), 240.

little in advance of our corps . . ." groused the surly Maj. Ellis Spear of the 20th Maine. "Apparently, a half hour would have given us the ridge without firing a gun." The Confederate cavalry's overnight delay had made all the difference.[61]

Stuart rushed more of Anderson's infantry onto the field to meet Bartlett's assault, plugging them in at just the right place at just the right time, still laughing, riding up and down the line, the ostrich plume in his hat trailing behind him. "Give it to them, boys!" he shouted.[62] He also extended the Confederate right by directing Brig. Gen. Benjamin Humphreys's four Mississippi regiments into line next to the 3rd South Carolina. The 55-year-old Humphreys once attended West Point with Jefferson Davis and Robert E. Lee but was one of the cadets expelled from the academy for his role in the infamous 1826 Eggnog Riot.[63] Now no-nonsense, Humphreys led one of the hardest-hitting brigades in Lee's army. Because of the topography, Humphreys's line jutted perhaps 175 yards forward of the main position.

Meanwhile, two batteries from Maj. John C. Haskell's First Corps artillery battalion rolled into position along Brock Road. On the west side of Brock Road rolled in Capt. John R. Potts's North Carolina Battery—Potts would be killed within hours of deploying—while on the east side of the road came Capt. Hugh R. Garden's Palmetto South Carolina Artillery. The Federals countered by deploying Capt. August P. Martin's Battery C, 3rd Massachusetts Light Artillery and Lt. George Breck's Batteries E and L, 1st New York Light Artillery.

On paper, Bartlett's brigade boasted seven regiments, but the 16th Michigan, 20th Maine, and the 118th Pennsylvania were on detached duty with Brig. Gen. Samuel W. Crawford's Pennsylvania Reserves division. Bartlett advanced the four regiments he had left, the 18th Massachusetts, 1st Michigan, 44th New York, and 83rd Pennsylvania, coming onto the field to the left of Denison and driving into "the very teeth of the enemy." Several regiments got close enough to lock bayonets with the South Carolinians, "which our men used freely over the enemy's works," wrote Lt. Col. DeWitt McCoy of the 83rd Pennsylvania, "from which the regiment was only driven by the force of superior numbers." They enjoyed a brief breakthrough before their repulse, though, descending on Confederates so quickly that some of them could not rise up from the ground quickly enough to

61 Ellis Spear, letter, undated, FSNMP BV 145.

62 Coxe, 357.

63 The Eggnog Riot was a drunken Christmas party on 24–25 December 1826, that spiraled out of control. Twenty cadets were court-martialed.

defend themselves. "[A] number of our men were bayoneted in the back," recalled a chaplain in Henegan's brigade.[64]

Griffin threw in his other two brigades as support—Brig. Gen. Romeyn Ayres and Col. Jacob Sweitzer—but Bartlett's men were already tumbling back by the time the other two brigades came forward.

"Colonel [George E.] Ryan called on the regiment to follow him, and he dashed ahead on horseback," recalled Lt. Porter Farley of the 140th New York in Ayres's brigade. A Zouave unit from around Rochester, New York, the 140th made it a habit to rush into a fray haphazardly. On the slopes of Little Round Top, the regiment had made a less-famous charge than their Maine counterparts, but secured the right of the Federal position there on July 2, 1863. In the Wilderness, they had rushed across Saunders Field to initiate the first major fighting of the Overland Campaign. Now, they plunged forward against yet another fortified foe, still wearing their knapsacks and still mostly in a marching column of fours. Suddenly, the ridgeline in front of them erupted in fire, and Colonel Ryan fell from his horse, mortally wounded. He would die at a field hospital later that afternoon, muttering incoherently. Then, Maj. Milo L. Starks fell dead with a bullet to the forehead.[65]

Adding to their woes, the 11th United States Infantry, assaulting in front of the New Yorkers, broke and fell back. As the Regulars streamed into their ranks, confusion set in. "Whatever the original expectation or plan may have been with reference to forming line before assaulting the position . . ." complained Farley, "the fatal error of not doing so was either allowed or persisted in and we rushed on in that mad, blind style. . . . [W]e fell back badly handled and in great confusion. . . ."[66]

Behind the New Yorkers rushed in the 62nd Pennsylvania, a veteran Pittsburgh regiment with only fifty-seven days of service remaining on their enlistments. Unbeknownst to them, they had entered a makeshift killzone: the newly placed Confederate batteries and Humphreys's extended line, which wrapped around like a cow horn, threw bullet and ball onto the entire left flank of the assault even as fire continued to roll in from the front. The farther they assaulted, the more exposed they became to the enfilading fire of the makeshift Confederate battleline.

64 Spear, letter. The 180 men of the 22nd Massachusetts from Sweitzer's brigade were also on loan to Crawford. Also see Robert Goldthwaite Carter, *Four Brothers in Blue: A Story of the Great Civil War from Bull Run to Appomattox* (Washington: Press of Gibson Bros., Inc., 1913), 393–95; William A. Throop, report, *O.R.* 36:1:581; DeWitt C. McCoy, *O.R.* 36:1:589; DuBose, 132.

65 Porter Farley, *An Unvarnished Tale: The Public and Private Civil War of Porter Farley 140th N.Y.V.I.*, ed. Brian A. Bennett (Wheatland, NY: Triphammer Publishing, 2007), 176–77.

66 Ibid., 190–91.

Pittsburghers fell wounded and dead from shrapnel and minié balls, and Lt. Col. James Hull fell with a bullet to the hip.[67]

Finally, as a sixth wave, Col. Richard Coulter advanced. Coulter commanded Robinson's third brigade and, with Robinson on his way to the rear to have his leg amputated, Coulter now commanded the division and Col. James Bates of the 12th Massachusetts commanded the brigade.

At about the same time Bates's men came on to the field, Lyle's men, still trapped in the punchbowl, decided to make another push forward. But even as they prepared to launch, Humphrey's Mississippians launched an attack of their own from the Confederate right. Their spot on the end of the line positioned them perfectly to swing around and hit Lyle's men in the flank, flushing them from the punchbowl. "The Federals seemed completely surprised, staggered, and as we continued our rain of lead into their ranks, broke and retreated in great disorder . . ." said South Carolinian John Coxe.[68]

Most of Lyle's men retreated westward, across the Brock Road, and then rearward from there. It became a "running fight when the brigade fell back," said Abner Small of the 16th Maine. "We all fell back in some confusion, but the men steadied when clear of the flanking fire. . . ." To Massachusetts soldier Charles Peirson, it almost felt like slow motion. "The sun was so hot, and the men so exhausted from the long run as well as from the five days and nights of fighting and marching, that this retreat, though disorderly, was exceedingly slow," he recalled, "and we lost heavily in consequence from the enemy's fire."[69]

One Federal soldier, at the edge of safety, stopped and turned around, running back up the Brock Road in the direction of the Confederates. He stopped next to a cherry tree growing alongside the road. "[H]e stooped down and picked up the body of one of his comrades, put it on his shoulder, and rapidly walked back into his own lines," Coxe marveled. "No Confederate gun was trained on that man. We all admired his pluck and imagined the picked-up body was that of his kinsman or friend."

The rest of the retreating Federals found protection in the advance of Coulter's brigade, which made it just far enough into Spindle Field to discourage a Confederate counterattack. Behind the line, Warren had grabbed the broken flagstaff of the

67 Ernest D. Spisak, *Pittsburgh's Forgotten Civil War Regiment: A History of the 62nd Pennsylvania Volunteer Infantry & The Men Who Served with Distinction* (Tarentum, PA: Word Association Publishers, 2020), 432–33.

68 Coxe, 357.

69 Small, 136; Charles L. Peirson, "The Operations of the Army of the Potomac May 7-11 1864," *The Wilderness Campaign,* Papers of the Military Historical Society of Massachusetts, Vol. IV (Boston: The Military Historical Society of Massachusetts, 1905), 215–6.

In his memoir, Charles Davis of the 13th Massachusetts recounts the story depicted in Alfred Waud's sketch: "The staff of the [13th's] national colors was shattered by a solid shot. During the repulse, General Warren took the flag with its shattered staff to rally a Maryland brigade, a picture of which appeared in *Harper's Weekly* for 1864, page 372." *Library of Congress*

13th Massachusetts's colors and tried to rally the dispirited Marylanders. The men reformed, but no one was going back out across that field.

"The field in our front was blue with the dead and wounded Federals," Coxe noted. Confederates settled back into their positions on the south edge of Spindle Field and waited for more.[70]

* * *

The morning had been hotter for Confederates than most people realized. Nearly all eyes focused across Spindle Field, but even as the first of Anderson's infantry had rushed onto the scene, word arrived of a threat in the Confederate rear.

While Grant's infantry column tried to bull its way down the Brock Road, a division of his cavalry had ridden to the east, to the Fredericksburg Road, which offered a back door into Spotsylvania Court House. At the head of the strike force was one of Grant's protégé's, 26-year-old Brig. Gen. James Wilson.

70 Coxe, 357, 358.

Wilson had begun the war as a topographical engineer, first at Fort Pulaski in Georgia and later in the Eastern Theater under George McClellan. He transferred to the Western Theater and served under Grant, who took a shine to the young officer for his efficient administrative skills. He transferred back east in early 1864, this time as chief of the Cavalry Bureau, although he had no experience in that area. When Grant decided to take to the field with the Army of the Potomac, he took Wilson with him and assigned him to duty under Sheridan.

A single regiment of Confederate cavalry, the 3rd Virginia, guarded the Fredericksburg Road. The Virginia troopers had started the day along the Brock Road, scrapping with Brig. Gen. Wesley Merritt's Federal horsemen and then Warren's infantry. As Lt. Col. Carter's Virginians approached Spindle Field, they were then ordered into Spotsylvania Court House "to hold the road if possible leading to Fbg." Posted on a ridge just to the west of the Ny River, the troopers served in Brig. Gen. Williams Wickham's brigade, gathering intelligence and guarding Stuart's rear. According to one source, Wickham himself started the campaign in Richmond, and was still on his way to the front on May 8, so command of the brigade temporarily devolved to Col. Thomas T. Munford of the 2nd Virginia Cavalry. Munford was "a nice gentleman, but not remarkably brilliant intellectually," according to crusty Jubal Early.[71]

The Virginians dismounted and assumed positions on the left and right of the road. With overpowering numbers, Wilson drove straight at them. A quick fight broke out on the south bank of the Ny, but Wilson's division brushed through with relative ease as his troopers found the Confederate left flank and caved it in. They then made their way into Spotsylvania Court House—and the rear of the Confederate army.[72]

The rest of Wickham's brigade rallied to the threat while also sending word to Stuart and Anderson, who was, even at that moment, sending the lead brigades of Kershaw's division—Henagan's and Humphrey's—to meet the Federal infantry advancing toward Spindle Field. The frantic messenger from Wickham arrived in time for Anderson to divert Kershaw's other two brigades—Brig. Gen. William T. Wofford's and Brig. Gen. Goode Bryan's—toward the village.

Seeing Confederates converging from all sides, Wilson recognized the precariousness of his situation. "[U]nless prompt supported by Burnside or other infantry from the rear, I should have to give up the advantageous position I had so easily gained . . ." Wilson realized. "As the perils were thickening and reenforcements nowhere in sight, I withdrew . . . without further encountering

71 F. Ray Sibley, Jr., *The Confederate Order of Battle, Volume 1, The Army of Northern Virginia*, 296n358.

72 William R. Carter, diary entry, 8 May 1864, FSNMP BV 18; Krick, *Lee's Colonels*, 86, 284.

the enemy." Wickham's cavalry closed the gap behind Wilson and, this time, Wickham's entire brigade—all four regiments—took up the position back along the Ny. They would pass the rest of the day in relative quiet, but Grant would set his eye on Spotsylvania's back door again soon enough.[73]

The contrast between Federal and Confederate cavalry at this stage of the campaign could not have been sharper. Stuart's troopers fought tenaciously, setting up ambushes, roadblocks, and preparing defensive positions as they deftly utilized their horseflesh and the terrain. Stuart and Fitz Lee were on the field, actively directing events, and Fitz's troopers performed effectively on the line for more than 24 hours. Elsewhere, Wade Hampton exercised direct supervision of operations of his division.

On the other hand, Sheridan's arrival on the field varies wildly among eyewitness accounts, and when he did arrive, he did so in a huff, his fragile ego bruised by the fact that his boss, Meade, had asked him, of all things, to do his job. For an offensive-minded officer, Sheridan was set to "defensive mode" on May 8—defensive of his mismanagement of his troopers.

Wilson, meanwhile, had missed the May 7 fighting entirely and then missed the opportunity to delay the Confederates as they pressed him in the village—just as Stuart's and Lee's troopers had done along the Catharpin, Brock, and Fredericksburg Roads—because he couldn't hold his own against a fatigued cavalry brigade and half of a footsore infantry division. Wilson had stepped into the command of the Cavalry Corps' First Division—boots once filled by the incomparable Brig. Gen. John Buford, an old dragoon best remembered for picking a fight with Lee's army in July of 1863—and was proving an inadequate substitute. Grant's handpicked westerners were costing the Potomac army when it counted the most.

* * *

With the crisis averted in the rear, Wofford and Goode led their men back toward the front at Spindle Field, where action had also begun to settle. The two brigades settled into the position just occupied by Henegan and Humphreys, who shifted to the right as they came back into line from their charge against Lyle. Stuart also packed Frank Huger's artillery into the Brock Road/Block House Road intersection.

The First Corps' main column, meanwhile, continued its hurried march forward. Next came Maj. Gen. Charles Field's division led by Col. John Bratton's

73 James Harrison Wilson, *Under the Old Flag; Recollections of Military Operations in the War for the Union, the Spanish War, the Boxer Rebellion* (New York: D. Appleton, 1912), 393–4. For the rest of his life, Wilson rued this lost opportunity. See "James Wilson, at Spotsylvania Court House, Wondered 'What If….'" by Chris Mackowski, posted 5 December 2023, at Emerging Civil War: https://emergingcivilwar.com/2023/12/05/james-wilson-at-spotsylvania-court-house-wondered-what-if/.

five South Carolina regiments, formerly commanded by Brig. Gen. Micah Jenkins, killed two days earlier in the same volley that had so seriously wounded Longstreet. Bratton's brigade extended the Confederate left across Spindle Field. Then came Col. Dudley DuBose's Georgians and Col. William F. Perry's Alabamians, eventually followed by Brig. Gen. John Gregg's Texas Brigade with their lone, stray regiment of Arkansans. "[W]e took position, began to build breastworks, and settled down to a death struggle," wrote John Coxe.[74]

The ever-increasing presence of Confederate infantry meant artillery could not be far behind. Colonel Henry C. Cabell rolled his 16-gun battalion into battery on Anderson's left, while Lt. Col. Frank Huger's 24-gun battalion took position on Anderson's right center. Huger's guns formed a semi-salient position that jutted northward and faced north east, his guns dominating the Brock Road and the adjacent fields and wood lots. Both Confederate battalions offered plunging fire against any blue mass to their front.

North of Spindle Field, Warren likewise scrambled to get the rest of his forces into position for renewed fighting. His final two divisions—those of Brig. Gen. Lysander Cutler and the Pennsylvania physician Brig. Gen. Samuel Crawford—moved forward past the shattered remnants of Robinson's division. Griffin's reformed ranks and the guns of Warren's artillery provided protection. Crawford aligned his two brigades on the east side of the road where Lyle's men had earlier advanced. Cutler aligned his three brigades on the west side of the road, where Denison, Bartlett, and Ayres had earlier advanced.

"The enemy were in position in the woods, skirting forward toward the center of the field and lying under cover of a slight elevation of ground," wrote one of Cutler's brigade commanders, Edward Bragg. "The troops advanced in good order for 250 yards across the field, when the enemy's advance opened a brisk fire, which checked the onward movement." Bragg said a wave of panic swept over the brigade, "and confusion instead of order, was the rule in the rear. But . . . they were once more rallied, and the Pennsylvania flag, with the stars and stripes, were carried to the top of the crest, planted upon the ground, the mob was straightened out. . . ." The "slight elevation" Bragg mentioned was the ridgeline occupied by the Spindle farm and which had caused trouble for Denison's Marylanders. Some of Bragg's beleaguered men took up positions in the farm's buildings and began sniping at the Confederate line.[75]

Sarah Spindle lived in a one-and-a-half story wood house and was sitting down to breakfast with four of her family members when the armies first arrived.

74 Coxe, 358.

75 Edward S. Bragg, report, *O.R.* 36:1:637; Edward S. Bragg to Earl M. Rogers, letter, 6 April 1900, Wisconsin Historical Society.

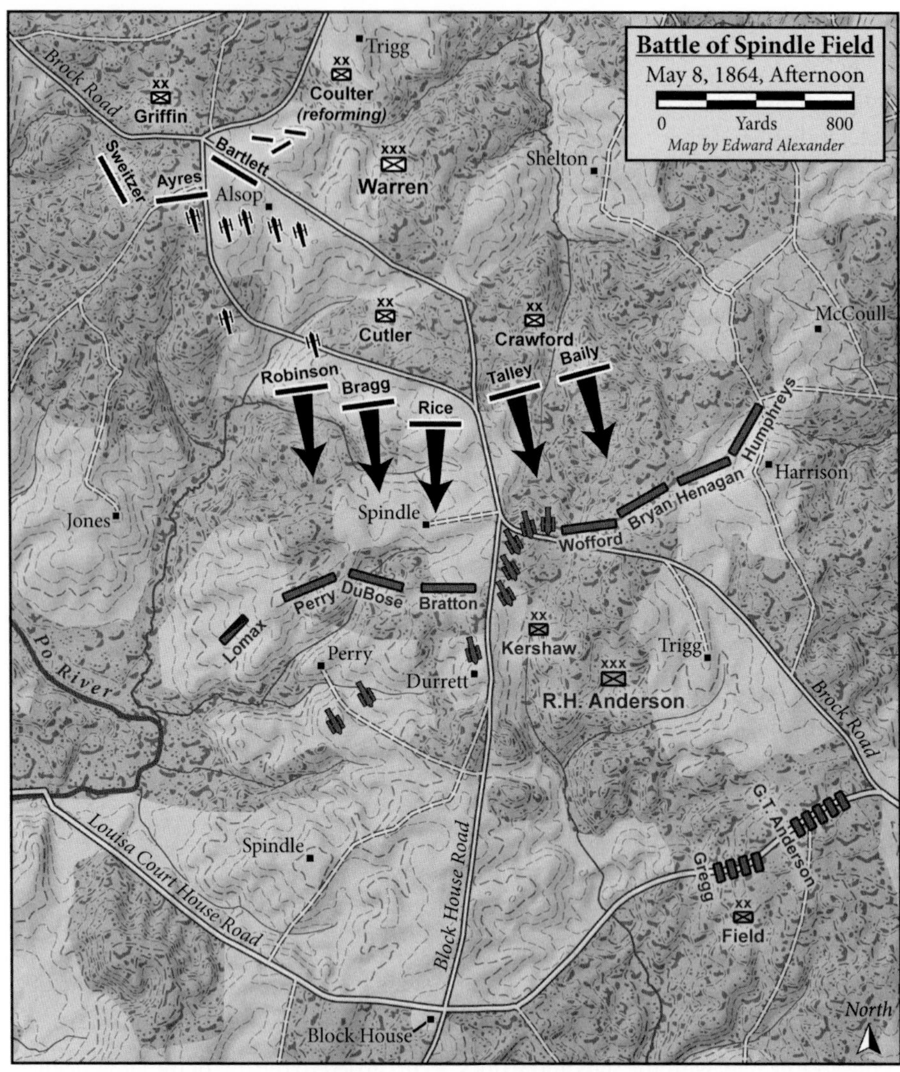


**Battle of Spindle Field, Afternoon**—After initial piecemeal attacks failed to dislodge Confederates, Federal V Corps commander Gouverneur K. Warren followed up with a more powerful attack by Cutler's and Crawford's divisions. Additional Confederate reinforcements strengthened the Southern position enough to repulse them.

---

They had sheltered in place during the first waves of fighting, but the Federals occupying the farm changed the dynamic. "Stuart ordered the artillery to burn the buildings, and the very first incendiary shell from the brass cannon fired the main building," Coxe recalled. "And then I saw a sight I never wanted to see again. A woman bareheaded, her long hairs streaming behind, ran out of the big house and

Conrad Freitag, a member of the 14th Brooklyn/84th New York, became a renowned artist after the war. One of his paintings depicted the experience of his regiment at Spindle Field, with the Spindle house aflame in the left of the image. *Fredericksburg and Spotsylvania National Military Park*

across the field to the left between the two fighting armies and reached shelter in the woods on the Po River."[76]

Spindle's oldest son, 26-year-old William, was serving with the 9th Virginia Cavalry that morning, elsewhere on the battlefield. Witnesses do not record what happened to the other four members of the family or the seventeen slaves who lived and worked on the Spindle farm. After Sarah's flight to the Po, her house burned down and was never rebuilt, and the Spindle family disappeared from history.

"[T]he dwelling was burning fiercely when the [84th New York] arrived at the clearing," recalled a member of the regiment, the "Red-Legs," "and here the fighting also became hot. Like hail the bullets spattered on the rail fences lining the road behind which the Red-legs took scant refuge. Besides those who had been struck by bullets, several were prostrated by the combined heat of the sun and the burning house."[77]

Colonel William W. Robinson's Iron Brigade anchored the right of Cutler's line, and the 6th Wisconsin anchored the far right of the Iron Brigade's right, although they themselves had nothing to anchor on. Their colonel, Rufus Dawes, threw skirmishers out to the regiment's right to keep watch for trouble, but the Wisconsinites soon found their attention drawn forward to the ravine on the back side of the Spindle

76 Coxe, 358.

77 MBCW I, N.Y., 422, 119. Quoted in Noel Harrison, *Gazetteer of Historic Sites Related to Fredericksburg and Spotsylvania National Military Park*, Vol. 1 (Fredericksburg and Spotsylvania National Military Park, 1986), 284.

farm ridge. Confederates there were blasting away at them. The pressure caused the regiment to Dawes's left to retreat "in confusion." And then more bad news arrived. "My skirmishers on the right were driven in, and reported the enemy moving without opposition around our right," Dawes wrote. "I endeavored to preserve the integrity of my command by retiring slowly through the woods, but outflanked both ways and pressed by the enemy from all sides, the line broke in disorder."[78]

On the east side of the Brock Road, the situation for Crawford went no better, from top down. The division took a position in "an oak forest," according to the perennially unhappy Ellis Spear, and "were subjected to heavy shelling, a most unpleasant experience and trying to the nerves. . . ." An exploding artillery shell knocked a tree into Crawford, which in turn knocked him out of the fight. Command devolved to Col. William McCandless of the brigade of Pennsylvania Reserves. "[W]ading knee deep through mud and water, and being raked by shrapnel," the men charged forward, but McCandless went down. His replacement, Col. William C. Tally of the 1st Pennsylvania Reserves, was soon thereafter captured. Colonel Wellington H. Ent of the 6th Pennsylvania Reserves and Col. Samuel M. Jackson of the 11th Pennsylvania Reserves both took turns in command, but the changes in command took their toll under the heavy Confederate fire. "Deprived of their leader, and more or less disorganized through the distance they had advanced, the Reserves fell back," wrote O. R. Howard Thompson of the 13th Pennsylvania Reserves. The rest of Crawford's division fell back, as well.[79]

Crawford's and Cutler's divisions withdrew to the north edge of Spindle Field where Griffin's division had begun throwing up earthworks. Cutler extended the Federal line on the right, Crawford on the left. Robinson's men were a little further to the rear at the Alsop farm—what was left of them—but the division had been so shattered by the morning's initial piecemeal attacks that Warren would dissolve it and split the remaining units among the corps' other three divisions.

For Warren, once the wunderkind of the Army of the Potomac, the morning had been an unmitigated disaster—and this on top of a few rough days in the Wilderness, where his corps suffered so many casualties that he doctored his troop returns lest army headquarters be too alarmed. He had criticized Federal cavalry commander Phil Sheridan because Sheridan's troopers had not cleared the road and now, more than six hours later, Warren hadn't cleared it yet, either.

78 Rufus Dawes, report, *O.R.* 36:1:619.

79 Ellis Spear, letter, *With a Flash of His Sword: The Writings of Major Holman S. Melcher 20th Maine Infantry*, William B. Styple, ed. (Kearny, NJ.: Belle Grove Publishing Co., 1994), 180–81; *O.R.* Howard Thompson, *History of the "Bucktails,"* (Philadelphia: Electric Printing Co., 1906), 300.

"[Anderson's] men left the trenches last night at 11 o'clock, and are as tired as mine," he wrote, exasperated. [80]

In a note to army headquarters, Warren admitted his befuddlement: "with the force I now have I cannot attack again . . ." but at the same time, "I dare not fall back, for then I shall disclose my feelings of weakness." He was low on ammunition. He had lost his old white horse. His staff was all tired out.[81]

"The rebels," he wrote a little while later, "are as tired out as we are."[82]

* * *

The advance of Cutler's and Crawford's divisions onto the field of battle did manage to produce one deleterious effect: it freed up some of the logjam along the Brock Road, making room for Maj. Gen. John Sedgwick's VI Corps to finally march to the front. "We pressed forward along a long narrow road leading through a thick growth of timber," wrote George T. Stevens of the 77th New York, who complained about the intensity of the heat. "The day had been the most sultry of the season. . . ."[83]

Soldiers saw the aftermath of the previous night's fighting at every turn. "We passed our ambulances loaded with our wounded comrades & saw lots of men laying by the road side that were wounded," recalled Simon B. Cummins of the 151st New York. "Some with a leg off, some with an arm off, some a hand, some a foot. I tell you it was a hard sight to behold." Such scenes hardly fortified men on the march into battle.[84]

As Sedgwick's men reached the split in the Brock Road, they marched to the left. This took them around the eastern edge of the Alsop farm. Warren moved his corps to the southern edge of the farm and deployed them to the right (west), then ordered them to dig in and wait for orders. The exception was Crawford's division, still deployed on the east side of the Brock Road; Warren did not move them lest, in doing so, he invite a Confederate attack against the Federal left. They stayed in place as Sedgwick's men arrived around them and began to fortify. As the senior officer on the field, Sedgwick should have taken command, but he deferred to Warren, in part because Warren had been there all day and had a clear idea of the

80 Morris Schaff, *The Battle of the Wilderness* (Boston: Houghton Mifflin, 1919), 210; Warren to Andrew Humphreys, 8 May 1864, *O.R.* 36:2:540–1.

81 Ibid.

82 Warren to George Meade, letter, 8 May 1864, *O.R.* 36:2:541.

83 George T. Stevens, *Three Years in the Sixth Corps* (New York: D. Van Nostrand, 1870), 328.

84 Simon Burdick Cummins, *Give God the Glory: Memoirs of a Civil War Solider,* Melvin Jones, ed. (Paris Press, 1979), 68.

situation, and in part because Sedgwick could see how prickly Warren was with his hackles up.

And Warren's hackles were definitely up. "General Sedgwick's corps was sent up to crush out Longstreet [Anderson]," the V Corps commander wrote resentfully. Yet the highest hackles belonged to Army of the Potomac commander George Gordon Meade. Warren's corps had spent an entire day failing to clear the road; in doing so, Warren had allowed Confederates to begin concentrating. In an effort to still muscle his way through, Meade sent Sedgwick forward to "join Warren in a prompt and vigorous attack on the enemy. . . . Use every exertion to move with the utmost dispatch." He reiterated this urgency to Warren: "It is of the utmost importance the attack of yourself and Sedgwick be made with vigor and without delay."[85]

Meade reinforced the point even further by sending his aid, Theodore Lyman, to the front, where Lyman found Warren, Sedgwick, and one of Sedgwick's division commanders, Horatio Wright, in conversation. "Was struck by their worn and troubled aspect," Lyman noted, "more especially in Sedgwick, who showed its effect more from contrast with his usual calmness. . . . And never, perhaps, were officers more jaded and prostrated than on this very Sunday."[86]

With two full corps now at the front—perhaps 34,000 men, nearly half the infantry—Meade expected them to advance together and, through sheer weight of numbers, overwhelm Lee's concentrating forces.[87] Rather that rush down the Brock Road again, though, Meade wanted to use troops to pin Anderson in place on the far side of Spindle Field while he concentrated the bulk of the attack on the Confederate right flank, off in the woods to the east of Brock Road. Confederates had arrived on the field via the Block House Road, which ran behind the Confederate left and westward across the Po River. If Meade could turn the Confederate right and force it, hinge-like, back onto the Confederate left, in theory, the Rebels would be forced back across the Po, or at least out of the Potomac army's way as it renewed the march to Spotsylvania Court House.

85 Warren, report, *O.R.* 36:1:541; Meade to Sedgwick, *O.R.* 36:2:545; Meade to Warren, *O.R.* 36:2:541.

86 Lyman, 145.

87 Calculating the exact number of men in the ranks at this stage of the campaign is problematic. The V Corps started the campaign with 24,423 officers and men and lost 5,132 officers and men in the Wilderness. The VI Corps started the campaign with 23,165 officers and men and lost 5,035 men in the Wilderness. Evidence suggests that Warren doctored his losses in the Wilderness. They could have been substantially higher. Also, the march to and from the Wilderness was taxing. Straggling was an issue. Then the losses at Spindle Field were not immediately reported and mostly folded in with the loses for the entire two-and-a-half-week battle. On paper, the units should have mustered some 34,000 men, but that number could be as low as 30,000. For more information, see the *O.R.* 33:1036; *O.R.* 36:1:119–137; Rhea, *The Battle of the Wilderness*, 34, 252; Schaff, 209–10.

New Yorker George Stevens, inspecting the landscape of attack, saw "the ground was rolling and partially wooded, admirably adapted for defensive warfare." Like the Federals, Confederates had used the afternoon lull to continue improving their position, creating "breastworks of logs, rails and earth," Anderson reported. Kershaw's division occupied the ground on the east side of the Brock Road/Block House Road intersection and Field's occupied the west, with Huger's artillery packed into the intersection itself. Lee reached the field by 6:00 p.m. at the head of Richard Ewell's Second Corps, with Maj. Gen. Robert Rodes's division in the lead.[88]

Meade had told Warren "to attack vigorously and without loss of time," but in a note to Grant, the army commander confided, "I fear the morale of his men is impaired." Meade's concerns turned into prophecy. Hours elapsed before the attack finally went forward, and when it did, Sedgwick's corps did most of the heavy lifting; Warren's men, exhausted and disorganized from the morning's fight, exerted little pressure comparatively. The one exception was Crawford's division, which found itself sandwiched between several VI Corps brigades.[89]

The Federal attack finally came at 6:20 p.m. The VI Corp swept down from its newly constructed position into low, swampy ground edged with pine, then up a forested slope "where we could see but little distance," said Mainer Ellis Spear. On they went, "with loud yells," and the Confederate line opened on them. "Yet though our companies seemed to melt away," wrote a member of the 15th New Jersey, "our gallant fellows plunged ahead through the soft mud."[90]

Confederates repulsed the assault, in Anderson's words, "without difficulty."

Crawford's once-proud Pennsylvania Reserves, in the vanguard, had but a few weeks of army life left, and their hearts were not in the assault. Gunfire, the dim glow of the setting sun, and the smoke of the battlefield intermingled shadows and light with the real and imagined horrors of the field. Crawford's division broke upon itself. The first line melted into the second, yet again creating confusion among the ranks.

Spear, in the second line, clutched a discarded flag as he tried to rally the soldiers. "The light was then so dim in the woods that the blue was hardly distinguishable from grey . . . clubbed muskets mixing with bayonets, and shooting," he said. A member of the 118th Pennsylvania—one of Bartlett's regiments on detail to Crawford—said "Men fought with desperation. Hungered, fatigued, discouraged, they were goaded to frenzied madness."

88 Stevens, 328; Anderson, report, 3.

89 Meade, endorsement, *O.R.* 36:2:540.

90 Spear, letter; Haines, 158.

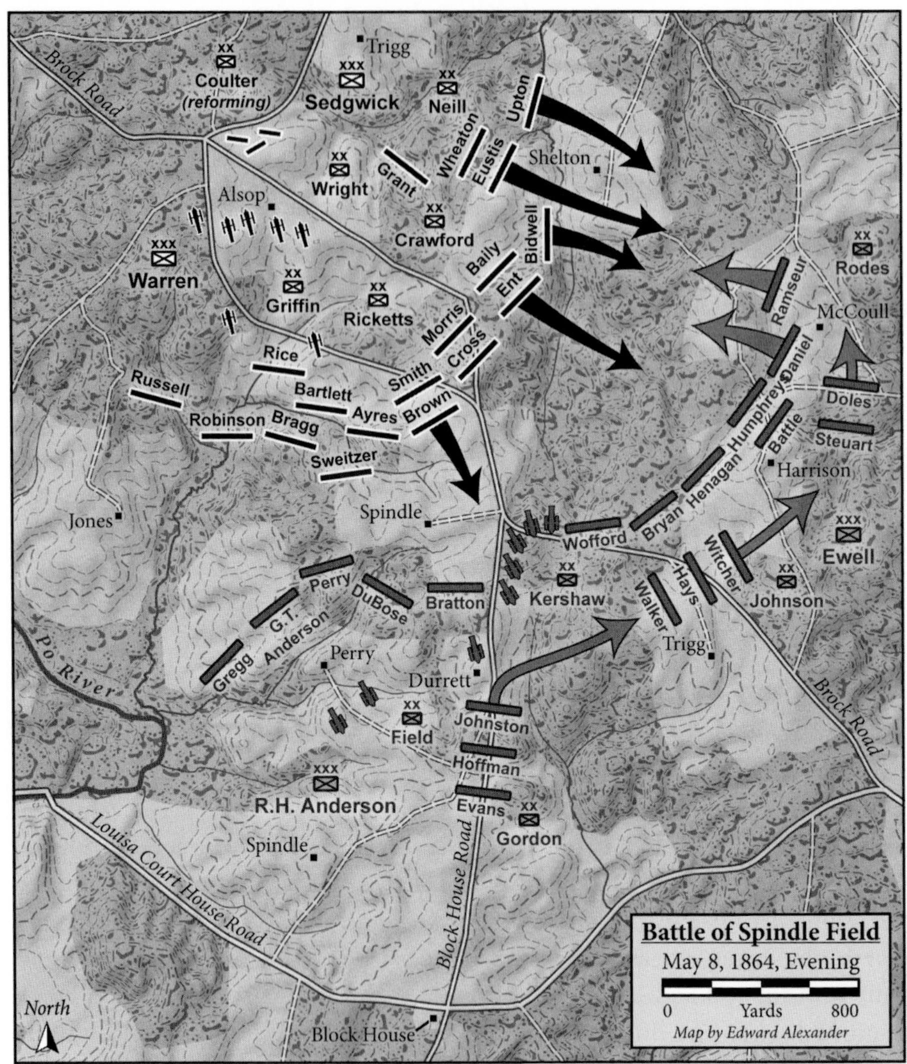


**Battle of Spindle Field, Evening**—The Federal VI Corps came onto the field for a coordinated attack with the V Corps. The Confederate Second Corps marched onto the battlefield in time to help repulse the attack and launch a counterattack of their own. By dark, the two sides settled into a stalemate and began to fortify.

---

Brigadier General Thomas H. Neill's division, on the Federal left, might have outflanked the Confederate position if not for the timely arrival of Maj. Gen. Robert Rodes's Second Corps division. Rodes was just deploying beyond Kershaw's right flank as Neill's men attacked. Rodes advanced his brigades to meet them. "[T]he enemy came pell-mell into our lines . . ." said Capt. Robert Carter of the 22nd Massachusetts. "There was no time to reload, men threw down their arms, and 'went in rough and tumble' where fists were freely used." In the melee, William Mulhearn of the 22nd Massachusetts was said to have killed "six or more" Confederates by rifle fire, bayonet, and rifle-butt. Captain Benjamin F. Davis of the 22nd Massachusetts's Company G successfully seized the flag of the 6th Alabama.[91]

But in the end, the Federals could not hold on. "Our men fired a volley or two, rose up, faced about, and moved back a few rods, to avoid being flanked," Carter reported.[92]

The counterattack turned into a rout, with Brig. Gen. Cullen Battle's five Alabama regiments pushing all the way to the Federal works. Battle's men had made a similar assault on the first day of the battle of the Wilderness, marching onto the battlefield and straight into an oncoming Federal assault. This time, though, they found Federal entrenchments and two battle lines behind them.

"Just at this time, too, there was much confusion on my right, caused in great measure by the crowding together of troops of my own and other brigades," Battle reported. Still, the Federals seemed evidently demoralized, and Battle felt he could carry the position. "I attempted to lead forward all the troops at that point," he recounted. He grabbed the colors of the 3rd Alabama and called for his men to follow. "I regret to say that the result did not correspond to my high hopes and confident expectations," he admitted, "a result no doubt greatly attributed to physical exhaustion from long marching, constant labor, and their rapid advance." Ramseur's men joined Battle's on the front, "with results scarcely better than before," Battle said. The two rebuffed brigades retired together.

Battle's men would later be accused of not going in. His brigade's reputation impugned, Battle's report reflected his indignant response: "The men are still much exhausted, and I have received a painful injury on my right foot, but if the service requires it, and the honor of my command requires it, we are ready for action." However, they would not be called on again that night.[93]

91 Pension record of Benjamin Davis, The National Archives, "Civil War Widows' Pensions, 1861–1910." Davis enlisted in the 22nd Massachusetts on 3 Sept. 1861, in Company B. He was promoted to captain of Company G on 12 February 1863. Davis was killed on 10 May 1864, near Laurel Hill while, "having gone to the front 'to view the enemys [sic] position.'" His father Daniel Davis submitted the pension application. The flag of the 6th Alabama was forwarded to the U.S. War Department on 6 October 1864, by Gen. Warren. The flag was assigned capture number 194, and was returned to the state of Alabama on 25 March 1905. See the Alabama Department of Archives & History https://digital.archives.alabama.gov/digital/collection/cw_flags/id/100.

92 Carter, *Four Brothers in Blue,* 393–395.

93 Cullen Battle, report, *O.R.* 36:1:1083–4.

The Federals felt just as rebuffed. "With overpowering numbers opposed, we fell back, and all this dash, so costly to us, accomplished nothing," lamented a member of the New Jersey brigade. The New Jersians had been posted near the spot where the two branches of the Brock Road reunited on the north end of Spindle Field, and it had fallen to them to pin Anderson in place on the field's south end. The Garden State boys had advanced only to run into a terrible hailstorm of lead from Huger's artillery.[94]

The gloaming settled into full dark. "Those who could walk came in by themselves; and later, those borne in the arms of their comrades," wrote the chaplain of the 15th New Jersey. "It was a terrible thing to lay some of our best and bravest men in a long row on the blankets, waiting their turn for the surgeon's care. Some came in with body wounds, and others with arms shattered and hands dangling."[95]

Meade and Grant had come to the front to watch the attack, although from their position on a little knoll, they could see little more than Neill's division advancing past them. "There was skirmishing just in our front," Lyman noted, "and the balls came clicking among the large trees, while a shell occasionally added its crashing to the general noise." The place, he said, "waxed hot." Grant soon left, followed shortly thereafter by a furious Meade.[96]

At headquarters, Meade let his anger loose: Sedgwick was constitutionally slow! Burnside was too late in the Wilderness to do any good! The men were now too tired to achieve anything![97]

By the time Warren and Sedgwick showed up for an after-dinner conference, Meade's fury had not abated. When Meade asked Warren for his opinion on events the day, the V Corps commander, perhaps thinking silence was the better part of valor, remarked, "I haven't any opinion to give."

Meade certainly had one: "You lost your nerve today," he snapped. Warren replied with indignance, but Meade would have none of it.[98]

Sedgwick was not safe from the old snapping turtle, either. Turning to him, Meade sneered, "I desire you to take command of your own corps."[99]

The conference broke up. Warren tried to buck up Sedgwick, who remained sullen. Everyone returned to their headquarters.

Four days old, the campaign was already unlike anything the army—either of the armies—had engaged in before. The Army of the Potomac had begun its march

94 Haines, 158.

95 Ibid., 159.

96 Lyman, 145.

97 Ibid., 146.

98 Ibid.

99 Rhea, *Battles for Spotsylvania Court*, 86.

on May 4, had fought pitched battles on May 5 and 6, skirmished all day May 7, marched overnight May 7–8, and resumed the fight on May 8 by 4:30 a.m.—all in intense heat.

Yet as soon as the Army of the Potomac began maneuvering on the Brock Road, things had begun to go awry. New Yorker Porter Farley, in his own private grousing, summed it up best: "[t]he affair was certainly very poorly managed. . . ." That mismanagement had started with Sheridan's failure to clear the road on May 7 and mushroomed to a grand scale involving nearly the entire Federal high command by the end of May 8.[100]

If one could see through the frustration, though, one might notice that Grant was achieving one of his main operational and strategic goals: nullifying Lee's army and bludgeoning it. Yes, Lee had blocked the road to the Confederate capital, but that same decision tied him in place. The Army of Northern Virginia couldn't break and run, nor could it retake the offensive initiative. Grant's army had Lee's by the arm, and although Lee was still a dangerous opponent, Grant was calling the shots.

VI Corps staff officer Thomas Hyde articulated the day's frustration in his journal. "The dim impression of that afternoon is of things going wrong, and of the general exposing himself uselessly and keeping us back, of Grant's coming up and taking a look, of much bloodshed and futility," he wrote. "Then the dismal night in the tangled forest, the hooting of owls, the embrace of the wood-tick, bang-bang from the picket lines, then a dozen more, then the dreamless repose of utter fatigue."[101]

Back at the front, Warren felt punch-drunk exhausted. Yet he was not so exhausted that he couldn't try to get the last word in. He had mulled over a reply—part indignant, part conciliatory, wavering back and forth—ever since leaving Meade's tent. "In truth, I only meant that there is but one thing left: to fight it out," he wrote. "I think it is very hard to do, but the object of war, a settlement, can never be come to without doing so." It was Grant's strategy sprung from Warren's pen: no turning back.[102]

Warren concluded his note abruptly: "I am so sleepy I can hardly write intelligently."[103]

And then the utter fatigue ended his day.

100 Farley, 176.

101 Thomas Hyde, *Following the Greek Cross, or, Memories of the Sixth Army Corps*, (Columbia, SC: University of South Carolina Press, 2005), 191–2.

102 Warren to Meade, *O.R.* 36:2:542.

103 Ibid.

Nelson Miles would one day go on to become general in chief of the United States Army, but late on the morning on May 8, 1864, the 24-year-old colonel was poking what looked to be a giant Confederate beehive. Already, a Confederate cavalry screen swarmed in Miles's front and, in the distance, he could see plumes of dust rising in the air, as if made by ten thousand marching feet rather than the buzz of wings. Separating Miles's five regiments from the Confederate force was the Po River, spanned only by Corbin's Bridge. Both sides seemed content to lob shells at each other with their field artillery and see what developed.

But this was the development as far as Confederate Maj. Gen. Wade Hampton was concerned. Cavalry commander Jeb Stuart had tasked Hampton with guarding the western leg of the Catharpin Road, an essential link in Lee's route from the Wilderness to Spotsylvania Court House. Lee had to cover that distance using exterior lines, which, in turn, required more time—compared to Grant's quicker, shorter interior line along Brock Road. Hampton, screening that movement, hoped the Federals would fall for his feint and not aggressively press forward to cross the bridge. Should they do so, they could block the Confederate line of march and defeat Lee's army in detail. So long as they didn't, though, the Army of Northern Virginia could continue its forced march to the battle shaping up on the edge of Spindle Field. Behind Hampton's screen, the lead elements of Ewell's Second Corps marched past: Maj. Gen. Robert Rodes's division, whose men would later find themselves thrown into the crucible of battle even as they arrived on the battlefield.

Federals felt almost exactly the same way. With the main Federal thrust pointed southward along Brock Road, Miles was more concerned with protecting the army's flank than with forcing anything against Hampton. Should Confederates aggressively push east and achieve a large-scale penetration in the vicinity of Todd's Tavern, Lee's army could get in Grant's rear, cripple part of the Federal supply chain, and cut off one of the major routes of retreat for the Army of the Potomac.

Miles had arrived at the Todd's Tavern intersection around 9:00 a.m. to find Brig. Gen. David M. Gregg's cavalry skirmishing with their Confederate counterparts along the Catharpin Road just west of the tavern. Miles ordered his men in as support, and the Confederates fell back as far as Corbin's Bridge, two miles to the rear. There, they set up their position on the west bank of the Po River and greeted Miles's approach with artillery fire. The Federal infantry advanced only as far as a treeline paralleling the east bank of the river. Miles wasn't sure what he was looking at—Confederate skirmishers, artillery, a heavy column of dust—but he worried it might come at him. He remained content to line up his regiments and wait, standing guard.

"The day is very hot and the roads dusty, a large force of cavalry and infantry are massed here ready for service at a moment's notice," wrote one of his men, Newton

Kirk of the 26th Michigan. "We improve the time in felling trees, and constructing defenses for we know not the moment when the enemy will be upon us."[104]

Col. Nelson Miles survived a gutshot at the battle of Chancellorsville in May 1863 where his "extraordinary heroism" earned him a Medal of Honor for "distinguished gallantry while holding with his command an advanced position against repeated assaults by a strong force of the enemy." *Library of Congress*

Miles lead the way for of Maj. Gen. Winfield Scott Hancock's II Corps, finally making its move from the Brock Road/Plank Road, where he had served as the Federal rear guard. Miles's primary concern was to prevent Confederates from attacking Hancock's new position around Todd's Tavern. "[A]s silence reigns, I suppose they are successful," Hancock reported to army headquarters.[105]

Hancock's defensive posture—unusual for the normally aggressive corps commander—sprang from lessons hard-learned during the three brutal days in the Wilderness. Hancock had launched a massive attack on the second morning of the battle, May 6, and in return absorbed a massive counterattack from Longstreet's corps later that morning. Confederates hammered at him late in the day, then harassed him throughout May 7. Now the corps had finally moved down Brock Road to reunite with the army, although the fighting ahead at Spindle Field bottlenecked the route enough that Hancock could not advance his men any farther than Todd's Tavern.

A member of the West Point Class of 1844, the 40-year-old Hancock had a well-earned reputation for intelligent aggressiveness and dependable grit. Even Confederate opponents gave him his due, "his attacks always meaning heavy pounding from start to finish." Grant, in his memoirs, would one day describe Hancock as "the most conspicuous figure of all the general officers who did not

104 Newton Thorne Kirk Papers, Michigan State University Archives and Historical Collections, Michigan State University, FSNMP BV 35.

105 Hancock to Humphreys, 8 May 1864, *O.R.* 36:2:531.

exercise a separate command." Admiring Hancock's service as a corps commander, Grant continued:

> his name was never mentioned as having committed in battle a blunder for which he was responsible. He was a man of very conspicuous personal appearance. . . . His genial disposition made him friends, and his personal courage and his presence with his command in the thickest of the fight won for him the confidence of troops serving under him. No matter how hard the fight, the 2nd corps always felt that their commander was looking after them.[106]

Other admirers simply called him "superb."[107]

At the battle of Gettysburg in the summer of '63, Hancock sustained an agonizing wound when a bullet passed through the pommel of his saddle and into his inner right thigh, carrying with it bits of leather, horse hide, a bent nail, and other material. The injury, which required hospitalization, festered for months before doctors finally located the last of the detritus. By the start of the 1864 campaign, the wound had not healed entirely, and Hancock was forced at times to ride in a carriage because horseback proved too physically uncomfortable.

And so it was, battle weary and in pain, that Hancock warily arrayed his four divisions facing west, from right to left: Gershom Mott, Francis Barlow, John Gibbon, and David Bell Birney. Despite Miles's screen, intelligence suggested Hancock should anticipate an attack. "I directed my division commanders to intrench their lines, to slash the timber in their front, and to obstruct the road leading to the enemy," he later reported.[108]

Around 1:20 p.m., in answer to a plea from Warren at the front, Hancock sent Gibbon's division down the Brock Road to the rescue. Gibbon would end up intercepted by army commander Meade at the Alsop farm, just shy of the action. "I am instructed to inform you that General Sedgwick is directed to re-enforce Warren with his whole corps," Chief of Staff Andrew Humphreys wrote to Hancock—a message that meant Gibbon was not going the rest of the way forward.[109]

106 Thomas Carter, *S.H.S.P.* 21:239; Ulysses S. Grant, *Personal Memoirs of Ulysses S. Grant*, Vol. 2 (Charles Webster & Co., 1885), 539–40.

107 George B. McClellan to Mary Ellen McClellan, telegram, 6 May 1862, *The Civil War Papers of George B. McClellan: Selected Correspondence, 1860–1865*, Stephen W. Sears, ed. (New York: Da Capo, 1992), 256–7.

108 Winfield Scott Hancock, report, *O.R.* 36:1:329.

109 Humphreys to Hancock, *O.R.*:2:533.

The afternoon passed tensely. "The greatest vigilance is required under the circumstances," Hancock's assistant adjutant, Francis A. Walker, wrote to II Corps division commander Gershom Mott. Mott sent skirmishers back up the Brock Road to keep eyes on the army's flank and down an eastward branch of the Catharpin Road to keep eyes on the army's rear.

At that critical moment and juncture, the Federal army was blinded. Gregg's troopers were removed eastward toward Chancellorsville. There, the undersized division would resupply and prepare for the trek toward Richmond Grant had foolishly approved.

"And so the Second Corps stood to arms, all the afternoon and into the evening," Walker wrote later in his capacity as II Corps historian, "believing that another of its great days of battle had come and that it was to be called upon to resist a supreme effort of a Confederate general who had shown such capacity for dangerous initiative. . . ."[110]

In fact, that Confederate general still had no a clear sense of Grant's intentions. Lee rode to the front himself to take stock. In the meantime, his Third Corps under Early operated under orders to strike east toward the Plank Road where it headed in the direction of Fredericksburg and, possibly, a chance to intercept Grant. That meant, after following the artillery road out of the Wilderness, the Third Corps would not follow the Second but, instead, follow the Catharpin Road to Todd's Tavern and then beyond. "[A] continuation of my march would have led through his [Meade's] entire army," Early realized.[111]

In the van marched Richard Anderson's former division, now commanded by Brig. Gen. William "Little Billy" Mahone in the wake of Anderson's recent assignment to the First Corps. Mahone's men materialized behind Wade Hampton's cavalry screen.

Unlike their Federal counterparts, the Confederate infantry and cavalry had communicated and cooperated well with one another throughout the day. Hampton pushed his newly attached Laurel Brigade, under Brig. Gen. Thomas L. Rosser, and Col. Gilbert J. Wright's mixed Mississippi and Georgia brigade northeast along the Catharpin Road. Some of Hampton's troopers dismounted and took to the woodlots along both sides of the road and began sparring with Miles's thin skirmish

110 Francis A. Walker, *History of the Second Army Corps in the Army of the Potomac* (New York: C. Scribner's Sons, 1886), 445.

111 Jubal Anderson Early, *Lieutenant General Jubal Anderson Early, C.S.A.: Autobiographical sketch and narrative of the War between the States* (Philadelphia: J. B. Lippincott Company, 1912), 352.

Artist Alfred Waud captured the Army of the Potomac as it marched down the Brock Road past Todd's Tavern. *Library of Congress*

line, which consisted of the 26th Michigan and the seven companies of the 140th Pennsylvania.[112] The exchange of fire along the line was brisk.

Lieutenant Thomas White, Company C of the 35th Virginia Battalion of Cavalry, was tasked with pressing the Federal line. He took hand-selected "sharpshooters"—simply men equipped with long rifles—into some of the dense woods near the Federals front. Miles began to pull back to the safer cordon the II Corps had formed around Todd's Tavern. White would be unable to press his own success, however. "In a few minutes I saw a small squad of our dismounted men making their way out of the woods carrying, as we thought, a wounded comrade," said a member of the 35th Virginia Battalion, "which proved to be the lifeless body of Lieutenant White, a gallant and appreciated officer who had led the 'Sharpshooters' into the woods."[113]

Meantime, Miles turned around to fend off Mahone's attack from the northwest. "The collision was sharp," recalled Walker.[114]

Mahone and Hampton worked in tandem to bring the Southern infantry to the field from the northwest, while Hampton's troopers pressed in from the southwest. The improvised plan came together better than Confederates could have hoped.

112 The 140th may have had eight companies on the skirmish line. In his post-battle report, Capt. Thomas Henry of the 140th stated that seven companies were on the line, but he was not in command that day of the regiment or the skirmish line. Another account written in 1906 claims that eight companies were on the line with Company K and another unknown company in reserve. See *O.R.* 36:1:383 and Benjamin F. Powelson and Aleck Sweeney, *The History of Company K of the 140th Regiment Pennsylvania Volunteers*, 34.

113 John E. Devine, *35th Virginia Battalion Virginia Cavalry* (Lynchburg: H.E. Howard, Inc., 1985), 50.

114 Walker, 445.

Major George Scott of the 61st New York complained, "We were suffering heavy loss from the enemy's cross-fire, and our right flank being in great danger. . . ." Miles was nearly killed while at the front and had to seek shelter from the enemy fire.[115]

Lieutenant Colonel Knut Oscar Brundin of the 61st New York countered by forwarding the reserve companies of the 140th Pennsylvania to the front, ordering the men to "cheer as we went in," recalled a member of the 140th's Company K. The fire was so intense that the battalion was forced to halt and established a base of fire some 150 yards to the left rear of the New Yorkers, using a fence line for cover. With the enemy's sights now set on the men of the Keystone state, the 61st New York took the opportunity to retire "slowly and in good order to the line of the 140th Pennsylvania Volunteers, bringing off all of our wounded."[116]

On the other end of Miles's line, things went from bad to worse. The Michiganders and Pennsylvanians on the skirmish line were in danger of being cut off. Miles dispatched his aide, Lt. Robert S. Robertson, to extract the skirmishers, which nearly cost Robertson his life. As the Confederates attacked, "I had to ride directly at them to get out to our own brigade and cross a stream," Roberston told his parents in a post-battle letter. "As I turned up the hill only a few rods in front of them, they gave a yell and fired at me, but my horse almost flew and none of their shot struck me." Robertson continued his flight, jumping a nearby fence. His saddle loosened, turned, and dumped him to the ground mid-air. Bullets whizzed about him as he remounted "and lay close to [the horse's] neck till I was safe with the brigade. . . ."[117]

115 Isaac Plumb, diary entry, 8 May 1864, USAHEC, Carlisle, PA, FSNMP BV 110.

116 Plumb, diary entry. Plumb was a captain in Company C, 61st New York. Lieutenant Colonel Kunt Oscar Brundin was also known as Oscar Brody and Oscar Broady. Born in Sweeden, Brundin was a former member of the Swedish navy, and a graduate of Colgate College. He entered the war at the head of Company C, 61st New York.

117 Robert S. Robertson to parents, letter, 14 May 1864, FSNMP BV 219.

Rosser's troopers sensed that the Yankees were breaking. "My men were very enthusiastic," he said, "and as soon as we came up with the main body of the enemy we charged him, capturing over two hundred prisoners, with their horses and arms, and drove them pell-mell before us." Three of Mahone's brigades continued the pursuit.[118]

Meanwhile, at apparently the least opportune moment, the brigade's commissary and quartermaster delivered beef on the hoof, boxes of hardtack, and other rations to Miles's men. Assuming that little was happening on this front, he thought it as good a time as any to resupply the men. Miles's men made a stand at the cracker boxes, which gave the battle its name, "The Cracker Fight." The Yankees allowed the Rebels to approach the boxes and, when they came close, the bluecoats "screamed 'Hard Tack' and we gave them a volley." Two successive Rebel waves were thrown back.[119]

A charge on disorganized Federal infantry was one thing, but an assault on a reformed line was another. Rosser rode to the front of his line but could not get his men to plunge in a third time. He recalled a Federal officer trying to do the same. Just then, Rosser recalled, "Private Holmes Conrad of the Eleventh Virginia, seized the regimental flag and with the sagacity of genius and the courage of Horatius he rode into the head of the enemy's column calling to his comrades to follow him and the flag they so honored." Rosser's men poured into the Federal position. At several points, the Federals attempted to seize Conrad's flag, but without success. "I counted five non-commissioned officers who were killed around that flag," Rosser noted proudly.[120]

As Miles's men gave ground, they gave up their rations. Pressure from two sides forced their withdrawal. The veteran 81st Pennsylvania's flank was exposed as the 183rd Pennsylvania gave way. The 183rd was a recent addition to the army, having been recruited in the Philadelphia area in the winter of 1863–64. While some of its officers had militia experience, the Overland Campaign was the unit's first taste of actual combat. Staff officer Robertson called its leaders "a cowardly lot of officers."

Miles sent Robertson in to rally the green Pennsylvanians. The aide seized the regimental colors and admonished the men to follow him back into action. That

118 *Philadelphia Weekly Times* (undated postwar account), FSNMP BV 201. Two hundred prisoners is a vast overstatement.

119 Robertson, letter.

120 *Philadelphia Weekly Times* (undated postwar account). Conrad was promoted to major after the action. He and five brothers served in the Confederate army. Holmes attended the University of Virginia and the Virginia Military Institute. He survived the war and went on to a successful career as lawyer, legislator, and Solicitor-General of the United States.

steeled the resolve of some of the Keystoners and allowed the unit to regain some of its honor, and Robertson' would receive the Medal of Honor for his.[121]

Without his full division on the field, Mahone backed off, and Miles resumed his withdrawal, sending word to Hancock about the unexpected Confederate assault. Hancock passed word to Barlow, who sent Col. Thomas A. Smyth's Irish Brigade in support of Miles. Although hardly now bigger than a regiment because of the ravages of battles like Antietam, Fredericksburg, and Gettysburg, the Irishmen were enough to fortify the frazzled spirits of Miles's men.

In the meantime, Hampton tried to get some of his cavalry on Miles's flank while Mahone resumed his frontal pressure. For the second time, Miles faced about to "beat back the enemy advancing upon him," Walker said.[122]

More bad news arrived at Hancock's headquarters. "About this time I was informed that the enemy's infantry was also advancing on the Brock road to attack my right," he reported.[123] Now it was Hancock's turn to send for aid. As word went out to army headquarters, Smyth pushed forward in time to cover Miles's final withdrawal into the II Corps line.

Was this Lee trying to get into Meade's rear? Meade almost hoped for it. He seemed delighted at the arrival of Hancock's message. In immediate response, he sent Col. J. Howard Kitching's heavy artillery brigade to bolster Hancock, although it withdrew "shortly thereafter."[124] A reconnaissance had revealed the additional Confederate threat to be all buzz.

Jubal Early, for his part, did not try to test the strength of the II Corps' full position. "[H]is designated route being barred against him by a force which would, at the least, have exacted a hard fight and a long delay before letting him pass, Early made no serious efforts to break through here," recounted Walker, who contended that Early "interpreted his orders to mean essentially that he was to go to Spottsylvania and not that he was to fight a battle at Todd's Tavern."[125] Indeed, Early withdrew back across the Po and encamped.

"[T]he sun went down, and darkness came on," said Walker, "and the great battle of Todd's Tavern was never fought."[126]

121 *O.R.* 36:1:381, 383, 385; Robertson letter; Robertson's medal citation reads. "While acting as aide-de-camp to a general officer, seeing a regiment break to the rear, he seized its colors, rode with them to the front in the face of the advancing enemy, and rallied the retreating regiment."

122 Walker, 445.

123 Hancock, report, 329.

124 Ibid., 330.

125 Walker, 444.

126 Ibid., 445.

Late on May 8, as the Confederate Third Corps wasn't fighting a battle of Todd's Tavern, the Confederate Second Corps was settling in after its fight with the VI Corps. Rodes's first two brigades had rushed into battle that day, but his third and fourth—those of Brig. Gens. Junius Daniel and George Doles—eventually settled into position along the same ridgeline John Henagan's men had first occupied across the Brock Road. As night wore on, Maj. Gen. Edward "Alleghany" Johnson's division filed in on Rodes's right.[127]

Once a regiment staked out a position, the men began to fortify. "[W]e found ourselves at a line of Confederate soldiers who were hastily constructing breastworks of poles, dirt, and everything they could lay hands on . . ." recalled Gordon Bradwell of the 31st Georgia, which arrived on the field late in the day and so found itself posted in a reserve position. "As far as to the right as could be heard there was the incessant noise of the pick, the shovel, and the ax."[128]

By the time Confederates finished settling in, their line at Spotsylvania ran for nearly five miles, winding along ridgelines that provided strong defensible positions and effective fields of fire. "The rebel works were constructed as follows," a New York soldier would later explain:

> A layer of stout logs close together & breast high was made and banked on the front side with earth. Above this with space to fire between was laced another log larger than the others protecting the heads of the defenders. For several rods in front the trees had been felled to fall outward and form by their entangled branches a dense abattis. Sometimes these branches of these trees had been sharpened so as to impale assailants. . . . Behind such works Lee's veteran army lay and was virtually unassailable.[129]

Brigadier General James "Stonewall Jim" Walker, commander of the Stonewall Brigade, justifiably bragged that "a very formidable line of fortifications frowned upon the foe, and our troops rested quietly and confident of victory, should the enemy attack them. . . . It was apparently impregnable. Just behind the intrenched line of infantry, artillery was placed at the most eligible points, to sweep the

127 Regarding the spelling of Ed Johnson's nickname, there are three correct spellings of "Alleghany/Allegheny/Allegany," depending on location and the topographical feature you're referring to. As someone who works in the town of "Allegany," New York, I'll defer to Johnson's biographer, Gregg Clemmer, on "Alleghany" as the correct reference for the general.

128 Gordon Bradwell, *Under the Southern Cross: Soldier Life With Gordon Bradwell and the Army of Northern Virginia*, Pharris Deloach Johnson, ed. (Macon, GA: Mercer University Press, 1999), 160.

129 Isaac O. Best, "Through the Wilderness With Grant," 22–3, FSNMP BV 38.

approaching enemy with shot and shell and cannister." From the morning of May 9 until the morning of May 12, Confederates worked incessantly to strengthen their works until, as Walker claimed, it "became one of the very best lines of temporary field works I ever saw."[130]

The left flank of the Confederate line was the strongest, anchored on the Po River and along the low crest on the south edge of Spindle Field. The right flank of the line terminated southeast of the village of Spotsylvania Court House itself. While it lacked the more dominating topography of the left flank, the Confederate right was relatively secure because the bulk of the Federal army was massed along the Confederate left and left center. For extra protection, though, Lee assigned cavalry to patrol the right flank. That cavalry presence would eventually avert disaster on May 14.

The weakest point on the Confederate line was its center. In following the natural contours of the land, the chief topographical engineer of Lee's army, 44-year-old Martin Luther Smith, had laid out a giant bubble in the center of the rebel line. A mile across at its base, it curved in a large arc that resembled a horseshoe or muleshoe, thus giving the position its eventual name: the Mule Shoe Salient.

Such a protrusion in a line—known as a salient—is inherently weak. A breakthrough at any point makes the entire position untenable because the enemy suddenly commands a position behind the entire salient. While a salient does provide interior lines for shifting reinforcements, the curved shape makes it difficult for any unit on the line to support those to its left and right. A salient is also susceptible to converging artillery and small-arms fire, which concentrates on defenders; meanwhile, the defenders' own fire diverges—it fans outward—muting its effectiveness against massed attackers.

Defenders are also vulnerable to crossfire, a problem Confederate infantrymen nestled in the tip of the salient recognized almost immediately. "After throwing up breastworks, we found that the Yanks had a cross fire on our regiment," one of them wrote in a letter published in the *Richmond Times-Dispatch*. "We then went to work and built pens, each holding eight or ten men." The "pens"—also called traverses—were earth-and-log breastworks built every 20–40 yards inside the line, perpendicular to the main works, that offered soldiers a degree of additional cover.[131]

The improvements did little to assuage the fears of the men posted in the Mule Shoe. "It was so liable to be enfiladed by artillery and would be a dangerous trap to be caught in should the line be broken on the left or right," one Confederate said. Another decried it as "a bad piece of engineering and certain to invite attack

130 Walker, 233.

131 R. C. Oakes, "The Twenty-First at Spotsylvania," Richmond *Times-Dispatch*, ca. 1906, FSNMP BV 139.

Maj. Gen. Martin Luther Smith commanded a division at Vicksburg and had also helped plan the defenses there, as well as those at New Orleans. He spent seven months as a prisoner before joining the Army of Northern Virginia. James Longstreet considered him "a splendid tactician as well as [a] skillful engineer and gallant withal." *Library of Congress*

as soon as the enemy understood it." It was, in short, "a wretchedly defective line."[132]

Confederate engineers who inspected the line found the salient worrisome, but they also feared the consequences of what might happen if they conceded the high ground within the salient to the U.S. army. That high ground, the site of Neil McCoull's farm, could potentially serve as an artillery platform for the Federals, who could deploy their batteries and then enfilade long stretches of Lee's line to both the west and south.

Lee, himself an engineer with an eye for terrain, became aware of the salient during an inspection of the line on May 9. Rather than correct the flaw by repositioning his line, he deferred to the judgment of Ewell—his de facto second in command—who oversaw the overall Confederate center. The 47-year-old Second Corps commander was convinced he could hold the salient if supported by enough artillery.

Martin Luther Smith was convinced, too, as were the artillerists themselves. "[T]he breastworks were good of the kind, and much of the ground in front was sufficiently open to see for a short distance the enemy's lines, when charging," one of them contended, "and had the artillery been in place the line could not have been carried." Lee allowed the position to stand.[133]

132 William S. Dunlop, *Lee's Sharpshooters; or, The Forefront of Battle: A Story of Southern Valor That Never Has Been Told* (Little Rock, Ark., 1899), 444; E. Porter Alexander, *Military Memoirs of a Confederate.* (New York, 1907), 219; Carter, 239.

133 Carter, 239; Walking from the Salient's "Bloody Angle" to its "East Angle," it is apparent how poorly laid-out that section of the Confederate line is. The forward sight-lines are terrible! (And could have been corrected). I speculate that Lee never visited that stretch of the line personally—although he did visit other stretches of the front line—because surely his engineer's eye would have caught the poor layout had he seen it for himself.

Soldiers from both armies spent the night of May 8–9 digging fortifications, and by the following morning, lines of breastworks stretched from the Po River on the western flanks to the Mule Shoe on the northeast. "Trees were felled and piled upon each other, and a ditch dug behind them with the earth out of it thrown against the logs," said General Walker, whose Stonewall Brigade was posted along the west face of the Mule Shoe. "The limbs and tops of the trees as cut off from the trunks were used to form abattis, by placing them in front of the breastworks with the sharpened points towards the enemy." Walker described the "very formidable line of fortifications" as "apparently impregnable."[134]

Neither army passed up the chance to make their positions even stronger, either. "Each army would fortify at night, and through the day, when not fighting, in order to hold the ground they had gained, and resist an attack," wrote John Casler of the Stonewall Brigade. The Confederates would eventually construct a secondary line of works behind their main line along the northwestern face of the Mule Shoe as well as a reserve line across the salient between the McCoull house and the Edgar Harrison house—the position John Brown Gordon's men occupied when they arrived on the field.[135]

The last Confederates to file into line were the exhausted men of the Third Corps. Early on the morning of May 9, the corps received orders to unite with the rest of the Army of Northern Virginia, recalling them from the Todd's Tavern area. Grant was not headed to Fredericksburg after all.

"After reaching the rear of the position occupied by the other two corps," Jubal Early later wrote, "I was ordered to Spottsylvania [sic] Court-House, to take position on the right, and cover the road from that place to Fredericksburg. No enemy appeared on my front this day, except at a distance on the Fredericksburg road."[136]

134 James Walker to editor of Richmond *Times*, *S.H.S.P.* 21:233.

135 John O. Casler, *Four Years in the Stonewall Brigade* (Guthrie, OK: State Capital Printing Company, 1893), 316.

136 Early, 353.

# May 5
# May 6
# May 7
# May 8
# May 9

John Sedgwick "looked the picture of buoyant life and vigorous health" on the morning he was killed.[1]

The most-senior major general in the Army of the Potomac, the bachelor Sedgwick had been married to the service his entire adult life. A native of Cornwall Hollow, Connecticut, Sedgwick came from solid Yankee stock that included Revolutionary credentials: his father had served as a lieutenant colonel in the Connecticut colonial militia and his uncle had served in the Continental Congress. Sedgwick attended West Point, graduating 24 out of 50 in the Class of 1837.

After graduation, he fought in the Seminole Wars and the Mexican-American War, and later he served in both artillery and cavalry units, including a stint as a trooper under then-Colonel Robert E. Lee. Sedgwick also became friends with future Confederate cavalry commander Jeb Stuart, who considered him "one of the best friends he had in the old army."[2]

A case of cholera kept Sedgwick out of the action at First Manassas in July 1861, but his work as assistant inspector general for the Military Department of Washington gained him recognition, and by the end of August 1861, Sedgwick earned promotion to brigadier general, which led to command of a division in the II Corps for the spring 1862 Peninsula Campaign. In the subsequent Seven Days' fighting, he suffered a wound at Glendale; at Antietam that September, he suffered three more—wrist, leg, and shoulder—which knocked him out of commission until the end of December. In January 1863, a cabal of officers plotted to have army commander Maj. Gen. Ambrose Burnside replaced; Burnside cleaned house

1 Porter, 89.

2 Alexander R. Boteler, diary, 9 May 1864, FSNMP BV 50.

instead, and in the ensuing shake-up, Sedgwick found himself at the head of the Federal VI Corps.

At the battle of Chancellorsville in May, Sedgwick scored the only success of the campaign for the Army of the Potomac, the victory at Second Fredericksburg. His large corps played a minor role at Gettysburg but would score a minor victory at Rappahannock Station, Virginia, on November 7 during the Mine Run Campaign.

What he lacked in razzle-dazzle, Maj. Gen. John Sedgwick made up for in dependability. That his men loved him enough to call him "Uncle John" was no small thing. *Library of Congress*

One of Sedgwick's staff officers, Charles A. Whittier, considered him "one of the truest and whitest souls ever known to any army."[3] Meade's aide, Theodore Lyman, described Sedgwick as "a stout, sturdy man, with a bright kindly eye, and a face full of intelligence." Lyman gauged him "a reliable officer," but over time came to the assessment that "Sedgwick was constitutionally slow."[4] That slowness often translated to a calmness and steadiness that served Sedgwick well in battle. He did not possess the dynamism of a Winfield Scott Hancock, but he was beloved by his men, who called him "Uncle John." "He was like a kind father to them, and they loved him really like sons," noted Lyman.[5] When Sedgwick campaigned, he slept in the field with his men under the stars.

Such had been the case on the night of May 8. After visiting Meade shortly before midnight, Sedgwick returned to his headquarters and bedded down near a haystack. The following morning, he arose early—"No tents or breakfast"—and proceeded to put out one small fire after another.[6]

3 Charles Whittier, memoir, typescript, Ms. "20th" Cab. 6.3, Boston Public Library, FSNMP BV 266.

4 Lyman, *Meade's Army*, 47, 145.

5 Ibid., 146.

6 Martin T. McMahon, "The Death of General John Sedgwick," *Battles & Leaders of the Civil War*, vol. 4, (New York: The Century Co., 1884), 175.

First, he received an order from Meade to assume control over the battlefield's Brock Road sector of the battlefield. Knowing that his V Corps counterpart, Warren, still smarted from the previous day's repulses, Sedgwick did his best to play peacemaker, downplaying his new assignment to a member of Warren's staff. "Just tell General Warren to go on and command his own corps as usual," Sedgwick told him. "I have perfect confidence that he will do what is right, and knows what to do with his corps as well as I do."[7]

Sedgwick then turned his attention from one of his peers to one of his subordinates, Second Division commander Brig. Gen. Thomas H. Neill. According to Whittier, Neill, "who had been an excelling brigade commander, had entirely lost his nerve." Neill had only risen to division command on May 7 after George W. Getty took a bullet to the shoulder in the Wilderness. Feeling "tension too great for him to bear," Neill seemed to suffered a mild nervous breakdown and began to withdraw his division from the front. Sedgwick reversed the order and soothed the situation. To make himself a visible example for his men, the VI Corps commander stayed along that section of the line "for a long time [and] supervised the digging of rifle pits and entrenchments."[8]

Next, Sedgwick turned his attention to his superiors when Grant and Meade arrived. Grant "expressed his intention to devote the day principally to placing all the troops in position, reconnoitering the enemy's line, and getting in readiness for a combined attack as soon as proper preparations for it could be made." Satisfied Sedgwick had his sector under control, the commanders rode on.

Through it all, Sedgwick "seemed particularly cheerful and hopeful."[9] Shortly before 9:30 a.m., he and his adjutant, Col. Martin McMahon, finally settled down to chat not far from the front on a pair of hardtack boxes. Sedgwick leaned back against a tree. Around that time, the 1st Massachusetts Light Artillery rolled a battery into position near a road junction where two branches of the Brock Road came together. Later, McMahon recalled their exchange with a plentitude of adverbs.[10]

"General, do you see that section of artillery?" McMahon asked. "Well, you are not to go near it today."

"McMahon," the general responded good naturedly, "I would like to know who commands this corps, you or I?"

7 Washington Roebling, memorandum, 9 May 1864, *O.R.* 36:2:574.

8 Whittier memoir.

9 Porter, 89.

10 The following account comes from McMahon, *Battles & Leaders*.

"Well, General, sometimes I am in doubt myself," McMahon replied playfully. But his tone then changed. "Seriously, General, I beg of you not to go to that angle; every officer who has shown himself there has been hit, both yesterday and today." Indeed, as a member of the 15th New Jersey Infantry later attested, "a rebel rifleman was posted on our right, in a tree. He seemed to kill at almost every shot, and was said to have taken twenty lives." Among those killed was the Fifteenth's color-bearer.[11] Brigade commander William H. Morris was wounded in the leg by the same sniping.

Martin T. McMahon received the Medal of Honor for action at White Oak Swamp in June 1862. His citation reads: "Under fire of the enemy, successfully destroyed a valuable train that had been abandoned and prevented it from falling into the hands of the enemy." *Library of Congress*

"Well," Sedgwick concluded, "I don't know that there is any reason for my going there."

That reason arrived soon enough. The 1st New Jersey Brigade deployed across the intersection, interfering with the position of the artillerists. "That is wrong," Sedgwick pointed out. "Those troops must be moved farther to the right; I don't wish them to overlap that battery."

McMahon rose to pass along the general's order even as Sedgwick himself stood. Forgetting their own admonitions to stay away from the intersection, the two men approached the infantrymen and directed them to the right. But as the Garden State men began to reposition themselves, "the enemy opened a sprinkling of fire." Men began to duck at the whiz and whine of the bullets zipping by.

"What! What!" Sedgwick cried. "Men, dodging this way for single bullets! What will you do when they open fire along the whole line? I'm ashamed of you. They couldn't hit an elephant at this distance."

11 Alanson A. Haines, *History of the Fifteenth Regiment New Jersey Volunteers* (New York: Jenkins & Thomas, 1883), 161.

Major General John Sedwick's loss, said Brig. Gen. Marsena Patrick, provost marshal of the army, "caused universal grief and sadness." A bas relief sculpture depicts the scene on the back of a monument to Sedgwick at West Point. *Kris White/American Battlefield Trust*

One of the artillerists dove to cover, landing near Sedgwick's feet. The general prodded the man with his boot. "They couldn't hit an elephant at this distance," Sedgwick repeated.

"General," the man said, "I dodged a shell once, and if I hadn't, it would have taken my head off. I believe in dodging."

That brought a chuckle from Sedgwick: "All right, my man. Go to your place."

Sedgwick turned back to McMahon, who resumed their conversation, but a "shrill whistle, closing with a dull, heavy stroke, interrupted our talk . . ." McMahon said. "[T]he general's face turned slowly to me, the blood spurting from his left cheek under the eye in a steady stream." Sedgwick collapsed on McMahon, and the two men tumbled to the ground.

Men scrambled to the general's side. A regimental surgeon posted nearby, Doctor Ludwig Emil Ohlenschlager, rushed over and poured water from a canteen over Sedgwick's face, hoping to clean the wound so he could get a better look at it. "The blood still poured upward in a little fountain," the despondent McMahon noted. "A smile remained on his lips but he did not speak." Observers noted the smile remained on Sedgwick's face as his body was carried from the battlefield.[12]

Command in the corps should have fallen to the senior division commander, Maj. Gen. James Ricketts, but Rickett's deferred, aware that Sedgwick had hoped his protégé, Brig. Gen. Horatio Wright, would get the call should anything happen to him. By 10:00 a.m., Wright got the word.

Horace Porter, who had been riding with Grant, was headed toward Sedgwick with a message from the commander when he saw a party carrying the body of an officer to the rear. The men tried to keep the officer's identity a secret, but Porter recognized McMahon among the cluster. It fell to Porter to take the news back to headquarters.

"Is he really dead?" Grant asked. "Is he really dead?" Grant needed time to collect himself from the shock. "His loss to this army is greater than the loss of a whole division of troops," he finally said.[13]

Porter had to agree. "[T]he news of his death fell upon his comrades with a sense of grief akin to the sorrow of a personal bereavement," he later noted.[14] A member of the 15th New Jersey attested as much: "We mourned his loss as irreplaceable, and of all the wounds which tore our hears, the most painful was caused by this unexpected fall of our commander."[15] Unexpected, indeed, admitted a shocked Pennsylvanian: "the thought that he would be killed never occurred to us."[16]

"But he has died with his armor on," wrote Wilbur Fisk of the 2nd Vermont, "and we cherish his memory, emulate his bravery so that, though dead, he still lives with us."[17]

Sedgwick would be the highest-ranking United States officer killed during the Civil War.

12 Porter, 90.

13 Ibid.

14 Ibid.

15 Haines, 161.

16 James M. Treichler, memoir, 59, FSNMP BV 41.

17 Fisk, 219.

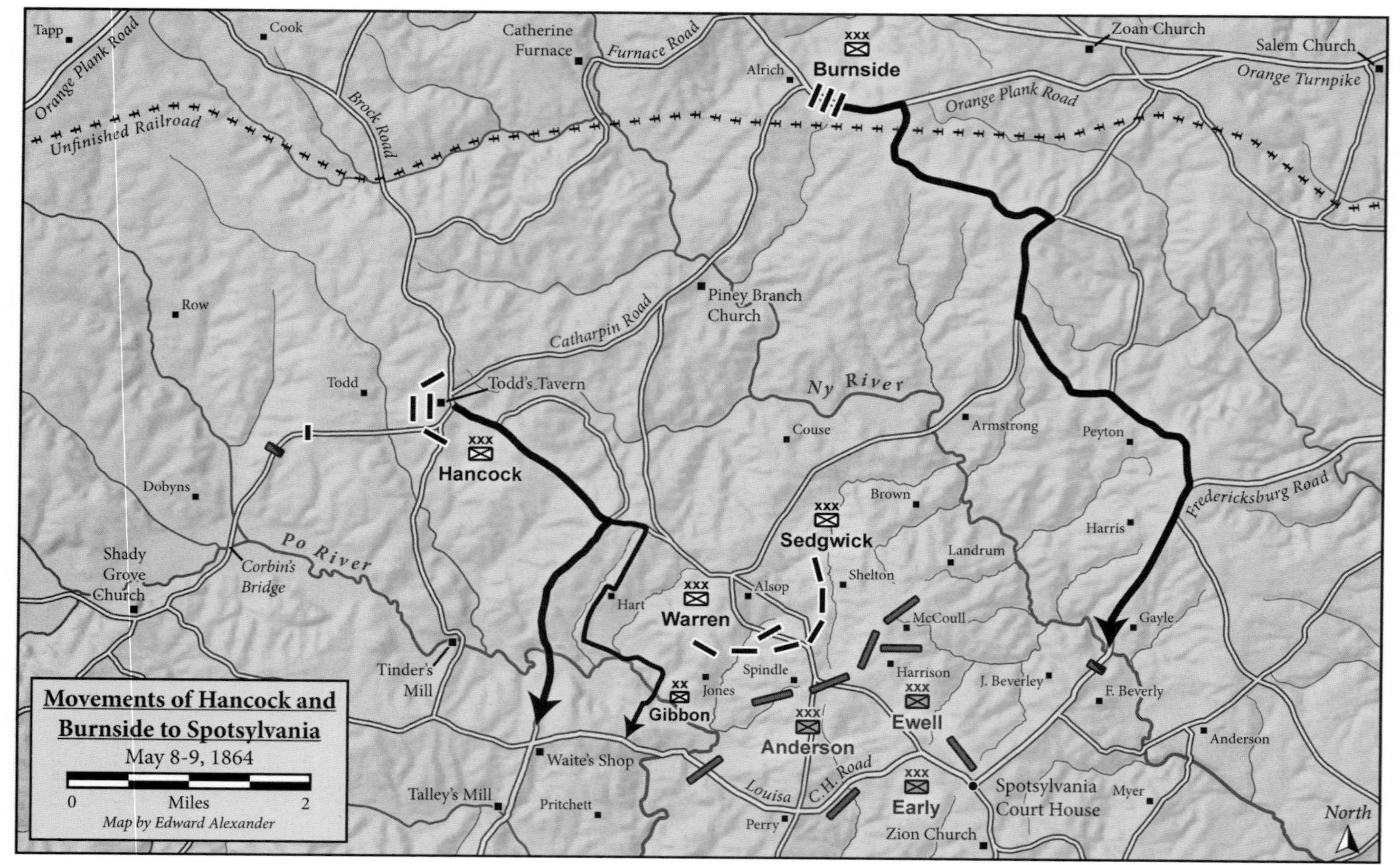
Movements of Hancock and Burnside to Spotsylvania
May 8-9, 1864
0
Miles
2
Map by Edward Alexander
North
Burnside
Hancock
Sedgwick
Warren
Gibbon
Ewell
Early
Anderson
Spotsylvania Court House
Fredericksburg Road
Orange Turnpike
Orange Plank Road
Unfinished Railroad
Brock Road
Furnace Road
Catharpin Road
Louisa C.H. Road
Ny River
Po River
Salem Church
Zoan Church
Alrich
Piney Branch Church
Catherine Furnace
Todd's Tavern
Todd
Cook
Tapp
Row
Dobyns
Shady Grove Church
Corbin's Bridge
Tinder's Mill
Talley's Mill
Pritchett
Waite's Shop
Hart
Jones
Spindle
Alsop
Couse
Armstrong
Peyton
Harris
Gayle
Anderson
F. Beverly
Myer
J. Beverley
Landrum
McCoull
Harrison
Brown
Shelton
Zion Church
Perry

**Movements of Hancock and Burnside to Spotsylvania**—The bottleneck created at Spindle Field by the Federal V and VI corps delayed the ability of the II Corps to get to the battlefield. Hancock led his men to the field on May 9, settling in on the Federal right—where they discovered a possible opportunity to outflank the Army of Northern Virginia. Meanwhile, Ambrose Burnside's IX Corps adjusted its route of march around the bottleneck entirely, moving eastward to the Fredericksburg Road and coming to Spotsylvania Court House via a back door.

---

To the east, as the VI Corps dealt with the death of "Uncle John" Sedgwick, another of Grant's army corps finally reached the battlefield.

Major General Ambrose Burnside's IX Corps had left the Wilderness on May 8. "The rays of a fierce and blazing sun poured down . . . untempered by any clouds save those of dust, which hung thickly above the marching column," wrote Henry C. Houston of the 32nd Maine. "Then, too, the men were burdened by the weight of weapons and equipments, the muskets, knapsack, haversack with such rations as it might contain, the canteen filled with water, and last, but by no means least, forty rounds in the cartridge-boxes, altogether making a heavy load."[18]

Their route took them through the old Chancellorsville battlefield, fought over by the same armies just one year previously. "The leaves of last autumn had covered most of the relics of that unfortunate affair," noted a grateful member of the 35th Massachusetts, "but groping among the rubbish of the road-side, a human skull was uncovered; a fit text for one disposed to moralize in the midst of the great events transpiring."[19]

As evening came on, the column pitched camp around the intersection of the Catharpin and Old Plank roads. "The main body, after a long day of painful exertion, at last made a welcome halt, and went into bivouac to snatch a few hours of sorely-needed rest," the Mainer recalled. The men by that point had been marching and fighting nonstop for five days. "To those of us who had realized that this was Sunday, as we had struggled on through the heat and dust, it had seemed a strange contrast to the quiet and peaceful Sabbaths to which we had been accustomed in our Northern homes."[20]

Grant originally intended the Burnside's corps to circle westward down the Catharpin Road, past Piney Branch Church (where he had made his headquarters),

18 Henry C. Houston, *The Thirty-Second Maine Regiment of Infantry Volunteers: An Historical Sketch* (Portland, ME: Press of Southworth Brothers, 1903), 110.

19 Committee of the Regimental Association, eds. *History of the Thirty-Fifth Regiment Massachusetts Volunteers, 1862-1865* (Boston: Mills, Knight & Company, 1884), 227.

20 Houston, 110.

and the advance toward Spotsylvania as support for the VI Corps. However, the bottleneck along the Brock Road created by the fighting in Spindle Field necessitated a shift in Burnside's marching orders. Grant directed Burnside to redirected his lead division toward the Fredericksburg Road—the same road James Wilson had taken the day before that had allowed him to stab straight into the Confederate rear.

Brigadier General Orlando B. Willcox's Third Division would lead the way, but at 4:00 a.m., as Willcox stirred his infantrymen into column, Phil Sheridan's cavalry "began to pour out from the neighboring farm." As it happened, the intersection where Willcox's men had encamped for the night was also serving as the cavalry's staging area for its raid toward Richmond. Willcox's men would lose an hour waiting for the cavalry to pass.[21]

The march was "fearfully warm and dusty," said one officer, and stragglers fell out by the hundreds. A sinister foreboding boomed in the distance. "As we marched down from Alrich's that morning, we had heard distinctly the sounds of battle, both artillery and musketry, away to the westward, where the Brock Road approaches Spottsylvania," recalled Lt. Col. Byron M. Cutcheon of the 20th Michigan.[22]

Grant ordered Burnside to "move your advance beyond (south of) the Gate," a spot marked on the map on the south side of the Fredericksburg Road a short distance east of the Ny River. The location of the Gate was mis-marked, though, leading to some initial confusion. Burnside would later correct the position as the Gayle house, "there being no such place as Gate in this section," and told Grant it was three miles farther than supposed. Even that didn't fully clarify the situation. Some of Willcox's subordinates confused the Gayle House with a home on the opposite bank of the nearby Ny called Whig Hill, which sat above the south bank of the Ny on the south side of the Fredericksburg Road. [23]

A two-story, L-shaped wooden house, Whig Hill belonged to 37-year-old Francis C. Beverly, who lived there with four family members. A farmer, Beverly had 200 of his 300 acres under cultivation. Twelve enslaved workers tilled the fields and tended crops of corn, oats, tobacco, Irish potatoes, and sweet potatoes. To add to the confusion, his younger brother, James, owned a house called Dixie

21 Cutcheon, *Story of the Twentieth Michigan,* 112.

22 Weld, 289; Cutcheon, *Story of the Twentieth Michigan,* 120.

23 Grant to Burnside, *O.R.* 36:2:548; Burnside to Grant, *O.R.* 36:2: 583. The Ny River—often spelled "Ni"—gets its name from a local tribe of Native Americans, the Mattaponi. They lend their name to four small rivers, the Ma, the Ta, the Po, and Ni, which all flow together to become the Matta and the Poni rivers and, ultimately, the Mattaponi River. I have chosen to use "NY" for consistency's sake because that is the spelling used most frequently in the Official Records. Some accounts also used "Nye."

This postwar image of Whig Hill—in the grove of bare trees in the distance—shows the driveway the 20th Michigan used as their initial position as the 60th Ohio advanced across the landscape from left to right. *Library of Congress*

on the opposite side of the road. Both houses appeared on maps as "Beverly." "The country about here seems to be supplied with Beverlys," quipped Cutcheon.[24]

With Willcox being so far in advance of his support—Brig. Gen. Thomas Greely Stevenson's First Division, still posted by the road to Piney Branch Church—confusion about Willcox's location and how to get reinforcements to him in the face of the enemy set nerves on edge, from the banks of the Ny River all the way up to army headquarters.

The reason for apprehension stood all too apparent across the roadway near the Gayle House. Williams C. Wickham's four cavalry regiments still guarded the Fredericksburg Road, with a screen of troopers deployed on the east side of the Ny River. Willcox couldn't gauge their strength so, despite his division's numerical advantage, he advanced cautiously. "The enemy show considerable force of cavalry and, I think, infantry, but it is hazy, and I am not sure," Willcox reported. "Their skirmish lines are deployed as though they meant fight."[25]

24 Harrison, 113–4; Cutcheon, *Twentieth Michigan*, 114.

25 Willcox to Burnside, *O.R.* 36:2:581.

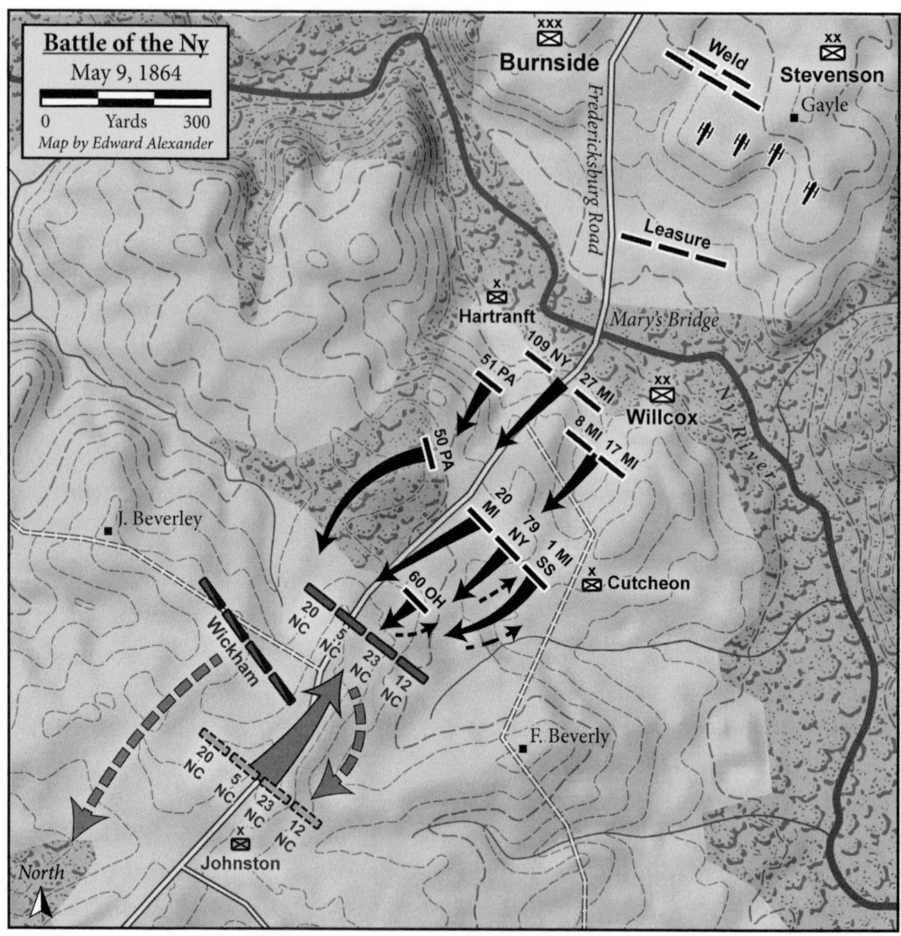


**Battle of the Ny**—Confederates from Robert Johnston's brigade prevented the Federal IX Corps from crossing the Ny River in force, allowing Johnston's outnumbered North Carolinians an opportunity to make a fight of it, aided by Williams Wickham's cavalry. A left-wheel by the 50th Pennsylvania finally broke the North Carolinians' grip, further dislodged by a Federal rally up the middle.

---

As Willcox prepared to engage, Wickham's troopers fell back across Mary's Bridge to the far side of the Ny. As one Pennsylvanian remembered it, "Our division found the enemy's pickets about one mile from the river, chased them back rapidly, seized the bridge, and crossed. . . ." Willcox offered Confederates additional discouragement by bringing up a section of artillery that opened fire and scattered the horsemen.[26]

The men of the 60th Ohio—six newly mustered companies from around Cleveland and Columbus—were first across the river as skirmishers. The road ascended toward a ridgeline about four-tenths of a mile ahead; a ridge also paralleled the road on the road's north side. The Ohioans "gained a hill beyond without serious opposition," reported Lt. Col. Martin Avery. Behind them, the 20th Michigan advanced as far as a farm lane that led to Whig Hill, with fifty men thrown forward with the Ohioans to complete the skirmish line on the right of the road.[27]

The 1st Michigan Sharpshooters and 79th New York advanced next, deploying on the 20th's left; the 50th Pennsylvania deployed on the right, across the Fredericksburg Road. "In our front was a wide, open field, some of it newly ploughed, extending southward to the line of a sunken fence, bordering a road leading southeast . . ." Cutcheon recalled. Beyond "was an old pasture, grown up with small sapling pines." Cutcheon ordered the 24 men of his Company I to take position behind the fence line with the Ohioans "and hold it till relieved." He believed the position offered an excellent field of fire except along the road, where the crest of the hill intervened. [28]

The Ohioans made it nearly to that crest before Confederates pushed back. Dismounted, Wickham's troopers had orders to "hold [the Yankees] in check as long as possible," recalled B. J. Haden of the 1st Virginia Cavalry.[29]

"[T]he fight now became quite sharp," Cutcheon admitted.[30]

The Sixtieth Ohio maintained its position valiantly, "though quite a number, both wounded and unhurt, were coming back." Cutcheon advanced more of the 20th Michigan in support. He also sent a dozen men to occupy the abandoned Whig Hill. "These dispositions had hardly been completed when a heavy line of the enemy . . . advanced rapidly from the direction of the Court House, on both sides of the road," Cutcheon said.

Four Confederate infantry regiments under the command of Brig. Gen. Robert D. Johnston—the 5th, 12th, 20th, and 23rd North Carolina—had come

26 William J. Bolton, *The Civil War Journal of Colonel William J. Bolton, 51st Pennsylvania, April 20, 1861–August 2, 1865*. Richard A. Sauers, ed. (Conshohocken, PA: Combined Publishing, 2000), 01.

27 Martin Avery, report, *O.R.* 36:1:978-9; Cutcheon, *Story of the Twentieth Michigan, 114*.

28 Ibid.; Cutcheon, report, *O.R.* 36:1:967–8.

29 Ibid.; B. J. Haden, *Reminiscences of J. E. B. Stuart's Cavalry* (Charlottesville, VA: Progress Publishing Co.), 31, FSNMP BV 138.

30 Cutcheon, *Story of the Twentieth Michigan,* 114.

to Wickham's aid. Initially part of Jubal Early's Second Corps division, Johnston and his men found themselves under the temporary command of Maj. Gen. Cadmus Wilcox of the Third Corps.

"It now became evident that the enemy were making preparations to drive us from the hill," an Ohioan remembered. "They opened a sharp fire of musketry on our front, which we soon silenced. They then, under cover of the woods, advanced on our left so as to enfilade our line." The Ohioans took advantage of the sunken road running perpendicular to their position and "changed front to rear on first company . . ." Avery recounted, "which still enabled us to retain the crest of the hill." The Buckeyes tried to maintain "a constant fire on the enemy, who advanced on our right and left, very nearly enveloping us"—but the pressure became too much. The 60th Ohio scattered. "In falling back we were in some confusion," Avery admitted.[31]

"Let us charge them!" hollered one of the Confederate troopers—"some man, not an officer," Haden pointed out. With a Rebel Yell, "every[one] mounted the fence and made for them."[32]

Seizing the high ground, Confederates set their sights on the regiment of Michigan sharpshooters who had deployed in support of the Buckeyes.[33] "[A] very severe raking flank fire was poured upon my whole line," lamented the sharpshooters' colonel, Charles V. De Land. Compounding their problems, Federal artillery shells began to fall in among them. "The action of our batteries was inexcusable, as they were within plain sight and must have seen, if they had tried to see at all, that they were firing upon us. . . ." DeLand wrote bitterly:

> Few veteran regiments would have better withstood a charge by double their numbers in front, a heavy flank fire, and the active practice of both the enemy's and our own batteries, but even under these circumstances the men would not have flinched had they not been deceived by the acts and orders of one of the line officers, who gave the order to retreat without any authority for doing so.[34]

As it was, the Michiganders "broke and fell back in much confusion," receiving "a severe fire from the enemy as they did so." Controversy would erupt over the

31 Avery, report, 978–9.

32 Haden, 31.

33 Company K of the 1st Michigan Sharpshooters was the "Indian Company" comprised of Anishinaabe indigenous people.

34 Charles V. De Land, report, *O.R.* 36:1:973.

In the Wilderness, Capt. Samuel K. Schwenk's "gallantry was conspicuous and remarked by all who witnessed it," said his brigade commander. At Spotsylvania, "he greatly distinguished himself, so as to draw the attention and admiration of the whole brigade."

*Library of Congress*

identity of the officer at fault for the collapse. Some blamed De Land for issuing "an order dictated by cowardice" while De Land pointed fingers, indistinctly, at a pair of lieutenants "for having absented themselves from their commands on the field and for cowardice," although he declined to say which of the two junior officers was actually responsible. Cutcheon later offered a sage if bland final assessment: "Cool-headed and steady officers are essential to cool-headed and steady men and regiments, and one panicky officer can bring disaster upon an entire command."[35]

As the Michiganders fled, they stampeded the nearby 79th New York. "Get out of here, quick! The rebels are right upon us!" the sharpshooters cried. The New Yorkers tried in vain to stop the sharpshooters panicky flight. Cutcheon's 20th Michigan remained firm, though, eventually buying time for the sharpshooters and the New Yorkers to rally.

As the Federal position disintegrated into pell-mell disarray on the left side of the road, "the whole weight of the attack on the right side of the road fell upon the 50th Pennsylvania." The road ran parallel to a ridge, and the Keystoners fell back to the far side of the slope to regroup, but "reverse seemed imminent." The topography blocked any supporting fire from the left side of the road.[36]

It was here, said the brigade commander, that the bravery of one man "was most conspicuous and did much to avert disaster." Captain Samuel K. Schwenk of the 50th Pennsylvania took command of the regiment's four right companies "and

35 Cutcheon, report, 967–8; Cutcheon, *Story of the Twentieth Michigan*, 117. For more on the controversy, see Raymond Herek, *These Men Have Seen Hard Service: The First Michigan Sharpshooters in the Civil War* (Detroit: Wayne State University Press, 1998), 133–4.

36 Cutcheon, report, 967–8.

In this rare image, the 79th New York advance past Whig Hill, which they referred to in their regimental history as the "Russell House." "There is a serious confusion in regard to the names of these houses," grumbled Col. Byron Cutcheon of the 20th Michigan, who referred to the house as "the Deserted House" as well as the "Beverly House." Others confused it with the Gayle house. *The Seventy-Ninth Highlanders*

charging with the bayonet, he drove back the enemy just as the Twentieth Michigan came up on the 'double quick' to his support, and the right was restored on the crest." The Michiganders "moved like a machine," a proud Cutcheon recalled.[37]

Federals finally surged on the left side of the road, too, as the Michigan sharpshooters and the New Yorkers fell in for the counterattack. "Come, Seventy-Ninth! You are wanted once more!" bellowed their colonel, David Morrison. "Shake out your colors! Forward!"

The 79th New York—the "Highlanders"—swept through Whig Hill's gardens as they advanced. "[F]ortunately the posts were rotten, and, yielding to the pressure of a hundred men, the fence was in a moment flat on the ground, and our line passed over without being broken," recalled Highlander William Todd of Company D. As they pushed forward, some of Johnston's men advanced to meet them, but the New Yorkers had the advantage of high ground. The North Carolinians fired

37 Ibid.; Cutcheon, memoir, 27, FSNMP BV 35.

a scattering of shots as the New Yorkers closed the distance. "Charge bayonets!" Morrison ordered. "Double quick! March!" Confederates fired one final volley then fled before the Highlanders, cheering as they charged. "[W]e were compelled to retire in haste," B. J. Haden admitted.[38]

Reinforcements from another of Willcox's brigades, Col. John F. Hartranft's, "dashed up the road" into the fray, raking the Confederate flank. Soon, "the enemy was repulsed all along the line." By noon, Confederates "retired behind a narrow strip of woods toward Spotsylvania Court House. . . ."[39]

"Thus, this division gained a foothold nearer Spotsylvania Court-House than any other part of the line," a Pennsylvanian proudly declared. The division "won this position in a very creditable manner," Cutcheon praised, "but at a cost of one hundred and eighty-eight killed, wounded and missing." The 79th New York, just four days away from the expiration of their enlistments, suffered three killed and eleven wounded, including both color bearers, wounded severely, and Morrison, who "received an ugly wound which shattered his right hand." Captured Federals quickly found themselves on their way to Andersonville. "The horrors of those ten months [in prison] could not possibly be described," J. B. Sanders of the 20th Michigan wrote much later.[40]

Confederates did not record their losses. "[W]e had lost a good many men—some killed," B. J. Haden wrote. No sooner had they retreated into the pine woods than Wickham's men received the order to join Stuart, who was even then in pursuit of Phil Sheridan toward Richmond. Johnston's infantry would hold the position on their own until more of the Third Corps could arrive.

Cutcheon, for his part, would later decree his overall satisfaction: "On the whole, it was a very neat affair, all in the open, on our side." It was not, he admitted, "a great battle" but rather, "a good, lively skirmish, and as a contest for position, was important."[41]

During the morning action—later called "The Battle of the Ny" in some reports—elements of two Federal brigades had piled into the fight. In the heat

38 Todd, 461–2; Haden, 31.

39 Cutcheon, report, 967–8; Bolton, 201.

40 Lewis Crater, *History of the Fiftieth Regiment, Penna. Vet. Vols., 1861-65* (Reading, PA: Coleman Printing House, 1884), 54; Cutcheon, report, 968; Todd, 462. Sanders and his comrades arrived in Georgia on June 4 and "were incarcerated until September 11, when we were moved to a similar prison at Florence, S.C. The latter part of February 186[5], we were turned loose, my weight reduced to 90 pounds from 162. . . ." As quoted from the 29 March 1893 *Ann Arbor Courier* in *The Civil War Diary of William Boston, A Union Soldier of Company H, Twentieth Michigan Volunteer Infantry, Ninth Army Corps. August 19, 1862–July 4, 1865*, FSNMP library.

41 Cutcheon, *Twentieth Michigan*, 116.

Colonel Byron Cutcheon's action along the Ny River on May 9, 1864, took place one day shy of the one-year anniversary of action at Horseshoe Bend, Kentucky, on May 10, 1863, where Cutcheon's regiment stormed "a house occupied by the enemy"—an action for which he received the Medal of Honor. *MOLLUS Collection, U.S. Army Heritage and Education Center*

of the battle, remembered one IX Corps soldier, "the First and Second Brigades had become thoroughly mixed up. . . . No attempt was made to restore these regiments to their proper brigades until [a] movement on the afternoon of the 11th." In view of this, Hartranft later reported, "I was placed in command of the troops on the right of the road. I immediately extended the right so as to secure the bank of the river and built breastworks."[42]

Cutcheon, meanwhile, assumed command of the troops on the left. "It was said that Col. Christ was sunstruck, or prostrated by the heat," the Michigander explained much later, but he carried suspicions with him for decades. He knew his superior was "not capable of great endurance" and "a man who indulged freely in the use of liquor."[43]

As mop-up got underway, Stevenson's IX Corps division arrived on the scene shortly after noon as reinforcements. A third division, Brig. Gen. Robert B. Potter's, was also readied for a move to the Ny River sector of the battlefield. Willcox directed their deployments from his headquarters at the Gayle house even as he kept a wary eye for more Confederate mischief. "I have massed my artillery on this side of the river in good position for their coming down the [opposite] crest," he told Burnside, referring to the field where the day's fight had taken place. If his men at the front were driven from their position, the Federal artillery would serve as a backstop.[44]

The later arrival of the two divisions triggered some men to wonder *What if. . . ?* "Of the importance of the foothold so gained there can be no doubt . . ." Cutcheon wrote, musing that, "had the entire corps been up when the first advance was made,

42 Houston, 118; John F. Hartranft, report, *O.R.* 36:1:949.

43 Cutcheon, memoir, 43.

44 Willcox to Burnside, *O.R.* 36:2:584.

and had the other divisions been in position to follow up the advantage when we repulsed the Confederate attack, it seems altogether likely that we might have pushed through to the Court House, and placed the rebel army in a precarious position."[45]

Brigadier General Orlando Willcox was "a negative looking man, with much whisker."
*Library of Congress*

Confederates, in fact, seemed to wonder why the Federals hadn't done just that. "It occurred to many of us at the time that the enemy here lost the best opportunity they had during the whole campaign to fall upon our flank and destroy our army . . ." wrote one of Jeb Stuart's aides, Theodore S. Garnett. If Gen. Grant could have known, and it seems to me that nothing could have been easier to ascertain . . . it would have been the work of a very few minutes to move against our right flank, throw it into confusion and seize the very ground on which we held him at bay for more than a week."[46]

Stevenson was "as he always was, more punctual than anyone else in the Corps," said his adjutant, Charles C. Mills, but the cascade effect of Burnside's revised marching orders had sent Stevenson's division unnecessarily over and yon. They had had their "usual luck of being obliged to wait for a couple of hours or more" because of the logjam created by the cavalry's departure, then they marched toward Piney Branch Church only to be turned around and sent to follow Willcox—except "We then proceeded to lose the road, owing to the neglect of higher authorities to provide us with a guide or map."[47]

45 Cutcheon, *Twentieth Michigan*, 116.

46 Theodore Stanford Garnett, *Riding with Stuart: Reminiscences of an Aide-de-Camp* (Shippensburg, PA: White Mane, 1994), 59.

47 Charles C. Mills, letter, 10–11 May 1864, FSNMP BV 108.

As it was, the IX Corps' arrival on the eastern side of the battlefield, opening a new front, would prove to be one of the most significant Federal successes at Spotsylvania. When Grant began his march from the Wilderness to the Court House, he pulled up his pontoon bridge behind him, effectively cutting the army off from its base in Culpeper, some 30 miles away along a tenuous supply line. Lee concluded that one of the logical options Grant might pursue would be a move toward Fredericksburg—thus Jubal Early's original route of march through Todd's Tavern—but Grant did not hold Fredericksburg as a clear objective. He sent his wounded from the battle of the Wilderness there, but he had not articulated a plan for supplying his army through the city. Federals had first occupied Fredericksburg in the spring of 1862, so infrastructure already existed there for moving supplies and reinforcements to the front and wounded men farther to the rear. Securing the Fredericksburg Road crystallized the city as a much more secure line of supply, just 10 miles away. "There is now regular communications with Fredericksburg," Theodore Lyman noted from Meade's headquarters.[48]

Seizing the Fredericksburg Road would also make it possible to better secure the Telegraph Road, the main road to Richmond, which ran just a few miles to the east of Spotsylvania Court House. Having both roads would, in turn, make it possible for Grant and Meade to better maintain a supply line as they advanced south, allowing them to receive more supplies from Fredericksburg as well as from the town of Port Royal, also on the Rappahannock River. That would become a huge operational boon for Grant as the campaign continued.

Burnside's men spent the afternoon and evening "fortifying our position at the crest of the hill, on both sides of the road," and Confederates did their best to disrupt the work. "The sharpshooters of the enemy were especially active and annoying throughout the day . . ." groused a member of the 32nd Maine. "Every clump of trees, every wooded ravine concealed a squad of these deadly riflemen."[49]

That night, the men on both sides finally hunkered down to await the next day's action. "The night of the 9th was spent in quiet," said Henry Houston of the 32nd Maine, "though the utmost vigilance was exercised to prevent a surprise."[50]

Their surprise would come the next day.

48 Lyman, *Meade's Army*, 156.

49 Ibid.; Houston, 111.

50 Ibid., 118.

Often associated with Spotsylvania, the photo that has become known as "Hancock and his generals" was actually taken in Cold Harbor. Seen here is a lesser-known variation of the photo, featuring (from left) Francis Barlow, John Bell Birney, and John Gibbon, with Hancock, experiencing discomfort because of his old Gettysburg wound, seated. *Library of Congress*

Winfield Scott Hancock, usually the hammer of Federal forces, began the ninth of May under a cherry tree. Joining him was one of his division commanders, Brig. Gen. Francis Barlow, "a queer, lean figure, in a cap, checked shirt and blue pantaloons," according to Theodore Lyman. Another of Hancock's division commanders, Maj. Gen. David Bell Birney, soon joined them. Birney, too, wore a checked shirt—"a strange contrast to his pale, dry, and rather precise face," Lyman noted.[51]

51 Lyman, *Meade's Army*, 147.

A small row of earthworks lined the road. Beyond, somewhere in a treeline on the far side of a wide field, the Confederates lurked. *The enemy is in our front,* a wary Hancock told his subordinates. Overnight, "the sounds reported from the picket line intimated a concentration of troops in our front," staff officer Francis Walker later claimed. As morning arrived, continued activity suggested an advance. "There is no doubt," Hancock assured army headquarters. All morning, he remained stapled in place.[52]

Confederate cavalryman Wade Hampton was, once again, up to his mercurial tricks, fixing Federal attention without giving anything away. This allowed Jubal Early to finish his movement to Spotsylvania unperturbed, which put the Third Corps in position in time to deflect Burnside's IX Corps. Had Sheridan left any Federal cavalry to disrupt Hampton, Early might not have made it to Spotsylvania in time to prevent Burnside from slipping in behind Lee's entire line.

By noon, the "interval of suspense" ended. The Confederates were no longer attempting to penetrate into the Federal rear by way of Todd's Tavern after all. Detailing Gershom Mott's division to guard the intersection, Hancock withdrew Barlow's and Birney's divisions down the Brock Road. They soon linked with John Gibbon's division, which Meade had floated between Todd's Tavern and the front as a possible reserve force for Warren and Sedgwick.

Rather than finish the trip down the Brock Road to join the bottleneck at the edge of Spindle Field, the II Corps instead followed "a wood road leading to the right, to the high open ground overlooking the Po River."[53] Hancock arrayed his three divisions in line of battle along the ridge, which commanded the valley of the Po. Across the river, he could see Confederate wagon trains still rolling down from the Wilderness, although the best he could do was harass the column with artillery. "Our batteries opened upon it and forced it to take another road," he wrote with some satisfaction.

But Hancock the Superb wanted to do more than just lob harassing artillery shells. He ordered his scouts to find a way for his infantry to effectively cross the river. "He thought he saw an opportunity of getting, in this way, upon the flank of the Confederate force at Spotsylvania," Walker recalled.[54]

By 6:00 p.m., those scouts found a path, and Hancock sent Barlow's division to the far side of the Po, with Colonel John R. Brooke's brigade leading the way. The Confederates offered minimal resistance, but the river itself worked against the

52 Walker, 446; Hancock to Humphreys, 9 May 1864, *O.R.* 36:2:565.

53 This and other quotes from Hancock in this section come from Winfield S. Hancock, report, *O.R.* 36:1:330.

54 Walker, 447.

Federals. "[T]he passage was extremely difficult owing to the depth of the water and the thick undergrowth along the banks," Hancock grumbled.

Birney, on the other hand, crossed farther upriver and "met quite a fierce resistance." The Confederates posted themselves behind the millrace of Tinder's Mill, which they used to good effect in their defense, although Birney finally flushed them out. Gibbon, crossing downriver, met no opposition at all.

Once across, Brooke advanced to a key intersection that gave him access to the Block House Road, which the Confederates had used to reach the battlefield. In theory, the road provided access to the Confederate rear, but the II Corps first had to unexpectedly cross the Po again. Their first crossing had put them on the inside curve of a bend in the river, which snaked in a narrow-mouthed "U" with the open end pointed away from the Confederate line, anchored on the riverbank. "I was anxious to reach the bridge on the Block house road, take possession of it, and effect the recrossing of the river before halting," Hancock admitted, "but it was found impracticable."

Darkness and dense woods hindered his corps' movements. When the skirmish line reached the river, "it was dark by the time we got up, and the rebels held the crossing in front," wrote Josiah Favill of the 57th New York, a Barlow aide.[55] Skirmishing quickly revealed that the river was "so deep that the flankers and skirmishers could not cross without swimming," Hancock reported.[56] The Confederates had thrown up earthworks on the far side.

"I was, therefore, compelled to wait until morning," the disappointed II Corps commander said.

Walker, who armchair-generalled much in his later capacity as the corps' historian, mused that, "Had the crossing been ordered earlier, a good beginning of a serious turning movement might have been effected."[57] As it was, Hancock inhabited a precarious position, pinned inside the "U," cut off from ready support. What once looked like an opportunity had, by nightfall, turned into a potential trap.

To cover his lines of communication, reinforcement, and retreat, Hancock ordered the construction of three pontoon bridges in the area where Brooke and Gibbon had crossed. Hancock also had his men keep an eye, as best they could in the darkness, on the wooden bridge across the Po in case the Confederates tried to torch it during the night.

55 Josiah Marshall Favill, *The Diary of a Young Officer Serving with the Armies of the United States During the War of the Rebellion* (Chicago: R. R. Donnelley & Sons, 1909), 293.

56 Hancock to Humphreys, 9 May 1864, *O.R.* 36:2:567.

57 Walker, 447.

And so Hancock ended the day as he had begun it, with his attention fixed exactly where the Confederates wanted it.

* * *

Lee had won the race to Spotsylvania Court House, and his forces had deployed on good ground, additionally strengthened by well-constructed earthworks. That did not mean he wanted to sit passively on defense. To do so would surrender the initiative—and the opportunities initiative created—to the Federals.

Lee had been reminded of this lesson the hard way during the previous November's Mine Run Campaign. The Army of Northern Virginia had staked out a strong defensive position on good ground, and Lee felt content to sit there and let the Federals try to come at him. The Federals didn't, though. Meade, then in his sixth month as the Army of the Potomac's commander, did not want to "knowingly and wilfully have thousands of brave men slaughtered for nothing" by assaulting such a formidable position, and so under the cover of night, he withdrew his army from the battlefield. By the time Lee decided on a sortie of his own, Meade had escaped. Lee's defensive-mindedness had cost him an opportunity to strike a much-needed blow.[58]

Lee would not repeat that mistake again.

Hancock's attack on the wagon train tipped Lee to the presence of the II Corps on the extreme Confederate left. Lee's first concern was to prevent them from working around the First Corps' left flank. Early's Third Corps—much of it still in motion—seemed the best option to counter the Federal II. Its lead division, under Cadmus Wilcox, needed to remain in place astride the Fredericksburg Road, but Early's other two divisions had yet to deploy.

Lee ordered the first, commanded by "Little Billy" Mahone, to reverse direction, so Mahone backtracked west along the Block House Road to the wooden bridge they had used to cross the Po. From there, they could block any Federal advance. Brigadier General Nathaniel Harris's four Mississippi regiments assumed a position left of the road, and Brig. Gen. Abner Perrin's five Alabama regiments followed suit on the right. Mahone's Virginians, now commanded by Colonel David Addison Weisiger, extended Harris's position, and Brig. Gen. Ambrose "Ranse" Wright's Georgians extended Perrin's. Three Florida regiments under Colonel David Lang hovered as reserves.

Even thus blocked, Hancock's Corps presented "a very threatening danger," Early noted, "as the position the enemy had attained would have enabled him to

58 Meade, *Life and Letters,* 158. For more on the story, see Chris Mackowski, *The Great Battle Never Fought: The Mine Run Campaign, November 26–Dec. 2, 1863* (El Dorado Hills, CA: Savas Beatie, 2018).

completely enfilade Fields's position [on Anderson's left flank] and get possession of the line of our communications to the rear."[59]

It would fall to Maj. Gen. Henry Heth's Division to drive Hancock out. The 39-year-old Heth often marched at the vanguard of the Third Corps—a position that stumbled him into a clash with Federal cavalry on the outskirts of Gettysburg 10 months earlier, inadvertently triggering one of the largest land battles in the history of the North American continent. No one would deny Heth was personally brave and willing to scrap, traits Lee now counted on. Rather than stack Heth's four brigades behind Mahone's, the Confederate commander devised a cunning plan to outflank the outflankers.

With Early accompanying him, Heth led his men south down Old Court House Road, away from the battlefield. They then turned west on the Louisa Court House Road, then onto the road to Waite's Shop, which would bring them north again. If all went well, Heth's Division would materialize in Hancock's rear or on his flank—in either case pinning the Federals in the interior of the Po River's "U" even as Mahone's Division attacked simultaneously from the front. Anderson's main line could lend artillery support.

"It was a great, an immense piece of luck for us, that Hancock made his move across the Po late in the afternoon, giving us the night to make preparations to meet him," noted First Corps artillerist E. Porter Alexander.[60]

59 Early, 354.

60 E. Porter Alexander, *Fighting for the Confederacy: The Personal Recollections of General Edward Porter Alexander*, Gar W. Gallagher, ed. (Chapel Hill, NC: University of North Carolina Press, 1989), 371.

# May 6
# May 7
# May 8
# May 9
# May 10

Dawn had hardly lightened the sky on May 10 before Hancock began searching for a way out of his predicament. The smartest thing would be to withdraw, he knew, but the general in chief of the army had decreed "no turning back" and seemed intent on that strategy. "Knowing that General Grant's intention was for the column to move on, I can still give the order, but do not think it wise, and await your instruction," he wrote to Meade overnight.[1]

Meade's instructions were brief: "[M]ove forward again at daylight in accordance with the directions issued to-night."[2]

Now operating with the advantage of daylight, Hancock sought a way around the Confederates on the far side of the river rather than through them. He sent a reconnaissance party south toward a branch of the river known as Glady Run and asked whether they could find an advantageous place to cross somewhere between the road and the run. Lieutenant John S. Hammill of the 66th New York led the "little advance," Favill recounted, and "dashed across the stream and almost into the enemy's rifle pits. He found the enemy in full force and was obliged to retire."[3]

Hancock looked for a way to follow up Hammill's excursion, but then word arrived from Grant for Hancock to withdraw the II Corps before trouble befell them. While this might have seemed like "turning back" after all, Grant actually had plans for other sections of the battlefield later that day and wanted Hancock to oversee part of the operation. Furthermore, he did not want the II Corps, isolated

1 Hancock to Humphreys, *O.R.* 36:2:567.

2 Humphreys to Hancock, *O.R.* 36:2:568.

3 Favill, 293.

and unsupported, to find itself in trouble while that other action was underway. For now, anyway, Grant "put an end to all thoughts of turning Lee's left flank."[4]

By midafternoon, Gibbon's and Birney's divisions had evacuated safely across the pontoon bridges, while Barlow's covered the retreat from "a singularly exposed and isolated position." To give himself a little extra security, Barlow ordered his brigades to erect a line of earthworks parallel to the Block House Road.[5]

"Many official reports are decorated with after thoughts, and some of them made to show things as they should have been, and not as they were," Josiah Favill warned in his memoir, which he described as "a narrative set down nightly after the day's march or the day's fight, telling of the marching, the fighting, and the catches of the breath between. . . ."
*The Diary of a Young Officer*

No sooner had the last of Gibbon's men withdrawn than Heth's skirmishers initiated contact. "It was not long before the rebels advanced in skirmishing order and opened fire," Favill wrote. "We could see their lines advancing, and as soon as they came within range, gave them a warm reception and expected to easily dispose of them, but the skirmish line was quickly followed by a line of battle, and it soon became clear we were in for a pitched fight."

Barlow seemed content to slug it out. If they had to fight, the Po at least offered better ground than most they'd seen, with an expanse of broad, open plain stretched out in front of the pontoon bridges. "A prettier field for such a contest was rarely to be found in that land of tangles and swamps," Walker later wrote.[6]

The Confederates "attacked with great vigor and determination," Hancock reported. "The combat became close and bloody. The enemy, in vastly superior numbers, flushed with the anticipation of an easy victory, appeared to be

4 Walker., 450.

5 Ibid.

6 Ibid., 451.

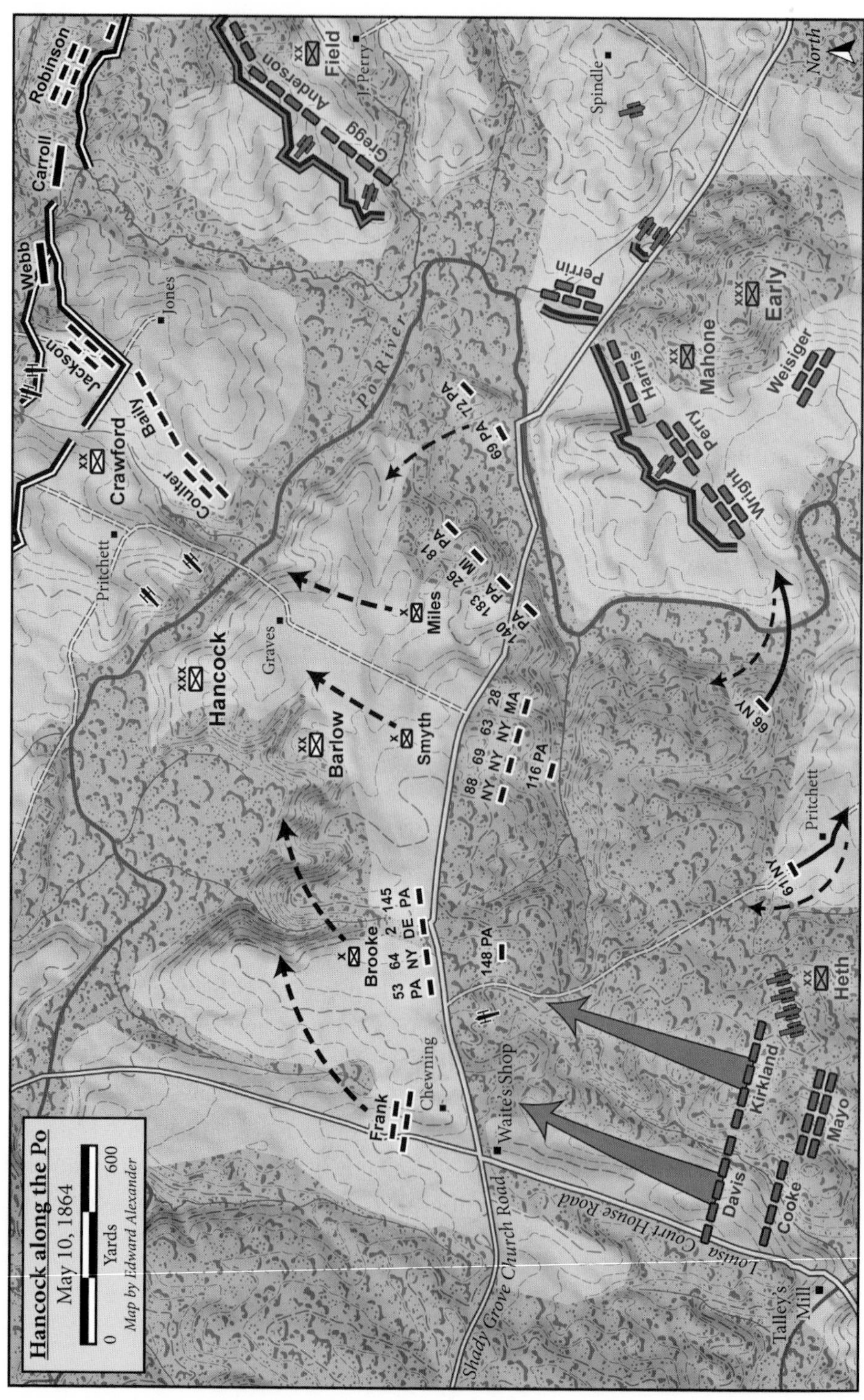
Hancock along the Po
May 10, 1864
0 Yards 600
Map by Edward Alexander
North
Robinson
Carroll
Webb
Jackson
Crawford
Baily
Coulter
Jones
Pritchett
Field
Anderson
Gregg
J. Perry
Spindle
Perrin
Early
Mahone
Harris
Perry
Wright
Weisiger
Po River
Hancock
Graves
Miles
Barlow
Smyth
Brooke
Frank
Chewning
Waite's Shop
Shady Grove Church Road
Louisa Court House Road
Talley's Mill
Davis
Cooke
Kirkland
Mayo
Heth
Pritchett
66 NY
61 NY
72 PA
69 PA
81 PA
26 MI
183 PA
140 PA
28 MA
63 NY
69 NY
88 NY
116 PA
145 PA
2 DE
64 NY
53 PA
148 PA

**Hancock Along the Po**—Barlow's division maintained a credible defense as it withdrew from an unenviable position on the south/west bank of the Po River. Heth's Confederates threatened to overrun the Federal position, but artillery from the north bank of the river provided decisive discouragement and allowed Barlow's men to withdraw to safety.

---

determined to crush the small force opposing them, and pressing forward with loud yells forced their way close up to our line, delivering a terrible musketry fire as they advanced." Federal infantry met the onslaught "with undaunted resolution."[7]

To support them, Capt. William Arnold's 1st Rhode Island battery opened an enfilading fire of shell and canister on part of the enemy advance. The Confederates, with the weight of numbers, pushed on, eventually flushing out the Rhode Islanders. In trying to withdraw, one of the battery's pieces became jammed between two trees and could not be extricated.[8]

As had happened in the Wilderness, sparks from the firefight set the dry leaves of the forest floor ablaze. Some Federals thought it was an intentional attempt by the Confederates to keep them hemmed in. "I had to throw away my knapsack to get out alive it was so dreadful warm & smoky," wrote a member of the 111th New York. "The rebs set fire to the woods & like to burn us all up, our dead & wounded were burned."[9]

During the melee, a group of officers from Barlow's Third Brigade, under the command of Col. Paul Frank, sought out their division commander. According to Favill, Frank was drunk on duty, and the officers "asked the general to relieve the Colonel from the command, stating that he was not in a fit condition to have charge of it, and asked the general to assign me [Favill] to it, offering to waive their rank, if he would do so." Barlow hesitated, looked at Favill, a mere captain, then seemed to think better of it. In refusing, Barlow told them, *Get along as well as you can.*

"How I hoped he would have consented," Favill wrote in his journal that night; "it seemed such an unheard-of opportunity, a captain to command his old brigade, but it was not to be." Colonel Hiram L. Brown would end up ascending to command.

Favill soon found himself on a separate mission instead. Hancock had been on a reconnaissance elsewhere on the battlefield in preparation for an assault Grant and Meade planned for later in the day. The eruption of gunfire and a stream of couriers from south of the Po began to worry the army commander, though. It

7 Hancock, report, *O.R.* 36:1:332.

8 Favill, 294.

9 Harry F. Smith to sister, letter, 17 May 1864, FSNMP BV 123.

would not do to have a Confederate threat on the army's right flank, particularly with an offensive planned, so Meade ordered Hancock back to the south side of the Po to take personal command of the situation. Hancock, in turn, ordered Barlow to withdraw. To cover that withdrawal, Hancock sent Favill to the north side of the river with a message to get artillery Capt. John G. Hazzard "with all his guns into position on the high bank of the river to protect the crossing."

As Hazzard mobilized, the first two brigades—Nelson Miles's and Thomas Smyth's—fell back to the pontoons and erected another line of works. By then, Hazzard's men were on line, providing covering fire for Barlow's other two brigades, Brooke's and Brown's, which began leap-frogging to the rear "in eschelon, frequently at the double quick." One brigade would lay down and open a covering fire while the other moved rearward for a hundred yards before it then stopped and laid down cover for the first. "The ground between them was alive with bursting shrapnel from Hazzard's guns," Favill recalled.

At that point, the action seemed to come to a swift conclusion. "[A]t last the enemy was obliged to retire under the murderous artillery fire," Favill summed up, "and the infantry recrosssed the river in good order, quite elated with their exploit."[10]

The Confederates had reason for elation, as well. Although Lee's little surprise didn't develop into a crushing blow as he'd hoped, Heth's men did at least drive the Federal II Corps away and secure the Army of Northern Virginia's left flank. "And after Barlow got across, Hancock's guns, as if specially mad with us for what we had done, dueled with us sharply for quite a while," chuckled E. Porter Alexander.[11]

Early detailed Mahone's men to stay back and continue guarding the position while he sent Heth toward the Confederate right. "I held, for a time, both of General Lee's flanks, which was rather an anomaly," Early later noted, "but it could not be avoided, as we had no reserves and the two other corps being immediately in front of the enemy in line of battle, and almost constantly engaged, could not be moved without great risk."[12]

But even as events began to cool for Early men's on the Confederate left, they would soon heat up for his men on the right.

10 Favill, 295.

11 Alexander, *Fighting*, 372.

12 Early, 354.

Aside from the nickname "Bad Hand," Ranald Mackenzie would later come to be known, not kindly, as the "Perpetual Punisher" for his strict discipline. *Library of Congress*

Ranald Slidell "Bad Hand" Mackenzie was two years out of West Point on the morning of May 10, 1864. Ulysses S. Grant would one day describe him as "the most promising young officer in the army"—a talented leader who, by war's end, would earn his way up to corps command in the Army of the James. But on this sultry May morning, the 23-year-old Mackenzie was a side-burned, fresh-faced captain, and the "bad" right hand that would give him his nickname, which he would later injure during the siege of Petersburg, still held all five fingers.[13]

Mackenzie had graduated top in his class at the academy, thus earning him a spot in the prestigious Engineering Corps. On this third morning at Spotsylvania, his superiors had tasked him, as a topographical engineer, with surveying the contours of the Confederate line. Grant and Meade hoped to launch an afternoon attack, and they were counting on Mackenzie to find the spot.

Mackenzie hunkered near the edge of a large punchbowl-shaped depression in the forest along the west face of the Confederate Mule Shoe Salient. VI Corps skirmishers had driven in the Confederate picket line, giving him close access to front. Ahead, slightly uphill and just outside the treeline, the rifle pits formerly occupied by the Confederate pickets dotted the edge of a field, with the main Confederate line some 200 yards beyond.

The Confederate works were "of a formidable character with abatis in front and surrounded by heavy logs, underneath which were loop holes for musketry," Col. Emory Upton would later remark after inspecting the position. The works consisted of chest-high fortifications with a protective head log across the top to shield infantrymen as they fired their rifles. Traverses perpendicular to the main

13 Grant, *Memoirs*, 2:371.

line appeared at scattered intervals as protection from enfilading fire, and about a hundred yards to the rear, a second, reserve line paralleled part of the first.[14]

As formidable as the Confederate position looked, though, Mackenzie saw much about the ground that he liked. From where he hunkered, the ground sloped upwards toward the Confederate line, but as it neared the earthworks, the ground also fell away to either side. While the terrain to the left was open and flat—and thus provided no cover—the terrain to the right had a pair of swales that would protect troops as they advanced.

This particular portion of the line also bulged outward from the main line, which itself was a big bulge. This small salient-on-the-side-of-the-Salient would result in some awkward fields of fire for defenders if any attackers broke through because the curve of the line would force Confederates to shoot through their own men in order to hit any Federal.

Mackenzie also knew the wood line in which he hid would limit the Confederate field of fire. Coupled with the topography behind him—the large punchbowl—the trees would offer additional concealment and protection, allowing the Federals to get within just a couple hundred yards of the Confederates before launching their attack.

Mackenzie reported his findings to Brig. Gen. David Russell, who now commanded Horatio Wright's division following Wright's promotion to corps command. The 43-year-old Russell, who sported a luxuriant carpet of a beard, had earned a rawhide-tough reputation in his army career. Theodore Lyman, always good for a keen description, called Russell "a man of extraordinary courage and, at the same time, a very plain and retiring man; one of his peculiarities was, that, when wounded, he never would make it public, but sought to conceal it."[15]

Wright had tasked Russell with finding the best place to launch an attack against the Confederates, and now it seemed Mackenzie had successfully done so. Russell verified the report by riding out with Mackenzie and looking at the ground himself. He brought with them one of his brigade commanders, Col. Emory Upton—the officer Russell had chosen to lead the assault.

A 24-year-old native of Batavia, New York, Upton had attended Oberlin College on Ohio, then the U.S. Military Academy at West Point, where he graduated eighth in the historic class of May 1861. An observer described the young colonel as having "a light mustache, high cheek bones, thin face, and a strong square jaw. He had a small mouth and thin, unusually closed lips, which made his mouth look

14 Emory Upton, report, *O.R.* 36:1:667.

15 Lyman, *Meade's Headquarters*, 268.

even smaller. His deep blue, deep-set eyes 'seemed to be searching all the time.'" One biographer described Upton as being "single minded in his purpose." He "never drank, smoked, or cursed, and seldom laughed. He was asocial to the point of being acutely uncomfortable in the presence of civilians."[16]

"At the start of the war [Emory Upton] had been willing to serve his nation in any manner required; by 1864 he was in search of personal glory," contends Upton biographer David Fitzpatrick, who adds, "These two desires were not mutually exclusive." *Library of Congress*

Upton was every inch a soldier, though, and unquestionably one of the finest combat leaders to come out of the Army of the Potomac. In late 1862, Upton was given command of the 121st New York Infantry, a unit later dubbed "Upton's Regulars" because of the discipline he instilled in them: although volunteers, they moved as crisply as professional, i.e., "regular," soldiers.

As they set out on their reconnaissance mission, Upton, Russell, and Mackenzie rode around the left flank of the VI Corps' position high atop an artillery-crowned plateau, then down to a farm lane that passed a home occupied by the Shelton family. The house, owned by William D. Scott and leased by the Sheltons, sat a quarter-mile in front of the Federal line and about one-half mile in front of the Confederates. The lane curved southeastward through this no-man's land and then skirted the edge of the punchbowl Mackenzie had earlier scouted. The position they examined would become known as Doles's Salient, named for Brig. Gen. George Doles, a Georgia lawyer turned brigade commander whose three Peach State regiments manned the works. This is where Upton first noted the works' "formidable character."

Accounts vary as to who came up with the overall operational plan for the VI Corps assault on Doles's Salient. Upton has ever since carried the lion's share

16 Isaac Oliver Best, *History of the 121st New York State Infantry* (Chicago: Jas. H. Smith, 1921), 31; Stephen Ambrose, *Upton and the Army* (Baton Rouge, LA: Louisiana State University Press, 1964), 3.

of credit for what history now remembers as "Upton's assault," but Mackenzie, McMahon, Russell, and Wright all had greater stakes in the plan's development. Upton came to the process late, although there is no doubt he executed the plan. His orders from Wright were simple: he was to assault the enemy's entrenchments in four lines at the spot indicated by Captain Mackenzie.

It fell to Wright's chief of staff, Col. Martin McMahon, to hand-pick 12 regiments of infantry selected from brigades in Russell's division and the division of Brig. Gen. Thomas Neill—some 4,500 men in all. Thomas Hyde, a VI Corps staff officer, noticed that among McMahon's picks was Hyde's former regiment, the 7th Maine infantry. "I coaxed McMahon . . . to substitute another," a less-than-confident Hyde later admitted. "They never knew it, and since I have not been quite certain if I did right."[17]

McMahon shared the final list with the young Batavian: "Upton, what do you think of that for a command?"

Upton eyed the line-up. "I golly, Mack, that is a splendid command," he replied, still examining it. "They are the best men in the army."

"Upton, you are to lead those men upon the enemy's works this afternoon," McMahon said, "and if you do not carry them, you are not expected to come back, but if you carry them I am authorized to say that you will get your stars."

"Mack, I will carry those works," Upton vowed. "If I don't, I will not come back."

McMahon filled Upton in on the rest of the plan. Gershom Mott's II Corps division, detailed to guard the intersection at Todd's Tavern, was finally called forward, but rather than reunite with the rest of the II Corps, Grant had directed the division to the army's left and instructed Mott to fill the gap between Wright and Burnside along Fredericksburg Road. When Upton attacked the western face of the Mule Shoe, Mott would simultaneously attack from the north. Upton was to peel open a hole in the Confederate line and then Mott, as his reinforcements, could slide into the breech and sweep down the works.

Word had come from the top: Grant considered Upton's the main attack, with Mott as support, but their combined action was just one of several that would happen in concert all along the line. Grant wanted to go all-in. On the Federal right, Hancock would lead a combined effort by his corps and Warren's against the Confederate line at Spindle Field, not necessarily with the intent to score a victory but to tie down those Confederates so they could not shift along interior lines as reinforcements against Upton and Mott. On the Federal left, Burnside was to push forward along the Fredericksburg Road with an eye on getting into the village of Spotsylvania Court House.

17 Hyde, 197.

Meade had asked Wright on the evening of May 9 to begin thinking through what the attack might look like on his front. This was also the reason Meade pulled Hancock from the far side of the Po River; he wanted the II Corps commander to familiarize himself with the situation and topography along Warren's front. Warren would be relegated to a secondary role subservient to Hancock's.

The more Upton heard about the plan, the more "enthusiastic and pleased" he became, McMahon noted, which reinforced his impression that Upton was the right man for the job.

"Mack, I'll carry those works," Upton said when he finally rode off to prepare. "They cannot repulse those regiments."[18]

* * *

As the sun hit mid-afternoon, Upton called together his 12 regimental commanders and crept with them up to the edge of the woods where he had surveyed the line earlier with Russell and Mackenzie. Upton laid out his plan and wanted his officers to see the ground for themselves so they could exactly envision what he had in mind. Upton explained his reasoning after the war: "[M]ost of our assaults had failed for want of minute instructions, and particularly at the moment of success." He would not let that happen today. "All the men knew what to do," he said.[19]

Upton's plan depended on *coup de main* tactics, incorporating speed and shock to gain the enemy works. He wanted to arrange his troops into a compact column three regiments across and four regiments deep—a formation reminiscent of the Greek hoplite phalanx or that of the Swiss Pikemen of the Middle Ages. The first line of the attack would consist of the 121st New York, 96th Pennsylvania, and 5th Maine. "We were ordered to fix bayonets, to load and cap our guns and to charge at a right shoulder shift arms," recalled Col. Clinton Beckwith of the 121st. "No man was to stop and succor or assist a wounded comrade."[20]

When the three regiments broke through, the New Yorkers and Pennsylvanians were then to wheel to the right and dislodge the Confederates in the southern stretch of works and silence the rebel battery while the 5th Maine was to wheel left and clear the northern stretch.

The second and third waves consisted of the 5th Wisconsin, 6th Maine, 49th Pennsylvania, 119th Pennsylvania, 77th New York, and 43rd New York, respectively.

18 Best, *History*, 135–6.

19 Upton quoted in David J. Fitzpatrick, *Emory Upton: Misunderstood Reformer* (Norman, OK: University of Oklahoma Press, 2017), 59.

20 Best, *History*, 128–9.

Following the first wave, they would pile into and onto the earthworks, keeping the line of retreat open while also supporting the forward movements of the first line.

The fourth line, which consisted of the 6th, 5th, and 2nd Vermont, would hold fast at the edge of the wood line as Upton's reserve. Because the topography to the left of the advancing column was open and flat—one of the disadvantages Mackenzie had noted on his first reconnaissance—the Vermonters would also have to supply supporting fire to help protect the regiments on that side of the formation, the 5th Maine, the 5th Wisconsin, and the 119th Pennsylvania.

The second, third, and fourth lines were to load their muskets and fix bayonets, but unlike the first wave, they were not to place percussion caps on the cones of their guns. The caps provided the spark that ignited a rifle's gunpowder. Upton wanted to thwart any intentions by his men of stopping to shoot at the enemy, which would inevitably cost the attack force momentum. Upton also instructed all the officers "to repeat the command 'forward' constantly, from the commencement of the charge till the works were carried." Otherwise, Beckwith later clarified, "He instructed us not to fire a shot, cheer or yell, until we struck their works."[21]

To soften the enemy position, Wright planned a pre-assault artillery barrage utilizing three VI Corps batteries—18 guns in all. If all went well, Upton's men would bore through the Confederate line, creating a gap for the rest of the Federal army to exploit. Mott's men, in theory, would support Upton's men and help expand the gap. The problem was that Upton and Mott did not coordinate closely with one another, and Mott's role in the assault seemed to be a mystery to him.

Across no-man's land, the Confederates were aware something was amiss. Their pickets had been driven in by companies of the 65th New York and 49th Pennsylvania, and there seemed to be an unusual amount of activity all across their front. Smoke from the skirmishing hovered in the humid air and "made it look hazy about us," said one observer. Another stated, more ominously, that "a death-like stillness hangs over the lines."[22]

Upton's men piled their knapsacks and followed the road through the woods past the Sheldon house. When they reached the punch bowl, they halted and, "at the edge of the heavy timber," began to align into formation. They listened for sounds of battle elsewhere on the field, but although they could hear the skirmishing along the front, and then the planned artillery barrage when it began, they could hear nothing else. The topography tucked them down beneath the

21 Upton, 668; Best, *History*, 129.

22 Ibid; Virginia Artillery, *Contributions to a History of the Richmond Howitzer Battalion* (4 vols.), Carlton McCarthy, ed. (Richmond: C. Marthy & Co., 1883), Vol. 2, 244.

soundscape, so they could not hear Burnside engaged on the battlefield's far side or even Mott's closer efforts.[23]

"We waited in suspense for some time," said Beckwith, whose nerves were getting the best of him. "I felt my gorge rise, and my stomach and intestines shrink together in a knot, and a thousand things rushed through my mind. I fully realized the terrible peril I was to encounter."[24]

* * *

Personally courageous, the 42-year-old Mott had earned his way to division command through misfortune after misfortune. A serious wound during the battle of Second Manassas earned him his brigadier's stars but knocked him out of service for months. He returned in time to lead a brigade in the Chancellorsville campaign but was again seriously wounded and again knocked out of service. He returned for the fall campaign of 1863, but because the entire III Corps performed so poorly during the campaign, it was disbanded during Meade's army reorganization in the spring of 1864. Officer attrition left Mott the senior man standing in his division and so he ascended to command as it was absorbed into Hancock's II Corps. Theodore Lyman thought Mott generally "showed a want of force and intelligence, though always a cool, brave man."[25]

Mott's division was the smallest in the corps. His seventeen regiments numbered only 1,500 men organized into two brigades. While many of the men were season veterans, Col. Robert McCallister of the 11th Jersey, commanding the first brigade, worried about their quality under fire. "The troops whose term of service is just coming to a close do not fight well," he complained. Indeed, Mott's division had broken and run during the battle of the Wilderness, raising grave doubts about their dependability. When Horatio Wright found out Mott was positioned to protect his left flank, he went to Meade to express concern. "I don't *want* Mott's men on my left," the new VI Corps commander said quietly but firmly. "They are not a support; I would rather have no troops there!"[26]

Mott had more to do than screen Wright's left, though. Meade had also asked Mott's division to stretch out and make contact with Burnside, farther east, who

23 Robert S. Westbrook, *History of the 49th Pennsylvania Volunteers* (Altoona, PA: Altoona Times Print., 1898), 189.

24 Best, *History*, 129.

25 Lyman, *Meade's Army*, 148.

26 Robert McAllister, *The Civil War Letters of General Robert McAllister*, James I. Robertson, Jr., ed. (New Brunswick, NJ: Rutgers University Press, 1965), 417; Lyman, *Meade's Army*, 149.

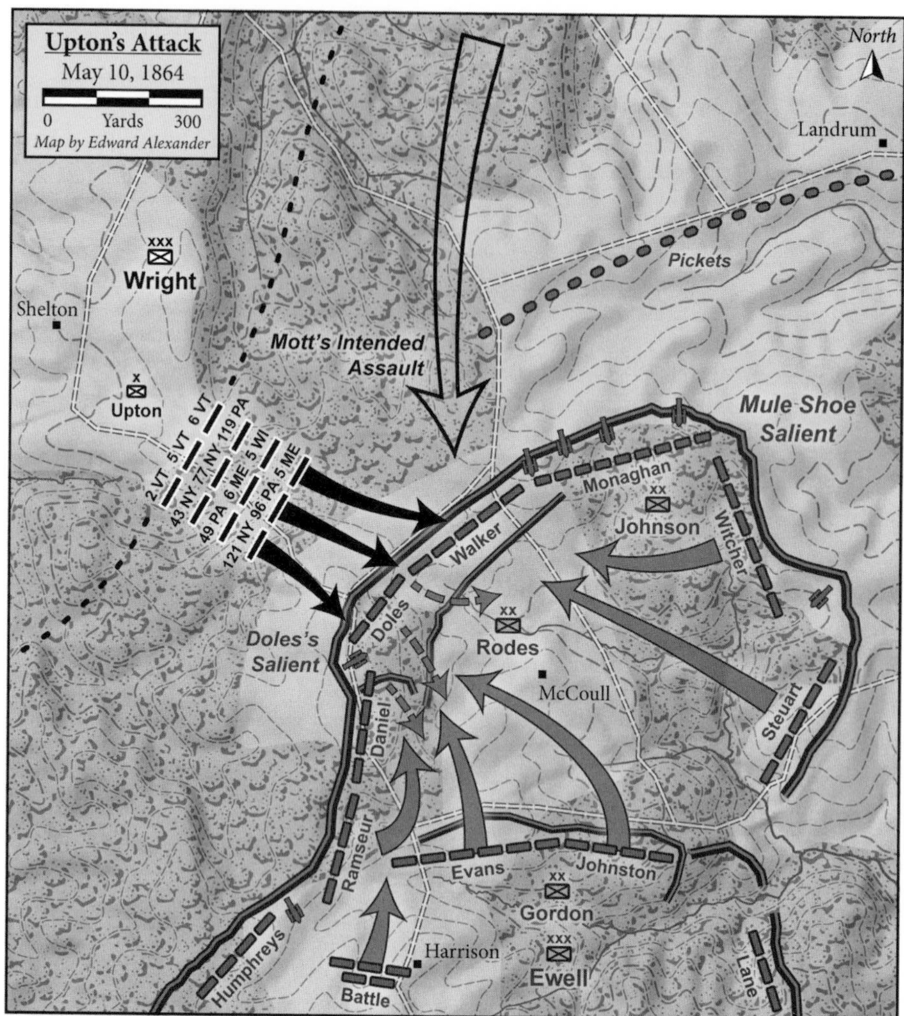


Upton's Attack—Upton's twelve-regiment attack force aimed at a bulge on the side of the Mule Shoe Salient that has become known as "Doles's Salient" after the Confederate brigade commander in that sector, George Doles. Once Upton's spear broke through, Gershom Mott's full (but undersized) division was supposed to pour in and help secure Upton's gains—but Mott and Upton did not advance in concert as originally planned.

hoped the division would help protect his right flank. "If you should need its aid make no hesitation in ordering it to your assistance," Grant's Chief of Staff, Brig. Gen. John Rawlins, told Burnside.[27]

27 Rawlins to Burnside, 10 May 1864, *O.R.* 36:2:610.

According to historian Greg Mertz, "Mott was offered little guidance on how to deal with the often-conflicting assignments. Everybody seemed to want help from Mott's division, but nobody wanted to accept responsibility for ordering Mott to follow a specific set of instructions."[28]

Even when assigned to support Upton's attack, Mott never had the opportunity to personally consult with Upton. Mott's men were just expected to "go in." Mott assembled his men about a mile north of the tip of the Mule Shoe Salient at the John C. Brown farm. When Wright's planned artillery bombardment began at 5:00 p.m., Mott likewise opened with his artillery, the 6th Maine Battery. "Loudly roared the brazen-mouthed cannon, chanting their deep bass notes of death," noted a Confederate artillerist, who appreciated the work if not the result of his Federal counterparts.[29]

What Mott did not know—and what no one told him—is that the wheels were starting to come off the caissons for the entire Federal attack. Hancock had been tied up beyond the Po and so was not yet in position with his men. In Hancock's absence, Warren launched his part of the attack early. Questions remained about whether Upton was in position.

Wright decided to postpone the attack for an hour while extending the artillery barrage to fill the time. But word never reached Mott about the postponement, and so his division dutifully stepped off at 5:10 p.m. as ordered.

Richard Ewell had told Robert E. Lee that Confederates could hold the Mule Shoe Salient if they packed it full of artillery. As Mott moved into range, Ewell proved himself right. Lee had positioned some 20 guns at the tip of the salient, and with nothing else to shoot at but Mott's division, the artillerists made quick work of the Federal advance.

"[W]e were repulsed when we ought to have been successful," wrote a rueful Robert McAllister.[30]

Defeat came so quickly that there was not time to get word back to VI Corps headquarters, and then down to David Russell at the front: Mott was out of the fight. Upton would not have support on his left.

* * *

28 Gregory A. Mertz, "Upton's Attack and the Defense of Doles Salient," *Blue & Gray Magazine*, August 2001, 20.

29 Virginia Artillery, 2:244.

30 McAllister, 417.

Sometime between 6:15 and 6:35 p.m., Upton's men burst from the tree line. "[A]t command, the lines rose, moved noiselessly to the edge of the wood, and then, with a wild cheer and faces averted, rushed for the works," Upton later reported.[31]

"Make ready boys," yelled one Southerner. "They are charging!"[32]

Vermonter Wilbur Fisk, in the fourth rank of the column, described the scene:

> At the signal, Col. Upton with his three lines of infantry jumped to their feet, and rushed ahead across the open field, to the enemy's works, while we cheered as lustily as we could to heighten the effect, and help create a panic among the enemy. How terribly the bullets swept that plain, and rattled like hailstones among the trees over our heads.[33]

Beckwith saw the action unfold almost in slow motion. A few steps into the field and "the rifle pits were dotted with puffs of smoke, and men began to fall rapidly," he wrote, "and some began to fire at the works, thus losing the chance they had to do something, when they reached the works to protect themselves."[34]

Confederates unleashed "a terrible front and flank fire," but Upton's men rushed across the open field, their officers urging them on: "Forward! Forward! Forward!" One member of the 96th Pennsylvania lamented, "Many a poor fellow fell pierced with rebel bullets before we reached the rifle pits. . . . When those of us that were left reached the rifle pits we let them have it."[35]

The battle at the Confederate line turned into "a deadly hand-to-hand conflict." Upton, on horseback, saw "The enemy sitting in their pits with pieces upright, loaded and with bayonets fixed, ready to impale the first who should leap over, [they] absolutely refused to yield the ground." He watched one of his men after another struggle with the sharp steel. One junior officer from Upton's own 121st New York was stabbed through the thigh. A Confederate used a bayonet to pin a Pennsylvania private to the parapet. A soldier in the 5th Maine, "having bayoneted a rebel, was fired at by the captain, who, missing his aim, in turn shared the same fate."[36]

Men thrust and threw their bayonet-tipped muskets at enemies, pinning them to the ground. Others used their muskets as clubs. Officers blasted away with their revolvers. One slashed with a cavalry sword. A color corporal "hit a big rebel with

31 Upton, report, 668.

32 Virginia Artillery, 2:244.

33 Fisk, 296–7.

34 Best, *History*, 130.

35 Upton, report, 668; Westbrook, 191.

36 Upton, report, 668.

his fist" only to be wounded himself a short time later. "No time now to load our pieces," wrote a member of the 49th Pennsylvania, "and many of our boys are using bayonets, butts of guns and fists—anything to get the rebels back out of our way."[37]

It was a scene of utter horror and pandemonium, yet the struggle lasted but a few minutes. Numbers prevailed, and "like a resistless wave," Upton said, "the column poured over the works. . . ."[38]

Private Thomas J. Dingler, a color bearer in the 44th Georgia, waved his regiment's flag to rally his comrades. He instead attracted special attention from Upton's men, who stabbed him fourteen times. "Killed at Spottsylvania, Va., by bayonet wound," a regimental roster later understated.[39]

Some of Dingler's fellow Georgians fell back about one hundred yards to a line of reserve works built behind the main line. Hundreds of other shocked Confederates simply threw down their rifles and surrendered. "[O]ur lives are worth something," realized Will Huie of the 44th Georgia.[40]

Scores of Southerners were pointed toward the tree line and told to make their way toward the Federal lines beyond. As they did so, "a rebel lieutenant, after passing to the rear, orders his men to pick up the guns that our dead and wounded have left on the field and fire on us from the rear," recounted one incensed member of the 49th Pennsylvania. To stop that from happening, Sgt. Sam Steiner put a "ball into the rebel's back, who threw his hands up and dropped to the ground. This stopped the picking up of guns."[41]

In all, Upton's men scooped up some 913 enlisted men and 37 Confederate officers. Among them was Confederate brigade commander Brig. Gen. George Doles, who, according to one Confederate, escaped by playing dead: "[W]hen the enemy was driven back he fell and, when our line came up, he arose and resumed command."[42]

Some Confederates, flushed from their trenches, leapt out of the front of their works into the no-man's land between lines and retreated along the front of their works before re-crossing and joining their comrades in a stretch free of Federals.

37 Westbrook, 191.

38 Upton, report, 668.

39 Rhea, 170; Henry W. Thomas, *History of the Doles-Cook Brigade of Northern Virginia* (Atlanta: The Franklin Printing and Publishing Company, 1903), 539.

40 George W. Beavers, Civil War Miscellany, Personal Papers, Drawer 283, Box 18, Georgia Archives, FSNMP BV 128.

41 Westbrook, 191.

42 Asbury H. Jackson Mrs. Luticia Jackson, 11 May 1864, Edward Harden papers Duke Univ.; FSNMP BV 26.

"The nomadic artist [Alfred] Waud said it was a fine sight to see the prisoners brought in on the double-quick in a great herd," Lyman wrote of Upton's attack. Waud titled his sketch "Rebel prisoners captured in the charge of Genl. Wrights Corps–running in." *Library of Congress*

"The Yankees fought with unusual desperation," one Confederate marveled, "and where the artillery was, contended as stubbornly for it as though it was their own." The artillery he referred to were four guns of the Richmond Howitzers, positioned in the western side of the salient. The topography had kept them out of much of the action, but once they had targets, the artillerists jumped to work. "[W]e poured a few rounds of canister into their ranks," a member of the battery said, "when we are ordered to 'Cease Firing—our men are charging!'" But the column of Confederates crossing the field in front of them was not counterattacking; they were the prisoners from Doles's Brigade, who "had no muskets," being hustled away. The Howitzers redoubled their efforts, angered that their comrades "had surrendered without firing a shot and were going to the rear as fast as their cowardly legs would carry them. . . ." Upton noted that "Many rebel prisoners were shot by their own men in passing to the rear over the open field."[43]

The Richmond Howitzers didn't have much time do keep firing, though. The VI Corps men inside the works soon made their way as far as the artillerists, who could not turn the cannon on the Federals for fear of firing upon their own men. In the end, "no artillerists could stem the torrent now nor wipe away the foul stain upon the fair banner of Confederate valor." The best the artillerists could do is take their firing implements with them as they fled, preventing the Federals from using the guns themselves.

A confused jumble of Pennsylvanians and Mainers clustered around the guns. "Who has a rat-tail file or a nail to spike these pieces?" asked a Pennsylvania captain.

"This is a hell of a place to ask for a file," one of his men replied, prompting laughter in the midst of the chaos.[44]

43 Upton, report, 669.

44 Westbrook, 191.

Beyond the artillery pieces, a long traverse offered Confederates a place to rally. The North Carolinians of Junius Daniels, who'd had their right flank stoved in by Upton's attack, clung to the traverse in an attempt to stay the flood. "Don't run, boys," bellowed Second Corps commander Richard Ewell. "I will have enough men here in five minutes to eat up every damned one of them!"

Ewell proved true to his word. For all of the weaknesses a salient presents, one strength it offers is its interior lines, which allow faster movement inside of the position. Ewell took full advantage of that strength as he effectively funneled reinforcements into the fray. It was one of Ewell's finest performances as a corps commander. "We were under a very hot fire for a time," admitted Ewell's chief of staff, his stepson, Campbell Brown. "I rather astonished myself by going forward as fast as anybody & urging the men up."[45]

The first to arrive were Brig. Gen. Cullen Battle's Alabamians. "[W]e were lying in reserve behind our front lines, when it gave way, letting the drunken villains in our works," said Eugene Blackford of the 5th Alabama. "[W]e went forward with a yell, and drove them out at the point of the bayonet. . . ." Colonel Clement Evans's Georgians came in on their heels.[46]

From his reserves, posted near Anderson's line, Ewell also summoned Brig. Gen. Robert D. Johnston's brigade of North Carolinians. They double-timed to the battlefield at about the same time Lee rode down from his headquarters near the Harrison house. Lee arrived on the scene to see, for the second time in four days, a portion of his army falling apart around him. At the Wilderness on May 6, he had watched his right wing crumble, only to be saved by the timely arrival of Lt. Gen. James Longstreet at the point of crisis at the last possible moment. Lee tried to lead Longstreet's foremost troops, the famed Texas Brigade, into battle to blunt the Federal assault, but they refused to let Lee put himself in harm's way. "Lee to the rear!" they cried. "We will not go forward unless General Lee goes to the rear!"

And so it was again here at Doles's Salient as Lee tried to rally Johnston's brigade and lead them forward to the point of contact: the Tar Heels refused to go. "Lee to the rear!" they cried.

"General Lee started for the breach . . ." a mortified Walter Taylor recalled. A bullet hit the pommel of Lee's saddle, and one witness later admitted that he expected the general at any moment to slump over, shot. Taylor and other members

45 Campbell Brown, *Campbell Brown's Civil War with Ewell and the Army of Northern Virginia*, Terry L. Jones, ed. (Baton Rouge, LA: LSU Press, 2001), 251.

46 Eugene Blackford to sister, 14 May 1864, Lewis Leigh Collection, U.S. Army Military History Institute, Carlisle Barracks, Pennsylvania, FSNMP BV 104.

of Lee's staff quickly boxed Lee in with their horses so he could not advance, begging him to stay back.

*I shall relinquish my purpose if you will see to it that the lines are reestablished,* Lee growled at them. *It must be done!*

The staff agreed, and Taylor himself drove his horse into the melee.[47]

On the north side of the breakthrough, the famed Stonewall Brigade fought desperately to stop the Federal onslaught. Brigadier General "Stonewall Jim" Walker refused his left—bending it back upon itself at a right angle—and poured fire into Upton's left flank. Meanwhile, he sent one of his staffers, Cpt. Randolph Barton, with an urgent plea for help to division commander Maj. Gen. Edward "Alleghany" Johnson. Johnson was some 300 yards away and, at that point, looking anxiously northward in the direction from which Mott's men had come. He expected a repeat performance, although no Federals had shown from that direction yet. "What troops can I send?" Johnson asked. Barton suggested the troops of yet another nicknamed general, Brig. Gen. George "Maryland" Steuart, who commanded a mixed Virginia and North Carolina brigade stationed on the right of the Mule Shoe.

"But if Steuart leaves his lines, the enemy will break through at that point," Johnson said, expressing his fears aloud.

"No, they won't," Barton blurted—impetuously, as he later admitted.

Johnson authorized Barton to deliver the order, and within moments, troops from the east face of the Mule Shoe began streaming across the interior of the salient to assist their comrades to the west. Joining them were Virginians from Brig. Gen. John Marshal "Rum" Jones's Brigade, now commanded by Col. William Witcher following Jones's death in the Wilderness. Most of these reinforcements would have been tied in place had Mott attacked simultaneously with Upton, unable to shift to Doles's aid. Instead, they swept into the clearing around the Neil McCoull farm and into the farthest advance of Upton's men, whose momentum had carried them that far but no more.

On the southern edge of the breakthrough, Confederates swarmed forward to retake the captured guns of the Richmond Howitzers. Ewell appeared, riding energetically, conspicuously, among the besieged elements of his corps, rallying them and directing reinforcements. "The excitement of the advance as they leaped the second line of works and charged the enemy, three new brigades . . . coming up

47 Walter H. Taylor, *Four Years with General Lee*, James I. Robertson, Jr., editor (Indianapolis: Indiana University Press, 1996), 130.

"Upton at the Salient" by Alfred Waud. *Library of Congress*

at once, was beyond anything I have ever felt," Campbell Brown said. "I shouted till I was hoarse."[48]

All became "a pandemonium of excitement and confusion," Walter Taylor later said.[49]

"[T]he whistle of balls seemed to come from all directions . . ." noted Colonel Beckwith of the 121st New York. "We could now see the flashes of the guns and knew they were coming in on us."[50]

Federal reinforcements, meanwhile, did not materialize.

48 Brown, 251.

49 Walter H. Taylor, *General Lee: His Campaigns in Virginia, 1861–1865* (Lincoln, NE: University of Nebraska Press, 1994), 240.

50 Best, *History*, 131.

An able commander with experience outside the Army of the Potomac, Maj. Gen. Horatio Wright took a little time to get up to speed as Sedgwick's replacement but ultimately served dependably at the head of "the Bloody Sixth Corps." *Library of Congress*

Upton, hard pressed, looked back for his fourth wave, which should have been positioned the edge of the tree line as reinforcements. They weren't there. The Green Mountain boys, like Upton, had their fighting blood up and had already charged across the field and into the fray. "The boys could not be restrained in their wild excitement, and without waiting for orders . . . they rushed in after the other brigade," admitted Vermonter Wilbur Fisk. Later, Upton graciously attested to their bravery—"[T]hey had already mingled in the contest and were fighting with a heroism which has ever characterized that élite brigade"—and Col. Thomas O. Seaver, commanding the three Vermont regiments, would earn the Medal of Honor for attacking and occupying the works "under a most galling fire." But in the moment, the Vermonters' absence must have caused a confusing drop in the stomach.[51]

For whatever reason, no one in the Federal chain of command had thought to ready a mobile reserve of troops to support Upton. The only other soldiers assigned to the assault were those in Gershom Mott's division, and he was no longer coming, although Upton still did not know that disheartening piece of information. "The enemy's lines were completely broken, and an opening had been made for the division which was to have supported on our left, but it did not arrive," Upton later wrote.

Behind the scenes, Wright had slowly come to the same realization Upton had quickly come to under fire. Wright reportedly rode to Grant directly,

51 Fisk, 297; Upton, report, 668.

circumventing Meade—a sign of the Army of the Potomac commander's increasing superfluousness. "What shall I do?" the new VI Corps commander asked.

"Pile in the men and hold it," Grant's replied.[52]

But it was too late. With ammunition running low, Upton had no choice but to reluctantly call for his men to withdraw. "We don't want to go," his dejected soldiers cried. "Send us ammunition and rations, and we can stay here for six months."[53]

But there was no ammunition, there were no rations—only orders from Russell to call off the attack. Upton obeyed. He first pulled his men to the outside of the works as a rally point, still fighting off the converging Confederates. A regiment of Georgians tried to outflank them from outside the works, but Upton's men held them off. Finally, shrouded in darkness, the VI Corps men managed to extricate themselves and withdraw.

North Carolinian Stephen Ramseur saw an opportunity to turn the withdrawal into a rout. With sword in hand, he leaped out of the Confederate works and ordered his men to follow. They didn't. "When the enemy retreated from our works they refused to charge them," one witness recorded. Ramseur pretended not to notice. In a letter to his wife the next day, he lauded the behavior of his men as splendid.[54]

Should Upton's men have stayed, as they claimed they could, they would have become Confederate prisoners. As it was, Upton's column lost some 1,000 men in the assault, with 216 of them from the 49th Pennsylvania alone—an exceedingly high number given the fact that only six of the regiment's companies were engaged. "Here is the saddest scene of our army life," a member of the regiment later lamented.[55]

Upton's own 121st New York lost one officer and thirty-two men killed "and a large number wounded. "[A]s we glanced along the terribly thinned ranks and upon the shattered staff and tattered colors, we were filled with sorrow for our lost comrades, and deep forebodings for the future," recounted Colonel Beckwith. "A splendid regiment had been nearly destroyed without adequate results."[56]

A VI Corps staff officer noted that evening that Upton was "much depressed" that his men had been driven back and "greatly grieved" by the losses. Upton had vowed that his men would take the works, and they had; that the assault

52 Charles Carleton Coffin, *Four Years of Fighting: A Volume of Personal Observations with the Army and Navy, from the First Battle of Bull Run to the Fall of Richmond* (Boston: Ticknor and Fields, 1866), 325.

53 Henry H. Houghton, memoir, FSNMP BV 400.

54 Creed T. Davis, diary, 11 May 1864, Mss 3:1 D2914:2, Virginia Historical Society, Richmond, Virginia, FSNMP BV 374; Stephen Dodson Ramseur, *The Bravest of the Brave: The Correspondence of Stephen Dodson Ramseur*, George C. Kundahl, ed. (Chapel Hill, NC: University of North Carolina Press, 2010), 220.

55 Westbrook, 192.

56 Best, *History*, 127, 133.

collapsed anyway was not their fault. "Our officers and men accomplished all that could be expected of brave men," he wrote. "They went forward with perfect confidence, fought with unflinching courage, and retired only upon the receipt of a written order, after having expended the ammunition of their dead and wounded comrades." The Federal high command had failed to properly reinforce the assault and had failed to properly coordinate support—a recurring theme not only during the three days of fighting at Spotsylvania but throughout the week-old campaign.[57]

Upton's men had their own guesses as to why their support failed to support. "The reason given at the time among the soldiers . . . was that the commanding officer [Mott] was intoxicated," one New Yorker groused. Although there was no truth to the rumor, Upton's men felt understandably cheated of their success and felt the need to assign blame. In the days ahead, events would unfold that would magnify the impact of the lost opportunity even more. "[H]ad the promised support arrived in time to protect our flanks," wrote J. M. Lovejoy of the 121st New York, "the battle of . . . May 12, 1864, would never have been fought."[58]

Spotsylvania lore tells how, in the wake of the May 10 assault, "Colonel Upton had been made a brigadier general upon the field by General Grant, and a popular and hard-won promotion it was. . . ."[59]

The telling comes third-hand, from Isaac Best's 1921 regimental history of the 121st New York, which quoted Clinton Beckwith recounting a conversation with Martin McMahon. As the tale goes, McMahon tried to comfort the "much depressed" and "greatly grieved" Upton that night of May 10.[60]

"Come see me again in the morning," he told the sad young colonel.

After Upton left, McMahon "hunted up a pair of brigadier general's shoulder straps," then went to Wright to remind him of the deal with Upton: *If you succeeded you are to have your stars, and if you do not you are not expected to come back?* With Wright's permission, McMahon asked Meade to ask Grant to ask President Lincoln to promote Upton to brigadier general. "Certainly," Meade replied, and he wired Washington that night and received a reply from the president that Upton's commission was approved and signed. Just like that.

The next morning, when Upton reported to headquarters, McMahon reminded him of the deal—as if Upton needed the reminder. McMahon took the brigadier's stars from his pocket and presented them to the grieved colonel. "Here

57 Ibid., 138; Upton, report, 669.

58 Best, *History*, 129; "Spotsylvania: A Sketch of the Grand Charge of the 12 Regiments at 'The Angle,'" *National Tribune*, 26 May 1887, 3.

59 Beckwith quoted by Best, *History*, 134.

60 See Best, *History*, 138–9.

they are," McMahon said. The pale face of an incredulous Upton "lighted up with animation." He cut off his colonel's eagles on the spot, the officers got some thread, and they sewed the stars on Upton's shoulders.

"The next day at the Bloody Angle he showed the stuff he was made of," McMahon said, underscoring Upton's worthiness for his new rank.

A voice no less authoritative than Grant cemented the story: "I conferred the rank of brigadier-general upon Upton on the spot," he (mis)rembered. He compounded the factual inaccuracy by adding, "Upton had been badly wounded in this fight." Porter, parroting his boss's account, explained, "Grant had obtained permission of the government before starting from Washington to promote officers on the field for conspicuous acts of gallantry, and he now conferred upon Upton the well-merited grade of brigadier general."[61]

Unfortunately, little of this was true. Upton *would* advance in rank, but not in the way legend has us believe. Meade would not request Upton's promotion until May 13, sent forward as part of a flurry of other promotion requests. The promotion would not be officially approved until May 28, backdated *not* to May 10 but to May 12.

And that much, at least, *is* true: On May 12, Upton would again throw his men into the fight and, indeed, show "the stuff he was made of."

* * *

As officers debriefed at headquarters, and enlisted men promoted themselves to armchair-generals around their campfires, Beckwith searched the corps field hospital for fallen comrades. "I . . . saw many of our regiment, shot in all shapes," he said, and as he looked around, "some idea of the awful loss we had sustained" took hold. Through the dark, he followed the farm lane back to the battlefield to continue his search. Dark forms covered the field, some moving, others not. The wounded cried and groaned. Confederates took random pot-shots in the dark. "Realizing how hopeless it was . . . I came back, tired out and heartsick," Beckwith said in admitting defeat. "I sat down in the woods, and as I thought of the desolation and misery about me, my feelings overcame me and I cried like a little child."[62]

On the far side of no-man's land, Confederates saw a similar landscape of woe. "Yankee dead were thickly strewn over the narrow field or clearing over which they charged. . . . Many were dead immediately outside our fortifications . . ." observed Cpt. Randolph Barton of "Stonewall Jim" Walker's staff. "Many of the Yankee

61 Grant, *Memoirs*, 2:225; Porter, 96. As we shall see, Grant didn't get this authority until May 16, well into the campaign.

62 Best, *History*, 132–3.

dead and wounded were within our lines and I recall one poor fellow, particularly, who was shot through the body and was suffering terribly. With one or two others I went to his relief, but cold water poured on his wound only intensified his pain, and we could literally do nothing for him. His groans were agonizing and we could only listen to them as they grew more and more feeble, until finally some time during the night he died."[63]

In the darkness, a Confederate band moved up to an elevated position on the line. They began to play, and "Nearer My God to Thee" drifted like a requiem over the field. According to one doleful witness,

> The sound of this beautiful piece of music had scarcely died away when a Yankee band over the line gave us the "Dead March." This was closely followed by the Confederate band playing the "Bonnie Blue Flag." As the last notes were wafted out on the crisp night air a grand old-style rebel yell went up. The Yankee band then played "The Star-Spangled Banner," and . . . it seemed by the response yell, that every man in the Army of the Potomac was awake and listening to the music. The Confederate band then rendered "Home Sweet Home," when a united yell went up in concert from the men on both sides. . . .[64]

Gouverneur K. Warren was having a bad week.

On May 4, when his corps left its winter camps around Brandy Station, Warren set a course for Spotsylvania Court House. The move required speed, with the V Corps at the lead, but because of the ponderous slowness of the army, the corps spent the first night of the campaign encamped in the Wilderness—exactly the one place Meade had hoped to avoid stopping.

On May 5, when Warren informed Meade and Grant he had encountered a portion of the Army of Northern Virginia there along the Orange Turnpike, Grant responded, "Pitch in at once."

"Attack with all your force," Meade added.

Warren did not have his whole force available, though. Part of his corps was strung out on the march and needed time to consolidate. He also anticipated reinforcements from John Sedgwick's VI Corps and needed to allow time for them

63 Cpt. Randolph Barton of Walker's staff, quoted in Margaretta Barton Colt, *Defend the Valley: A Shenandoah Family in the Civil War* (Oxford: Oxford University Press, 1999), 310–12.

64 Thomas, 479.

to arrive. So, instead of pitching in at once, Warren orderd his available men to dig in, creating a fortified position they could fall back to in the event of calamity. *Then* he ordered them forward. The delay gave the Confederates time to fortify their own position—an advantage they used to excellent measure, repulsing everything Warren threw at them.

And it seemed like the Confederates had been fighting from behind works ever since.

On May 6, a portion of Warren's corps under Brig. Gen. James Wadsworth was handled roughly for the third time in two days, and Wadsworth himself mortally wounded while trying to fend off a successful counterattack by Longstreet.

On the night of May 7-8, there had been the stubborn cavalry resistance during the advance down the Brock Road. Had Sheridan's cavalry only done their job, Warren believed, the march would have gone as planned—and Warren told Sheridan so in a conversation every bit as hot as the fighting going on around them. Warren did not know it yet, but that particular blowup would come back to haunt him in rueful, career-ending ways.

Then the Confederate infantry showed up and further stymied Warren's progress. Then there were the scattered, shattered assaults. And the indignity of having to "cooperate" with a man for whom Warren had evaporating patience: Sedgwick. In fact, Warren was writing a note to Meade the morning of May 9 to articulate that very frustration when word arrived of Sedgwick's death. "General Sedgwick does nothing for himself," Warren groused in a note that also lambasted Hancock's capability. The note was now moot—at least as far as Sedgwick was concerned—and Warren wisely tucked it away.[65]

The indignity continued through May 9 and now on to the 10th. When Meade had revealed plans for his May 10 assaults—with Emory Upton's spear thrust in the middle supported by Burnside on the left and Hancock on the right—Warren realized he was being subordinated to another corps commander yet again, one whom he had just described in his unsent note as "not capable." Yet Hancock was to take command of the army's entire right wing and oversee efforts by both the II and V Corps.

Hancock had been on the far side of the Po, but Meade recalled him midmorning May 10 and laid out the plan. "An assault was to be made on the enemy's works . . . in front of General Warren's position . . ." Hancock later wrote. "I was directed to move two of my divisions to the left to participate in it, and to

65 Historian Gordon Rhea found the note, which had sat undiscovered in Warren's papers for nearly a century and a half. He quotes it in *The Battles for Spotsylvania Court House and the Road to Yellow Tavern, May 7–12, 1864* (Baton Rouge, LA: LSU Press, 1997), 95.

assume command of the forces to be engaged in the attack." He shifted Gibbon's and Birney's divisions, once across the Po, over to Warren's right.[66]

But that's when Henry Heth attacked Barlow's division, still inside the "U" of the Po, forcing Hancock to return to give his "personal supervision" to the action there.[67]

That left Warren as senior man on the Federal right once more.

* * *

Warren had grown up across the Hudson River from West Point and seemed almost predestined to attend the academy. He graduated at age 20 in the Class of 1850, ranking second of 44. After engaging in a wide variety of engineering work for the army, he was teaching mathematics at the academy when war broke out. By September, he had earned promotion to colonel, and by the Seven Days' Battles in June–July 1862, he was commanding a brigade. He was also assisting army headquarters by scouting topography and roads, which eventually led him to service as the army's chief engineer for its commander, Maj. Gen. "Fighting Joe" Hooker, in the Chancellorsville campaign.

Warren's star climbed at Gettysburg. Recognizing the vulnerability of the Federal left, he rushed reinforcements to an eminence that came to be known as Little Round Top just in time to prevent it from falling into Confederate hands and threatening the entire Federal position. Meade rewarded Warren for his service by promoting him to temporary command of the II Corps for that fall's campaign, filling in for the Gettysburg-wounded Hancock. At Mine Run, Warren made a controversial decision to call off an attack in the face of fortifications Confederates had unexpectedly thrown up overnight—a call Meade conceded to.

The reorganization of the army in the spring of 1864 created a permanent command for Warren in the V Corps. When Grant assumed command of all U.S. forces later that month, Warren impressed him. "Warren was a gallant soldier, an able man . . ." Grant later said of him, "and he was, beside, thoroughly imbued with the solemnity and importance of the duty he had to perform." Were anything to happen to Meade, Grant saw Warren as the best candidate to replace him.[68]

66 Hancock, report, *O.R.* 36:1:331.

67 Hancock, 331.

68 Grant, *Memoirs*, 543. Grant offered this gracious characterization of Warren as a bit of a make-good in his 1885 memoir. Warren had died in 1882 after trying for decades to clear his own name after a late-war injustice inflicted on him by one of Grant's cronies, Phil Sheridan. Grant, as general in chief of the army and, later, as president, obstructed Warren's demands for the inquiry. The army did eventually clear Warren of wrongdoing, but the judgment was published shortly after Warren's death.

Once hailed as the "Hero of Little Round Top," Maj. Gen. Gouverneur K. Warren's star would fall so far that his biography would be titled *Happiness Is Not My Companion,* a phrase plucked from Warren's wartime correspondence. *Library of Congress*

"Warren, it is but fair to observe, was a gallant West Point officer of great experience and fine ability, who was generally regarded as one of the most capable corps commanders our army ever had," cavalryman James Wilson would write of him after the war, "but he was captious and impatient of control."[69]

That lack of control fired his belly on May 10. He knew of the broad plan for Upton's attack, and the role of the II, V, and IX Corps as support. He knew Hancock, by virtue of seniority, was supposed to oversee activity on this wing of the army. But so eager was Warren to somehow fix his bad week, he created an opportunity.

All day, the New Yorker had been pushing troops forward, sometimes "in considerable force," along the Confederate line, probing for weaknesses. Whether he finally found one or just convinced himself he'd found one remains unclear, but he sent word to army headquarters that he'd not only found a soft spot but that he had an excellent window for exploiting it—*right now*.[70]

"The opportunity for attack immediately is reported to be so favorable by General Warren that he is ordered to attack at once," Chief of Staff Andrew Humphreys wrote to Hancock, still trying to extricate Birney's division from the far side of the Po. "At once" translated to some point shortly before 4:00 p.m.—more than an hour ahead of Upton's scheduled assault. Allured by the surety of Warren's report, Grant rode to the front to watch the action for himself.[71]

69 Wilson, 397.

70 Walker, 458.

71 Humphry to Hancock, *O.R.* 36:2:600.

The Confederate line ran along the top of a steep hill that crossed a freshly plowed field of the J. Perry farm. A narrow band of woods separated the farm from Spindle Field just to the northeast. Another band of trees and a boggy waterway separated the position from the Federals to the north and northwest. While Charles Field's brigades here had tolerated skirmishing, they had not yet contended with a major attack, which had given them time to fortify their position. "They had formed an almost impenetrable abatis by dragging trees and bushes up on the hillside, with the limbs all pointing downward and every twig and branch thoroughly sharpened," wrote P. S. Potter of the 8th Ohio. "Without axes it was impossible to get through."[72]

Even approaching the position seemed particularly "difficult and hazardous." As Hancock noted following his morning reconnaissance, "a heavy growth of low cedar trees, most of them dead, whose long, bayonet-like branches interlaced and pointing in all directions presented an almost impassable barrier."[73]

Potter and his comrades in Col. Samuel S. Carroll's "Gibraltar Brigade" slipped forward to the skirmish line in twos and threes so they could look at the position for themselves. "As each group returned to the line it was plainly written on each face that they considered it an almost hopeless job," Potter admitted.

Old "Brick-Top" Carroll seemed to know it, too. "Boys, we have got a hard job before us!" he called to his soldiers. Potter noted: "Our brave Colonel knew his men would do all that men could do, and the charge must be made if every man went down. [N]o jest or gay banter now; every face wears a serious but determined look; that strange hush which precedes a battle was over all."[74]

Boom—boom—far down the line. "That's the signal," said Potter, and the assault stepped off. Humphreys oddly noted Warren was "wearing his full uniform" as he watched. Cutler's and Crawford's divisions swept forward, accompanied by Webb's and Carroll's brigades of Gibbon's II Corps division, which "suffered severely," Hancock would later note.[75]

The main attack came against the far left of the Confederate line, occupied by Field's Division. A Kentuckian, Field was one month into his 38th year. His five brigades included men from South Carolina, Georgia, Alabama, Texas, and Arkansas, and more Georgians. Brigadier General George T. "Tige" Anderson's brigade anchored the far left along a tributary of the Po, with four full batteries

72 P. S. Potter, "Reminiscences of Spottsylvania," *National Tribune*, 15 April 1882, 3.

73 Hancock, 334. This description of the cedars gets picked up and repeated verbatum in a surprising number of other people's accounts, unattributed to Hancock.

74 Potter, 3.

75 Walker, 457; Hancock, 333–4.

packed around him in well-constructed redoubts. Four other batteries lined up on higher ground behind the line. Gregg's Texas Brigade protected Anderson's right flank and connected with Perry's Alabamians.[76]

The Federals descended a slope into the obstructing cedars, which threw their ranks into disorder as they pushed through. Emerging into the open ground beyond, they met "a tremendous volley from the rebel works." Heavy musketry and artillery fire—some direct, some flanking—swept the ground. Some regiments made it as far as the abatis before finally being driven to ground. A few even made it as far as the crest of the parapet and into the works, but their numbers were so few Confederates quickly repulsed them or took them prisoner.

"We are so close that the troops cannot stand up without drawing a volley from the enemy," Crawford complained to Warren from the right flank. He would hold his position along the crest of a ridge as long as he could, he said, but "Our troops suffer in their present position severely."[77]

Warren, perhaps feeling the pressure of his shaky performance thus far in the campaign, decided he needed to see for himself. Colonel Rufus Dawes, commanding the Iron Brigade's 6th Wisconsin close to the center of the advance, saw the corps commander come "running up the hill to have a look." Dawes snagged Warren by his yellow sash and pulled him violently to the ground. "To have exposed himself above the hill was certain death," the frazzled Wisconsonite explained. He showed Warren a safer place from which to view the action.[78]

Grant, watching the battle intently through his field glasses, had a close call of his own. Hot iron came screeching in, and "a piece of shell struck the head of one of his orderly's horses, carrying away a portion of it, causing the horse to plunge madly about, creating a great panic among the other horses," a Massachusetts infantryman observed. "During it all the general remained as unconcerned as if nothing had happened, not even removing the glasses from his eyes."[79]

As if to make the fight more hellish, sparks from the gunfire ignited the grass in between the lines. "At times the heat of the fire was suffocating," a member of Carroll's brigade complained. Bodies of dead and wounded Federals began to

76 William Meade Dame, *From the Rapidan to Richmond and the Spotsylvania Campaign* (Baltimore: Green-Lucas Company, 1920), 143–44. Dame was a member of the Richmond Howitzers, whose guns—posted there along the line—were protected by Gregg's men. Dame wrote, "Our service together on this spot, and our esteem of one another's conduct in battle, made the Texans and the 'Howitzers' ardent mutual admirers, and fast friends, to the end."

77 Crawford to Warren, *O.R.* 36:2:607.

78 Dawes, 266.

79 Charles Davis, *Three Years in the Army. The Story of the Thirteenth Massachusetts Volunteers from July 16, 1861, to August 1, 1864* (Boston: Estes and Lauriat, 1894), 338.

Brig. Gen. James C. "Old Crazy" Rice hailed from Massachusetts, graduated from Yale in Connecticut, taught in Mississippi, and practiced law in New York City. His brigade of four New York regiments also included a random regiment of Pennsylvanians. *Library of Congress*

burn. One corpse, a captain from the 2nd Wisconsin, lay above the brow of the hill. As the fire crept toward the dead officer, a lieutenant crawled close and tried to lasso the dead captain's foot with a pair of suspenders in order to drag the body away, but to no avail.[80]

To the left of the Iron Brigade, Brig. Gen. James Clay Rice's brigade of New Yorkers and Pennsylvanians had the least amount of ground to cover to reach the Confederate lines. Rice, however, noticed a gap between his brigade and the supporting brigade to his left, Ayres's. Rice rode rearward to look for his commander, Lysander Cutler, in the hope that Cutler could send someone forward to fill the gap. "I do not know whether it was the form of the man—for he was a splendid-looking officer—or the beautiful charger that he rode, or the tone of voice in which he delivered his message, that impressed me most," a witness later wrote. Called "Old Crazy" by his men because of his enthusiasm in a fight, Rice seemed at this moment to be almost depressed, the witness noted. "The tone in which he spoke had not the firm ring which one is accustomed to hear in battle and on the march," the soldier wrote, "but rather that of a man who asks another for a favor."[81]

Having passed on his message, Rice disappeared toward the front. A short time later, that same witness reported seeing four men carrying a fifth in a blanket between them, running rearward, Rice's handsome black charger trotting behind. "The spectacle of that riderless horse told plainer than words the fate of his owner," the soldier wrote.[82]

80 Theodore G. Ellis, report, *O.R.* 36:1:456; Dawes, 266.

81 Thomas Chamberlain, *History of the One Hundred and Fiftieth Regiment Pennsylvania Volunteers, Second Regiment* (Philadelphia: F. McManus, Jr. & Co., 1905), 231.

82 Ibid.

Shot in the leg—some reports say the knee, others say the thigh, none specify left or right—Rice was taken to a field hospital in the rear, where doctors amputated the leg. At some point, he called out from his stretcher to Meade, who was passing by. "Don't you give up this fight!" Rice cried. "I am willing to lose my life, if it is to be; but don't you give up this fight!" Doctors tried to soothe Rice and offered to turn him that he might rest more easily. "Turn me with my face to the enemy," he replied. He died shortly thereafter.[83]

Warren, meanwhile, seemed everywhere at once, trying through sheer force of energy to somehow make the attack succeed. "Wearing his full uniform, he was conspicuously prominent," noted a member of the 118th Pennsylvania, posted on Warren's left. "He was on all parts of the field, encouraging his soldiers by his presence and stimulating them by his example to unusual activity." Later, on the far right, a witness saw Warren bucking up Crawford's men. They had "acted abominably, breaking all to pieces, so that Warren was obliged to rally them himself, colours in hand," observed artillerist Charles Wainwright. "He held it short, for it had been shot in two in his hand just before. The little general looked gallant enough at any rate. Mounted on a great tall white horse, in full uniform, sash and all, and with the flag in his hand, he must have made a prominent mark. . . ."[84]

But not even Warren's personal exertions or wishes could push his men any farther forward. After two hours, he called off the futile struggle.

General Hancock returned to Warren's sector of the battlefield in time to see the final withdrawals. He noted that the two II Corps brigades involved in the attack had "lost heavily," and Gibbon growled that, "The only result . . . was to kill and wound a large number of men, many of whom were burnt to death by the fierce conflagration which raged in the dry timber." The same was true of the V Corps divisions that had participated in the assault. "My loss was quite heavy," Cutler reported in terms similar to Hancock's.[85]

Despite the losses, the fighting in Spindle Field had not yet finished. At the center of the Federal line, Emory Upton was launching his flying column at Doles's Salient, and on the far side of the battlefield, Ambrose Burnside was sweeping toward Spotsylvania Court House. Action on Warren's front needed to resume in order to prevent Confederates from shifting reinforcements to either of those other threatened locations. Unfortunately, V Corps forces were in disarray following

83 Lyman, *Meade's Army*, 151; J. William Hofman, report, *O.R.* 36:1:625.

84 Survivors Association, *History of the 118th Pennsylvania Volunteers: The Corn Exchange Regiment* (Philadelphia: J. L. Smith, 1905), 417; Wainwright, 364.

85 Hancock, rport, 334; Gibbon, report, *O.R.* 36:1:430; Cutler report, *O.R.* 36:1:611.

Warren's latest failed attempt at a breakthrough. Not until 7:00 p.m. were troops ready to launch another attack in Upton's support—too little, too late.

* * *

Federal Brig. Gen. John Henry Hobart Ward was an officer who, according to historian Ezra Warner, had amassed a reputation as someone "almost universally eulogized by his superiors for bravery and ability." Yet Ward was also dogged by odd stories of battlefield conduct unbecoming an officer—a perplexing mix that would come to a head at Spotsylvania. He had served as colonel of the 38th New York through the Second Manassas campaign and was then promoted to brigadier. While he continued to serve ably, during the May 1863 battle of Chancellorsville, his III Corps brigade entangled itself in a nighttime friendly fire incident. Ward panicked and fled to the rear, accidentally trampling two Federal soldiers with his horse.[86]

At Gettysburg, Ward's III Corps brigade was posted near Devil's Den. During the corps' rout at the Peach Orchard, Ward was wounded, but he returned to serve during the "forgotten fall" campaign of 1863. When the war department reorganized the army over the winter, Ward's brigade transferred to the II Corps under Hancock. On May 6, during the battle of the Wilderness, a forest fire roared through the area where Ward's men were posted. As at Chancellorsville, Ward again fled to the rear. "They say he was in liquor in the Wilderness and that he rode away from the fight on a caisson," Meade told Lyman on the evening of May 8 after placing Ward under arrest.[87]

By May 10, Ward's division commander, Birney, had found time to speak up on his behalf, telling his commanders, "Gen. Ward has hitherto maintained a high reputation in the Country & Army for bravery & soldierly qualities."[88]

Birney's testimonial worked. Ward was back in command, but the charge of "misbehavior and intoxication in the presence of the enemy" hung over him.[89]

Now on May 10, Hancock—trying to regain some semblance of control over the Spindle Field sector of the battlefield from the overeager Warren—chose

86 Ezra J. Warner, *Generals in Blue: Lives of the Union Commanders* (Baton Rouge: Louisiana State University Press, 1964), 538.

87 Lyman, *Meade's Army*,16; Charles Dana also makes note of the arrest in a May 9 letter to the War Department, *O.R.* 36:1:65.

88 D. B. Birney, letter, 10 May 1864, J. H. H. Ward Collection, New York Public Library, FSNMP BV 50, 6.

89 Lyman, *Meade's Headquarters*, 106.

Upton's assault could be compared to Brig. Gen. Hobart Ward's in Dickinsian terms: it was the best of breakthroughs, it was the worst of breakthroughs. *Library of Congress*

Ward to spearhead the latest attack against the Confederate left flank. He would be supported on the right by the other brigade in Birney's division, Col. John S. Crocker's, and on the left by Carroll's brigade from Gibbon's division. The rest of Gibbon's command would serve as the reserve along with Crawford's harried V Corps division. Hancock's other division on the field, Barlow's, was settling in on the army's extreme right flank, keeping close watch for any potential threat from beyond the Po.

As with Upton's attack, Ward's would be a spear thrust. Eight regiments, stacked one behind the other in a single column, would rely on speed and surprise: the 86th New York, 3rd Maine, 124th New York, 99th Pennsylvania, 141st New York, 20th Indiana, 110th Pennsylvania, and 40th New York. When they advanced, they were "to take double quick steps for the works but hold our fire until we carried the works," one of the Mainers explained.[90]

After the violent struggles of the day, infantrymen had little appetite for more. "The men regarded the effort as hopeless from the start," wrote David Craft of the 141st Pennsylvania, "and the officers failed to secure any enthusiasm in their troops." It was little wonder. "This is sheer madness," fretted a hand-wringing Crawford, still posted on the far right of the line. "This is sheer madness, and can only end in wanton slaughter and certain repulse."[91]

By contrast, Ward's brigade had enjoyed a relatively easier few days than Warren's men around them. The brigade started May 10 on the far side of the Po, but by early afternoon had shifted to the left and settled into position opposite an

90 Amos G. Bean, "The Life of Amos G. Bean as a Soldier," 18, FSNMP BV 273.

91 David Craft, *History of the One Hundred Forty-first Regiment* (Towanda, PA: Reporter-Journal Printing company, 1885), 190; Charles H. Weygant, *History of the One Hundred and Twenty-Fourth Regiment, N.Y.S.V.* (Newburgh, NY: Journal Printing House, 1877), 310.

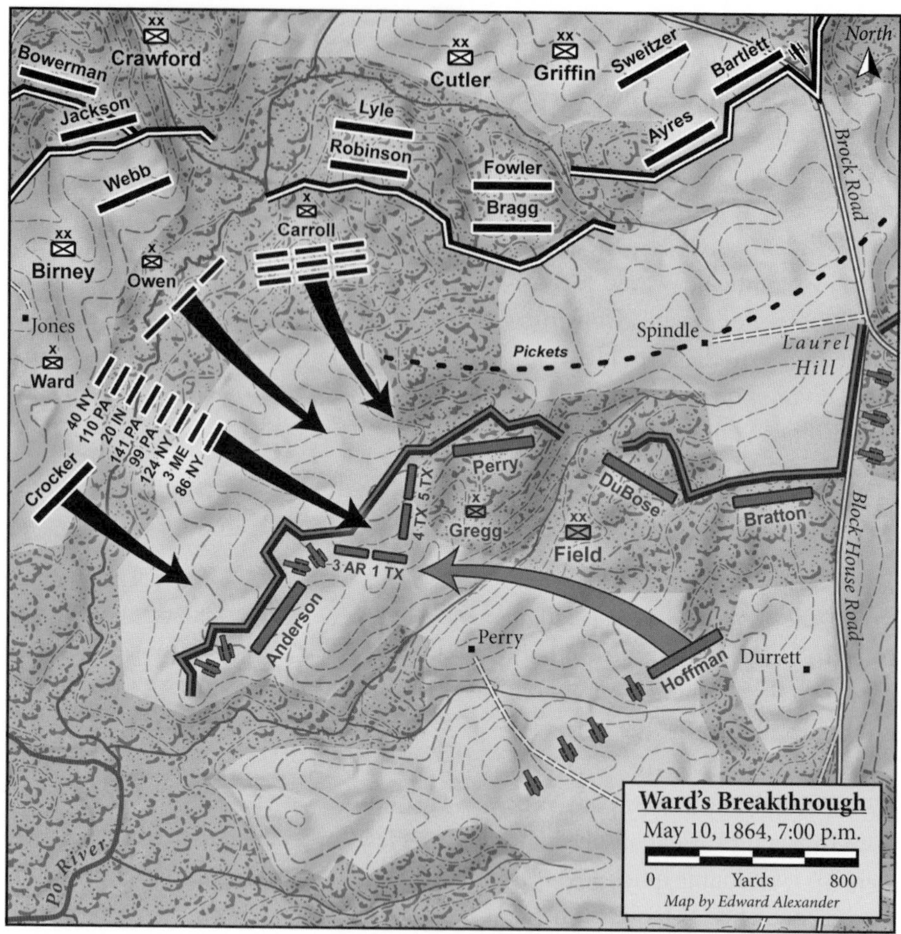


**Ward's Breakthrough**—Ward's eight regiments sprang forward in single file and, despite heavy artillery fire, managed to pierce the Confederate line. Gregg's enraged Texans and Arkansans counterattacked. Pressure from additional Federal brigades did not exert enough pressure to exploit Ward's breakthrough.

artillery redoubt in Field's line. A first shell came arching in and exploded in front of the brigade's breastworks, showering the men with "bushels of dirt and gravel stones." Moments later, Col. Moses "Mose" Lakeman of the 3rd Maine, sitting on a stump and leaning back against another tree, had a cannonball rip a hole in the tree just above his head.

"The Colonel began coolly to poke out the slivers," a witness recounted, "and remarked, 'See what the carless cusses have done to my chair-back.'"

"Colonel, haven't you better move before they hit you?" someone asked.

"Oh no, they have not got the bullet molded yet to kill old Mose."

But then a second sold shot came crashing in, this one "several inches lower and very near his head," the witness said. Lakeman rose to his feet. "If you want that chair, you can have it," he said to no one in particular. "I am not going to sit there any longer."[92]

The time for sitting soon passed, anyway, as the order came for Ward's attack. The brigade advanced down a thickly wooded slope into low ground and, along the banks of a small stream that trickled through the bottomland, they awaited the signal to charge. Almost every man filled his canteen. All fixed bayonets. "[T]he cannon shot was passing over our heads from each side," Bean recalled. He watched the shrapnel of one exploding Confederate artillery shell nick Ward, sitting on horseback about 50 feet away. "I saw him put his hand to his right temple and next the sight of blood," Bean said, "but he did not fall."

*Should I take your place?* asked Thomas Egan of the 40th New York, the senior colonel in the brigade.

"No sir!" Ward barked. "I am in command yet. When I want help, I will call for you."

A few moments later, Ward called for Egan after all. "[A]nd he went to the brook and washed his head, tied a handkerchief around it and came back to command," Bean noted.[93]

Time crept as the artillery duel continued. One member of the 141st Pennsylvania described "a half-hour of weary waiting, during which our minds were filled with anxious forebodings of coming evil." As J. D. Bloodgood, a fellow member of the 141st, explained, "The troops had witnessed the failure of Warren's men to take the ridge and the terrible slaughter which resulted, and moved forward with a good deal of reluctance, for they all felt it to be a hopeless undertaking and that they were like sheep being led to the slaughter."[94]

The "go" order arrived. "[U]p the hill, at a rapid gait we started, tearing our way through the brush, leaping across ditches, and clambering over felled trees," wrote Charles H. Weygant of the 124th New York.

Confederate artillerist William Meade Dame of the Richmond Howitzers said the breath was "about knocked out of us" by the suddenness of the attack. "There, pouring out of the woods, yelling like mad men, came the Federal infantry, fast as

92 Bean, 18.

93 Bean, 18.

94 Weygant quotes throughout this section, 310–11; J. D. Bloodgood, *Personal Reminiscences of the War* (New York: Hunt & Eaton; Cincinnati, OH: Cranstons & Curts, 1893), 248.

they could run, rushing straight upon our line," Dame said. "The whole field was blue with them!" Knocked-out breath or not, Confederates soon gathered their wits and opened fire.[95]

"The expected storm of battle now opened with horrid crash and roar…" Weygant saw from the Federal side. "But onward and upward, tumbling into ditches, tripped by tangling vines, lacerated by springing branches and pierced and torn by the dry pointed cedars,—onward, right onward through the gathering gloom, filling with whizzing, whistling bullets, we forced our way." Amos Bean of the 3rd Maine said, "It seemed as though the air was full of bullets as honey bees at swarming time."[96]

As historian Greg Mertz has noted, no account seems to exist that suggests anyone scouted the location for Ward's assault the way Ranald Mackenzie had scouted the location for Upton's. The terrain certainly worked against Ward's men more than it did against Upton's. Ward's three lead regiments became "so intermixed that they had to be handled as one body."[97]

Coming up from the low ground gave the column one advantage, however: Confederates overshot badly. That allowed Federals to push up to and through the abatis—only to run up against the Confederate battlement. Sharpshooters atop the works poured down fire as artillerists inside began to shout orders for point-blank engagement. Several quick-thinking Federal officers, recognizing the peril, ordered their men to ground. "The order to *lie down* was obeyed with alacrity," Weygant said—"not a moment too soon."[98]

"Fire!" yelled the Confederate gunners. Out leaped the powder flames and a volley of canister. "[T]he very earth beneath us seem[ed] to shiver," Weygant would write. It was, recalled a member of the 141st Pennsylvania, "such a fire as to sweep the front lines completely away." As another member of the regiment attested: "All went steady under a perfect shower of bullets until the grape and canister began to come, when we broke and run in all directions."[99]

But even as much of the attack column began to melt away, the lead elements surged to their feet and, "like a great blue wave," swept over the top of the works. Fighting became terrific, intense, personal. One Federal began stabbing

95 Dame, 165.

96 Bean, 19.

97 Gregory A. Mertz, "General Gouverneur K. Warren and the Fighting at Laurel Hill During the Battle of Spotsylvania Court House, May 1864," *Blue & Gray Magazine*, Summer 2004; Weygant, 310–11.

98 Ibid., 311.

99 Craft, 191, 190.

at Confederates with his bayonet, crying, "Squawk, Damned you! I like to hear you squawk." Color-bearers for the 3rd Maine and 86th New York planted flags on the Confederate parapets. Picks and shovels became hand weapons. Muskets, once fired, became clubs. One Confederate officer even used a frying pan to direct action. "We must hold this position!" shouted Col. Robert S. Taylor of the 3rd Arkansas as he swung his pan "round and round by his head, scat[t]ering hot gravy in every direction."[100]

The Texans and Arkansans met the assault with all the frontier ferocity they could muster, but the brigade had suffered dreadfully in the Wilderness on May 6. Now only a third of the size it had been less than a week earlier, the exhausted survivors could not hold back the desperate attackers. As Upton's men had done, Ward's began pushing open a breech for reinforcements, forcing the Texans back. In doing so, the Texans left the two Napoleons of the Richmond Howitzers unprotected—but they also cleared the artillerists' field of fire. With no fellow Confederates in the way, the gunners opened with double cannister, delivering what Dame called an "awful mauling." A post-battle count would tally "nearly one hundred dead and wounded Federals . . . at the muzzle of our guns."[101]

The Texans used the respite to rally. "Perfectly furious," they "came leaping like tigers upon [the Federal] flanks," Dame observed. "It was the first time in the whole war they had been forced from a position, under fire, and they were mad enough to eat those people up."[102]

Just as reinforcements had failed to materialize for Upton, so too did they fail to show for Ward. Carroll's column turned back as soon as the artillery began blasting away. Webb's brigade, which had fought in the burning field earlier in the day, didn't move forward at all. Webb later reported that the brigade's "rear line broke to the rear." He could find only three of his nine regiments, and ended up putting officers under arrest. Ward's surviving men were left to themselves.[103]

"We had to get and get right smart soon," realized Mainer Amos Bean. For Bean, "right smart soon" wasn't soon enough. Even as he made his escape, he watched the color-bearer of the 3rd Maine fruitlessly try to rally men on the parapet. Then, just four rods from the works, Bean took a bullet through his left thigh. "I leaned on

100 Bean, 19; J. B. Minor, "Rallying with a Frying Pan," *Confederate Veteran* XIII (1905), 72. Minor incorrectly places the action on May 6—the day the Texas Brigade famously came to Lee's rescue in the Wilderness. A May 1905 reply in *Confederate Veteran* by a member of the 3rd Arkansas corrects the date.

101 Dame, 170; W. P. Johnson, "Third Arkansas and Richmond Howitzers," *Confederate Veteran* XIII (1905), 210.

102 Dame, 168.

103 Alexander S. Webb, report, *O.R.* 36:1:437.

A resident of Texas before the war, Brig. Gen. John Gregg served in the Western Theater until the spring of 1864, when he was assigned to command the Texas Brigade in the Army of Northern Virginia. *Library of Congress*

my gun for a crutch and made only a few hops when another went through my right hip completely using me up," Bean recounted. "Then I threw off all my rig and tried to drag myself by my elbows but soon I fainted and supposed I was dying but I soon came to myself to find the Rebs had made eight bullet holes in my hide." Bean would lie on the field for two days before Confederate pickets would evacuate him from the field and send him south to prison camp.[104]

The Texas Brigade, its dander up, chased the last of the scattered blue infantry down the slope and into the woods. Some of Tige Anderson's Georgians joined in the pursuit, although the Confederates soon gave up the hunt in the gloaming. Efforts turned instead to foraging and plunder. "Quite a number of our men went out in front of the breastworks and gathered up the spoils—such as muskets, cartridge boxes, etc.—and distributed them along the line," wrote W. P. Johnson of the 3rd Arkansas.[105]

Inside the works, Gregg congratulated his brigade for their rally, then turned his attention to the Richmond Howitzers who had supported them. "Boys," the general said, "Texas will never forget Virginia for this!" General Field rode over to add his praise. "Men, it was perfectly magnificent," he told them.[106]

On the opposite side of the battlefield, Ward's men crashed through the cedar thickets and up the far slope, where it took Birney's and Hancock's staffers to corral them. Ward himself, though, was conspicuous in his absence. Upton had led from the front during his attack, and witnesses saw him all over the battlefield; no one seems to have left a single account of Ward. Perhaps he had excused himself from the field because of his injury, although no textual evidence exists to offer an explanation.

104 Bean 19.

105 Johnson, 210.

106 Dame, 168.

And Ward's fall from grace was not yet over. Two days later, in the midst of the hardest fighting yet, General Birney would encounter Ward making his way rearward. *I need my horse*, claimed Ward, who had gone into the battle unmounted. Birney instructed an orderly to give his horse to Ward and then ordered the brigadier back to his brigade on the front line. "I attributed his excitement at the time to the extraordinary success of the assault," Birney later explained. But moments after meeting Ward, Birney met Hancock, who expressed concern that Ward was "drunk on the field." The abstemious Birney immediately rode to the rifle pits to find his subordinate. "[W]atching his movements, I felt it my duty to order him to the rear under arrest," Birney concluded. "I believed him to be grossly intoxicated."[107]

Colonel Thomas Egan would be promoted to command of the brigade while Ward would be shuffled to the rear and eventually cashiered from the army. He would spend the rest of his life petitioning the army for a formal hearing on the matter, to no avail. "I think the reason why he failed," said one of his former men, "was that the government and army officers thought such a cowardly case was too disgraceful to be aired by a hearing."[108]

For Gouverneur K. Warren, May 10 likewise proved to be one more bad day in a string of them. That Ward's failed attack fell under Hancock's command, and not Warren's, didn't matter—Warren still received the blame for it. "[I]t was executed with the caution and absence of comprehensive *ensemble* which seem to characterize that officer [Warren]," wrote Assistant Secretary of War Charles Dana in a dispatch to the war department. Even the sympathetic Theodore Lyman shook his head. "Warren is not up to a corps command. . . . [H]e cannot spread himself over three divisions. He cannot do it, and the result is partial and ill-concerted and dilatory movements."[109]

Lyman was diagnosing a problem with Warren that likewise plagued Meade and Grant, although that larger pattern seemed lost on the aide. He saw the piecemeal failures on Warren's front as Warren's fault. However, Grant was beginning to see the pattern, which had dogged the campaign since its opening.

But he recognized something else, too, more immediate: the accumulated failures of May 10, perhaps, suggested an unexpected opportunity.

107 D. B. Birney to Francis Walker, 4 June 1864, J. H. H. Ward Papers, New York Public Library, FSNMP BV 50, 8.

108 Wyman White, "The Civil War Diary of Wyman S. White, First Sergeant of Company 'F' of the 2nd United States Sharpshooter Regiment (New Hampshire Men) in the Army of the Potomac, 1861–1865," FSNMP BV 150.

109 Dana to Stanton, May 11, 1864, *O.R.* 36:1:67; Lyman, *Meade's Army*, 151.

Major General Ambrose Burnside and the loneliness of command—well-liked by his peers but not necessarily well-respected. *Library of Congress*

---

History tends to forget that, of all the Federal commanders operating against Spotsylvania Court House on May 10, 1864, the affable but ill-starred Ambrose Burnside enjoyed the greatest success.

Less than two weeks shy of his 40th birthday, the commander of the IX Corps had already proved himself a mismatch for operations under Grant—not that Burnside wanted to be back in Virginia in the first place. He had commanded the Army of the Potomac during its ill-fated battle at Fredericksburg in December 1862 and its miserable, morale-crushing "Mud March" in January 1863. He also had to stare down a cabal of disgruntled subordinates who tried, behind his back, to have President Lincoln oust him. Fed up, he asked for and was granted transfer from a command he had not wanted in the first place.

Burnside soon found himself in command of the much-quieter Department of the Ohio, although November 1863 found him in the field again, successfully overseeing the defenses of Knoxville, Tennessee.

When Grant came east in the spring of 1864 and looked to bolster Federal forces there for the planned campaign against Lee, he called Burnside's IX Corps—which had served under him during part of the siege of Vicksburg—to join the concentration. But because Burnside had once commanded the Army of the Potomac, and because Burnside outranked its current commander, George Meade, Grant made the IX Corps its own autonomous force—essentially a small independent army that reported directly to Grant. Just as Grant directed Meade, he also directed Burnside.

Try as he might to coordinate both bodies of troops with each other, Grant was already discovering the challenges of that arrangement. In the march to the Wilderness, Burnside had brought up the rear and moved with such lethargy that other corps commanders exhibited little to no faith in getting him into the fight in any meaningful way. "He won't be up—I know him well," cautioned James C. Duane, the Army of the Potomac's chief engineer, as the generals drew up their plans. And indeed, on the morning of May 6, Burnside did not show on time. "I knew it!" exclaimed an exasperated Hancock, who sorely needed him at that moment. "Just what I expected!" According to Theodore Lyman, Burnside possessed "a genius for slowness."[110]

Burnside's route to Spotsylvania had put his corps, alone, on the eastern side of the battlefield. A thin line of skirmishers—the 4th and 10th U.S. Regulars—stretched from his right flank through the swampy bottomlands of the Ny River's headwaters northward to link with Gershom Mott's orphaned II Corps division near the Brown farm. Mott, in turn, connected with Horatio Wright, who was unhappy to have Mott floating out there on his left flank. Such was Burnside's tenuous connection with the rest of the army. Orders between Burnside and army headquarters had to travel miles of circuitous back roads.

Once upon a time, Burnside might have seemed the perfect candidate for such an isolated command. In early 1862, he captured national headlines by capturing the Outer Banks and closing the northern North Carolina coastline, an important step in the U.S. government's "Anaconda Plan" to choke off the Confederacy's ability to supply itself. Lincoln thought so much of Burnside's effort that he twice offered Burnside command of the Army of the Potomac. Burnside took it only on the third offer because command would have otherwise gone to one of his rivals if he didn't.

Burnside even looked every bit the soldier, almost regal in his bearing. His distinctive moustache swept down almost walrus-like from his upper lip, flanking his bare chin and instead sweeping back along his firm jawline and up the sides

110 Lyman, *Meade's Army*, 135, 136.

of his balding head. To cover his bare top, he often wore a tall hat with a rounded top that, in a later era, might make him look like a "Keystone Cop" of early 20th century lore. Morris Schaff, an Army of the Potomac staff officer, described him as "agreeable and well-groomed," although Schaff did not necessarily intend that as a compliment. Schaff considered Burnside one of "the California-peach class of men, handsome, ingratiating manners, and noted for a soldierly bearing,—that is, square shoulders, full breast, and the capacity on duty to wear a grim countenance, while off duty all smiles and a keen eye to please."[111]

In short, Burnside was spectacularly mediocre as a commander. Nevertheless, his presence along the Fredericksburg Road had provided immediate dividends for Grant by shortening and strengthening the Federal supply line. On the late afternoon of May 10, Burnside would use that same road as his axis of advance in his effort to support Emory Upton.

* * *

Once in possession of the Fredericksburg Road, the IX Corps spent its time improving its holdings. "I immediately extended the right so as to secure the bank of the [Ny] river and build breast-works," wrote Col. John Hartranft, whose brigade made up the right flank of Burnside's position, occupying the north side of the road. "During the next day [May 10] I continued strengthening the works, advancing, and re-establishing the picket line."[112]

Similar work continued all along the line. To Hartranft's left, Orlando Willcox's other brigade, under Col. Benjamin Christ, fortified the south side of the road. Brigadier General Thomas G. Stevenson's division came up to extend the line to the left with Col. Daniel Leasure's brigade, with Lt. Col. Stephen Minot Weld's brigade as reserves.

Because Willcox's division had taken the lead in the fighting on May 9, it fell to Stevenson's men on the morning of May 10 to feel out the enemy further and develop the situation. That task, in turn, trickled down to the 57th Massachusetts, which threw forward skirmishers to test the Confederate lines. "General Stevenson was present and directed the movement in person fearless of all danger," one of them recalled.[113]

111 Schaff, 226-7.

112 John F. Hartranft, report, *O.R.* 36:1:949.

113 John Anderson, *The Fifty-Seventh Regiment of Massachusetts Volunteers in the War of the Rebellion: Army of the Potomac* (Boston: E. B. Stillings & Company, printers, 1896).

"No more officer was devoted to his duty," wrote Massachusetts Gov. John Andrew of Brig. Gen. Thomas Greely Stevenson. "No officer more fully won the respect and love of his men, whom it may be most truly declared that he always led rather than commanded." *Author's Collection*

The 28-year-old Stevenson came from a well-connected Boston family. He started the war by raising his own regiment, the 24th Massachusetts, and saw his first action as its colonel during Burnside's North Carolina Expedition in early 1862. At the beginning of that summer, the regiment stayed in the Carolinas when Burnside first joined the Army of the Potomac, although Burnside made time to recommend Stevenson for promotion. "I know no Colonel in the army who makes a more efficient brigadier-general," Burnside attested. "He has shown great courage and skill in action, and in organization and discipline he has no superior." Stevenson's star came through on December 27, 1862.[114]

Continued service found Stevenson's brigade among the forces besieging Charleston, South Carolina, in the summer of 1863. Stevenson commanded the reserves during the attack on Battery Wagner. Most of his brigade's subsequent assignments were dutiful if unremarkable, but he earned the respect and admiration of his troops. "A sagacious, cool, and dauntless soldier, he was an inspiring leader of men, and a gentleman of the noblest stamp," one of them said.[115]

"He would have been . . . with the experience of large operations—which he would have gained so rapidly and so thoroughly in the campaign of 1864—one of the best, if not the very best division commander in the Army of the Potomac," predicted his assistant adjutant general, Charles Mills, in a comment that seemed

114 Joshua Thomas Stevenson, *Memorial of Thomas Greely Stevenson, 1836–1864* (Boston: Welch, Bigelow, & Company, 1864), 21.

115 Charles Folsom Walcott, *History of the Twenty-first Regiment, Massachusetts Volunteers, in the War for the Preservation of the Union, 1861-1865: With Statistics of the War and of Rebel Prisons* (Boston: Houghton, Mifflin and Company, 1882), 320.

prescient of Stevenson's reassignment to Burnside's IX Corps in April 1864. Burnside was pleased to see his former young star.[116]

Satisfied with the deployment of the troops along his front, Stevenson retired some distance behind the line. "On the left of the road were three or four terraces," said one Federal officer; there, Stevenson breakfasted with Colonel Leasure, commander of his second brigade. When Leasure went forward to inspect the trenches of the 3rd Maryland, Stevenson stayed behind, "talking with staff officers and reclining on the grass in the rear of the Union trench." A member of the 100th Pennsylvania, posted nearby, reported seeing Stevenson "laying under a tree in the shade." It was, an officer said, "a comparatively secure place." And another said they gaggled there "without the slightest idea of any danger."[117]

At some point, Colonel Christ rode by, accompanied by Col. Zenas Bliss, a brigade commander from Brig. Gen. Robert Potter's Second Division. *We wish we could trade places with you!* they joked with Stevenson, lounging under his shade tree.

*I'd rather remain under my tree, eating lunch, than be out in the heat reconnoitering as you are*, he laughed in reply.[118]

Meanwhile, along the front line itself, the colonel of the 20th Michigan described "a strong and vigilant skirmish line" that had opened a lively firefight. "[A] raking fire from the enemy's skirmishers," opened on the 1st Michigan Sharpshooters, complained their colonel, "and from which the regiment suffered severely, until extending and strengthening my skirmish line I succeeded in driving the rebels back out of range."[119]

As these back-and-forth dustups erupted, died out, and erupted again, Daniel Leasure conducted his inspection. As he walked the line, his presence sparked another of these eruptions. Confederate sharpshooters began firing, and "About half a dozen [bullets] passed over his head," wrote a witness from the 100th Pennsylvania. "One of them passed through the rear and crashed through Lt. S. G. Leasure's canteen, then continuing on, struck General Stevenson in the head."[120]

116 Charles Mills, letter, USAHEC, Carlisle, PA, FSNMP BV 108.

117 Stephen Minot Weld, *War Diary and Letters of Stephen Minot Weld, 1861-1865* (Boston: Massachusetts Historical Society, 1979), 290; "Joe Templeton's father" to Alex Adams, letter, 23 May 1864, FSNMP BV 507. Templeton was a member of the 100th Pennsylvania. He relayed news of Stevenson's death to his father, who then passed the news on to Adams, another member of the regiment, then convalescing in the hospital; Weld, 291; Charles Mills, letter, USAHEC, Carlisle, PA, FSNMP BV 108.

118 Rhea, *Battles for Spotsylvania Court House,* 182.

119 Cutcheon, *report, O.R.* 36:1:977; Charles DeLand, report, *O.R.* 36:1:973.

120 William Gilfillan Gavin, *Campaigning with the Roundheads: The History of the Hundredth Pennsylvania Veteran Volunteer Infantry Regiment in the American Civil War 1861-1865: The Roundhead Regiment* (Dayton, OH: Morningside, 1989), 410.

Several correspondents recorded Stevenson's death as instantaneous, but staff officer Edwin Rufus Lewis of the 21st Massachusetts—who trained as a doctor after the war—had the most proximate view of the incident:

> We had breakfasted and had had coffee and the general was enjoying his pipe reclining on the ground and resting on his right elboy [*sic*], his head and upper body up, when report came that some of our men behind killed in action had been left uncared for. Stevenson began to give us an order for having proper care taken of the bodies. He removed his pipe and began speaking. I stood near listening to him. Stray bullets were coming over and whistling around, burying themselves in the ground. It was a part of our routine experience. One was heard coming that seemed to be VERY near. The general stopped in the middle of a sentence. I heard the bullet strike with a peculiar dull thud as if striking in a pumpkin. I stood waiting the completion of the order. But the general was silent. He had not moved. He was holding his pipe up in hand and looking me in the face. No movement of hand or eye betrayed him, but soon his hand began to drop and his head to droop. Lieut Jones, an aide standing near by, exclaimed "Good God! the general is struck." I sprang forward and put my hand under his head to support it and felt a gruesome damp liquid oozing out. The ball had entered back of the left ear. On searching we saw it pushing out below the right temple. It had passed through the brain but had stopped short of emerging. The general never knew what hit him. He was unconscious, of course, and soon a comative sleep developed. In an hour or so he died.[121]

In subsequent reports, Stevenson's death would most often be attributed to a sharpshooter, but Mills, who was there and spent the day in sober reflection over the tragedy, described it as "one of the occasional shots from rebel skirmishers which passed to our rear." Being tucked behind the slope of the ridge would have kept them safely out of the line of sharpshooter fire, but an overshot by a skirmisher could fly past the crest of the ridge and, on its downward trajectory, still carry lethal—if unlucky—velocity. Stevenson's fellow division commander, Willcox, reported the news back to IX Corps headquarters that Stevenson was "hit by some chance shot."[122]

121 Edwin Rufus Lewis, letter, FSNMP BV 415.

122 Willcox to Burnside, 10 May 1864, *O.R.* 36:2:613.

A bas-relief memorial to General Stevenson, installed in 1905 stands in Nurses Hall, at the entrance to Memorial Hall, in the Massachusetts State House. *Chris Mackowski*

"We all of us felt dreadfully to-day on account of Tom Stevenson's death," wrote Weld, another Boston Brahman and commander of Stevenson's First Brigade. "He will be a sad loss to us all." Weld had his men make a coffin for Stevenson, whose body was then sent rearward on the long journey back to Massachusetts. Major Nathaniel Wales and John Jones, friends from home who had served with Stevenson, accompanied the body. "It made me feel blue enough to lose such a fellow as he was," Weld wrote after watching the sad little procession leave.[123]

Burnside was visibly shaken by the death of his division commander. Horace Porter, Grant's aide, rode into Burnside's camp shortly after the general heard the news. Burnside "felt his loss keenly," Porter noted, "and was profuse in his expressions of grief." Stevenson's "course was invariably marked by the most cheerful and untiring devotion to his duties and the most conspicuous gallantry,"

123 Weld, 290; Committee of the Regimental Association, 228; Weld, 291.

Burnside later wrote of his young protégé; "and his death was deplored by the many new friends, who had in that time of trial, learned to respect him, as well as by those older friends, to whom his worth had long been known."[124]

* * *

Porter had arrived from Grant's headquarters after a harrowing ride past the tip of the Confederate position at the Mule Shoe. Grant had pulled him aside at 10:30 that morning and outlined, in great detail, his plans for the afternoon attack and Burnside's role in it. Porter was to explain all this to Burnside and answer any questions the commander might have. Grant handed Porter a letter to deliver that outlined these details, then sent him off.

Two roads led to Burnside: one that circled to the rear of Mott's position in a northeasterly direction, which then intersected with a road Burnside had used to get from Chancellorsville to the Fredericksburg Road—a distance of seven miles. The second involved a farm lane that ran along the outside of a wood line and exposed any Federal rider to enemy fire, although running the gauntlet cut nearly four miles off the trip. Porter put his horse on the run and, throwing his body down along the horse's neck on the opposite side from the enemy, charged across 600 yards of open space. Bullets kicked up dust on the road around him and clipped nearby tree branches, at times showering him with leaves. A few shots nicked the horse, only slightly. "[T]hey were considerate enough to skip me . . ." he later preened. "I succeeded in reaching Burnside rather ahead of scheduled time."[125]

Porter passed along Grant's instructions: Burnside "was to move forward for the purpose of reconnoitering Lee's extreme right, and keeping him from detaching troops from his flanks to reinforce his center. If Burnside could see a chance to attack, he was to do so with all vigor, and in a general way make the best cooperative effort that was possible." Porter then passed Burnside the dispatch that articulated the same thing.[126]

Burnside had three divisions at his disposal: Willcox's, Potter's, and Stevenson's, now temporarily commanded by Leasure. A fourth, under Brig. Gen. Edward Ferrero, consisting of United States Colored Troops (USCT) hung several miles to the rear, guarding the army's wagon trains, and was unavailable for service. As Burnside considered Grant's instructions and the current deployment of his forces,

124 Porter, 94; Stevenson, 51.

125 Ibid.

126 Ibid.

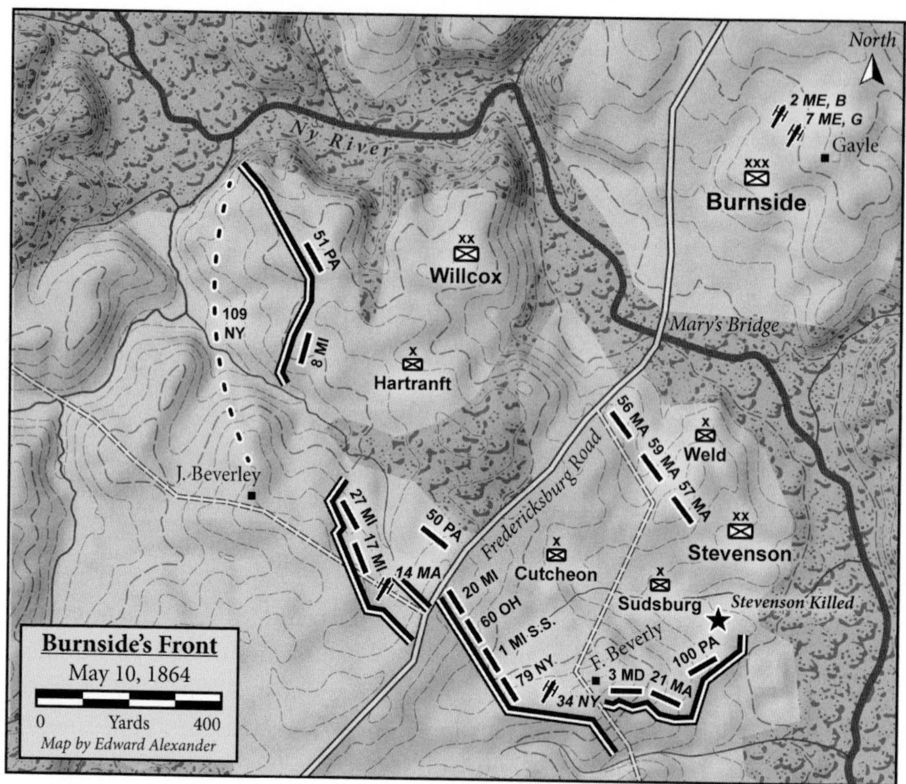


**Burnside's Front**—After securing its position along the Fredericksburg Road, the IX Corps kept up pressure along the front to tie Confederates in place so they could not shift as reinforcements elsewhere on the battlefield. As part of that ongoing skirmishing, Brig. Gen. Thomas Greely Stevenson was hit by a stray shot despite being in a relatively protected location behind a ridge. Possession of the Fredericksburg Road gave Federal forces a major operational advantage because it created a shorter route for supplies, reinforcements, and the evacuation of the wounded.

he somehow wondered whether to attack with all three divisions or just demonstrate with two, despite the phrases "with all the force you can bring to bear" and "all the show you can" in Grant's dispatch. Porter felt certain about the choice Grant would make, but Burnside sent an orderly to hear from Grant himself.[127]

The IX Corp commander's dithering did not bode well. His caution—a carryover of the old "McClellanism" that had infected the Army of the Potomac since its days under the command of Burnside's close friend, Maj. Gen. George B.

127 Grant to Burnside, *O.R.* 36:2:610.

McClellan—did not mesh well with Grant's more active style. This new general-in-chief expected prompt attacks with force and show and vigor. Most important, Burnside needed to get the timing of the attack right so it could most effectively support Upton's assault against the center of the Confederate line.

In the time Burnside's question got to Grant and the response came back, more than two hours elapsed. Grant correctly predicted in his response, "It will now be too late to bring up your third division," he wrote. "I will have to leave it to your judgment. . . . I want the attack promptly made in one or other of the modes proposed."[128]

To his credit, once he heard from Grant, Burnside mobilized. He ordered Potter's division to cross the Ny and serve as a reserve for Willcox and Leasure, whom he ordered to advance toward Spotsylvania Court House. "Open with your artillery promptly at 5 o'clock this p.m.," he ordered Willcox at 4:00 p.m., "and have your command ready to follow up the effect at once."[129]

Burnside directed them to use the Fredericksburg Road for their advance, but they were to do so in a sweeping right-wheel maneuver. John Hartranft, on Willcox's extreme right, was ordered to "hold on to my right," and as the line swept forward and rightward, "I should swing my left with it." The 51st Pennsylvania—the regiment on the far-right of Hartranft's brigade—acted as the pivot upon which the entire wheel swung, like a giant clock hand moving clockwise, with the Pennsylvanians at the center.[130]

Unknown to Burnside, the "cooperative effort" Grant envisioned among his corps commanders—and about which Burnside had been lectured—was already breaking down. On the far side of the Po, Hancock was dealing with the Confederate surprise against his last division. Gouverneur Warren launched his premature attack across Spindle Field under Grant's own gaze. Upton had been ordered to delay for one hour so Warren could reorganize and try to support him still. Only Mott, on Burnside's far right, was advancing as originally ordered. And as the dominos tumbled, none of them in concert, no one notified Burnside. Like Mott—with whom he had no direct contact—Burnside launched his attack as ordered. He rode to the front to watch, accompanied by Porter.

With the 109th New York serving as the skirmish line, "the troops moved out of the works and advanced on a general right wheel," reported Byron M. Cutcheon of the 20th Michigan. Depending on their location along the line, regiments advanced as much as a mile or not at all. "Being the right, which was the pivot,

128 Grant to Burnside, *O.R.* 36:2:611.

129 Burnside to Willcox, *O.R.* 36:2:613–4.

130 Hartranft, 949.

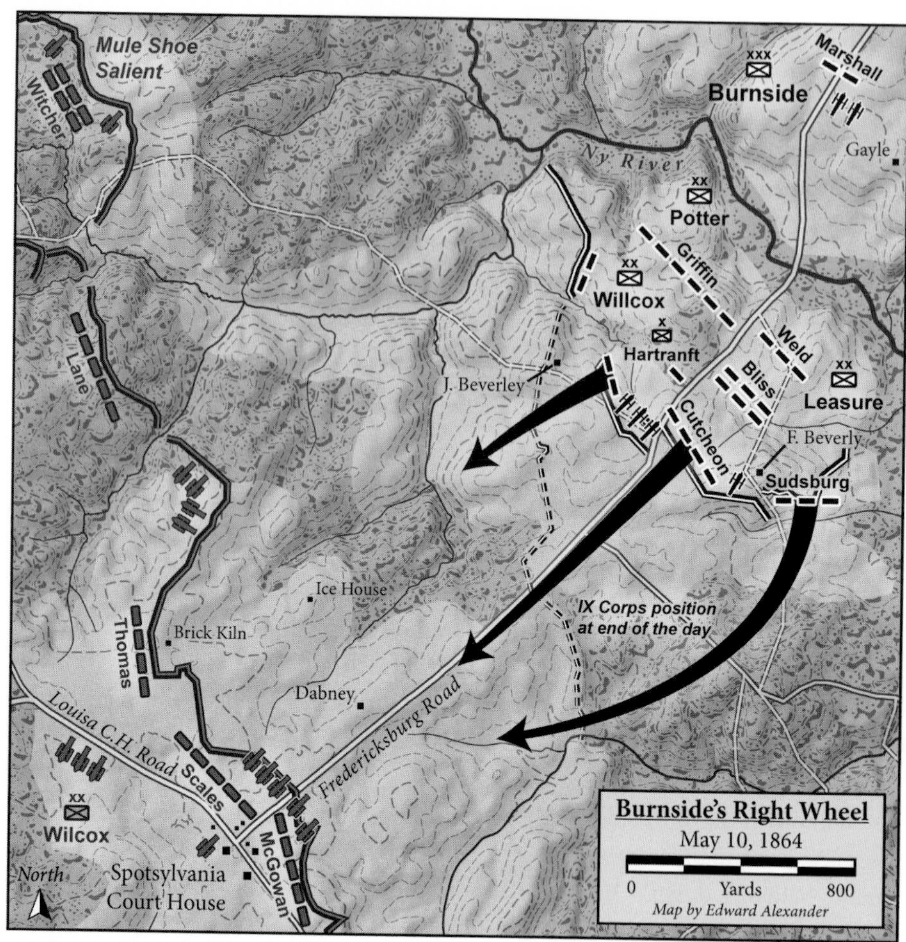


**Burnside's Right Wheel**—Stevenson's division, now commanded by Daniel Leasure, made up the far end of Burnside's advance, moving the greatest distance on the outside of a large right wheel. Envision the hand of a clock moving from four to seven, with the center of the clock, Willcox, staying fixed along the Ny River for protection. Burnside's line advanced to within a few hundred yards of the village.

this regiment did not move far," Cutcheon said. Colonel Constant Luce of the 17th Michigan "advanced my regiment with the brigade nearly three-quarters of a mile, or near the enemy's line." Some units even went a little farther.[131]

"I held on to my right," Hartranft attested, "but the line on the left of the road continued its advance to the front nearly a mile. I was compelled to fill in and

131 Cutcheon, 977; Constant Luce, report, *O.R.* 36:1:958.

lengthen my line in order to keep up the connection until I had much less than a line of battle." The reserve brigade of Col. Simon G. Griffin from Potter's division had to advance to fill the gaps that began to open in Hartranft's line as it stretched.[132]

Along their sweep, the Federals met "comparatively light resistance," Cutcheon said. By 6:00 p.m., they were within easy view of the village. "After pretty smart skirmishing we halted within about quarter of a mile of the Court-House," Potter reported. Willcox offered a sanguinary assessment. "We hold all the ground," he wrote to Burnside. "The enemy's lines are in rear of a strip of woods. He looks like throwing up some slight breast-works, and there are some indications of planning batteries. . . . We have thrown up fence-rail breastworks along the whole line, and will do heavier work to-night."[133]

Willcox referred to the "heavier work" of building stronger fortifications—which they would eventually do—but the work got heavier in a different way as Confederate resistance stiffened. Fighting intensified, yet Willcox remained confident. "All quiet. Well intrenched. Feel perfectly easy," he told Burnside.[134]

Burnside may have come to the front for a look himself. In a report to Grant, he noted "a pretty heavy fire close up to the enemy's lines,"[135] and informed the commanding general of the IX Corps's position a half-mile outside Spotsylvania Court House before directing his division commanders to hold those positions. In the dark, the soldiers began to construct more formidable works, digging and chopping in shifts so men could rest after the afternoon's fighting. "The line was regulated and intrenched before morning," Burnside would happily note.[136]

Porter, as Grant's on-site emissary, seemed equal parts stunned and stymied by the outcome of events. "The advance . . . completely turned the right of the enemy's line," he admitted; "but the country was so bewildering, and the enemy so completely concealed from view, that it was impossible all the time to know the exact relative positions of the contending forces. Toward dark, Willcox's division had constructed a line of fence-rail breastworks, and held pretty securely his advanced position." Porter sent two separate riders to Grant with updates. One never arrived, "having probably been killed," and the other couldn't find the general, who was on the front line.[137]

132 Hartranft, 949.

133 Cutcheon, 969; Robert B. Potter, report, *O.R.* 36:1:928; Willcox to Burnside, *O.R.* 36:2:614.

134 Ibid.

135 Burnside, 909.

136 Ibid.

137 Ibid.

Alfred Waud mis-dated his sketch "The Advance on Spotsylvania" as being May 9, but it depicts events on Burnside's front on May 10. The village of Spotsylvania Court House is visible in the background, with several clearly distinguishable buildings in sight—a perspective the Federal army only saw from the Fredericksburg Road and no earlier than the late afternoon of May 10. An inscription on the image says, "Rebels firing from the dwarf pine on the slope to the ct. house." A line of pine trees still marks the position, near the Confederate Cemetery. *Library of Congress*

---

Willcox believed he could hold on, so long as the IX Corps received proper cooperation from Meade's forces. "If Mead [*sic*] holds his own [position], he will occupy the enemy too much to enable them to mass on me . . ." he told Burnside. "The least attempt to withdraw would be actively followed up by the enemy and enable him to mass everything here suddenly on Meade's left." So much for feeling "perfectly easy." He might have felt even less so had he known about Meade's difficulties coordinating anything all day.[138]

At Grant's headquarters, the lieutenant general had begun to feel concerns of his own about the IX Corps. "Burnside's isolated position alarms me . . ." he confided to Meade. "[H]e is within a mile and a half of Spotsylvania court house." In fact, Burnside's men were even closer than that. Unknown to anyone, the Federal high command had plotted Burnside's location on poor maps that inaccurately showed

138 Willcox to Burnside, *O.R.* 36:2:614. For the evidentiary trail on the mis-dated sketch, see the four-part series "Alfred Waud's Sketchy Spotsylvania" by Chris Mackowski, published Sept. 7, 9, 14, & 22, 2021, at Emerging Civil War: https://emergingcivilwar.com/tag/wauds-sketchy-spotsy/

the Ny River a mile farther from the village than it really was. The "Gate/Gayle" mix-up had only added to the confusion. Federal cavalry might have easily dispelled the confusion with timelier intelligence, but of course, Sheridan had ridden away with most of the army's troopers. As a result, Grant had difficulty understanding exactly where Burnside's command was situated.[139]

Soon thereafter, Burnside's message arrived informing Grant that the IX Corps was a mile closer to the court house than Grant had realized. The miles between Burnside's and Meade's forces meant Grant could not quickly or easily reinforce or protect the IX Corps. The closest support, if needed, was Mott's bullied division, which no one had any faith in, particularly after that afternoon's debacle.

Grant seems not to have had faith in Burnside either, for he decided to order the IX Corps into a more protective posture rather than ask Burnside to probe for any additional opportunities. In a 10:30 p.m. dispatch, Grant said that, because the IX Corps was "entirely isolated and without support," it was imperative that Burnside use one of his divisions to extend his right. Grant decided to pull Mott's division from its ineffectual post so Burnside would connect directly with Wright.[140]

Such concerns were perfectly legitimate, but Grant's prescribed remedy was entirely impractical. His imperfect understanding of the geography, terrain, and distance—the fault of his poor maps and an absence of cavalry—led him to ask of Burnside the impossible. After the war, Grant would write that Burnside "was not aware of the importance of the advantage he had gained, and I, being with the troops where the heavy fighting was, did not know of it at the time. . . . I attach no blame to Burnside for this, but I do to myself for not having had a staff officer with him to report to me his position."[141]

That statement was both true and false. Porter had been with Burnside all day at Grant's behest. He might have been able to offer a clearer picture for his commander, but rather than run the gauntlet, he took the long way back to headquarters—and got lost. "[O]wing to the intense darkness, the condition of the roads, and the difficulty of finding the way," the young aide did not reach headquarters until after midnight. By then, the message to Burnside had been sent. The day was done. Grant was already spinning up plans for his next swing at Lee.

139 Lyman, 151.

140 Grant to Burnside, *O.R.* 36:2:612.

141 Grant, *Memoirs*, 550.

# May 7
# May 8
# May 9
# May 10
# May 11

As was his custom, Lee arose on the morning of May 11 at 3:00 a.m. He had snatched perhaps four hours of sleep after the nerve-testing 10th, but duty called. That he had gotten even that much sleep was a small blessing: he had gone to bed expecting Grant to launch a night attack, a "favorite amusement of his at Vicksburg," Lee had learned. No such night attack came, though, for which he thanked Providence.[1]

The army commander took a quiet breakfast in his tent by candlelight, then set about his work for the day. Grant's breakthrough at Doles's Salient underscored Lee's initial concerns about the overall position. "It will be necessary for you to re-establish your whole line tonight," Lee had told Ewell before retiring for the night. "Set the officers to work to collect and refresh their men and have everything ready for the renewal of the conflict at daylight tomorrow."

They had been meeting at Ewell's headquarters at the otherwise-deserted McCoull house, with Rodes, Ramseur, Doles, William Nelson Pendleton, and Robert D. Johnston. Quiet had been restored after the chaos of Upton's breakthrough. "General, what shall we do with Gen. Doles for allowing those people to break over his lines?" Lee asked Rodes, a question that must have mortified Doles had he been sitting there as the eyewitness claimed.[2]

"We shall have to let Doles off this time," Rodes replied, "as he has suffered quite severely for it already."

1 Lee quotes in the first two paragraphs come from Lee to Ewell, *O.R.* 36:2:983.

2 The tale and quotes that follow come from "Gen. Lee's Story" by Richard D. Johnston, quoted in Noel G. Harrison's *Gazetteer of Historic Sites Related to the Fredericksburg and Spotsylvania National Military Park*, Vol. 1 (Fredericksburg, Va.: Fredericksburg and Spotsylvania National Military Park, 1986), 293.

A scout arrived with an update for Lee. Overhearing, Ramseur chimed in. "The impression was general in the army that the Federal Troops were moving to the left toward Richmond," he said.

Lee turned to him and "playfully remarked": "I do not know which one of you may be called to the command of the army when I am gone. Until then you could not know the difficulties which beset the commander of an army, the greatest of which is to distinguish the true from the false reports which come from the scouts." He thereafter ordered precautions, then sent everyone back to their respective commands.

One observer described Robert Rodes during the battle of Spotsylvania as "a man of very striking appearance, of erect, fine figure and martial bearing. He constantly passed and repassed in rear of our guns, riding a black horse that champed his bit and tossed his head proudly, until his neck and shoulders were flecked with white froth, seeming to be conscious that he carried Caesar." *Library of Congress*

With daylight soon coming, Lee wanted to be sure his orders had been followed. Rodes, in particular, had needed to "rectify his line and improve its defenses." Lee had made his headquarters that night near the home of Edgar and Ann Harrison, just behind Rodes's position, so he would inspect that first, but afterward he intended to ride the entire line with his chief engineer, Brig. Gen. Martin Luther Smith. Recently arrived from the West where he had commanded a brigade in the Vicksburg garrison, Smith knew Grant, at least on the battlefield, so perhaps the engineer might have insights to share. Perhaps he knew what sorts of weakness to look for in the line that Grant might well notice.

Lee also needed intelligence. Grant had surprised him with his move out of the Wilderness, moving to Spotsylvania rather than Fredericksburg. Then, since the armies' arrival there, Grant had hammered at Lee almost continuously. What would he do next?

Confederate division commander John Brown Gordon would one day credit Lee with a preternatural ability to understand his opponents. "He read the mind of the

Union commander, and developed his own plans accordingly," Gordon wrote. Lee had easily taken the measure of the blustery but overly cautious McClellan; the indecisive Burnside; the blowhard "Mr. F. J. Hooker"; the deliberate but worthy Meade.[3]

Alas, Grant posed a more puzzling problem for Lee's mind-reading powers, if such existed. Lee had misjudged him several times already because he could *not* read his mind. Longstreet's absence as the "Grant Whisperer" in this moment must have felt keen.

* * *

Grant arose that morning a little later than Lee, feeling refreshed and ready. He sat with his staff at a mess table, alive with morning fellowship and chatter, and downed a cup of coffee. He then breakfasted on a small piece of beef "cooked almost to a crisp." The man who would be vilified by political foes and former enemies as "Grant the Butcher" could not stand the sight of blood and so preferred his meat well-done. "[T]he nearer [the cook] came to burning up the beef the better the general liked it," Horace Porter later noted.[4]

Grant lit a cigar, moved to a camp chair set up outside his tent, and held good-natured court. Among the gathering was Grant's political patron, Illinois Representative Elihu B. Washburne, who was also a close political ally of President Lincoln. Washburne had opened the campaign with the army but now needed to return to the capital. "General, I shall go to see the President and the Secretary of War as soon as I reach Washington," he informed his friend. "I can imagine their anxiety to know what you think of the prospects of the campaign." If Grant had a message to send, Washburne offered to carry it to them on Grant's behalf.

Grant puffed and thought. "We are certainly making fair progress," he finally said, "and all the fighting has been in our favor; but the campaign promises to be a long one, and I am particularly anxious not to say anything just now that might hold out false hopes to the people."

He puffed some more and thought some more, then offered to set pencil to paper. He disappeared into his tent to write.

3 John Brown Gordon, *Reminiscences of the Civil War* (New York, 1903), 297.

4 Porter, 97-98; Ironically, on that very day, May 11, the first-known reference of Grant as a butcher appeared in print—"if the butcher Grant can be snubbed in the South"—in the *Washington* (Pa.) *Reporter*, quoting a Copperhead critic. Southern papers quickly picked up the phrase. Gary Gallagher provides a brief but illuminating summary of the phrase's origins, "which had everything to do with politics and very little with the Overland Campaign," in "Two Generals Who Resist Each Other: Perceptions of Grant and Lee in the Summer of 1864" in *Cold Harbor to the Crater: The End of the Overland Campaign* (Chapel Hill: UNC Press, 2015).

Congressman Elihu Washburne's calling card explains his political patronage of U. S. Grant: "Galena"—their mutual home town.

*Library of Congress*

"We have now ended the sixth day of very heavy fighting," Grant scribbled. "I . . . propose to fight it out on this line if it takes all summer."[5]

Indeed, by referring to May 10 as the "sixth day" of fighting, Grant offered insight into his overall strategic view. The series of engagements that began on May 5 in the Wilderness was, in Grant's mind, a single long conflict rather than separate battles. He intended to continue pushing.[6]

"The arrival of re-enforcement here will be very encouraging to the men," he continued, "and I hope they will be sent as fast as possible, and in as great numbers. . . . I am satisfied the enemy are very shaky, and are only kept up to the mark by the greatest exertions on the part of their officers, and by keeping them intrenched in every position they take."

That Grant saw Lee's army as "very shaky" would become a blind spot for the Federal commander as the campaign continued. Having made up his mind on the matter, he would tend to see intelligence through that lens and would interpret battlefield results toward that conclusion, which would have bitter consequences by early June at Cold Harbor, outside Richmond.

Grant addressed the note to Henry Halleck, his one-time superior in the West and predecessor as general-in-chief, now relegated to chief of staff of the army and the person at the war department through whom Grant channeled his correspondence. But Grant knew his friend Washburne would pass word directly

5 Ulysses S. Grant to Henry Halleck, *O.R.* 36:2:627.

6 Meade viewed events from a similar perspective. "We have been fighting continuously for six days," he wrote his wife on that same day, May 11, "and have gotten, I think, the better of the enemy, though their resistance is most stubborn." Meade, *Life and Letters*, 194.

to Lincoln, as well. The congressman shook Grant's hand, thanked him warmly, then mounted his horse and rode off.

Next: the day's plans. First, he ordered "every wagon that can be spared" to head to the new supply base at Belle Plains on the Potomac, beyond Fredericksburg, to stock up. He detailed portions of the USCT serving in General Ferrero's division to oversee the mission, although some continued their current duty of guarding the roads to the rear and protecting the army's wagon train.[7]

He then sent his aide-de-camp, former engineer Cyrus Ballou Comstock, to "make lines between Burnside & Wright correct"—a follow-up to the order Grant had sent the previous night. Elsewhere, Theodore Lyman noted "the whole army, along its front of some miles, was strongly entrenched, with pickets in pits, and the batteries covered by strong epaulements." Having seen the benefit the Confederates had made of strong works, the Federals chose to emulate them, although most soldiers suspected they wouldn't be sitting still for long.[8]

As Comstock shuttled back and forth, Grant turned his attention to the next task: what lesson could be learned from the previous day's assaults? Grant had "but little doubt" that Upton's breakthrough "would have proved entirely successful" if it had been timed better and properly supported. Mott continued to take the blame on that count, but interestingly, Grant had also come to believe that the IX Corps should have "heartily entered" the fray, despite having never been ordered to do so. Grant had clearly outlined his expectation that Burnside attack in coordination with the other attacks, but he had never said anything about being *part* of those other attacks.[9]

That curious question aside, Grant understood that any chance at success would require proper timing and adequate reinforcements. With those criteria in mind, he began to formulate a new plan quite similar to Upton's, but on a much larger scale. And this time, he intended to target the very tip of the salient, which, by its very nature, was the weakest spot in the Confederate line. He intended to hit that weak spot with a quick, powerful strike, similar to Upton's. But rather than send just twelve 12 regiments, Grant planned to send Hancock's entire II Corps.

And as Hancock attacked the tip of the salient, Grant's plan called for Warren to once more push against the Confederate left at Spindle Field. Grant did not expect a breakthrough, but he did want Warren to attack with enough vigor to prevent Lee from shifting men from that part of the line to reinforce the center.

7 Grant to Meade, *O.R.* 36:2:628, 629.

8 Lyman, *Meade's Army*, 152.

9 Grant to Meade, O.R. *O.R.* 36:2:629.

Burnside's IX Corps would reposition itself to push against the east face of the salient. Wright's VI Corps would reinforce Federal efforts wherever needed.

The idea was simple, and it resembled the parameters Upton had put forward on May 10. The formation would be compact, with a tight two-division front aimed at the tip of the Mule Shoe. The first line would break open the Confederate position. The second wave could then secure the gap. To widen the breakthrough, one division could swing to the east and one to the west. The potential existed for Wright's reinforcements to flood forward and exploit the breakthrough. With Burnside and Warren putting pressure on the other fronts, Lee would not be able to shift reinforcements into the breach and would have to retreat or face the destruction of his center and possibly his army.

The attack would form near the farm of John C. Brown, just under a mile from the salient's tip. Between lay plenty of open land that would afford the II Corps a relatively unencumbered approach to the Confederate position, although a wood lot closer to the Brown house would allow the men to get into position under cover. To the immediate front of the apex was a clearing about 400 yards wide, with a large swale that cut diagonally across it—a topographical feature that would come to play an oversized role as the day's events unfolded.

"Several of the staff-officers were on that part of the field a great portion of the day," Porter noted of the reconnaissance work.[10]

To help preserve secrecy, Grant ordered the men to assemble under cover of darkness and begin the attack at 4:00 a.m. He passed the orders on to Meade, who then went over them that afternoon with Hancock, Wright, and Warren. "[E]very effort [was] made to have a perfect understanding on their part as to exactly what was required in this important movement," Porter recalled.[11]

Burnside, as an independent command, received his orders directly from Grant: "You will move against the enemy with your entire force promptly and with all possible vigor at 4 o'clock tomorrow morning." Comstock returned from his errand just in time to deliver Grant's orders personally. Accompanied by fellow aide Orville Babcock, they were to spend the night and ensure Burnside carried out Grant's orders.[12]

When Comstock arrived back at Burnside's headquarters, he discovered the commander "had withdrawn all his forces to the north side of the Ny to occupy

10 Porter, 99–100.

11 Ibid., 100.

12 Ulysses S. Grant to Ambrose Burnside, *O.R.* 36:2:643. I don't want to read too much into the fact that Grant did not send Porter back even though Porter had been his emissary to Burnside the previous day. However, I can't help but wonder, considering how disappointed Grant was with Burnside's May 10 performance, whether Grant blamed Porter for not serving as a more forceful voice for headquarters.

the worst line." Midafternoon, orders had arrived for Burnside "to withdraw to the north side of the Ny and take a new position"—in other words, give up everything he had won the day before on his advance to the outskirts of the village, plus everything they had established upon their arrival on May 9.[13]

"[I]t was a profound mystery to the men in the ranks, at this time, why such a movement should have been made," one soldier said. "We failed to comprehend why, after having struggled so near to the Court House that we could plainly discern the Stars and Bars flying above the principal building of the little hamlet, we should then be faced to the rear and withdrawn, without having accomplished, or even attempted to accomplish, anything whatever." The unexplained back-tracking, in the rain, to give up ground so close to the enemy undermined morale.[14]

Burnside reported the entire move dutifully: "The recrossing was affected, and whilst the line was being formed in the new position, the command was ordered to recross the Ny and occupy the position we had just left." Comstock noted that the normally affable Burnside complied "at once without difficulty, but with some grumbling at the change."[15]

By that point, a heavy storm had opened, obscuring the infantry's movements, and the men were able to reoccupy their works without Confederates resistance. "The threatening sky was not propitious for the movement . . ." Porter said. "[T]he preparations went on regardless of the lowering clouds and falling rain. All those who were in the secret anticipated a memorable field-day on the morrow."[16]

Along with adjustments to his lines, Burnside also adjusted his line-up. Daniel Leasure, temporarily commanding the First Division following Stevenson's death, returned to command of the 2nd Brigade, replaced by newly arrived Maj. Gen. Thomas L. Crittenden. A Kentuckian, 44-year-old Crittenden—just four days shy of his 45th birthday—had commanded a corps in William S. Rosecrans's Army of the Cumberland. Scapegoated for Rosecrans's defeat at the September 1863 battle of Chickamauga, Crittenden had recently been fully exonerated and transferred to the Eastern Theater. "He is the queerest-looking party you ever saw," observed Lyman, "with a thin, staring face, and hair hanging to his coat collar—a very wild-appearing major-general, but quite a kindly man in conversation, despite his terrible looks."[17]

13 Cyrus B. Comstock, *The Diary of Cyrus B. Comstock*, Merlin E. Sumner, ed. (Dayton, OH: Morningside, 1987), 266.

14 Houston, 118.

15 Burnside, 909; Comstock, 266.

16 Porter, 100.

17 Lyman, *Meade's Army*, 116–17.

In fact, the entire situation was about to look terrible. "With anxious hearts the men stood around their camp-fires in the pitiless storm, speculating as to the chances of the morrow, and with sad but heroic hearts wondering if they should survive the terrible carnage which they knew well was before them," wrote Leander Cogswell of the 11th New Hampshire. "The men of different regiments mingled together—for many pleasant friendships had been formed—and many hasty but earnest good-byes were spoken." The men milled about, in the rain, in a landscape of woe. "[T]he drenched earth and dripping trees made our positions anything but a comfortable one . . ." said Henry Houston of the 32nd Maine. "There was no moon, the heavens were obscured by heavy clouds, the rain fell in soaking showers, and the whole situation was a dismal and dreary one."[18]

* * *

As Grant formulated his plans, Confederate mapmaker Jedediah Hotchkiss was scouting the field on an intelligence-gathering mission, observing the Federal left. He reported back to Lee that the poor configuration of Burnside's position left the Federals "exposed to a flank movement." As the afternoon passed, more reports suggested that Burnside's wagons and infantry were on the move in an apparent withdrawal—which, Lee reasoned, explained why Burnside's position was vulnerable.[19]

To be sure Lee stayed in place and didn't prepare an offensive of his own, Grant ordered a reconnaissance in force against the Confederate left flank. The subsequent probes by Col. Nelson Miles attracted Lee's attention, and Lee countered by shifting two brigades from Early's Third Corps from the Confederate right to reinforce the Confederate left.

All the while, Lee kept his eye on the activity along the Fredericksburg Road. As he came to understand it, Burnside was stripping his position, and the probes against the Confederate left had been intended to draw focus away from the Federal withdrawal. "Gradually," wrote Ewell staffer Campbell Brown, "the conviction spread that they were retiring towards Fredericksburg." If anyone had given thought to *why* Grant might be withdrawing, no record of the conversation exists. "I should not wonder if they retired today as it has just commenced raining, which may frighten them for their communications—& [would] much impede

18 Cogswell, 363; Houston, 121.

19 Jedediah Hotchkiss, *Map Me a Map of the Valley*, Archie P. McDonald, ed. (Dallas, TX: Southern Methodist University Press, 1973), 203.

their march on Richmond as they pass our Army," Brown wishfully thought.[20] The simplest answer is that Lee had expected such a movement from the start, and it now biased his reading of his intelligence.

Lee wanted to pursue Grant should the opportunity arise, which meant Confederate wagons, artillery, and other equipment needed to be ready "to march at any hour."[21] Lee gave special consideration to the artillery at the tip of the Mule Shoe that supported "Alleghany" Johnson's division. That artillery would have the furthest to travel and the hardest time moving because of the poor condition of the few farm roads that accessed the area. "[W]ithdraw the artillery from the salient . . . to have it available for a countermove to the right," Lee ordered.[22]

Lee also suggested that the infantry prepare to move, but Ewell countered. *In the rain*, he said, *the men would be more comfortable in the trenches than if moved, as they already had shelters there*. Lee demurred in the interest of his soggy men but encouraged Ewell to have them ready to go on short notice.

Withdrawal of the artillery began in late afternoon "with as much caution as possible to prevent observation," noted Second Corps artillery chief Brig. Gen. Armistead Lindsay Long. Along Johnson's line, 30 guns from the battalions of Lt. Col. William Nelson and Maj. Richard C. M. Page pulled out, leaving only two batteries—eight guns—behind. On the western face of the salient, the batteries of Captains William A. Tanner and Benjamin H. Smith sat on a knoll overlooking the brigades of Brig. Gen. Julius Daniels and Col. William Monaghan, covering the ground Upton had crossed in his attack on May 10. To the right, James Carrington's four Napoleons covered Walker's Stonewall Brigade.[23]

No one told Johnson about the move of his artillery, though, and he was alarmed when he found out about it. That section of the line, occupied by "Maryland" Steuart's Brigade, was "a point which with artillery was strong, but without it weak," Johnson said.[24]

The artillerists themselves professed a strong desire to stay. "The breastworks were built, we would be in place and, supported by infantry, absolutely impregnable against successful assault," one of them said.[25]

20 Campbell Brown, 253; Ibid., 252.

21 William N. Pendleton, report, *O.R.* 36:1:1044.

22 Taylor, *Campaigns in Virginia*, 242.

23 Armistead L. Long, *Memoirs of Robert E. Lee, his military and personal history; together with incidents relating to his private life, also a large amount of historical information hitherto unpublished* (London: Sampson, Low, Marston, Searle, and Rivington, 1886), 399.

24 Johnson, report, *O.R.* 36:1:1079.

25 Thomas Carter to editor of Richmond *Times*, *S.H.S.P.* 21:240.

But, the artillerist added, orders were orders. So off they went.

The Confederates were not the only ones on the move as night settled in. On the right flank of the Army of the Potomac, Hancock began to shift elements of the II Corps toward the staging area around the Brown farm. "Arms and accoutrements, canteens, haversacks and tin dippers were to be carried so as to make no noise, and all commands were given in whispers," recounted a member of the 19th Maine. "Staff officers were seen whispering to regimental commanders and pointing the way." Everyone moved "with the utmost quiet and secrecy."[26]

"Nobody knew where were going," an anonymous Pennsylvanian penned to his hometown newspaper, "but a rumor was started that we were going back to the rear to rest and wash our clothes. And this proved partially true, as it rained so hard all night that our clothes were thoroughly washed, but they needed wringing badly."[27]

Rain fell in torrents. The roads turned to quagmires and streams to raging rivers. Guides became lost as the Federals slogged into position. "[M]ud was the prevailing power, and when darkness set it, it was *black* . . ." wrote John Haley of the 17th Maine. "The wind sobbed drearily over the meadows and through the trees, rain fell steadily, and the night was so dark men had to almost feel their way." It was follow-the-file-leader, said the anonymous Pennsylvanian, "not by sight or touch, but by haring him growl and swears, as he slipped, splashed and tried to pull his feet out of the mud."[28]

"The movement was necessarily slow with frequent halts," another soldier recalled, "at which time the men, worn out by loss of sleep and the terrible nervous and physical strain they had endured during the past eight days, would drop down for a moment's rest, and be asleep almost as soon as they touched the ground."[29]

During one such stop, some of the men had an unexpected scare. A pack mule, strapped down with blankets and cooking utensils from an officer's mess, got spooked and broke away from its attendant. "The kettles and frying pans struck the trees along the mule's flight and every few leaps the mule let off panic-stricken brays that could be heard a mile, followed by disembowelled [*sic*] groans, that struck terror to the hearts of the tired soldiers," wrote John Day Smith of the 19th Maine. "It seemed for a minute as though a legion of devils armed with frying pans and mounted on mules were charging the Union lines." Some regiments scattered

26 Smith, 153.

27 Anonymous author (probably Sylvester Hildebrand of the 139th PA), Apollo (Pa.) *Sentinel*, ca. 1911, 13, FSNMP BV, 362.

28 John Haley, *The Rebel Yell and the Yankee Hurrah*, ed. Ruth L. Silliker (Camden, Me.: Down East, 1985), 154; Anonymous, Apollo *Sentinel*.

29 Black, "Reminiscences," 422.

through the woods "as though his Satanic Majesty was after them." No one fired any shots, however, and the stampede was soon checked.[30]

Aside from that burst of excitement, the dull drudge of the march continued. "[W]ere on the road all night," complained Capt. George A. Bowen of the 12th New Jersey. "[G]uess we did not make much distance as the roads were simply awful, rained continuously and mud was almost knee deep in places." It was, another Federal officer said, "an intensely dark night."[31]

And the morning ahead was about to get darker.

30 Smith, 153-54.

31 George A. Bowen, May 12, 1864, typescript diary entry, FSNMP BV 228; Francis Barlow, Papers of the Military Historical Society of Massachusetts, Volume 4, "Capture of the Salient 1864," (Boston, Mass., 1905), 248-249.

# May 8
# May 9
# May 10
# May 11
# May 12

They stood in the predawn quiet, waiting, some 20,000 of them. "Surrounded by the silence of night, by darkness and by fog, they stood, listening to raindrops as they fell from leaf to leaf," one of them remembered.[1]

The drizzle soaked their clothes, the mud sucked at their boots, the fog seeped into their bones. Yet some of the men of the II Corps still managed to doze on their feet, exhausted as they were from seven straight days of fighting and marching. When the time came, when the word came down, they would rouse themselves, shake hands and bid each other goodbye, and advance south across the fields to attack the Confederate salient.

In the meantime, some of them prayed. Some of them complained. Some of them fidgeted. Still, they all maintained their tight formation, and they waited.

Details of the assault were kept mostly secret, even from many of the officers who'd lead it. "We were told that it was a movement of more than usual importance," Francis Barlow, whose First Division would form the left wing of the attack. Barlow expressed obvious frustration that "[n]o information, so far as I can remember, was given to us as to the position or strength of the enemy, or as to the troops to be engaged in the movement . . . or as to the plan of the attack, or why any attack was to be made at that time or place."

Officers and soldiers alike "loudly expressed indignation" about being kept in the dark about the details of such an important movement. "It was an exquisitely ludicrous scene, and I could hardly sit on my horse for laughter," Barlow said. "I

1 George A. Bruce, *The Twentieth Regiment of Massachusetts Volunteer Infantry 1861–1865* (Boston, 1906), 371.

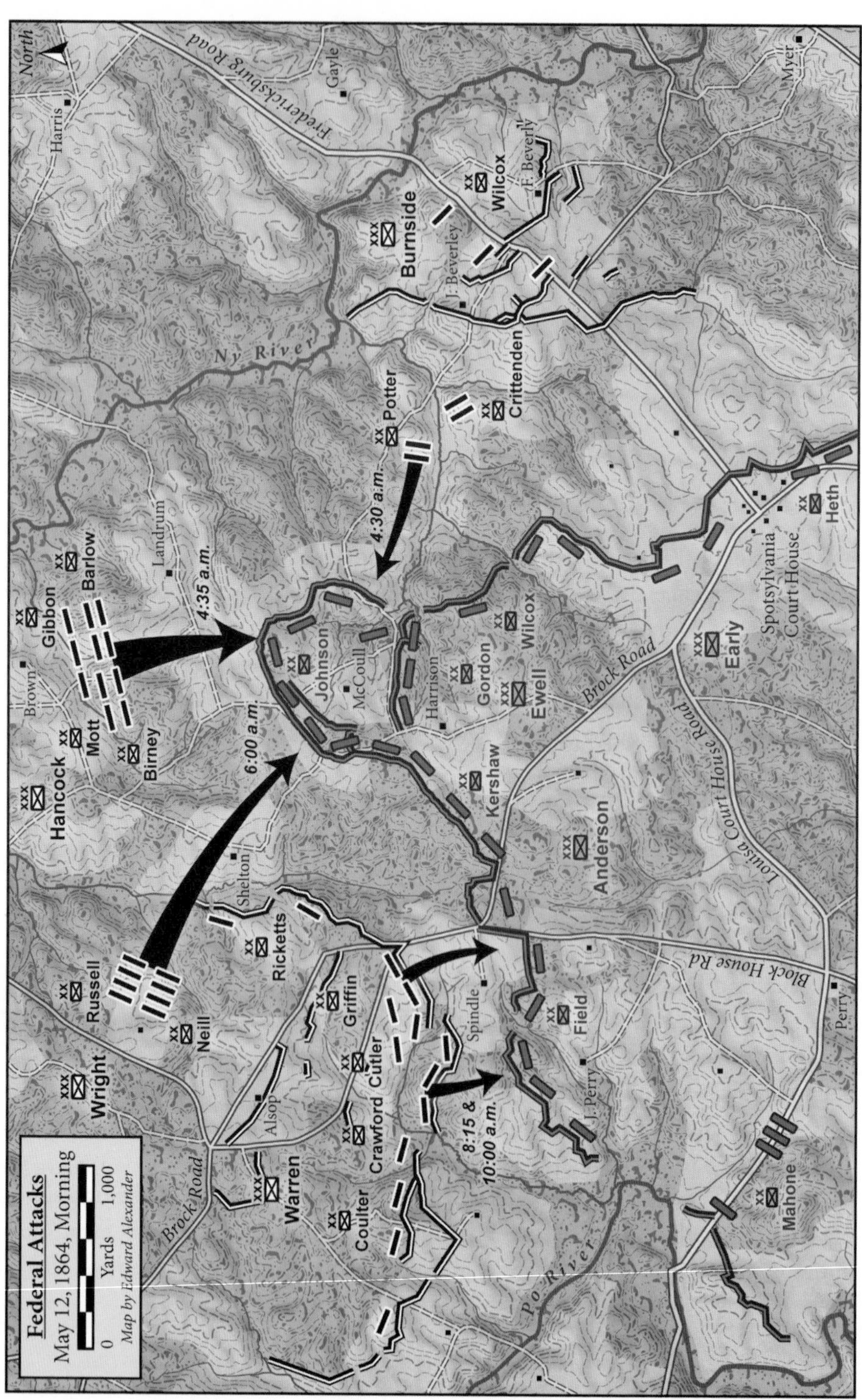
Federal Attacks
May 12, 1864, Morning
0 Yards 1,000
Map by Edward Alexander
North
Brock Road
Fredericksburg Road
Louisa Court House Road
Block House Rd
Ny River
Po River
Harris
Gayle
F. Beverly
J. Beverley
Myer
Landrum
Brown
Shelton
McCoull
Harrison
Spindle
Alsop
J. Perry
Perry
Spotsylvania Court House
Hancock
Gibbon
Barlow
Mott
Birney
Wright
Russell
Neill
Ricketts
Warren
Griffin
Cutler
Crawford
Coulter
Burnside
Wilcox
Potter
Crittenden
Johnson
Gordon
Ewell
Kershaw
Anderson
Field
Early
Heth
Mahone
4:30 a.m.
4:35 a.m.
6:00 a.m.
8:15 &
10:00 a.m.

**Federal Attacks**—Grant's plan for May 12, 1864, called for a II Corps-sized thrust at the tip of the Confederate Mule Shoe, with the VI Corps ready as a reserve to flood into the breakthrough. Simultaneous attacks by the V and IX Corps would tie down the Confederate left and right.

---

remember that I finally said to Colonel [Charles] Morgan, 'For Heaven's sake, at least, face us in the right direction, so that we shall not march away from the enemy, and have to round the world and come up in their rear.'"[2]

Barlow aligned the brigades of Colonels Nelson Miles and John R. Brooke to lead the advance, followed by the brigades of Colonels Thomas A. Smyth and Hiram R. Brown. David Birney's Third Division, advancing alongside Barlow's, made up the right wing of the assault. Barlow's formation—a narrow front stacked several regiments deep—resembled a large-scale version of Emory Upton's attack formation two days earlier. Birney, by comparison, aligned his men in a more traditional line of battle. Gershom Mott, whose undersized Fourth Division had advanced over this very ground on May 10 in its failed attempt to support Upton, followed behind Birney's division. John Gibbon's Second Division held back as a reserve to support both attack wings as necessary. The 1st and 2nd U.S. Sharpshooters and the 66th New York spread across the front of the formation as skirmishers.

Soldiers were ordered to carry their arms at right shoulder shift. Officers were ordered to give no commands above a whisper. The skirmish line, deployed at a one-pace interval, was ordered to hold their fire under any circumstances, "but as soon as they drew the first of the enemy's pickets, to rush forward and capture every man of them, allowing none to escape to the rear and give alarm to the main line." Orders were to advance without firing a shot, said another of Barlow's staffers, "and by simple weight of numbers crush everything in front of us."[3]

Opposite the Federal army, hunkered down in the Mule Shoe Salient, the men of Ewell's Second Corps waited. Since their repulse of Upton's breakthrough on May 10, everyone had spent their time refortifying. Robert Rodes's Division still occupied the westernmost leg of the salient, where it began its northward jut from the main Confederate line. Cullen Battle's Brigade connected with Stephen Ramseur's and Junius Daniel's North Carolina brigades. George Dole's all-Georgia brigade, which had once occupied the front line but had been pierced by Upton's attack, had been pulled back in reserve.

2 Ibid., 248–49.

3 Ibid.; Favill, 296.

To the right of Daniel's Brigade, where the salient began to turn to the northeast, were five Louisiana regiments commanded by Col. William Monaghan. The men had formerly belonged to Brig. Gen. Harry T. Hays's large, consolidated brigade, but following the fight in the Wilderness, Hays's five regiments had been combined with the five Louisiana regiments of Leroy Stafford's Brigade because both brigades had taken such frightful losses, including Stafford, fatally shot through the spine on May 5. As part of the command shuffle that resulted from A. P. Hill's illness and Early's subsequent elevation to temporary corps command, the reconstituted brigade had been assigned on May 8 to Edward "Alleghany" Johnson's Division. On May 10, however, brigade commander Hays sustained a serious wound from a shell fragment during that day's fighting, and the brigade was again split in two.

Next to Monaghan's Louisianans were the members of the famed Stonewall Brigade, commanded by "Stonewall Jim" Walker. To Walker's right, leading to the tip of the salient, was the other half of Hays's former brigade, now led by Col. Zebulon York. As the salient then dipped southeast, it was covered by the Virginia brigade of Col. William Witcher, who had recently taken over command of the six regiments from John "Rum" Jones, also killed in the Wilderness. Occupying the final segment of the salient were Virginians and North Carolinians under George "Maryland" Steuart. Beyond Steuart's right, a hundred-yard gap in the line separated him from Brig. Gen. James H. Lane's five regiments of North Carolinians, part of Cadmus Wilcox's Division in Jubal Early's Third Corps.

Johnson, who oversaw the brigades of Walker, York, Witcher, and Steuart, was a 48-year-old grizzled veteran of the "old army," a West Point graduate from the Class of 1838 who had seen action in the Mexican and Seminole wars. He got his nickname, "Alleghany," from his early-war service at Camp Alleghany in the mountains west of the Shenandoah Valley. At the battle of McDowell in May 1862, while serving with Stonewall Jackson, Johnson sustained a severe wound in the foot that took more than a year to heal. When he returned to service, he relied on the use of a hickory walking cane, which earned him another nickname, "Old Clubby." Jackson once praised Johnson's "high qualities as a soldier"; a Georgia infantryman praised Johnson as "a Stirring old Coon always on the alert." "There was no sturdier, truer, braver division commander than General Edward Johnson," one of his artillerists said.[4]

Johnson made his headquarters in the home of Neil McCoull, a one-and-a-half-story wood house that sat near the center of the salient about two-tenths

4 James I. Robertson, Jr., *Stonewall Jackson: The Man, The Soldier, The Legend.* (New York: Macmillan, 1997), 73; Thomas Carter, *Southern Historical Society Papers,* Vol. 21, 242.

Major General Edward Johnson was so colorful, says his biographer, Greg Clemmer, that "Anyone, it seemed, who crossed paths with this man and later put pen to paper, left behind some 'gem' on Ed Johnson." Historian Harry Pfanz called Johnson "a character in an army that had more than its fair share of eccentric general officers." *Library of Congress*

of a mile behind the line. All night, Johnson had been getting reports of Federal movements, and his brigade commanders started getting edgy. "The enemy is moving and probably massing in our front and we expect to be attacked at daylight," Steuart wrote in a message to his division commander. "The artillery along our front has been withdrawn, by whose orders I know not, and I beg that it be sent back immediately."[5]

When Johnson sent word to his superior, Ewell, the Second Corps commander explained away the noises as part of Grant's purported withdrawal to Fredericksburg. It took an in-person visit by an agitated Johnson to convince Ewell—reluctantly—to return the artillery, although it would end up taking hours for the batteries to make their way back to the salient.

Johnson also took the time to visit the few batteries that did remain in the salient and admonished the gunners to remain vigilant. Upon his return to the McCoull house, Johnson sent orders to his brigades "to be on the alert, some brigades to be awake all night, and all to be up and in the trenches an hour or so before daylight. This order was obeyed." Finally, he and his staff settled in to try to catch some sleep, although they remained fully clothed, "ready to leap to a horse at a moment's notice."[6]

Later critics looking to pin blame for what was about to happen would turn Johnson into a scapegoat. They would unfairly charge him with negligence,

5 McHenry Howard, *Recollections of a Maryland Confederate Soldier and Staff Officer Under Johnston, Jackson, and Lee*, (Baltimore, MD 1914), 294.

6 Robert Hunter, "Major Hunter's Story," *S. H. S. P.* 33:337; Johnson, report, *O.R.* 36:1:1080; Hunter, 336.

claiming that the Federal army caught him unaware. Even Lee—who had just, days earlier, described "my friend Ed. Johnson" as "a splendid fellow" when considering him for corps command—would express dissatisfaction with "Old Alleghany" by transferring him to the Army of Tennessee in August.[7] A number of Johnson's officers would come to his defense, though. Major D. W. Anderson of the 44th Virginia was typical. "[N]either General Johnson nor his men were surprised at the attack at the time it was made . . ." he attested, adding, "I am quite sure, so far as Jones's [Witcher's] brigade was concerned, all of us were expecting it."[8]

Defenders such as Anderson would largely go unheard, however, and some would even be silenced. Ewell's stepson, Campbell Brown, who would devote considerable energy in the postwar years trying to exonerate the Second Corps, would eventually be warned to pipe down. "[S]omehow I feel reluctant to suffer anything to distract from Gen. Lee's fame," one influential former Confederate cautioned. "It is all we have left to us and of the great shipwreck we have suffered."[9]

But, in the early morning hours of May 12, Alleghany Johnson had done all he could to prepare his men to meet the growing threat that loomed in front of them, somewhere in the darkness to the north.

* * *

The rain had let up, but in its place it had coaxed a heavy fog to rise from the bottomlands that drained into the Ny River. When 4:00 a.m. came and the assault on the salient was to begin, Hancock demurred. *The fog is too thick*, he said. Barlow agreed. They decided to wait just a bit a longer in the hope that the white veil would lift.

The men in the ranks, too, peered through the swirling early morning mists. "In front of us was a long open slope up a hill nearly clear, but in places covered with a thicket of young pines," wrote Robert Robertson of Nelson Miles's staff. "On the summit, twelve hundred yards from our front, was supposed to be the Confederate intrenchments . . . but all invisible as yet in the gray darkness of approaching dawn."[10]

7 Sorrel, 243.

8 D. W. Anderson, *S. H. S. P.* 21:252.

9 Gregg S. Clemmer, Johnson's biographer, wrote a thorough and enlightening exploration of this controversy. See "Bringing Back the Mule Shoes Guns" in *Old Alleghany: The Life and Wars of General Ed Johnson* (Staunton, VA: Hearthside Publishing Company, 2004), 679–87.

10 Robert Robertson, "From the Wilderness to Spotsylvania," *Sketches of War History 1861-1865: Papers Read Before the Ohio Commander of the Military Order of the Loyal Legion of the United States, 1883-1886 Volume I,* (Cincinnati, Ohio: Robert Clarke & Co., 1888), 280–81.

Alfred Waud sketched Hancock's II Corps assembling around the Brown farm prior to the battle. *Chris Mackowski*

As 4:30 a.m. approached, Hancock met with his brigade commanders near the 20th Indiana, positioned on Birney's left and at the center of the overall line. That regiment, Hancock told his officers, would serve as the guiding regiment. He reminded everyone of their orders to advance without firing. "Gentlemen, are you all ready now?" he asked. *Yes*, they answered. "Then join your regiments and move forward," he said.[11]

"And then," wrote John Black of the 145th Pennsylvania, "in the dim gray light of that early spring morning, with a mist rising from the field and thicket, and while the birds were faintly chirping in the bushes and trees as they noted the coming of dawn, the grand old First Division moved forward in almost perfect silence." It was 4:35 a.m.[12]

Hancock, sitting on horseback, watched them advance. "I know they will not come back!" he exclaimed. "They will not come back!"[13]

11 Erasmus C. Gilbreath, typescript, Erasmus C. Gilbreath Papers, Indiana State Library, IN, FSNMP BV 55.

12 John D. Black, "Reminiscences of the Bloody Angle," *Glimpses of the Nation's Struggle* (St. Paul, MN: H. L. Collins Co., 1898), 425–26.

13 J. W. Muffly, *The Story of Our Regiment: A History of the 148th Pennsylvania Volunteers* (Des Moines, IA: The Kenyon Printing & MFG. Co., 1904), 255.

Because of the secrecy of the plan, coupled with the foggy weather, few infantrymen knew the exact position or nature of the Confederate works or the ground they had to cross to get there. "[A]nd so we had to take our chances, moving forward till we struck them," wrote a lieutenant on Barlow's staff. "[O]n we went, a solid mass, moving very rapidly." Barlow's division crossed open rolling fields, while Birney's men advanced through "a marshy place, and a dense wood of low pines."[14]

As both divisions approached the east-west farm road that led to the Landrum house, they encountered the first line of Confederate pickets. "I don't see how we could ever have gotten so close without giving alarm to their pickets, but so it was," wrote one member of the 86th New York under Birney's command. "[T]hey had to do one of two things, surrender or skip, and I think every picket in front of our line skipped for dear life."[15]

Any Confederate picket who did try to challenge the Federal advance found more than he bargained for. "As they challenged," Black wrote, "the low order was passed along our line, 'Double-quick,' replied to by a scattering volley from them, and then with a mad rush our boys were upon them and a dull thud here and there, as the butt of a musket compelled a more speedy surrender, told how well the order had been obeyed, and the way was open for the attack."[16]

A few yards to the south of the Confederate picket line, the Federal assault crested a ridge that ran alongside Landrum Lane, which ran to a small farmstead on the northeast corner of the field. Many infantrymen mistook the sunken lane for the main Confederate works. As they bounded over, many of them disobeyed orders and "let forth a yell which woke people in Washington, I would think." The soldiers quickly realized their error. "[M]ounting this crest, the red earth of a well-defined line of works loomed up through the mists on the crest of another ridge, distant about two hundred yards with a shallow ravine between," Black wrote. Realizing their yell had blown any cover they might still have, the Federal assault immediately picked up speed and "with a prolonged cheer, at the double quick," dashed across the remaining space toward the new line of works.[17]

Although some Confederate pickets had by now made it back to the main line to sound the alarm, it was "the yells of thousands on our front" that provided the true wake-up call, one Southern infantryman said. Confederates readied

14 Favill, 297; Gilbreath.

15 Stephen P. Chase, memoir, US Army Military History Institute, Carlisle Barracks, Carlisle, PA, FSNMP BV 38.

16 Black, 425–26.

17 Gilbreath; Favill, 297.

themselves, "their muskets cocked, peering through the gloom for the first glimpse of their foes," recalled "Stonewall Jim.[18]

Several moments passed—"which seemed very much longer to the anxious and expectant Confederates," Walker said—before the Federals came into view.[19] They materialized out of the fog about a third of the way across the field, charging down into the ravine from Landrum Lane.

The attacking Federals, too, finally got a clear look at what they faced: "We see the frowning earth-works in our front lined with the now thoroughly aroused enemy, whose every eye was taking deadly aim over the long line of glittering muskets resting beneath the logs which crowned the rampart."[20]

As the Federals reached the bottom of the ravine, "there belched forth from the works a volley of shot and shell that would have proved disastrous had we been in range," Black recalled. "But, fortunately for us, the guns, in anticipation of a night attack, had been trained on the ridge we had just crossed, and so the shells passed over our heads, doing no damage."[21]

Onward the Federals charged, "line after line, one behind another on they came," wrote James L. McCown of the 5th Virginia, part of the Stonewall Brigade."[T]hey came in seventeen lines, one line just behind the other, and we counted them," wrote Thomas Reed of the 9th Louisiana, "and some fellow said: 'Look out! boys! We will have blood for supper.'"

"Well," Reed continued, "before supper-time we had lots of blood."[22]

* * *

"The moment for the Confederate line had come," pronounced "Stonewall Jim."[23]

The general stood on the Confederate breastworks in front of his men "and with perfect safety and without a shot coming in any direction" watched as the first waves of blue ascended the slope from the bottom of the ravine. "One well-directed volley, such as our men knew so well how to give . . . would have thrown them into confusion, and made their future movements too slow and dispirited," he said. Standing to full height behind the earthworks, Confederates "leveled their

18 James L. McCown, diary entry, May 12, 1864, FSNMP BV 16; Walker, *S. H. S. P.* 21:235.

19 Ibid.

20 Robertson, "From the Wilderness," 280–81.

21 Black, "Reminiscences," 425-26.

22 McCown, diary; Thomas B. Reed, *A Private in Gray* (Camden, AR: T.B. Reed, 1905), 75.

23 Quotes from "Stonewall Jim" throughout this section from Walker, 235.

trusty muskets deliberately . . . with a practiced aim which would have carried havoc" into the ranks of the advancing Federals.

But "instead of the leaping line of fire and the sharp crack of the muskets," the Confederate guns went *pop! pop! pop!* Infantrymen pulled their triggers, the hammers fell, and the caps exploded—but the muskets, which had been stacked all night in the rain, barrels up, were soaked. Their powder was damp. The weather had effectively disarmed a large portion of the Confederate army.[24]

As the Confederates frantically tried to reload, the Federals reached the abatis and slashings in front of the trenches. According to one Michigan private, the obstacles "greatly retarded our progress at this critical time, and they created havoc in our ranks, while we were getting through." Some men tried tearing it away while others crawled through it. "[T]his we were obliged to destroy ere we could get to their line of battle," recalled a Federal officer.[25]

And then suddenly they were through—and just as suddenly, said Robertson, "The mad mass surges on over the intrenchments, in a resistless terrible wave which sweeps all before it." The lack of Confederate fire even made it possible for Federal officers to ride up to the breastworks on their horses and step from their stirrups onto the fortifications without harm.[26] At 4:50 a.m., the 26th Michigan planted its regimental colors atop the earthworks, followed quickly by the veteran troops of the 140th Pennsylvania—with the rest of Barlow's division flooding in close behind.

Fresh caps on the Confederate muskets "only produced another failure" for most soldiers, Walker said. "A muzzle loading musket with damp powder behind the ball is as useless to a soldier in an emergency like that as a walking-cane."

Ironically, Alleghany Johnson was proving just how useful a walking cane could be.

When the Federal attack hit the salient, Johnson had positioned himself with William Witcher's Virginians at the salient's tip. There, John Brooke's Federal brigade made first contact with the Confederate line, slamming into Witcher's front almost dead-on and curling around the outer tip of the salient. Brooke said his men "poured in one irresistible mass upon them." Johnson prowled along the top of the fortifications, clad in his long, gray military overcoat, swinging his hickory walking cane at Federals who scaled the works. As they tried to stab at him

24 Ibid.

25 Newton T. Kirk, typescript memoir, Newton Thorne Kirk Papers, #1397, Michigan State University Archives and Historical Collections, FSNMP BV 35; George A. Bowen, diary entry, May 12, 1864, FSNMP BV 228.

26 Robertson, "From the Wilderness," 280–81; Walker, 236.

with their bayonets, Johnson used his cane to parry their jabs. Their sheer weight of numbers dragged him down.[27]

Somewhere behind Johnson, the artillery pieces of Capt. William Carter arrived on the field. The missing artillery, which Johnson had tried all night to have returned, finally arrived—literally at the moment of crisis. It would be too late. "Most of this battalion reached the salient point just in time to be captured," recalled artillerist Thomas Carter, William's brother. Only one of Carter's four guns managed to unlimber and get into position—it would fire off a single round of canister—before Federals overran the guns. "Don't shoot my men," Carter pleaded. While the Federals took Carter and his men prisoner, they couldn't haul away Carter's guns: Confederate infantrymen shot the horses to prevent the guns' capture.[28]

Other batteries weren't even that lucky. Lieutenant Charles L. Coleman of Capt. Charles R. Montgomery's Battery fell mortally wounded even as he led his piece onto the field behind Carter. "It is said that while lying on the ground a corporal, in the confusion, asked him which way he should point the gun. 'At the Yankees!' [Coleman] replied, and those were his last words," recounted former battery commander S. V. Southall. Coleman's body was never recovered.[29]

Brooke affected his breakthrough against Witcher "after a sharp, short fight" in which his men "killed and captured nearly all who occupied the works. Those who still resisted were driven in confusion. . . . The bayonet was freely used on both sides, the enemy fought desperately, and nothing but the formation of our attack and the desperate valor of our troops could have carried the point." Never during the war, Brooke said, had he seen such desperate fighting.[30]

Brooke's brigade made up the right wing of Barlow's division; Miles's brigade led the left wing. As Barlow's formation crossed the field beyond Landrum Lane and reached the bottom of the ravine, the left elements of Miles's brigade encountered a small stand of timber and brush, which forced them to move farther left on their course of attack. A depression in the terrain, which provided a small degree of cover, funneled them left even farther. As a result, Miles hit the Confederate line along the breastworks near the middle of Steuart's brigade on the eastern face of the salient.

27 John R. Brooke, report, *O.R.* 36:1:410; William P. Carter, "'Allegheny' Johnson at Spotsylvania Courthouse," *The Southern Bivouac*, III (1885), 272-73.

28 Carter, "The Bloody Angle."

29 S. V. Southall, "The Captured Guns at Spotsylvania Court House—Correction of General Ewell's Report," *S.H.S.P.* 7:536.

30 Brooke, 410.

As the Federals neared the breastworks, "The first line seems to melt before the terrific volley which salutes us," said Robertson. Miles said he could hear "the sputtering sound, like the fall of hail, as the thud of their bullets fell on the head or shoulders of the men in our ranks." But even as the men in front fell, the men behind them continued forward until, as one Pennsylvanian said, "the great mass of men, with a rush like a cyclone, sprang upon the entrenchments and swarmed over." Steuart's left-most regiments, already overwhelmed by the fleeing remnants of Witcher's Brigade, surrendered with hardly a fight once the Federal assault broke through. Unit cohesion was failing due to the enemy, panicked comrades, and terrain.[31]

"The inside of the enemy's works was one of disorder and confusion," wrote Newton Kirk of the 26th Michigan. "[T]he trenches were crowded with their men, hardly aroused from their slumbers and many only partly dressed. They fired on us as we advanced toward them, and we promptly returned their fire. As we drew nearer, they threw down their arms, and cried out that they surrendered. We ordered them over the works, leaving their arms behind them, and in a few minutes the route over which we had just come was filled with rebels, who were being hurried as prisoners of war to the rear."[32]

One of those prisoners was Steuart, who surrendered after the Federals overran his position and scattered his command. The Federal colonel who accepted his surrender, James A. Beaver of the 148th Pennsylvania, at first mistook him for the more famous Confederate cavalry officer.

"I would like to surrender to an officer of rank," the Confederate brigadier said. "I am General Steuart."

"What," exclaimed Beaver, "are you 'Jeb' Stuart?"

"No, I am George H. Steuart." He'd been given the nickname of his home state, "Maryland," because of this very kind of confusion.

"I will accept your surrender," Beaver said. "Where is your sword, sir?"

"Sir," Steuart responded coldly, "you all waked us up so early this morning that I didn't have time to get it on."[33]

Steuart walked at the head of a long column of prisoners bustled to the Federal rear by members of the 3rd Pennsylvania Cavalry.[34] Major James W. Walsh,

31 Robertson, *From the Wilderness*, 279-81; Nelson A. Miles to Francis C. Barlow, January 6, 1879, *Papers of the Historical Society of Massachusetts* IV, (Boston, 1881–1918), 260-261; St. Claire Augustine Mulholland, *The Story of the 116th Pennsylvania Volunteers in the War of the Rebellion: The Record of a Gallant Command*, (Philadelphia, 1899), 197.

32 Kirk memoir.

33 Muffly, 857-58.

34 As part of the provost guard, the 3rd Pennsylvania Cavalry did not accompany Sheridan's raid.

commanding the cavalry, recognized Steuart and ordered an aide to bring Steuart a horse to ride. Then, turning to the Confederate general, Walsh explained that he had served in the prewar army with Steuart for a stretch in the 1850s. "I am very glad to meet you again, sir," Walsh said, extending his hand.

Steuart rebuffed Walsh's handshake. "We were friends then, sir," Steuart snapped, his voice dripping with contempt. "We are enemies now!"

Walsh turned to his aide and said, "Never mind about that horse. General Steuart shall walk to the rear with the other prisoners, by God, sir!"[35]

Johnson, who had likewise ended up a prisoner, scowled at his subordinate. "Don't be a damned fool!"[36]

The Federals herded the two officers and their men rearward. Impatient chaperones began poking, prodding, and "punching" the Rebels onward with their bayonets. Johnson, hobbling on his walking stick, his ire already seething, jerked to a stop. "'Clubby' Johnson . . . halted in the road and waving his 'club' in the air, cursing, swore he would not move another step, but die there if they did not quit bayoneting his men," said a member of the 10th Virginia, also a captive. Johnson "worked his ears backward and forward and was in a terrible rage." Whether startled by the mad outburst or amused by it, the Federals stopped their poking.[37]

While Confederate foot soldiers marched to the rear, Steuart and Johnson, as general officers, were escorted to II Corps headquarters, which Hancock had established at the Landrum farm. Sixty-five-year-old Willis Landrum and his wife, Lucy, along with five other family members, had abandoned their four-room home, and Confederate pickets had incorporated boards from inside the home—including the wooden staircase—into part of their earthworks. The house sat close enough to the front for Hancock to see the action but far enough back to be out of rifle range.[38]

Hancock and Johnson—"Win" and "Ned," as they called each other—had known each other well in the old army, and Hancock greeted his old friend warmly. "I am glad to see you, Ned," he said, offering a kindly smile and a handshake. With tears coursing down his face, Johnson returned the grasp. "Under other

35 William Brooke Rawle, *History of the Third Pennsylvania Cavalry*, (Philadelphia: Franklin Printing Company, 1905), 425-26.

36 Oliver Edwards, memoir, 143, FSNMP BV 55.

37 Casler, 328.

38 The Landrums owned no slaves. Upon the family's return after the battle, they would find the two chimneys of their home still standing, the four walls pocked with cannonball holes, and 28 Federal soldiers buried in their yard. Their home essentially destroyed, they would build another home elsewhere on their 170-acre farm.

As prisoners, Generals Steuart and Johnson eventually found themselves under guard by members of the United States Colored Troops.
*Library of Congress*

circumstances, I would be pleased to meet you," Johnson said, admitting, "This is worse than death to me."

Exact reports of the conversation vary. "This is damned bad luck," Johnson said, "yet I would rather have had this good fortune fall to you than to any other man living." Or, instead, Hancock said, "I'm sorry for your misfortune, but if you had to be captured I am pleased that it my good fortune to entertain you." In either event, both men seemed glad to see each other, despite the circumstances.[39]

Hancock then offered his hand to the far pricklier Steuart. "Under existing circumstances, Sir, I cannot take your hand," Steuart responded.

"And under any other circumstances," Hancock replied coolly, "I should not have offered it." Another version of Hancock's reply gives him more snark: "Under no other circumstances would it be offered to a rebel."

And so ended Hancock's hospitality to Maryland Steuart, unable to give up being a "damned fool." Hancock motioned for the provost guard to haul the Marylander away. He turned back to Johnson. "Pray be seated," Hancock said. "We will have breakfast directly."

The war continued around them, and Hancock continued to issue orders. "Johnson put his hand to his heart as though it pained him," a Federal soldier observed, "and as he gazed upon his fellow prisoners and the earthworks, which,

39 This particular scene has become a bit of a hash in the last 160 years, but the version here is based on two eyewitness accounts: Black, "Reminiscences," 428-29, and Charles B. Brockway, *Across the Rapidan,* July 1, 1882, *Philadelphia Weekly Times*, FSNMP BV 141. Hancock's wife offered a version in her edited *Reminiscences of Winfield Scott Hancock by His Wife* (New York: Charles L. Webster & Company, 1887), 103-06, and other fragments from interested parties circulate, as well.

but an hour before were under his command, heavy tears coursed down his cheeks and his whole frame heaved with emotion."[40]

Johnson was eventually bundled off to Grant's headquarters. Steuart, for his surliness, was not given the opportunity. "No further attempt was made to extend any courtesies to this prisoner, who was left to make his way to the rear on foot with the others who had been captured," recounted Horace Porter. Johnson and Steuart were two of more than 3,000 Confederates taken prisoner in the initial assault.[41]

"I am very sorry to inform you that our Div[ision] has suffered very severely and the small remnant we had left of the Reg[iment] were nearly all captured. We now have about 20 left," wrote surgeon Abram S. Miller of the 25th Virginia, one of Witcher's units. "I think our brigade was to blame for the most of it. They have run on three occasions and no doubt they are to blame. The Brig[ade] has never stood very high and never will."[42]

* * *

As Barlow's assault swept through Witcher's and then Steuart's brigades, Birney's attack swept down the northwestern face of the salient. His lead elements had pierced the Confederate line in front of the Louisianans of Leroy Stafford's old brigade, commanded by Zebulon York. "Then ensued one of those hand-to-hand encounters with clubbed rifles, bayonets, swords, and pistols which defies description," wrote a New York officer.[43]

"Every Confederate realized the desperate situation and every Union soldier knew what was involved," wrote John Haley of the 17th Maine. "For a time, every soldier was a <u>fiend</u>. The attack was fierce—the resistance fanatical. We captured one of their strongest entrenchments, but it was done in a tempest of iron and lead, in a rain of fire."[44]

During the melee, the color-bearers of two opposing regiments—one from New York, the other from Louisiana—planted their flags within feet of each other atop the earthworks as the members of the units struggled for supremacy. Without warning, a New Yorker leapt up, grabbed the Louisianans' colors, and ducked back to safety.

40 Charles B. Brockway, *Across the Rapidan,* July 1, 1882, *Philadelphia Weekly Times*, FSNMP BV 141.

41 Porter, 105.

42 Abram S. Miller, letter, May 18, 1864, FSNMP BV.

43 Weygant, 322–23, 332–33.

44 Haley, 156.

When the Louisianans then tried capture the New Yorkers' colors, the Empire State men were ready for them and repulsed several waves.

As the entire II Corps continued to flood the gap that had been punched through the line, the Louisianans in York's Brigade crumbled away. Beyond them lay the right flank of the Stonewall Brigade, positioned next down the line. "We were ordered to reserve our fire until near enough to tell on them with effect," wrote James McCown. "Then now warmly we gave it to them, line after line recoiled before the withering fire from our line. Another coming up. They recoiled and on they came."[45]

The Stonewall Brigade could hardly keep up an effective rate of fire, however, since wet muskets and soggy ammunition plagued them as badly as it did their compatriots in York's and Witcher's brigades. They were also plagued by stray gunfire from across the salient, where Federals had fanned out behind the Confederate works in Steuart's sector. "We were exposed to a front and side line," McCown recalled. "It was terrific beyond any description."[46]

Many of them simply threw down their useless muskets and ran back into the interior of the Mule Shoe and southwestward down the breastworks. Others "were captured without hardly firing a shot." The color-bearer of the 5th Virginia tore the regiment's flag from its pole and folded it into his shirt, determined that it not fall into enemy hands even as he was taken captive as the Federal army continued its sweep.[47]

Walker, frantic to plug the hole, sought help from the artillery of James Carrington posted nearby. "Carrington, can't you help my men with your Battery?" Walker asked, raising his arm and pointing at the Federals now behind his lines. "General," Carrington replied, "it is difficult to get these guns out here in the woods, and if I could see where your men are, they are between me and the enemy, and if I attempted to use canister, it would be more distructive [*sic*] to them than to the enemy."[48]

Just then, a bullet struck Walker in the left arm, wheeling him around and "eveidently [*sic*] producing terrible shock and great pain," Carrington recalled. While an aide helped Walker from the field, Carrington had to attend to more pressing matters: The rout of the Stonewall Brigade meant his guns faced capture. "I saw many of these brave old Stonewall men using their bayonets and buts [*sic*] of their muskets around the gun until they were overwhelmed by masses of the enemy,"

45 McCown.

46 Ibid.

47 George P. Ring, letter, May 15, 1864, Louisiana Historical Association Collection, Tulane University.

48 James Warwick Carrington Papers, typescript memoir, Hotchkiss Papers, R59, F227, Library of Congress, Washington, DC, FSNMP BV 62.

Carrington wrote. "We continued desperately not dreaming of capture until we were completely surrounded by their overwhelming numbers," McCown wrote.[49]

In all, 22 guns fell into Federal hands, Carrington and 50 of his men were taken prisoner, and the collapse of one of the most famous units in the Confederate army continued unabated. "All that escaped had to 'run for it' some distance . . ." recalled John O. Casler of the Stonewall Brigade. "Men in crowds with bleeding limbs, and pale, pain-stricken faces, were hurrying to the rear."[50]

"[T]he old brigade was annihilated," Walker would lament. "On the 12th of May, 1864, the famous Stonewall brigade, which had won renown on so many battlefields, ceased to exist."[51]

The battle of Spotsylvania Court House could effectively be called "The Last Days of 'Stonewall Jim' Walker and the Stonewall Brigade." Walker would live to fight another day, albeit in the political arena. This lesser-known Congressional portrait comes from 1896. *The United States Red Book, An Illustrated Congressional Manual*

* * *

A stream of reports from the front kept Meade and Grant informed of Hancock's progress, such as: "Our men have the works"; "All of my troops are engaged"; "Wright . . . slightly wounded, but still in command"; and "Prisoners come in rapidly. . . . General Johnson among them."[52]

"Aides galloped up one after the other in quick succession with stirring bulletins," Porter remembered. Grant sat on his camp chair by the fire, huddled against the rain, unmoving except to read the updates aloud as they came in.

49 Ibid; McCown.

50 Casler, 212.

51 Walker, 236, 235.

52 See Hancock's correspondence to Meade, *O.R.* 36:2:656–57.

Perhaps John Rawlins, Grant's chief of staff, showed enough enthusiasm for both of them. According to Lyman, Rawlins's "hard hollow voice, broke out into loud, coarse exultation." "By God! They are done!" Rawlins grinned. "Hancock will just drive them to Hell!"

Lyman, a refined Boston Brahmin, initially had "a very disagreeable first impression" of the rough Rawlins: "loud and profane in talk, fiery and impulsive of temper, and with a general demeanor of the bad 'Western' kind." But Lyman eventually found himself won over by the irresistible and impressive officer. "In truth he is a man of a cool, clear judgment, and well gifted with common sense; despite his temper too, he is a good hearted man," Lyman concluded. "His flashes of anger & of over confidence depend perhaps on his pulmonary tendency; for he seems hopelessly consumptive." Indeed, Rawlins would eventually die of tuberculous in 1869 after serving five only months as President Grant's first secretary of war.

Close to 6:30 a.m., a Confederate officer surprised them by riding up to the campfire. He was, said Lyman, "a stout built man, with a coarse stern face. He had on riding boots, a blue-grey, double-breasted coat and a very bad black felt [hat]." The officer carried himself gravely, but Porter, also present, had to keep from smirking: from a hole torn in the crown of the officer's hat, a tuft of hair protruded, "looking like a Sioux chief's warlock."[53]

As the officer dismounted and saluted, Meade looked at him attentively, and then recognition registered. "Why, how do you do, general?" Meade shook his hand warmly, then introduced him to the general-in-chief. "General Grant, this is General Johnson—Edward Johnson."

Grant extended a similarly warm handshake. "How do you do?" Grant asked. "It is a long time since we last met."

"Yes," replied Johnson, "it is a great many years, and I had not expected to meet you under such circumstances."

"It is one of the many sad fortunes of war," Grant answered. He offered Old Alleghany a cigar, then moved a camp chair close to the fire for him. "Be seated," Grant invited, "and we will do all in our power to make you as comfortable as possible."

"Thank you, general," Johnson said. "Thank you; you are very kind." Porter noted Johnson seemed "deeply touched by these manifestations of courtesy." Lyman, meanwhile, noted that Johnson seemed "terribly mortified and kept coughing to hide his nervousness."

53 Quotes from this section come from Porter, 103-04 and Lyman, *Meade's Army*, 153-54.

But it was Porter who ended up putting Johnson at ease. As Porter recounted:

> [Johnson] had been in the corps of cadets with General Meade, and had served in the Mexican war with General Grant, but they probably would not have recognized him if they had not already heard that he had been made a prisoner. I had known Johnson very well, and it was only four years since I had seen him. We recognized each other at once, and I extended a cordial greeting to him, and presented the members of our staff. He was soon quite at his ease, and bore himself under the trying circumstances in a manner which commanded the respect of every one present.

Even as Johnson "chatted freely with his captors . . ." one newspaper correspondent noted, "he eyed General Grant with an evident feeling of great curiosity."[54]

Missing from the chat was General Steuart. "[L]ittle Baltimore Stewart, behaved like a donkey," Lyman recounted derisively, sent with the other prisoner to Fredericksburg "on foot, for his pains, with the mud ankle deep!"

Dispatches continued to flood in. Burnside reported that his right flank had lost contact with Hancock's left. Grant replied briefly but clearly: "Push the enemy with all your might; that's the way to connect."

Next came a note from Hancock: "I have finished up Johnson, and am now going into Early." Grant passed the note around but did not read it aloud "out of consideration for Johnson's feelings." Johnson nevertheless seemed to anticipate the news from the front. "Doubtless you have gained an advantage," Old Alleghany said, "but you are much mistaken if you think we are beaten yet!"

And as Lyman would recall, "He was right!"

* * *

Winfield Scott Hancock had just peeled open a gap in the Confederate line that stretched for nearly half a mile. Barlow had "done splendidly," Hancock thought, and he ordered his division commander "to hold what he has captured at all hazards" and "protect his flank as best he can."[55] Barlow did so by sending a request to Burnside to link their flanks together.

54 W. H. Cunnington, quoted in Clemmer, 573.

55 Black, 429–30.

Edwin Forbes sketched the action as seen along the Fredericksburg Road, which appeared as the woodcut "The Fight on the Left: Burnside's and Hancock's Corps Engaging the Enemy" in *Frank Leslie's Illustrated Newspaper.* *Library of Congress*

Burnside had attacked with two of his divisions: Potter's on the right and Stevenson's, now commanded by the newly arrived General Crittenden, on the left. Willcox's division served as the reserve. "[W]e formed into line of battle and moved forward a little to the right of the road running toward the court house . . ." said Ephraim Myers of the 45th Pennsylvania. "While making the movement, I remarked to the boys upon the character of the firing on our right [Hancock's main attack]. I said, 'I don't believe those fellows are putting in all their powder. . . . [But] I found out the next day . . . that there had been no half charges there. The field was strewn with dead and wounded."[56]

The men found themselves pushing through marshy areas around the Ny River bottomlands and crossing two of its small tributaries, and then assaulting uphill, often through thick woods. "[F]or some time, shells were plenty," one officer bemoaned. All the same, Potter succeeded in capturing part of the Confederate line, but in the process, managed to lose his connection with Hancock. In consequence, Burnside reported, "our right was seriously pressed and driven out of that portion of the enemy's line just captured, losing a few prisoners."[57]

James Lane's North Carolinians, occupying the Confederate line south of Maryland Steuart's position, had "[i]n the best of spirits . . . welcomed the furious assault . . . with prolonged cheers and death dealing volleys." Colonel R. V. Cowan of the 33rd North Carolina, hat in hand, "was constantly running along his line and cheering his men, though himself all the time exposed to a storm of Yankee

56 Ephraim E. Myers, "Three Years' and Five Months' Experience of an Orange Recruit," *History of the Forty-Fifth Regiment, Pennsylvania Veteran Volunteer Infantry, 1861-1865*, Allen D. Albert, ed. (Williamsport, PA: Grit Publishing Company, 1912), 287.

57 Weld, 292; Burnside, report, *O.R. 36:*1:909.

bullets," Lane noted. But no sooner had the Tar Heels repulsed Burnside than they faced pressure from Barlow on the flank because of Steuart's collapse. Lane ordered his men to hold their ground at all hazards: "The honor and the safety of the army demand it."[58]

Just then, "urgent orders" from Grant arrived for Burnside—the terse "push the enemy with all your might" missive—so the IX Corps commander threw Potter and Crittenden in again—and again—"which resulted in severe loss, but did not succeed in driving the enemy from his main line." Allen D. Albert of the 45th Pennsylvania, surveying that "severe loss," was struck by the cost of the morning's assaults:

> When we got upon high ground that morning where we could look back over the territory we had passed over, dead and wounded men were scattered thickly over the fields as far back as we could see. Being a farmer's boy the scene reminded me right away of a harvest field on the old farm in Tioga County [Pennsylvania], and forsooth it was a harvest field we were on—the harvest field of Death with human forms as the ghastly sheaves![59]

On Birney's side of the salient, the blue advance continued its sweep past the Stonewall Brigade and on to Monaghan's Louisianans. "I have as you know been in a good many hard fights," one Pelican State captain would write, "but I never saw anything like the contest of the 12th."[60]

Just beyond, the Federals finally ran into a strong line of Daniel's North Carolinians, bolstered by three Georgia regiments from Col. Clement Evans's Brigade. Daniel had wheeled his brigade around to a position that allowed his men to fire on the Federals as they moved down the trenches. A few pieces of artillery also wheeled around to provide backup. "[T]his combined fire of infantry and artillery was more than human flesh could stand and it was impossible for them to reach our lines," said Maj. Cyrus B. Watson of the 45th North Carolina.[61]

58 James Lane, "Battle of Spotsylvania Court-House," *S.H.S.P.* 9:146; William S. Speer's reports, James H. Lane Collection, Special Collections, Auburn University Libraries.

59 Burnside, report, *O.R.* 36:1, 909; Allen D. Albert, ed., *History of the Forty-Fifth Regiment, Pennsylvania Veteran Volunteer Infantry, 1861–1865.* (Williamsport, PA: Grit Publishing Company, 1912), 128.

60 Ring.

61 Cyrus B. Watson, "Forty-Fifth Regiment." *Histories of the Several Regiments and Battalions From North Carolina in the Great War, 1861-65,* ed. Clark, Vol. I, 35-61.

In the interior of the salient, the II Corps had pursued retreating Confederates beyond the McCoull house. "We followed up the enemy, driving them before us through the woods and brush up to another interior line of entrenchments occupied by another line of troops," wrote Capt. George Bowen of the 12th New Jersey.[62]

That interior line, set up by Gordon and Lee as a reserve and occupied by Virginians under Col. John S. Hoffman, provided a rallying point for some of the retreating Confederates. "[T]hey were very hard to rally," admitted an artillerist who had retreated with the infantrymen. "[M]any of them were still running and looked as if they had no idea of stopping at all."[63]

Still, the Federals found the second line "now fully on the alert and too strong to be carried," although they did have limited success penetrating the line's easternmost end. Confusion, too, worked against the advance. "[P]assing through the woods, our line had become broken," Bowen said. Other Federal regiments faced similar problems. "We have no regimental or company organizations left, but a disorganized and shattered line devoid of organization," Robertson noted. No one in the scattered units seemed to know what to do next.[64]

Just as Johnson had received reports overnight of Federal activity, fellow division commander John Brown Gordon had heard similar news. When fighting broke out, Gordon received a message that "there's something wrong down in the woods where General Johnson's men are," but he and his staff officers could hear nothing through the forest and fog.[65] Not until the stream of refugees began filing rearward did Gordon understand the situation. "There was little or no shooting in the front line to indicate any fighting, and this alone informed us of the disaster," said a soldier in one of Gordon's brigades.[66]

Gordon immediately sent Brig. Gen. Robert D. Johnston's men forward, but they quickly found themselves outnumbered. Twice, Federal officers demanded that Johnston surrender. "Our answer in both instances was a volley," replied a member of the 23rd North Carolina. As the firefight intensified, Johnston was hit in the head with a bullet, "causing some confusion among the men," Walter Taylor recorded. Although Johnston would live, the injury knocked him out of the fight, and command devolved to his senior colonel, Thomas M. Garrett of the 5th

62 George Bowen, diary, FSNMP BV 228.

63 "Frank," undated letter, Charlottesville Art., J. W. Daniel Papers, University of Virginia Library, 7.

64 Favill, 297; G. Bowen; Robertson, "From the Wilderness," 279–81.

65 Gordon, *Reminiscences*, 274–75.

66 Bradwell, 166.

North Carolina. Garrett was soon killed, and command fell to Col. Thomas F. Toon of the 20th North Carolina.[67]

To buy time, Gordon redeployed the brigade and sent them sweeping forward into the Federal ranks, screaming as they charged. Surprised, the Yankees fell back, surprising Johnston and his outnumbered men in turn. Gordon, meanwhile, wheeled around to find more men to throw into the fight. A bullet nearly clipped him, but he managed to ride back toward the brigades of Hoffman and Evans.

Major General John Brown Gordon painted a surreal battlefield scene in his memoirs: "The mist and fog were so heavy that it was impossible to see farther than a few rods. . . . The sudden and unexpected blaze from Hancock's rifles made the dark woodland strangely lurid." *Library of Congress*

Gordon formed the men into line of battle, with Hoffman's five Virginia regiments on the left wing and three of Evans's six Georgia regiments on the right (the other three regiments were still entangled in fighting along the western face of the salient near Daniel). As Gordon assembled his battle line, Lee arrived on the scene, alerted to the pending disaster by a member of "Alleghany" Johnson's staff. "Not a word did he say, but simply took off his hat, and as he sat on his charger I never saw a man look so noble, or a spectacle so impressive," observed one Confederate.[68] But another soldier recalled something else revealed on Lee's face: "The General's countenance showed that he had despaired and was ready to die rather than see the defeat of his army."[69]

67 R. D. Johnston, memoir, August 6, 1895, John W. Daniel Papers, Box 1849–1904, Folder 1890–1899, Duke University; Charles S. Venable, "The campaign from the Wilderness to Petersburg—Address of Colonel C. S. Venable (formerly of General R. E. Lee's staff), of the University of Virginia, before the Virginia division of the Army of Northern Virginia, at their annual meeting, held in the Virginia State Capitol, at Richmond, Thursday evening, October 30th, 1873," *S.H.S.P.* 14:529.

68 Anonymous, Pegram's brigade, May 25, 1864, Richmond *Sentinel*, FSNMP BV 61.

69 Bradwell, 168.

As demoralized men streamed past him, Lee spoke to them in a voice as "deep as the growl of a tempest": "Shame on you, men; shame on you! Go back to your regiments; go back to your regiments!" His face, said an observer, "was more serious than I had ever seen it, but showed no trace of excitement or alarm."[70]

The spell broke, and Lee rode over to the front of Gordon's formation, as if to lead it into the breech. Gordon intercepted him and took Lee's horse, Traveller, by the bridle. Lee was far too valuable to the Confederacy to expose himself to fire, Gordon warned. Then, in a fiery tone intended to inspire the assembled infantrymen, Gordon pointed out that they were Virginians and Georgians. "These men have never failed! They never will!" he yelled. "Will you, boys?"

"No! No!" they cried back. "We will not fail!"

Then the chorus arose, "General Lee to the rear! Lee to the rear!" The throng pressed in around Traveller, turning the horse around and preventing the commanding general from advancing, until a sergeant from the 49th Virginia led the horse rearward.[71]

This was the third "Lee-to-the-rear" incident in a week, first at the Wilderness on May 6, and again during Upton's attack on May 10. "This habit of exposing himself to fire—as they sometimes thought, unnecessarily—was the only point in which his soldiers felt that Lee ever did wrong," a Confederate memoirist said after the war. As a soldier in the excited moment, Lee forgot his larger duty as a commanding general, but his men did not. They recognized his increasingly isolated role as the army's—and the Confederacy's—indispensable man.[72]

"Forward!" Gordon commanded. "Charge!"

"And with a shout and yell," said one infantryman, "the brigades dashed on, through bog and swamp, and briers and undergrowth, to the breastworks."[73]

"All saw that a crisis was upon us. If we failed the consequence would be disastrous in the extreme," that same soldier said. Another added: "At no time did the fortunes of our army seem to be so desperate."[74]

* * *

Dawn slowly broke across the slate-gray sky, diffused by the rain clouds, as Gordon led his men into the fight. While Lee hoped they would solve the immediate

70 Stiles, 259.

71 Gordon, 279.

72 Stiles, 260.

73 Anonymous, Pegram's brigade.

74 Ibid; Thomas F. Wood, memoir, FSNMP BV 293.

crisis, he knew he still had a larger problem: the Mule Shoe was untenable. If he pulled back to a new line with no protective earthworks, however, the open-field fight that would result would play right into Grant's hands.

Lee set his engineers to work—with remnants of Johnson's shattered division pressed into labor beside them—cutting a line of works across the base of the salient. They would seal off the Mule Shoe and, at the same time, shorten the Confederate defensive line.

The men set to work with a purpose, "building breastworks, cutting down trees, which fell in every direction, some carrying them and piling them up, other with picks, shovels, bayonets and tin-cups throwing up earth on top of the logs," said John Casler of the Stonewall Brigade. Bullets whistled around them as they worked.[75]

The engineers needed enough time to do their work, and so Lee made one of his most difficult battlefield decisions: he would sacrifice lives for time. He would feed men into the salient to try to hold back the Federals, perhaps even plug the gap in the line, while the engineers constructed the stronger new position.

Lee could pull men from other portions of the Confederate line that remained quiet. Grant's planned assaults were not happening simultaneously. Burnside and Hancock had attacked, but Burnside did not hit with enough force and was now bogged down. Warren's V Corps, which was supposed to move against the Confederate left, remained dormant—a situation that would nearly cost Warren his job.

Lee sent word to move more units to the front even as Gordon's two brigades hit Hancock's men in the salient. "Onward they swept," Gordon wrote, "pouring their rapid volleys into Hancock's confused ranks, and swelling the deafening din of battle with their piercing shouts." The dead and dying of both armies lay in the wake of the charge "[l]ike the debris in the track of a storm."[76]

Gordon's push forced the Federals back across the salient and into the works, where other Federal soldiers had already begun to reverse the trenches in an effort to transform them into a reserve line for their own men. "[B]efore they were completed, however, the enemy came forward in immense numbers and made the most desperate attempt to recover their lost ground," wrote Lt. Josiah Favill of Barlow's staff. "They seemed determined to gain back at any cost what had been lost, and the most severe close fighting of the war ensued."[77]

75 Casler, 213. "I was digging with a pick, and every time I would stick it in the ground it would get fast in the pine roots, which was very aggravating," Casler complained.

76 Gordon, *Reminiscences*, 280.

77 Favill, 297.

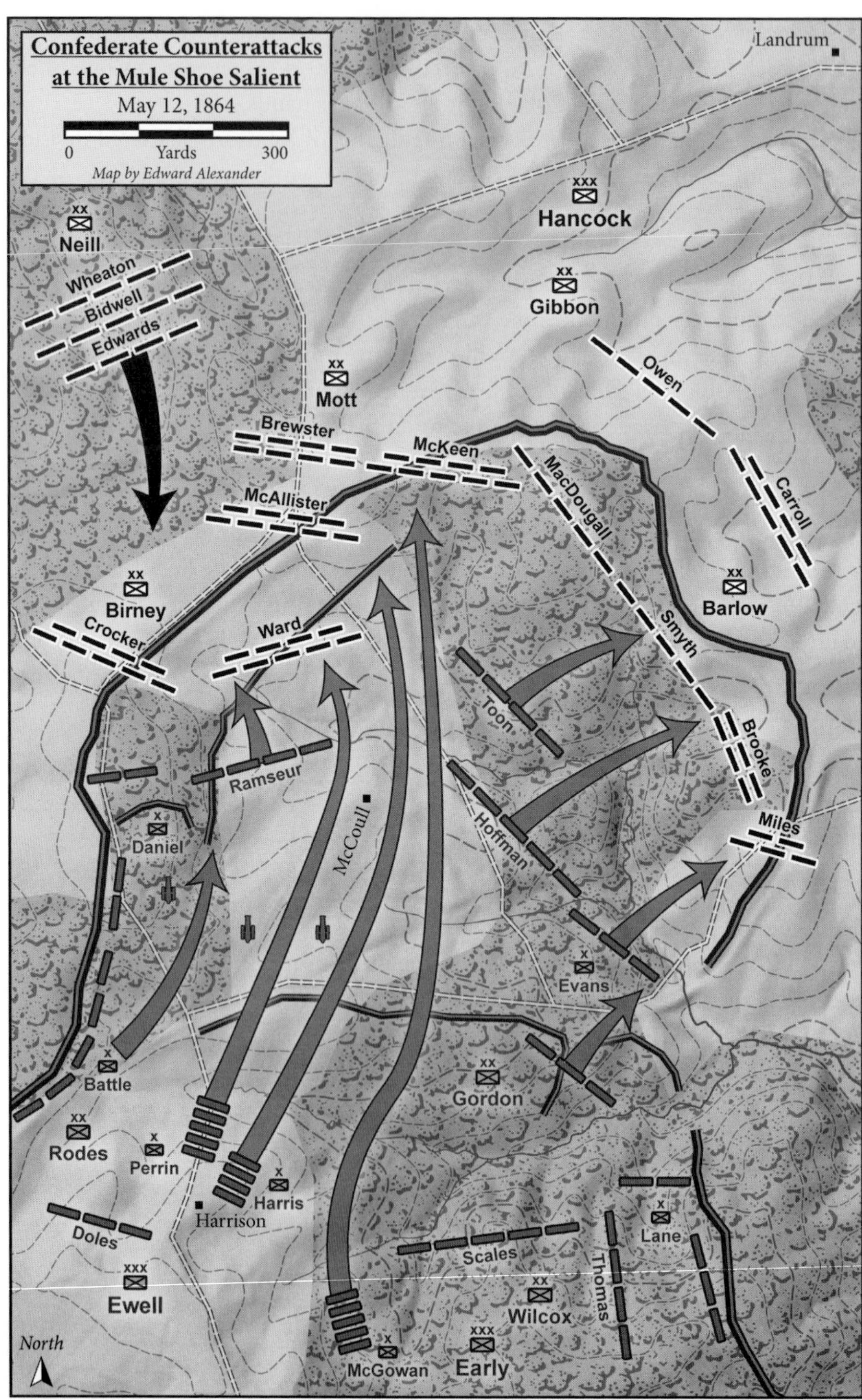
Confederate Counterattacks
at the Mule Shoe Salient
May 12, 1864
0 Yards 300
Map by Edward Alexander
Landrum
Hancock
Neill
Wheaton
Bidwell
Edwards
Gibbon
Mott
Owen
Brewster
McKeen
MacDougall
Carroll
McAllister
Birney
Barlow
Crocker
Ward
Smyth
Toon
Brooke
Ramseur
McCoull
Hoffman
Miles
Daniel
Evans
Gordon
Battle
Rodes
Perrin
Harris
Harrison
Lane
Doles
Scales
Thomas
Ewell
Wilcox
Early
McGowan
North

**Confederate Counterattacks at the Mule Shoe Salient**—Initial Confederate counterattacks against the Federal breakthrough came from a reserve line occupied by Gordon's division. Subsequent reinforcements came from the Third Corps, pulled from the Confederate right in front of the Federal IX Corps, which attacked against the Mule Shoe but not across its entire line.

---

Hoffman's brigade fought its way to the northernmost stretch of works that Steuart originally occupied, driving out Brooke's brigade. On Hoffman's right flank, Evans's men regained the works by pushing back Miles's brigade. Evans had a tougher time holding his position, though, and seemed ready to collapse. The color-bearer of the 31st Georgia, Jim Ivey, urged his regiment to hold on. "A few of us rallied around him and fought while he waved his colors and encouraged us to fight until there was no hope," one of his fellow Georgians said.[78]

Beyond Evans, Lane had successfully managed to stave off attacks by Burnside's IX Corps, although he urgently needed reinforcements. On May 11, Lee had stripped two brigades—Thomas's and Scales's—from Lane's sector of the field and sent them to bolster the left flank against the probes Grant had ordered. Now, as Thomas and Scales returned to their original positions on the battlefield at the most propitious moment possible, division commander Cadmus Wilcox funneled them directly into the fight to reinforce Lane. The surge of Confederates drove Col. Simon Griffin's brigade out of the works, securing the eastern face of the salient, albeit tentatively. A vigorous Confederate artillery barrage from Early's guns soon helped.

The Federals did not withdraw far, though, and they began to construct a series of defensive works of their own, sometimes only yards away from the Confederates. They also "piled dead bodies one on top the other to lie behind for protection," said a soldier from Massachusetts.[79]

On the western face of the salient, Daniel's brigade and Evans's three regiments, held, although Daniel himself was mortally wounded, shot through the bowels. The grisly stalemate broke when Cullen Battle threw his Alabamians into the fight. The assault pushed the Federals backward like "a solid wedge driven into the very heart of the enemy."[80]

78 Bradwell, 39.

79 Nathaniel W. Bunker, War Record, University of Michigan, William L. Clements Library, FSNMP BV 34.

80 Cullen A. Battle, "The Third Alabama Regiment," Alabama Department of Archives and History, Montgomery, 104–5, FSNMP BV 125.

Birney's men gave ground grudgingly, though. "We sought shelter from the storm behind stumps and trees, anything that offered a suggestion of safety," said John Haley, whose 17th Maine had been part of Birney's first wave. But not only did the Federals have to contend with the Confederates, they also had to contend with the weather, which continued to snarl equipment. "Men tore off pieces of their clothing to wipe out their gun with, and then went to work firing again," recalled Erasmus C. Gilbreath of the 20th Indiana.[81]

Rodes then ordered Ramseur's Brigade into the fray. Rather than attack up along the works, Ramseur was to form in a field west of the McCoull house and drive northwestward into the secondary works from the rear. The fog had thinned to reveal their objective, just a few hundred yards away. "The stars and stripes were floating proudly all along our works when the order was given to 'forward without firing,'" recalled one of Ramseur's men, Walter Raleigh Battle of the 4th North Carolina. "We commenced moving up pretty briskly, when our men commenced falling so fast that the order was given to 'double quick.'" Their ranks "very much depleted," Ramseur's men carried the secondary line of works without firing.[82]

Stopping to catch their breath, the Confederates noticed a Federal flag-bearer taunting them with his colors. "Genl Ramseur being a good artillery shot, called for volunteers to go and bring him some canister shot," recalled T. J. Watkins of the 14th North Carolina. "Genl. Ramseur sighted for his saucy flag bearer, the Lieut fired the gun, cutting down the flag bearer and, and [*sic*] mowing a lane through their lines, this was several times repeated; before we charged the enemy."[83]

The Federals soon had their revenge, though. Gunfire hit Ramseur in the arm, knocking him out of the fight. Colonel Bryan Grimes, who assumed command because he saw "no one to apply to," ordered a charge from the secondary line of works forward to the main line. "[W]e rushed on the yankees with fixed bayonets," Grimes said. "[T]he yankees allowed our lines to get in a few paces of their lines before firing. [T]hey cut down at least one third of our boys. . . . [N]ot withstanding this withering fire our boys made no halt, other than to pour into the enemies ranks, if possible a more deadly fire, for as we drove them the land we charged over was litterally covered with the enemies dead." "The field," said Grimes, "was perfectly blue with them."[84]

81 Haley, 156; Gilbreath.

82 Walter Raleigh Battle, letter, 14 May 1864, FSNMP BV 85; William E. Ardrey, diary, May 12, 1864, William E. Ardrey Papers, FSNMP BV 55.

83 T. J. Watkins, memoir, FSNMP BV 85.

84 Bryan Grimes, 14 May 1864 letter, Grimes Papers, University of North Carolina, FSNMP BV 55; Watkins; Grimes.

The second assault had carried the North Carolinians along the works as far as the left flank of Walker's former position with the Stonewall Brigade. There, Ramseur's Brigade, with Grimes leading them, bogged down into a grueling slugfest with mixed elements of Birney's division. But as the line of works continued to Grimes's right, they rose along a gentle slope, giving the Federals in the traverses along that stretch an elevated position from which they could fire down into Grimes's men. "Men were killed while squatting just as low and as close to the breastworks as it was possible for them to get," one of the North Carolinians noted. Making matters worse, the Federals began to flank Grimes, taking huge chunks of his men prisoner.[85]

The only option, Grimes, decided, was to keep pressing onward. Traverse by traverse, his men fought his way along the line. The Federals, enjoying the advantage of being uphill, hurled themselves down at the advancing Tar Heels. "Charge after charge came rushing on us," said a member of the 2nd North Carolina. "[W]e fought fearful odds, and it was here for the first time that I ever knew the enemy to run upon our bayonets, but they came down with such fury that we pitched many of them with the bayonet right over into the ditch."

"The water was so bloody in the ditches," he continued, "that one inexperienced would have taken it for blood entire, though the water was about one foot deep in the trenches where we fought."[86]

Between each assault, Confederates and Federals fired at each other over the earthworks. "There is not a man . . . who will ever forget the sad requiem which those minie balls sang over the dead and dying for twenty-two hours," said Walter Battle. "They put one in mind of some musical instrument; some sounded like wounded men crying; some like humming of bees; some like cats in the depth of night; while others cut through the air with only a 'Zip' like noise."[87]

Although the Federal soldiers held the high ground, the Confederates held an advantage of their own. Each fresh Confederate unit advancing into the Mule Shoe had good order and discipline and a clear-cut job: secure what they had lost. The Federal regiments, in contrast, were now broken and disjointed, with all semblance of order gone. No one knew the next step in the plan. The tactics drawn up by Emory Upton had been new, and the way Grant had scaled them up had been new, as well, so "what to do next" puzzled officers and enlisted men alike. Their only option seemed to be to keep slugging it out.

85 Battle, letter, 17 May 1864.

86 D. Lane, memoir, FSNMP BV 2.

87 Battle, letter, 14 May 1864.

It was, by now, nearing 6:00 a.m., and already the fighting was among the most intense and the most miserable any of the soldiers on either side had ever seen. "I know it to be the hottest and hardest fought battle that has ever been on this continent," wrote Walter Battle. "Every one looks as if he had passed through a hard spell of sickness, black and muddy as hogs. . . . Brigadiers and Colonels lay as low in the trenches and water as the men."[88]

"There is a point in battle beyond which flesh and blood can not pass and we had found that point," Robertson would write. "The 'Horse-shoe' was a boiling, bubbling and hissing caldron of death."[89]

* * *

Richard Ewell had not handled the collapse of his center with much poise. At one point, Gordon found "Old Baldy" sputtering and pulling on his beard in a state of near apoplexy. Shortly thereafter, as the remnant of Johnson's shattered division streamed to the rear, Ewell mocked and berated them. "Yes, goddam you, run," he bellowed. He was, according to one witness, in a "towering passion" emitting a "terrible volley of oaths."

Ewell's fury did little to inspire the fleeing men to rally, so he began to slap some of them with the flat of his sword. For Lee, arriving on the scene, that was too much. The Confederate commander gently urged the retreating men back into line, and then he turned his ire on his corps commander. "How can you expect to control these men when you have lost control of yourself?" Lee asked. "If you cannot repress your excitement, you had better retire."[90]

With an entire army to save, it is little wonder Lee expressed even that much patience with Ewell. The reinforcements he had sent in had managed to plug all but a few hundred yards of the gap that the Federal advance had opened in the line—but those few hundred yards still remained open. Lee called on the brigades of Abner Perrin, Nathaniel Harris, and Samuel McGowan to fill them.

In direct contrast to Ewell, Robert Rodes portrayed the picture of coolness. Riding his horse along the lines behind Daniel's position, he would "stop to attend to some detail of the arrangement of his line or his troops, and then ride on again, humming to himself and catching the end of his long, tawny mustache between his lips," said one observer. When reinforcements arrived from Joseph Kershaw's

88 Ibid.

89 Robertson, "From the Wilderness," 282-83.

90 Donald C. Pfanz, *Richard S. Ewell: A Soldier's Life*, (Chapel Hill, NC: UNC Press, 1998), 388–89.

Alfred Waud captured a lot of action in his depiction of the fighting at the Bloody Angle, but he did not witness the scene firsthand. He visited the battlefield the day after the fight and recreated events based on interviews he conducted with soldiers. He incorporated Meade and Hancock for artistic license in the lower-right of the image, although based on their location, the generals in real life would have been perilously close to the front. *Library of Congress*

First Corps division—Brig. Gen. William T. Wofford and his Georgians—Rodes personally directed them into line. These troops might not have been available had Warren attacked with any vigor on his front, but thus far, activity in Spindle Field remained quiet.[91]

On the Federal side, Hancock, too, was calling for reinforcements. "A tremendous attack has just again been made on my right, and it requires all my troops to repulse it," he wrote to Meade. His own attack had stalled, but he still had Wright's entire VI Corps to back him up—plus elements of Warren's V Corps, if needed. The battle hung in the balance, and one more wave of reinforcements could make the difference. "Someone must attack on my right, if possible," Hancock pleaded repeatedly.[92]

Wright already had three of his brigades readily available, those of Brig. Gen. Frank Wheaton and Colonels Daniel Bidwell and Oliver Edwards, all from

91 Robert Stiles, *Four Years Under Marse Robert*, (New York, 1903), 261.

92 Hancock to Meade, *O.R.* 36:2:659.

Thomas Neill's division. Edwards went in first, approaching the western face of the angle in front of Ramseur's Brigade. Edwards's men could not pierce the Confederate line, so they hunkered down on the outside of the works. "[M]y men and theirs were firing under the same head logs on top of the breastworks," Edwards said, "and while 'old Glory' waved over the works for one side, so did the 'stars, and bars' from the other side."[93]

Bidwell wheeled to form on Edwards's right, and Wheaton then wheeled to form on Bidwell's right, approaching the works where Ramseur's and Daniel's brigades met. The Confederates had ample time to prepare for the Federal advances and, with much hot work, repulsed them.

Soon, Wright himself appeared, but no sooner had he arrived than an exploding artillery shell threw the general several feet. A witness said a fragment bruised Wright's thigh, "injuring him severely, but fortunately not disabling him." Wright sat close to the lines "in a little hollow where the road from the woods came into the open." From there, he directed his corps while sipping whiskey to ease the pain of his wound. "[M]issiles of all kinds were so plenty," recalled one observer, with "a good number of bullets flying about and clicking among the trees." Unfortunately Wright could not see much from behind the hill and many of his men were directed to one spot, creating a traffic jam of Federal soldiers.[94]

As Wright continued to mass his troops across from the western face of the salient, Lee's reinforcements also continued to flow into the area. Leading the way was Abner Perrin's brigade from Mahone's Third Corps division. Perrin swung his five Alabama regiments into line and looked for any ranking officer to give him direction on what to do next. He soon found Lee, Ewell, Rodes, and Gordon in a conference, and he reported for orders. Gordon took charge and pointed the men into battle, ordering Perrin to help Ramseur secure the works on Ramseur's right flank. "Then Perrin spurred his horse to the front and around the left flank of our regiment, and with the accustomed yell, our brigade drove at the enemy at a rushing step," one of his Alabamians said. Perrin, who had earlier remarked that he expected to become a live major general or a dead brigadier, was killed "almost at the very first."[95]

The brigade swept through the open field around the McCoull house. "As I passed under a large cherry tree near the front gate I distinctly remember the shower of the bits of leaves floating to the ground in the still sultry air," recalled

93 Oliver Edwards, typescript, Illinois State Historical Society, FSNMP BV 70.

94 Hancock, 359; Lyman, *Meade's Army*, 154; Theodore Lyman, *Papers of the Massachusetts Historical Society*, 4:238; Lyman, *Meade's Army*, 154.

95 Alfred L. Scott, *The Boys of Belair*, Norman E. Wilhelm, ed., Virginia Historical Society, Richmond, VA, FSNMP BV 63.

Alfred Scott of the 9th Alabama. "They were falling in a constant shower from the whole tree, and, as I passed through them, I remember that the sight at the moment suggested to my mind, a constant fall of snow falling to the ground with that easy quiet motion peculiar to it, when there is not a breath of wind. The enemy must have been overshooting us wonderfully, for, if the bullets had been sweeping close to the ground as thick as they were through that tree, I don't see how any of us could have gotten through."[96]

Abner Perrin is buried in the Fredericksburg city cemetery. *Chris Mackowski*

Three of the 9th Alabama's color-bearers went down in the clearing, but the regiment continued moving. They soon came under fire on their right flank. Turning to meet the threat, they drove back the Federals only to come under fire on their right flank again. They assumed they were victims of friendly fire because the shots came from the direction from which they had just come, so the Alabamians "never thought of returning their fire, but called to them to cease their fire, that we were friends, and called our color bearer to 'show the flag.' He held the colors up as high as he could, waving them emphatically. . . . But the more our colors were waved the more the fire seemed to pour into us."

The fire came from a group of Federals still clinging stubbornly to a position in the secondary line of works not entirely cleared out by Ramseur. The Alabamians were saved by a nearby Confederate battery. Said Scott: "[T]here came a crash which nearly lifted the top of my head off and I saw the bushes in front of me swept by the blast of a cannon, and its charge of grape fired straight into the line that was firing on us. . . . We recognized them at once, and our boys didn't treat them as friends any more."

96 Ibid.

Behind Perrin's Alabamians came Brig. Gen. Nathaniel H. Harris's Mississippians. Lee met them and, again, seemed on the verge of leading them into battle but, again, the men refused unless Lee stayed back. "General Lee," said one of the officers, "you are worth all of us put together! Can't you trust us?"

Lee sent them forward: "Yes, I can trust you. Go, and may God go with you."[97]

The four undersized regiments—800 men in all—advanced through a gentle valley and came on line just northeast of Perrin's men. "The morning was dark and rain was falling slowly from the lowering clouds," one of Harris's men recalled. "An almost impenetrable fog hovered near the surface of the ground, which with the smoke of battle, rendered it difficult to see beyond a short distance."[98]

Some of the units were able to guide along a road that led to the McCoull farm and, from there, directly into the heart of the fighting. Others passed close to the secondary line of works where some Yankees still lurked. Those Federals opened on the flank of Harris's column, killing Sam Baker, colonel of the 16th Mississippi, leading the way.

The Mississippians nevertheless managed to push their way into the line on Perrin's right. They found themselves in a low, boggy stretch formerly occupied by the Stonewall Brigade. "[T]he mud fought for us . . ." said David Holt of the 16th Mississippi. "Many of them were shot dead and sank down on the breastworks without pulling their feet out of the mud." Fighting was so close men could not put rifle to shoulder to fire, Holt said, "so we shot from the hip."[99]

Harris ordered the 12th and 16th Mississippi to fight their way up the works—as much to get out of the fire as to continue to close the breech. Like Ramseur's brigade had done earlier under Grimes's leadership, Harris's men went traverse by terrible traverse, moving slowly closer to the west angle, taking back positions that had once been theirs. "The fighting was horrible," one of them said. "The breastworks were slippery with blood and rain, dead bodies lying underneath half trampled out of sight."[100]

The 16th Mississippi's flag bearer, Sgt. Alexander Mixon, led the way. Eventually, he was shot while climbing over one of the traverses. Only wounded, he picked up his flag, staggered forward, but was then shot through the head. The flag remained standing at the very apex of the west angle. Federal soldiers charged forward to capture the colors, but Harris's and Perrin's men counterattacked with equal ferocity.

97 David Holt, *A Mississippi Rebel in the Army of Northern Virginia*, Thomas D. Cockrell and Michael B. Ballad, eds. (Baton Rouge, LA: LSU Press, 2001), 255.

98 Rhea, *Battles of Spotsylvania Court House*, 270.

99 Holt, 256.

100 Rhea, *Battles of Spotsylvania Court House*, 271.

Mississippi graves near the McCoull house on the Spotsylvania battlefield. *Archives and Special Collections, United States Military Academy Library*

As the fight at the west angle seesawed, Neill asked for reinforcements. Wright and Hancock first turned to Brooke, who had fallen back to the Landrum house after running out of ammunition. Brooke resupplied his men and moved around to the western face of the salient to assist Edwards, still pinned to the outside of the works. Wright also sent in another of Neill's brigades, the five Vermont regiments of Col. Lewis Grant. One Vermonter described it as "the thickest of the battle, nothing but a breastwork of logs between us and the enemy, where we would stab over with our bayonets, men would jump up on the works and his comrad[e]s would hand him our muskets and he would stand there and fire until shot down when another would take his place and so continue."[101]

One young Federal, after seeing one of his officers gunned down from atop the works, hurled his musket like a spear at the Confederate who had fired the shot. "The force with which he threw it," said a witness, "drove the bayonet entirely through his chest, burying at least four inches of the muzzle of the gun in the breast of the Confederate, who uttered the most unearthly yell I ever heard from human lips, as he fell over backward with the gun sticking in him."[102]

The next Confederate unit into the fight were the 1,300 men in Samuel McGowan's Brigade—the 1st, 12th, 13th, and 14th South Carolina infantry regiments, along with Orr's Rifles. They arrived in the salient about 9:00 a.m., falling in along Harris's right "with a cheer and at the double quick, plunging through mud knee deep, and getting in as best we could." According to one soldier, their enthusiasm quickly faded once they realized their position: "The sight we encountered was not calculated to encourage us. The trenches, dug on the inner side, were almost filled with water. Dead men lay on the surface of the ground and in the pools of water. The wounded bled and groaned, stretched or huddled in every attitude of pain. The water was crimsoned with blood."[103]

McGowan took a bullet in the right arm—his fourth wound of the war. His senior colonel, Benjamin T. Brockman, was mortally wounded shortly thereafter; Brockman's brother Jesse, a captain, was mortally wounded at about the same time and place. Colonel Joseph N. Brown took command, and he and his men prepared for a long, punishing struggle. The five veteran regiments were about to face horrors that would pale in comparison to what they had seen at Fredericksburg, Chancellorsville, and Gettysburg. "It was plainly a question of bravery and endurance now," Brown said. "We entered upon the task with all our might."[104]

The earthworks to Brown's right took a slight bend to the east as it neared the apex. Federals in that stretch of the line continued to fire on Brown's flank and rear, so Brown ordered his men to continue pushing in that direction. He ordered Lt. Col. Washington Pickney Shooter of the 1st South Carolina to lead that push. "I know we are all about to be destroyed," Shooter said, "but I cannot consent to retire." He

101 Houghton.

102 Black, 431–32.

103 J. F. J. Caldwell, *The History of a Brigade of South Carolinians* (Philadelphia: King & Baird, 1866), 191.

104 Joe Brown, typescript of speech, FSNMP BV 5.

waved his sword overhead, urging his men onward, when Federal bullets cut him down. "I am a dead man," he gasped. "I die with my eyes fixed on victory."[105]

In the charge, bullets shattered the staff of the 1st South Carolina's flag. Flag-bearer Charlie Wilden snatched up the fallen flag and wrapped himself in it, pushing forward through the knee-deep mud. Reaching the spot where Alexander Mixon of the 16th Mississippi had, only a short time earlier, been gunned down, Wilden planted his Palmetto flag. Wilden's regiment, following close behind, clashed with the elements of the 124th and 86th New York occupying the position, eventually driving them out.[106]

By 9:30 a.m., David Russell's division from the VI Corps—including the brigade of Col. Emory Upton, whose May 10 attack had inspired this one—joined the fight. Upton had a particularly difficult time getting into position because the cacophony and confusion of battle made it nearly impossible for him to determine where he was supposed to deploy. A tiff with Edwards and Col. Joseph Parsons of the 10th Massachusetts annoyed Upton so badly that he decided to simply order his men to charge the Confederate works in three separate waves. Confederates repulsed all three assaults with heavy losses, and Upton's men fell back into the ravine for protection. "[T]roops cannot live over that slope," Upton declared. From there, Edwards bitterly complained, Upton's troops were useless and "might as well have been at the bottom of a well, firing up at the sky, for all the loss they did or could inflict upon the enemy."[107]

As morning wore on, Federal troops became so stacked in front of the west angle that one II Corps officer pleaded, "For God's sake, Hancock, do not send any more troops in here."

* * *

But still the Federals came, directed toward the west angle by topography as much as by Wright's poor design. A ravine ran diagonally across the field between Landrum Lane and the salient, and advancing soldiers crouched under the protection it afforded for as long as they could. As a result, moving southwest through the ravine funneled them away from the salient's tip—where Birney and

105 1st South Carolina papers, collection of South Carolina letters, FSNMP BV.

106 16th Mississippi papers, collection of Mississippi letters, FSNMP BV 430. For more on Charlie Whilden, see Gordon Rhea's excellent account *Carrying the Flag: The Story of Private Charles Whilden, The Confederacy's Most Unlikely Hero* (Basic Books, 2003).

107 Edwards typescript.

Mott hunkered relatively unmolested and where a gap in the line still existed—toward the west angle.

The area around the west angle area encompassed perhaps 150 yards of the works, but those few yards witnessed some of the most hellacious fighting of the Civil War. "At every assault and every repulse new bodies fell on the heaps of the slain, and over the filled ditches the living fought on the corpses of the fallen," said a New Jersey officer. "The wounded were covered by the killed, and expired under piles of their comrades' bodies."[108]

"I have heard that blood-drenched, bullet-swept angle, called 'Hell's Half-acre,'" recalled Robertson. A Pennsylvanian called it "a literal saturnalia of blood" and "a panoply of horror." Other soldiers described it as a "the slaughter-pen of Spottsylvania," "a pandemonium of terror," and "a Golgotha," a place of skulls. Theodore Lyman referred to it as "the Death-Angle."[109]

But most simply remembered that bend in the works as the Bloody Angle.

"The ground drank its fill of blood, and grew slippery to the foot," said Robertson. "Fresh troops from the other corps were continually being pushed up to the salient, in vain endeavors to make a new assault on the enemy's line within. But the heaps of dead, the pools of blood, and the terrific volleys of musketry, were too much for man's endurance." Indeed, Robertson thought the frenzied combatants looked less like men than demonic hordes who fought like wild beasts to destroy each other.[110]

"All around that salient was a seething, bubbling, roaring hell of hate and murder," said Haley. "In that baleful glare men didn't look like men. Some had lost or thrown away hats and coats. Some were gashed and cut, and looked like tigers hunted to cover."[111]

Some looked worse than that. "I was splashed over with brains and blood," complained Col. Comillus McCreary of the 1st South Carolina. "In stooping down or squatting to load, the mud, blood and brains mingled, would reach up to my waist, and my head and face were covered or spotted with the horrid paint."[112]

Getting out of the mud and mire proved impossible, though. The lines were only feet apart. Breaking cover, said one Confederate, meant certain death: "[W]ith every

108 Haines, 177–78.

109 Robertson, "From the Wilderness," 284; Muffly, 859-60; Anonymous author Apollo (PA) *Sentinel*; 16th Mississippi papers; Thomas T. Roche, "The Bloody Angle," Philadelphia *Weekly Times*, September 3, 1881, FSNMP BV, 144; Lyman, *Meade's Army*, 155.

110 Ibid., 283.

111 Haley, 157.

112 Comillus W. McCreary, *Charleston Daily Courier*, 26 May 1864, FSNMP BV 236.

kind of shot and shell whistling over us, among us, in us and about us . . . it was as much as your life was worth to raise your head above the works."[113]

John Haley of the 17th Maine authored an extraordinary Civil War memoir, and his account of the fight at the Mule Shoe is one of the most compelling ever written. After the war, he returned to his hometown of Saco and became a librarian. This never-before-published image of Haley shows him late in his retirement.

*Dyer Library and Saco Museum/Brian Swartz*

To fire their rifles, some soldiers held their firearms as far over the breastworks as they could and depressed the barrels, firing blindly. "Sometimes they would grab one of our guns and wrench it from us," explained a New Yorker, who said the Confederates "lost a number of guns in the same way." Other soldiers shot through the gaps in the breastworks or through the openings beneath the headlogs that lay atop the fortifications.[114]

Combatants were so close, said one Virginian, that their heads were at the ends of gun muzzles as they shot each other. "When ammunition ran out or got wet they crushed each other's skulls with gun butts," he added. "They stabbed each other with swords. The mud of the breastworks became a mass of torn bodies as fresh troops rushed into the mouths of cannon firing double loads of canister."[115]

The canister came courtesy of the 5th U.S. Artillery, which rolled a section onto the field and began firing on the angle. Two of the guns, commanded by Lt. Richard Metcalf, fired from nearly point-blank range: one discharged nine rounds, the other 14. Mississippians flooded out of the works in an attempt to take the guns, but loads of double-canister quickly dissuaded them. Still, Metcalf's section

113 Anonymous, 28 May 1864, Montgomery, AL, *Daily Advertiser*, FSNMP BV.

114 Chase, memoir.

115 Andrew D. Long, *Stonewall's "Foot Cavalryman"* (Austin, TX: Walter Long, 1965), 22.

suffered a fearful toll in their advanced position: he lost all of his horses, and all but two of his men were killed or wounded. Infantrymen from the 5th Wisconsin then took over operation of the gun until they ran out of ammunition. The guns, mired in mud, had to be abandoned.

Metcalf's strike wasn't the only artillery Hancock sent into the battle. He placed nearly 30 guns along the Landrum farm lane, opposite the Confederate works, hoping to blast out the Confederates at a range of only 400 yards. Other guns, 24-pounder Coehorn mortars intended to lob shells into and over the works, were moved to the front. Unfortunately, the green cannon crew was firing the guns for the first time in anger. Many of their shells fell short, hitting their own men lying in front of the Angle. Hancock's idea failed.

By early afternoon, the pre-carious back-and-forth nature of the morning's battle had settled into a grim stalemate, with the armies slugging it out at close quarters in the pouring rain for the rest of the day. Soldiers used their bayonets freely. Some of Harris's Mississippians used the camp hatchets they had carried with them into battle. Bullets, said one soldier, "sang like swarming bees, and their sting was death."[116]

Soldiers reported firing as many as 300–400 rounds. "Toward evening I had great difficulty in getting the balls down on account of the dirt and dust that had accumulated inside by my gun getting wet so often during the day," wrote Benjamin Jones of the 49th Pennsylvania. "The guns were so badly used up that they were condemned afterward, and we drew new ones."

Small-arms fire flew so intensely that a 22-inch oak was "hacked through by the awful avalanche of bullets packing against it." The oak, located in the fourth traverse from the Angle, toppled on members of the 1st South Carolina, injuring several of them. Musketry fire also mowed down an 18-inch red oak and an 8-inch hickory in the same traverse. In all, some three acres of woods were all but destroyed. "The north side of the trees which stood in the rear of our works there was not a vestige of bark left," Roche said. "Every small branch had been cut away and the large limbs were hanging frayed, frazzled [*sic*] and twisted." It looked like an army of locusts had swarmed through, said another eyewitness.[117]

The hail of lead made it difficult for prisoners to get to the rear or for the wounded to get to safety. A member of the 5th Maine, Edwin C. Mason, was among several wounded Federals who "had to lie in the mud of the ploughed field with only a rail to keep our shoulders above the mire into which the body sunk by its own

116 Robertson, "From the Wilderness," 283.

117 Dr. Charles Macgill, June 1, 1864, Richmond *Examiner*, quoted in Jno. Robertson, *Michigan in the War* (Lansing, MI: W. S. George & Co., 1822), 466; Roche, "The Bloody Angle"; Macgill, 466.

weight until in some cases the mud and water met over the hips."[118]

In the Confederate trenches, conditions were no better. "The lips of the dead were incrusted with powder from biting cartridges," said Brown. "It was a horrible scene." Wounded soldiers found themselves buried in the mud or trapped beneath piles of corpses. Soldiers still in the fight inadvertently trampled them. Some drowned in the shin-deep water. Andrew Long of the 5th Virginia, shot in the shoulder early in Hancock's assault, was one of the lucky ones. "When I came to I crawled to a puddle of water through which men had been walking and fighting all day—and drank," he said. "All I wanted was water regardless of how dirty. There was mud, blood and brains in this puddle."[119]

The infamous Bloody Angle oak stump remains on display at the Smithsonian Institution's Museum of American History. *Library of Congress*

Although the air was alive with lead, a Confederate captain and 12 men, covered with blood and mud, threw down their guns, jumped the works, and ran into the lines of the 96th Pennsylvania. "The Devil couldn't stand it in there," the captain said, explaining his defection and surrender.[120]

About 2:00 p.m., two other Confederates hunkered in the

118 Edwin C. Mason, *Through the Wilderness to the Bloody Angle at Spotsylvania Court House: Glimpses of the Nation's Struggle, 4th Series* (St. Paul, MN: H.L. Collins Co., 1893), 311.

119 Brown, 103; Long, 22.

120 Henry Keiser, diary, May 12, 1864, FSNMP BV 41.

earthworks on the far right of McGowan's line also tried to surrender. They affixed a white flag to the end of a ramrod, which they then waved tentatively over the works. Soldiers on both sides mistakenly thought their opponents were surrendering. "The Yankees have surrendered!" a number of McGowan's men began to shout. "This caused a burst of exultation on the Confederate side," recalled Thomas T. Roche of the 16th Mississippi. "The Federals were frantic with delight, throwing up their caps and waving their flags, sending up cheer after cheer, and calling on 'Johnny' to lay down his guns and come over, while the Confederates were making the same polite request to the Yankees." The confusion led to a five-minute cessation of hostilities while officers on both sides denied authorizing the white flag. A Federal officer, who had exposed himself to parlay, was shot at when he refused to surrender, triggering renewed firing all along the line.[121]

That was not the only white flag waved that day. Federal soldiers complained that Confederates waved white flags at various points during the day only to blast away at any Federals who stopped to honor the truce. On one occasion, William W. Noyes, a private in the 2nd Vermont, responded by leaping onto the fortifications and shooting a Confederate on the other side. He then had members of his regiment pass him loaded rifles, 15 in all, before leaping back to safety. He would receive the Medal of Honor.

* * *

On the Federal right, Gouverneur Warren's V Corps had remained on alert but largely immobile, even after orders arrived for Warren to support Hancock with an assault of his own. "Attack immediately and with all the force you can, and be prepared to follow up any success with the rest of your force," Meade ordered Warren at 8:00 a.m.[122]

Some men later swore that silence reigned over the battlefield up to that point, despite the cacophony at the Mule Shoe. "I am quite sure we heard no sound of it . . . ," Abner Small of the 16th Maine would attest. "[P]erhaps the conditions were right for one of those local silences occasionally remarked in the vicinity of a battle. As I remember it, the quiet was almost unbearable."[123]

If so, it was the quiet before the fatal storm. Warren felt certain his men faced calamity by assailing—yet again—the nearly impregnable Confederate earthworks

121 Roche, memoir.

122 Meade to Warren, May 12, 1864, *O.R.* 36:2:662.

123 Small, 139.

"Batteries on Warren's front." *National Park Service*

edging Spindle Field. "[S]kirmishing was going on as usual and we had no evidence that the enemy was weakened in our front . . ." wrote Warren's aide, Washington Roebling. "[I]t is not a matter of surprise that they had lost all spirit for that kind of work. Many of them positively refused to go forward as their previous experiences had taught them to do so was certain death on *that* front."[124]

Warren sent three regiments forward—the 9th Massachusetts, 32nd Massachusetts, and 62nd Pennsylvania—to poke at the Confederate position. Encountering "a heavy fire of musketry and canister" they "soon came back in disorder, having suffered heavily." The 13th Massachusetts, which also crept forward on recon, found Confederate "in about as social a condition as a Hornet or Yellow Wasp would be in when their nest is disturbed. No one else advanced, despite Meade's orders, which Warren had "issued and reiterated." One Pennsylvania officer blamed the inaction on "underbrush . . . of such a dense character that it was found impossible to push the line through it . . . " although the Confederate artillery on the far side of the brush had far more to do with it.[125]

"It does not take many men from the enemy to hold the entrenchments in my front," Warren wrote to headquarters, as though it explained his lack of an all-out attack. While certainly an accurate assessment earned over four days of fighting, his observation came across as dithering.[126]

124 Roebling, report, FSNMP BV 55.

125 James A. Cunningham, report, *O.R.* 36:1:570; Stearns, 266. William S. Tilton, report, *O.R.* 36:1:566; J. W. Hofmann, report, *O.R.* 36:1:625.

126 Warren to Meade, May 12, 1864, *O.R.* 36:2:662.

Grant had had enough. "If Warren fails to attack promptly, send Humphreys to command his corps, and relieve him," he told Meade, referring to the army's chief of staff.[127]

Whether Humphreys knew he might be tapped to take command of the V Corps remains unclear, but he laid out Meade's expectations to Warren in straightforward and unconditional terms: "The order of the major-general commanding is peremptory that you attack at once at all hazards with your whole force, if necessary." In a second note a few minutes later, he added in an encouraging tone: "Don't hesitate to attack with the bayonet. Meade has assumed the responsibility and will take the consequences."[128]

"General Meade reiterates his order to move on the enemy regardless of consequences," Warren passed the grim news to his division commanders. He then—finally—gave the signal to launch a thrust against Field. "[A] commotion ran down the line," wrote Abner Small; "there was a great stir of troops; and we heard the command to go forward." Charles Griffin's, Lysander Cutler's, and Samuel Crawford's divisions pushed out into Spindle Field. Confederate artillery opened on them immediately. "The moment we rose from the ground a perfect hailstorm of balls from three sides were poured into us—men fell by the dozens," said Charles T. Bowen of the 12th U.S. Infantry. "At every moment I could hear the dull peculiar thud sound of a ball as it entered some poor fellow."[129]

Griffin's men, attacking parallel to the Brock Road, dashed uselessly against the Confederate line. "I had just got my feet on the works," recalled Bowen, "and was about to jump down when a shot hit me on the knapsack and knocked me full ten feet on the other side, flat as a flounder in a puddle of mud and water. Here I lay for a moment with the breath knocked clean out until one of the 146th [New York] picked me up. When I looked at my knapsack I found a musket ball had gone clean through my dry goods and was only stopped by my razor which happened to be about the last article between my back and the ball. It made a smash of the handle, but I was mighty glad it didn't do the same by my spine."

Griffin's division collapsed quickly, exposing the left flank of Cutler's men, who went to ground in a ravine beyond the smoldering ruins of the Spindle farmhouse. "Time dragged" for the men there, according to Abner Small. "We had no hint of what was developing elsewhere." Cutler's four intermingled brigades made several attempts to storm the works on the uphill slope to no avail.[130]

127 Grant to Meade, May 12, 1864, *O.R.* 36:2:654.

128 Humphreys to Warren, May 12, 1864, *O.R.* 36:2:663.

129 Warren to Cutler, May 12, 1864, *O.R.* 36:2:671; Small, 139; Charles T. Bowen, diary, FSNMP BV 209.

130 Small, 139;

A worried Warren could not get a clear picture of what he otherwise knew was happening. "Report to me in writing if you think your troops cannot carry the position in their front," Warren wrote, in part to assess the situation and in part to cover his backside. Cutler gave Warren the answer Warren hoped for. "My brigade commanders report they cannot carry the works," the division commander wrote. "They are losing badly, and I cannot get them up the hill."[131]

Austin Stearns of the 13th Massachusetts found about a dozen stragglers from different regiments huddled for protection behind a huge oak tree. He and another sergeant were sent back to order them forward, "but just before we reached there, a shell struck the tree, knocking about a cord of wood in every direction, and completely routing those who had taken refuge behind it."[132]

Cutler's men had to withdraw under withering fire. "The fire from the enemy was unusually fatal, a large proportion of the wounds proving mortal," said Rufus Dawes of the Iron Brigade's 6th Wisconsin. Abner Small concurred: "[D]eath had been furiously busy."[133]

Beyond Cutler, Crawford collapsed, as well. "[T]he same staggering fire that told so fearfully upon our ranks on the morning of the 10th, was again experienced," said the chaplain of the 11th Pennsylvania Reserves, who mourned the casualties left "behind on that fatal hill, as an additional sacrifice to its evil genius."[134]

Humphreys, who by that point had arrived on the scene, "gave the order to the assaults there to cease, as soon as [he] was satisfied they could not succeed."[135]

The attacks were "all for nothing but foolishness," Bowen grumbled.

Colonel Edward Bragg lamented that "every assault made was swept by artillery, wrecking the whole front that we attacked, until we were obliged to fall back, many of the men killed, and many more bleeding and wounded, and the wood thick with smoke from burning leaves, adding danger of suffocation to the dangers from artillery and musketry."[136]

Warren wrung his hands over "suffering heavy loss, but failing to get in," as he wrote in his official report. "The enemy's direct and flank fire was too destructive. Lost very heavily." His men rightfully had little appetite for more slaughter over ground that had already seen more than its share; however, a more artful approach

131 Cutler to Warren, *O.R.* 36:2:671.

132 Stearns, 266.

133 Rufus Dawes, report, *O.R.* 36:1:620; Small, 139, 140.

134 William Henry Locke, *The Story of the Regiment* (Philadelphia: J. B. Lippincott & Co., 1868), 337.

135 Andrew Humphreys, *The Virginia Campaign of '64 and '65 The Army of the Potomac and The Army of the James* (New York: Charles Scribner's Sons, 1883), 101.

136 Bragg to Rogers.

to the day's heavy work might have accomplished Grant's overall goal where futile assaults did not. By not exerting effective pressure against the Confederate First Corps, Warren allowed Lee to strip units from that sector of the field at several points during the day to send in as support at the Salient.[137]

As morning turned to afternoon, Grant stripped Warren of two of his divisions—Cutler's and Griffin's—and send them to the direct support of the II and VI Corps at the Angle. That left Warren with Crawford's division and the Maryland Brigade "presenting a line of battle not as strong as a single rank." Even as Warren continued to fret, Lee felt no need to move his First Corps out of its highly effective position and made "no serious effort" to press the Federal right.[138]

* * *

On the opposite side of the battlefield, Capt. William Thorne Nicholson listened carefully as General Lee gave him instructions. "Captain, I am sending you on a dangerous mission, and I leave it to your discretion whether to go or not," Lee said, "but the fate of my army depends upon it, and for God's sake don't lose any time."[139]

The 23-year-old Nicholson served in the 37th North Carolina from James Lane's Brigade. The son of a prominent planter from Halifax, North Carolina, Nicholson graduated from the University of North Carolina with distinction in 1860. He had risen through the ranks from private and now served as judge advocate in Wilcox's division court. A colleague called him "a most gallant officer."

With events at the Mule Shoe bogged into a gruesome slugfest, Lee sought to find some way to relieve the pressure on his beleaguered Second Corps. Warren's attacks against Lee's left, unenthusiastic as they were, prompted the army commander to instead look to his right, along Jubal Early's front, for a possible opportunity. Was Grant's left flank along the Fredericksburg Road protected? Lee could see artillery there: was it supported by infantry? Did an opportunity exist for Lee to strike? If so, Lee hoped that offensive action by Early would draw Federal forces away from the Mule Shoe to counter the new threat.

Lee needed intelligence, and he identified Nicholson as the man to get it. Nicholson agreed and, grabbing a companion, he ventured to the picket line. Skirmishing had been brisk along the front all day, and Confederates had recently torched a house—"Dixie," owned by James Beverley—that the Federals had been using as a sharpshooters' nest.

137 Warren, report, *O.R.* 36:1:541.

138 Ibid.

139 "Warren," "North Carolinians in the Recent Battles," *Raleigh Weekly Confederate*, June 8, 1864, 4.

*I can't raise my head without getting shot at,* the captain of the pickets warned Nicholson.

*I'll be okay,* Nicholson assured him, then he and his partner scurried, under cover of the foliage, into the no-man's land between the lines.

Nicholson might be okay, but the same could not be said for his unidentified companion. As they nudged close enough for Nicholson to glass Willcox's line, something caught the eye of Federal pickets, and they began taking potshots at the two North Carolinians. Nicholson remained unscathed, but his companion took a bullet. Nicholson hoisted his comrade on his shoulders to evacuate him, but as soon as they reached the safety of the line, artillery shells began raining in, and shrapnel killed the wounded man.[140]

A subordinate of William T. Nicholson said he was a man "born to command men." *Histories of the Several Regiments and Battalions from North Carolina in the Great War*

But Nicholson brought back the intelligence Lee needed: the battery was unsupported.

Lee would attack.

The Confederate army commander ordered Early to use Lane's and Mahone's brigades for an assault against "the flank of the columns of the enemy which had broken Ewell's line, to relieve the pressure on him [Ewell], and, if possible, recover the part of the line which had been lost." The two brigades were to move forward from the Confederate line and swing northward into the flank of Burnside's and Hancock's forces on the outside of the Mule Shoe. This would amount to a chance for payback for Lane, whose brigade had spent all morning staving off attacks from the IX Corps.[141]

When Lee had pulled Sam McGowan's South Carolinians from Early's line to help staunch the bleeding at the Mule Shoe, Early shifted Lane's men into McGowan's former position so they could rest. Mahone's Brigade, commanded by

140 W. P. Alexander, memoir, FSNMP BV 55.

141 Early, 356.

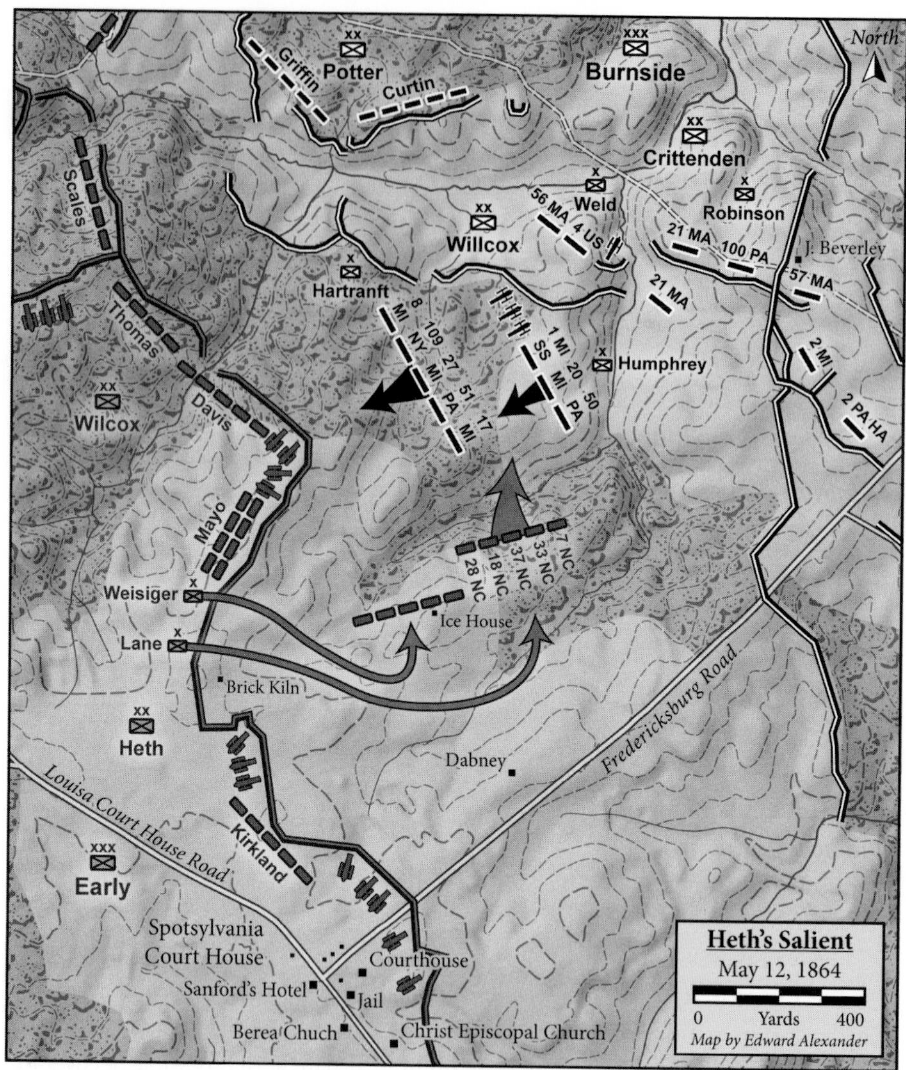


**Heth's Salient**—Lee and Grant launched simultaneous, albeit coincidental, attacks in the sector of the battlefield now known as Heth's Salient, near the Fredericksburg Road. Burnside advanced two of Willcox's brigades as Early advanced a pair of brigades (neither of which belonged to Heth). Confederates got the drop on the Federals and won the exchange, but neither side accomplished its overall objective.

---

Col. David Weisiger, occupied the center of the position as its reserve. The entire position formed a small salient that jutted out from the main line and, like the Mule Shoe Salient, was vulnerable to attack from multiple sides. In fact, artillery fire from the IX Corps raked the position mercilessly.

Early tried to compensate by shuffling some of his own artillery, with several batteries packed into the salient's tip. At one point during the day, Spotsylvania native Chew Coleman, a private serving in Capt. Thomas Ellet's (Virginia) Battery, repositioned a gun and its caissons under shells "skimming so close to the mounted cannoneers and the horses' heads." No sooner had Coleman parked his piece than a Federal shell came screaming in. "When it struck it exploded one chest of the caisson, and the heat set fire to the next one, but it did not explode immediately," recalled artillerist Charles P. Young. "The driver of the lead team, in his fright, tumbled from his horse, and the team made straight for the enemy's lines." As Young recalled:

> [Coleman] kept his seat, although next to the exploded chest, and the heat set fire to his jacket, which burned through to the skin, and, notwithstanding the flesh was crisping up, and he was suffering the most excruciating pain, he did not let go the reins, but stopped the horses, thereby preventing them from taking the team into the enemy's lines.

A couple of cannoneers unlimbered the burning chest and got it out of the way before it exploded "with a terrific noise." Young called it "the bravest exploit that came under my observation in the four years of the war."[142]

As it happened, Grant was also looking to the eastern front—at the same time as Lee—for a possible opportunity to break the stalemate at the Bloody Angle. About 2:00 p.m., he wrote to Burnside, pressing "The necessity for an attack, with a view to attracting the attention of the enemy from other parts of the line, if nothing more."[143]

With Potter and Crittenden already in the fight, the IX Corps commander ordered Willcox to move forward. Their target: a small bulge in the Third Corps's front manned by the Alabamians, Tennesseans, and Virginians of Archer's and Walker's brigades from Henry Heth's Division. Like the Mule Shoe Salient, Heth's Salient—as it would come to be known—jutted from the main line and was vulnerable to attack from multiple sides.

Hartranft's brigade, on the right, led the way. Christ's brigade—now commanded by Col. William Humphrey following Christ's debilitation the day before by another case of "sunstroke"-in-a-bottle—followed *en echelon*, behind and to the left of Hartranft. Although terrain across the entire Spotsylvania battlefield proved challenging, this was arguably the worst any Federal soldiers had to cross. Once beyond the marshy lowlands that fed into the Ny, part of the lead

142 Charles P. Young, *S.H.S.P.* 21:375.

143 Burnside, report, *O.R.* 36:1:910.

Best known for inadvertently starting the battle of Gettysburg, Maj. Gen. Henry Heth is memorialized with a landscape feature at Spotsylvania, "Heth's Salient." *Library of Congress*

brigade moved through "a bushy, small growth of trees" that offered concealment; another part moved through "a dense growth of pine timber difficult to pass in line of battle," and another crossed "a belt of perfectly open ground, extending up quite to the enemy's works." And they did all, wrote Lt. Col. Byron Cutcheon, "under the most terrific fire of shells, canister, and musketry." As Burnside later testified, "The dense woods through which a portion of our troops had charged was the scene of a most fearful conflict."[144]

The advance closed on the well-constructed works of Heth's Salient and, in Jubal Early's words, "got up to within a very short distance . . . before it was discovered." Robert Mayo's Virginians and Edward Thomas's Georgians opened up and, as Cutcheon later wrote, "the first line was soon checked and melted away." The 1st Michigan Sharpshooters, in Humphrey's line, pushed to the front and onward, soon joined by the 27th Michigan from Hartranft's line. Both regiments advanced within 50 yards of the Confederate line and took cover behind a breastwork of rails thrown up earlier by Confederate skirmishers. Artillery from Heth's line worked against them with "tremendous effect."[145]

Before other Federal units could gird their loins to join the two Michigan units, an unpleasant surprise appeared on their left flank. Unaware that Burnside had launched an attack, Early unleashed one of his own, as Lee had earlier ordered. Lane's and Weisiger's brigades sallied forth and, as things worked out, Lane got the drop on the Federals. "It was now soon discovered that the enemy were at the same time moving through the thicket in front of my left," reported an unpleasantly surprised Hartranft, whose left-most regiments absorbed the blow.[146]

144 Cutcheon, 969; Burnside, report, 910.

145 Early, 356; Ibid.

146 Hartranft, 950.

Colonel Constant Luce commanded the 17th Michigan, posted on Hartranft's far left. A private from the skirmish line first raised the alarm about the approaching Rebels. "I stooped over to see them," Luce remembered, "when he was knocked across my back, killed by a piece of shell. I fell on my face, the man across my back. While in this position the enemy's line passed over me and surrounded my regiment and captured all." Of the 225 Michiganders engaged, 189 became casualties: 98 prisoners, 73 wounded, and 23 killed.[147]

Those who didn't fall fought their way out. "After the regiment was surrounded and all resistance seemed useless," Sgt. Charles Thompson "fought single-handed for the colors and refused to give them up." Sergeant Daniel McFall captured Col. William Barbour of the 37th North Carolina, rescuing Lt. George W. Harmon on the way. Lieutenant Charles H. Todd was rescued by Frederick Alber, who shot one Confederate, knocked over another with the butt of his musket, and took them both prisoner. Thompson, McFall, and Alber each received the Medal of Honor for his heroics.[148]

Lane's and Hartranft's men became entangled, which "resulted in the loss and gain of some prisoners," Hartranft said—as well as the loss of the 51st Pennsylvania's colors. Hartranft chose to pull back. "The enemy's cannon poured their shot through my lines from the front," he said, "and his infantry being in superior force on my left, my line was compelled to retire."[149]

As Hartranft struggled to extricate his men, the North Carolinians swept through his brigade and into Humphrey's. "In our immediate front was a thick wood, into which we charged, when the enemy succeeded in getting upon our flank and rear," a member of the 50th Pennsylvania recalled, "then a most desperate hand to hand conflict took place. The bayonet and butt end of the muskets were freely used." The 50th Pennsylvania lost nearly 100 men, but the survivors "rallying around their colors, gallantly fought their way out, contending hand-to-hand in many instances with bayonets and butts of guns."[150]

The 20th Michigan, next in line, almost met the same fate, but their commander, Maj. George C. Barnes, wheeled the regiment to the left to face the attackers, which had by then broken into disorganized fragments. "[E]xposing himself where it seemed impossible for a man to live, encouraging and steadying his men regardless of danger," Barnes's conspicuous bravery emboldened his

147 Luce, 958. A monument on the Spotsylvania battlefield to the 17th Michigan lists 26 killed, 70 wounded, and 100 missing or captured.

148 Charles Thompson Medal of Honor citation.

149 Hartranft, 950.

150 Crater, 56; Cutcheon, 970.

regiment. Most of the men were, "at some stage of the fight," prisoners "and some were captured and recaptured several times," but Barnes managed to lead his men out of the woods. By the end of the fight for Heth's Salient, Spotsylvania had sapped the 20th Michigan of half its effective strength.[151]

Beyond Humphrey's men, posted to the left of the assault column, Willcox had stacked his artillery on an open plateau. For most of the day, artillery there had been harassing Early's line. These were the unprotected guns Nicholson had seen earlier in the afternoon, unaware that their protection—Hartranft's and Humphrey's—weretn't visible because they were organizing for attack. When first ordered to make that attack, Willcox had expressed concern about his left flank, which was not only the left flank of the assault but of the IX Corps and the entire Federal army. Colonel Elisha G. Marshall's provisional brigade—a mishmash of four converted cavalry and artillery regiments just that day assigned to Crittenden's Division—straddled the Fredericksburg Road as Willcox's only sort of reserve.

To provide additional protection, he ordered his chief of artillery, Lt. Samuel N. Benjamin, to bolster the artillery position, and Benjamin complied by advancing two additional batteries past the still-smoldering ruins of the Beverly house onto the plateau. Deployed with the others, they could not only enfilade part of Heth's Salient but also any potential Confederate counterattack. Willcox detailed the 2nd Michigan to provide support for the artillery on the far left.

Lane's assault had attracted the artillerists' attention almost as soon as the Confederate attack opened. "Our men commenced yelling too soon and drew upon themselves a terrible fire of canister," Lane admitted.[152]

Their forward momentum nonetheless swept them to within ten paces of the left-most section, commanded by Capt. Joseph W. B. Wright. "[I]t was but a few minutes before nearly every man belonging to this section was either killed or wounded, and the pieces ceased firing," recalled the 2nd Michigan's William Humphrey. To save the guns, one of Humphrey's subordinates, infantry Capt. James Farrand, jumped into action. "After all the gunners were killed or wounded, he manned the guns from his regiment," Humphrey wrote, "but he was killed soon after while bravely directing the fire of the pieces he had so hastily manned." Farrand's quick thinking, however, had "repulsed the enemy handsomely." So close

151 Ibid., 969, 977. Regimental losses were reported at 4 officers and 13 men killed, 3 officers and 92 men wounded, and 31 men missing, for a total of 143. That tally does not distinguish how many men were lost in each action at Spotsylvania, only that they reflect losses up to this point during "this period," i.e., the "Second Epoch" of the Overland Campaign.

152 Lane, 148.

LEFT: Brigadier General James Lane led skillful defensive efforts for Confederates throughout the day on May 12. *National Park Service*

RIGHT: Colonel John Hartranft demonstrated nimble adaptability throughout the Federal army's time in Spotsylvania. *Library of Congress*

was it that Lane, in his after-action report, believed his men had actually captured the pieces but had been unable to take them from the field for lack of horses.[153]

When Lane's men swept forward, Lieutenant Benjamin was "severely wounded in the neck in the hottest of the fight." He stayed with his pieces until the Confederate momentum broke. According to Hartranft, Willcox then took personal command of the guns and "opened fire upon the enemy and did good execution in driving him back."[154]

Lane looked for help, but Weisiger didn't respond. The North Carolinian would later accuse Weisiger of never leaving "the oak woods in which he formed line of battle." As a result, the Tar Heels withdrew "in some confusion" as the woods "rendered it almost impossible" to preserve cohesion. Somewhere along the way, Lane evaded a close call with death. "I am indebted for my own life to private

153 William Humphrey, report, *O.R.* 36:1:955.

154 Hartranft, 950.

P. A. Parker, Company D, Thirty-seventh regiment," Lane reported, "who killed the Yankee that had leveled his gun and was in the act of firing upon me—the Yankee was not more than ten paces from us at the time."[155]

The withdrawal of Lane's Brigade opened a way out for the 1st Michigan Sharpshooters and 27th Michigan, still holding onto their forward position in front of Heth's Salient. The collapse of Hartranft's brigade had left them exposed "to a murderous cross-fire of shell, grape, and canister," but they had had nowhere to go. "To advance was impossible," said sharpshooter Col. Charles DeLand; "to retreat difficult." They fought from their position for an hour, and when the chance finally came to escape, they took it. They were the last of Willcox's men to leave the field.[156]

This "mêlée in the woods," as Michigander Byron Cutcheon described it, seemed a wash for both sides. "This was a repulse to my line," Hartranft admitted, "but the enemy failed equally in his objects, with a slight advantage of prisoners in his advantage. My loss in killed and wounded was heavy." Humphrey's spin was that Federals "so severely repulsed" the Confederates that the Confederates, in turn, were "unable to take advantage of a serious repulse of part of our own lines at about the same time."[157]

Willcox's men did not give up the field entirely. Along the base of the hill where their artillery was positioned, they "commenced throwing up temporary works," said Capt. Edwin Evans of 109th Pennsylvania, "which were gradually enlarged until they were considered defensible." Burnside would remain in that defensive position for the next week.[158]

Lee had watched the Heth's Salient attacks for himself. The assault had not, as he'd hoped, rolled up the Federal IX Corps, but it did rob Burnside of what little initiative he possessed. Nor did the action do anything to alleviate the pressure on Ewell's line at the Mule Shoe. Mahone's and Cooke's brigades tried again later against the provisional brigade along the Fredericksburg Road but found the IX Corps too well-entrenched. "The ground between the lines was very rough, being full of ragged ravines and covered with thick pines and other growth," Early later complained, and flanking fire made the Confederate approach too precarious. With Lee's approval, Early used the two brigades to strengthen his own defense of the Fredericksburg Road.

155 Lane, 149–51.

156 DeLand, 975.

157 Hartranft, 950; Humphrey, report, *O.R.* 36:1:955.

158 Evans, 962.

For Lane's ill-starred brigade, the afternoon had offered one more vicious fight for which they would get no credit. As the men who'd accidentally shot Stonewall Jackson at Chancellorsville the year before, they carried with them a stigma that no hard fighting could shake. After a desperate morning defense that had saved part of Lee's army, the thanks they received was a mission they were too small to reasonably accomplish with no support and with verbal abuse at the end. As they filtered back to the Third Corps line, "Little Billy" Mahone materialized on the scene. Although commanding a division on the Po River sector of the battlefield, he'd heard Weisiger was leading his former brigade into action and rode over to snoop on the results. Lane said Mahone began "abusing my brigade generally" and accusing "the damned North Carolinians [of] deserting his brave Virginians." Lane countered with charges that Weisiger's men had, through incompetence, fired into Lane's when the attack began and then refused to advance. "I had far better opportunities of witnessing the performance of Mahone's brigade than did General Mahone himself," Lane snarled. "I was in the oak woods, I was in the open field, and I was also in the pine thicket beyond the opening."[159]

The episode led to years of postwar animosity, despite corps commander Jubal Early's attempt to put the matter to definitive rest: "Mahone's brigade did not become seriously engaged."[160]

* * *

As Grant's hopes for Burnside wilted into disappointment, he turned his attention back to his center. Although Burnside did not relieve the pressure at the Mule Shoe, Grant believed the Army of the Potomac might still have a chance at a breakthrough there. Grant hoped the V Corps reinforcements he had shifted from Warren would be enough to bolster Wright and Hancock for a renewed attack—and at first, Wright sounded optimistic about his chances. As the afternoon wore on, though, he began to sound more cautionary.

Wright, the least experienced of Grant's corps commanders, was losing his nerve.

It didn't help that Wright, who had a fondness for alcohol, had been drinking all afternoon in an attempt to dull the pain of his wounded thigh. When Cutler's division arrived shortly after 3:00 p.m., Wright misinterpreted Grant's order and misdeployed them, thereby muting any effectiveness Cutler might have had in assisting with an attack. By 5:00 p.m., when the brigades of Romeyn Ayres and

159 Lane, 151.

160 Early, 356.

Jacob Sweitzer appeared from Griffin's division, Wright opted not to send them in at all, being "not so strong as I supposed," he said. In his communications with Meade, he cited doubts about "a reasonable prospect for success" and worried about "a disaster which would possibly follow a failure." Most of all, he feared a Confederate counterattack.[161]

Meade responded, with Grant's assent, by ordering Wright and Hancock to shorten their lines and allow as many of their men as possible to rest. The Federal army would resume offensive operations the next day. That was easier said than done, though, with the II, V, and VI Corps all so entangled with the Confederates on the western face of the salient. "I have to say that I can't shorten my line a single foot," Wright griped.[162]

When darkness fell, Confederate fire slackened enough that several Federal units were able to pull back, including Bidwell's, Upton's, and Grant's brigades. Edwards, whose men had been in the fight the longest, pinned down in front of the Confederate works since 6:30 a.m., also asked permission to withdraw. Instead, he was told to hold the entire position himself. The 10th New Jersey was sent in to help, but Edwards expressed bitterness over the unfairness of the arrangement. When his men ran low on ammunition, they began to strip it from the dead and wounded.

Fatigue set in across the battlefield. "We cut some cedar boughs & lay down to sleep not knowing when a ball would hit us, but so tired were we that I slept first rate although the rain poured down all night," said Charles T. Bowen of the 12th U.S. Infantry, part of Ayres's brigade. "Every hour or two some fellow would get hit & cry out but the remainder would merely look up to see who it was & say poor fellow poor something like it & then go to sleep again."[163]

The Regulars had suffered especially badly thus far in the campaign. On May 14, the original nine companies of the 12th U.S. would be consolidated into three companies of 50 men each. The 2nd U.S., meanwhile, was down to 60 men, "having been terribly cut up," Bowen said. "At the rate we are being slaughtered it will only take a few more days to finish us off entirely."[164]

On the inside of the works, the Confederate brigades of Ramseur, Perrin, Harris and McGowan continued to hold. On the angle's eastern face, Hoffman and Evans still kept Birney and Barlow at bay, although several Federal brigades had pulled back into the relative safety of the woods a few hundred yards to the

161 Wright to Humphreys, May 12, 1864, *O.R.* 36:2:675.

162 Ibid., 676.

163 C. Bowen diary.

164 Ibid.

northeast. At the tip of the salient, elements of Mott's and Birney's divisions were still stacked tight against the works, although they had not become nearly as jumbled as the brigades in front of the Bloody Angle.

And so it was in "the dark of the moon and a drizzling rain" that Confederates at the Angle continued their grim work. "[T]he darkness was only broken by the flashing of the guns to light up the horrid scene . . ." said Joseph Brown of McGowan's Brigade. "Every flash of the guns lights up the ghastly faces of the dead, with whom the ground is thickly strewn."[165]

* * *

Orders for the Confederate withdrawal came down the line about 3:00 a.m. The remnants of Johnson's Division had completed the new fallback position. The salient could be abandoned.

In twos and threes, the Confederates slipped ghostlike to the rear, occupying the new line of works Lee had ordered south of the Harrison house. Edwards managed to capture the last handful—some 60 men and their captain—but the rest of the Confederates escaped undetected, leaving behind empty trenches and thousands of casualties. Befuddled Federals, advancing for attack, found only the carnage and detritus of war. "In many places the dead and wounded lay three and four deep, with muskets, cartridge boxes, blankets, and everything pertaining to a soldier's gear, all in the wildest confusion," wrote one Ohio soldier. "The face and parallel ditches were filled with water and blood, and the dead, from the rains, were bleached and ghastly. In many cases the wounded were so tangled and wedged in among the dead as to be utterly unable to extricate themselves without our help."[166]

The apparent withdrawal of the Confederate army bolstered Federal morale. It appeared that Lee had abandoned the field, leaving open the road to Richmond. Hancock needed to know for sure.

Men from the United States Sharpshooters, accompanied by Carroll's Gibraltar Brigade, advanced into the new no-man's land. They pushed beyond the battle-scarred trenches and into the interior of the Mule Shoe, but they advanced no farther than the reserve line of trenches before they stumbled across Confederate skirmishers. "In front[,] the 2nd Sharp Shooters were briskly popping away at the rebel skirmish line, and the infantry were altering the rebel works into defenses for

165 Brown, 103, 105.

166 Fred Larue, Xenia (OH) *Torch-Light*, June 1, 1864, FSNMP BV 198.

themselves," wrote George A. Marden, quartermaster of the 1st U.S. Sharpshooters. "The ground was almost a sea of mud."[167]

In the exchange, Carroll took a bullet in the left arm. He been injured once already, in the right arm during the fighting in the Wilderness, but after that wound he'd still managed to stay in command. This time, his injury knocked him out of the fight. Command devolved to Col. Thomas Smyth, the experienced brigade commander from Barlow's division.[168]

The Federals continued their push, scattering the Confederate skirmishers, and moved forward toward the McCoull farm. With Confederates gone, soldiers from the 140th Pennsylvania took advantage of the opportunity to dart forward and claim a pair of cannons and a limber chest that had been abandoned by their adversaries during the previous day's fighting. In two days, the II Corps had captured 22 cannon, 3,500 men, and two generals.[169]

Meanwhile, the Federals who advanced into the clearing around the McCoull house finally saw the new Confederate line less than half a mile away, just beyond the Harrison farm. Unsure of the Confederate strength, the Federals withdrew back to the Mule Shoe. Other reconnaissance missions discovered that Lee's flanks still held.

The Army of Northern Virginia had not gone anywhere after all—other than into a new, stronger line.

167 George A. Marden, journal, May 16, 1864, FSNMP BV 363.

168 Warner, *Generals in Blue*, 465–66. The Irish-born Smyth would eventually have the distinction of being the last general killed in Meade's army.

169 Robert Stewart, *History of the One Hundred and Fortieth Regiment Pennsylvania Volunteers* (Regimental Association, 1912), 197-200.

# May 9
# May 10
# May 11
# May 12
# May 13

The magnitude of the carnage left behind at the Mule Shoe Salient remained invisible until dawn. But as daylight whispered across the drizzling sky, and the morning fog gave way to thick humidity, soldiers of the Army of the Potomac began to see a landscape of carnage unlike anything they had seen in three previous summers of fighting. "The one exclamation of every man who looks on the spectacle," wrote a *New York Times* correspondent, "is, 'God forbid that I should ever gaze on such a sight again.'"[1]

"[T]here has been no one spot like it in the whole war," one soldier said.[2]

Dr. Daniel Holt of the 121st New York, who was no stranger to gore because of his work as a surgeon, found himself speechless. "No tongue can describe the horrors of the scene around me," he wrote. "Dead and dying men by scores and hundreds lie piled upon each other in promiscuous disorder."[3]

As Federal soldiers wandered into the abandoned earthworks, they saw "scenes of horror" on the inside of the salient just as grisly as the sea of blue corpses on the outside. One Confederate lieutenant had 21 bullet holes in his body and an iron ramrod through his neck. Rufus Dawes of the 6th Wisconsin saw the body of a Confederate soldier sitting the corner of one of the traverses "in a position of apparent ease, with the head entirely gone, and the flesh burned from the bones of the neck

1 Special Correspondent, "From Gen. Grant's Army: The Latest. Additional Casualties," May 18, 1864, *New York Times*, 1.

2 Wainwright, 367–68.

3 Daniel Holt, *A Surgeon's Civil War: The Letters and Diary of Daniel M. Holt, M.D.* James M. Greiner, Janet L. Coryell, and James R. Smither, eds. (Kent, OH: Kent State University Press, 1991), 188.

"I cannot but shudder at the thought of the carnage which it seems to me to be inevitable to follow upon the meeting of the two armies," Dr. Daniel Holt had predicted before the spring campaign opened. *National Park Service*

and shoulders." Charles Brewster of the 10th Massachusetts "saw one [Confederate] completely trodded in the mud so as to look like part of it and yet he was breathing and gasping."[4]

"Even at the bottom of the pits as they took out the bodies to burry them the[y] found some men still alive that had laid for 30 hours thus unnaturally & unhumanely buried alive," said a New York lieutenant.[5]

Nor was the scene where "the boys in blue" lay less cruel, Holt noted: "They were mostly in the open,—many nothing but a lump of meat or clot of gore where countless bullets from both armies had torn them; all ploughed with many wounds, but each by himself on the greensward, lying in his last line of battle." Isaac Best, a member of Holt's regiment, was awed by the sight. "For fully a quarter of a mile I could have walked upon the slain, stepping from body to body on our side of the works," he sighed.[6]

It would take several days for the Federals to attend to the army of corpses strewn across the field. "The ghastly upturned faces of the numerous dead, stared grimly at us between our lines, the bountiful fruit of the harvest of death," grieved one soldier. "[U]ntil the 17th, their decomposed and worm-eaten bodies lay uncovered, filled with worms and polluting the atmosphere with their foul stench."[7]

Some remains had been so mutilated by the battle, and corrupted by the weather, that stretcher crews could not move them without first maneuvering

4 G. W. P. Boutan, diary entry, May 12, 1864, typescript, FSNMP BV 55; Dawes, *Sixth Wisconsin*, 269; Charles Brewster, *When This Cruel War Is Over: The Civil War Letters of Charles Harvey Brewster*, David W. Blight, ed. (Amherst, MA: University of Massachusetts Press, 1992), 296.

5 Amos Stanton, typescript letter, FSNMP BV 183.

6 Hyde, 202; Best, *History of 121st*, 18–9.

7 John C. Gorman, memoir, FSNMP BV 293.

them onto blankets to help hold them together. "Some lying between the lines are so completely riddled that it is impossible to raise them," Holt would write. "A hole has to be dug side of them and they rolled into it for burial. They were a *complete jelly*! Hundreds of balls had passed through them."[8]

One Federal officer, searching for the body of a soldier from the 26th Michigan, could not believe what he found. "[W]e would never have recognized it as having been a soldier," he said. "There was no semblance of humanity about the mass that was lying before us. The only thing I could liken it to was a sponge."[9]

A Federal stretcher bearer, Maurus Oestreich of the 96th Pennsylvania, wrote in his journal that he had seen so much horror that "I can't nor will put it in this book. I will seal this in my memory by myself. God have mercy on those who started this cruel war."[10]

Henry Kaiser of the 96th Pennsylvania assisted in the battlefield burial of some of his former comrades. His description was typical of such interments: "We buried them in one trench, first placing a blanket underneath and one on top, placing a board of a cracker box, with the name, company and regiment marked thereon, at the head of each." One corpse, so mutilated as to be unrecognizable, sparked a debate between the regiment's commander, Colonel William Henry Lessig, and a subordinate. Lessing contended the body was J. M. Ferree:

> [W]hile the Lieut. as strongly contending that it was not, saying that he had seen Ferree shot in the thigh and get behind a stump. The Colonel then directed me to examine his pockets, which I did. In the right hand pocket I found an old knife with the blade broken. When I went to reach in the left hand pocket, I got the full length of my fingers into a pile of maggots, which had filled the pocket. When an examination showed that he had been shot through the thigh, as the Lieut. said, but the rains had washed away the blood on the outside, while the maggots gathered in the pocket where the blood was not washed away. It was the crossfire that had killed him while setting behind the stump. Of course the Lieutenant gave in.[11]

In all, the fight for the Mule Shoe cost some 17,000 victims, most of whom carpeted the area around and within the salient. Lee lost roughly 8,000 men killed,

8 Daniel Holt, 190.

9 Black, 432-34.

10 Maurus Oestreich, journal, FSNMP BV 44.

11 Henry Keiser, diary entry, May 13, 1864, FSNMP BV 41.

Confederate prisoners amassed in the "punch bowl" at Belle Plain along the Potomac, waiting for transportation that would take them to more permanent detention facilities, such as Point Lookout, Maryland, and Elmira, New York. *Library of Congress*

wounded, or missing, including 3,000 captured from Johnson's Division. Grant lost as many as 9,000 altogether.

A long line of wagons filled with wounded men streamed wearily toward Fredericksburg. "A painful spectacle!" Theodore Lyman would exclaim on May 14. "As the wheels would jolt into the deep sand holes, we could hear the cries of the poor sufferers mingled with the voices of the drivers shout to their mules as they struggled through the hard pulling. It was the best we could do." The campaign had transformed Fredericksburg into a city of hospitals.[12]

The condition of the wounded never seemed far from Lyman's mind. He wrote about it often in his journal throughout his time at Spotsylvania. "In an army thus constantly fighting and moving the Medical Department is called on for labors almost impossible," he marveled. "With the number of medical supply wagons so limited and even the ambulances reduced as much as possible, the surgeons are still called upon to care for enormous numbers of wounded. By great system and economy of force they accomplish wonders."[13]

12 Lyman, *Meade's Army,* 157.

13 Ibid., 165.

Because of the size of his army and the relative availability of reinforcements, Grant could bear the losses more easily. But Grant discovered yet one more downside of his superior numbers—aside from the army's sluggish reaction time, slow pace of march, and inability to coordinate well. The fight for the Mule Shoe extended over a front of perhaps 1,500 yards along the face of the salient. "Within that narrow field two corps were piled up to assault and in support," Lyman noted. "Indeed we had *too many* troops, as the generals justly said. The lines got mixed and jammed together and were hard to handle."[14]

The Confederates, meanwhile, already diminished by the campaign's hard fighting, felt their losses keenly. Between the Wilderness and the middle stages of the struggle at Spotsylvania, Lee had lost 19,000–23,000 men. "There is but a very few of this 2d Brigade left with the exception of this regt which has more men than all the remaining five regts and we have only 173 left," decreed Lt. Overton Steger of the 21st Virginia. "Our Col and Lt. Col are both wounded. We've not a Brigadier left."[15]

May 12 had cost Lee one division commander and seven brigade commanders, killed or wounded, and that was on top of the significant leadership losses he had taken at the Wilderness, including two corps commanders.

Alleghany Johnson's Division, hit especially hard in the initial Federal assault, was so devastated that only 1,400 men remained. "Jackson's old division was annihilated," wrote a rueful member of the 21st Virginia, John Worsham, who called it "a terrible blow to the army." "[T]his was [Stonewall] Jackson's old division, and those were the men who had done so much fighting, and who had made those wonderful marches for him . . ." Worsham said. "The number was small it is true for a division, but they were such trained soldiers that they counted as many in a fight."[16]

Lee parceled the division's survivors to other units. "What was left of Stafford's Brigade of Louisianians has been attached to Hay's Brigade of Early's command," reported Powell Reynolds of the 50th Virginia, part of William Witcher's Brigade. "The two N.C. Regiments in Stuart's [*sic*] Brigade have been put in Ramseur's Brigade of Rhode's [*sic*] Division. The six Va. Regiments in our Brigade and the five Va. Regiments in the 'Stonewall' Brigade and the three Va. Regiments in Stuart's Brigade have all been thrown together and make one Brigade."[17]

14 Ibid., 155–56.

15 *O.R.* 36:2:1075; Overton Steger, memoir, FSNMP BV 104.

16 John H. Worsham, *One of Jackson's Foot Cavalry* (New York: The Neale Publishing Company, 1912), 213.

17 Powell Reynolds, letter, May 19, 1864, FSNMP BV 3.

The grim math of war was beginning to tell on Lee, who saw his offensive capability shrinking with each passing day.

* * *

"It has been nothing but one scene of horror and blood shed since we crossed the Rapidan," wrote Ransom F. Sargent of the 11th New Hampshire. By the morning of May 13, both armies felt shell-shocked. "[A]n almost unbearable stillness prevailed" over the battlefield, reflected North Carolinian John C. Gorman. "The armies still confronted each other, but an unacknowledged truce prevailed."[18]

As the Federals hurriedly cleared the dead and wounded, some units began to refashion the landscape around the Bloody Angle by digging new works. "Our division occupied the ground they had taken from the rebs . . ." wrote sharpshooter George A. Marden. "There were few signs of a fight. . . . In front the 2nd Sharp Shooters were briskly popping away at rebel skirmish line, and the infantry were altering the rebel works into defenses for themselves. The ground was almost a sea of mud." Marden noted that "the 5th corps [dug] away at breastworks ten times as industriously as they ever did on the [P]eninsula. This didn't look like advancing."[19]

Grant tried to make sense of the situation, and initially he misread the intelligence that had filtered up from skirmishers on the front line. "I do not infer the enemy are making a stand, but [are] simply covering a retreat, which must necessarily have been slow with such roads and so dark a night as they had last night," he decided.[20] Others felt less confident about Lee's intentions.

Lee, of course, had no intention of retreating. His second line, which stretched across the base of the former Mule Shoe Salient, followed the crest of a ridge that dominated most of the open, rolling ground to the north. Nearly 30 cannon lined the works, which were initially manned by the remnants of Johnson's Division before Lee began to parcel them away.

The new line made Lee's overall position stronger than ever. To the west, his left flank remained on the steep banks of the Po River. The line ran east across the Brock Road and linked with the newly established line south of Harrison farm, then continued to just north of the town of Spotsylvania Court House. A salient still bulged out from the line in front of Henry Heth's position, but it was well-situated on high ground, overlooking a stream and marsh, with clear fields

18 Ransom F. Sargent, letter, May 19, 1864, FSNMP BV 253; Gorman, memoir.

19 Marden, journal.

20 Grant to Meade, letter, May 13, 1864, *O.R.* 36:2:698.

of fire and strong fortifications, and Heth's men had already proved they could defend position.

By 9:00 a.m., it was obvious that Lee had not only not withdrawn closer to Richmond, but had actually entrenched in preparation for more fighting. "Found [Lee] in full force, rather stronger than the day before," reported one of Grant's subordinates. "Our skirmishers have found the rebels along the whole line," wrote Assistant Secretary of War Charles Dana in a dispatch that morning to Washington, D.C., "and the conclusion now is that their retrograde movement of last night was made to correct their position after the loss of the key-points taken from them yesterday, and that they are still before us in force."[21]

Not only did the new Confederate center look strong, but the fighting since May 8 on the Confederate left, at Spindle Field, had convinced Grant that the Confederate position there was impregnable—the same conclusion Warren had reached by May 10. Grant began to look instead at the Confederate right. Lee had not been seriously tested on the right and so, Grant reasoned, there could be a weak point there.

The Federal high command cut the orders for a shift from the Brock Road sector of the field to the Fredericksburg Road—from Grant's right to his left. But Grant was not interested in just moving and probing: he wanted a fast move immediately followed by a quick strike. He directed Meade to have Warren shift the V Corps from the Federal right to the Federal left immediately after dark and then attack down the Fredericksburg Road toward Spotsylvania Court House, similar to Burnside's attack on May 10. He directed Horatio Wright to move the VI Corps "in like manner at the same time, if roads can be found" and get into position on Warren's left for an attack down the Massaponnax Church Road farther to the southeast. Hancock would be cued to then attack the center to hold potential Confederate reinforcements in place. "These attacks will be made at 4 o'clock [a.m.] if practicable," the order read. Warren and Wright spent the rest of May 13 preparing to march.[22]

As Grant set into motion his next move, Lee allowed many of his own men to get some much-needed sack time. He considered the loss of the salient nothing more than a temporary setback, and he was much satisfied with the newer configuration of his lines, but he began to worry about the toll Grant's headlong charges were taking on his army. The men's morale remained high, but they suffered

21 Dana to Stanton, 13 May 1864, *O.R.* 36:1:69.

22 Seth Williams, special order, *O.R.* 36:2:700.

from exhaustion. "We are outnumbered and constant labor is impairing our men," he wrote to President Jefferson Davis in a request for more troops.[23]

Richmond had no men to spare. For one, Maj. Gen. Benjamin Butler's 30,000-man Federal Army of the James was advancing toward the Confederate capital. To the west, Maj. Gen. Franz Sigel had advanced into Virginia's Shenandoah Valley, and farther west Brig. Gen. William Averell had moved into western Virginia. Although no single action threatened to break the Confederacy's back, the simultaneous movements tied down Confederate troops at a time when Lee desperately needed reinforcements. Grant's grand strategic plan, dependent on coordinated offensive movements, was working.[24]

As Lee took stock of his situation and mulled his options, a courier arrived at his headquarters with more bad news—perhaps the worst Lee had received in the campaign. The rider, a young officer named Andrew Reid Venable Jr., who served on the staff of Jeb Stuart, came from the south astride one of Stuart's favorite horses, a gray charger. Venable passed a note to Lee, who read it in silence.

Lee leaned forward and placed both hands over his face to conceal his emotion, although it was evident to all that he was "greatly moved." Collecting himself, he spoke slowly. "Gentlemen," Lee announced, "we have very bad news. General Stuart has been mortally wounded." He paused a few moments longer, then added, "He never brought me a piece of false information."[25]

Stuart had taken a gutshot from a dismounted Federal cavalryman during a May 11 battle with Phil Sheridan's troopers at Yellow Tavern, a small village on the northern outskirts of Richmond. He died the next evening in Richmond, just before 8:00 p.m. When Lee staffer Alexander Boteler broke the news to other members of the headquarters staff, "those brave men bowed their heads and wept like children." Campfire services that night, held by the lights of the campfires, "were among the most solemn and touching" the army ever held.[26]

This was a huge personal blow to Lee, who had known Stuart for years and looked on him as a surrogate son. "[H]is devotion to Lee was so thoroughly appreciated," a Confederate staff officer attested. It took Lee several days to process the loss. "A more zealous, ardent, brave & devoted soldier, than Stuart, the Confederacy cannot have," he would write to his wife, Mary, on May 16. If he reported Stuart's death to

23 Lee, *Wartime Papers*, 729.

24 Ibid., 18-25.

25 Charles Marshall, quoted in Jeffry Wert, *Cavalryman of the Lost Cause: A Biography of J.E.B. Stuart* (New York: Simon & Schuster, 2008), 365; W. Gordon McCabe, "Major Andrew Reid Venable, Jr.," from *Richmond Dispatch*, *S.H.S.P.* 37:68.

26 Alexander Boteler, "On 'J.E.B.' Stuart's Staff," diary, 8, FSNMP BV 50.

officials in Richmond, that correspondence has been lost, although President Davis would surely have heard the news almost immediately because Stuart was already in the capital when he died. Not until May 20 would Lee issue General Orders No. 40 to formally inform the full army "with heartfelt sorrow":

> Among the gallant soldiers who have fallen in this war General Stuart was second to none in valor, in zeal, and in unfaltering devotion to his country. His achievements form a conspicuous part of the history of this army, which with his name and services will forever be associated. To military capacity of a high order and all the nobler virtues of the soldier he added the brighter graces of a pure life, guided and sustained by the Christian's faith and hope. The mysterious hand of an all wise God has removed him from the scene of his usefulness and fame. His grateful countrymen will mourn his loss and cherish his memory.[27]

The issue of Stuart's replacement at the head of the Army of Northern Virginia's cavalry would remain unresolved for the time being. Lee had two candidates to consider: one was his nephew, Fitzhugh Lee; the other was the highly competent South Carolinian, Wade Hampton. Lee probably realized, even then, that Hampton deserved the nod more, but in Lee's Virginia-centric command structure, Hampton's Palmetto State residency weighed against him, even if subconsciously. In addition, the hand of nepotism placed at least a finger on the scale in favor of Fitz.

It is easy to see May 13 as one of Lee's loneliest days in command. Stuart's death came on the heels of Longstreet's wounding, which had taken place just a few miles from where Jackson had been mortally wounded, under eerily similar circumstances, a year and four days earlier. Lee had lost the "eyes and ears" of the army, and he had lost the counsel of his "Old Warhorse." On top of that, A. P. Hill remained too sick to take the field. Richard Ewell had cracked under pressure when Federals had broken through at the Mule Shoe. Down the chain of command, dependable division and brigade commanders had been knocked out of the fight. In his May 16 letter to his wife, a disheartened Lee would admit: "I grieve the loss of our gallant officers & men, & miss their aid & sympathy."

* * *

Grant, meanwhile, was similarly assessing the condition of his own army, starting at the top. He sent a dispatch to Washington recommending the promotion

27 Sorrel, 255; Lee, *Wartime Papers*, 731; Lee, general order, May 20, 1864, *Wartime Papers*, 736.

of Army of the Potomac commander George Gordon Meade. Meade's rank came from his position as commander of volunteers, not the "regular" army—a situation Grant decided to rectify, in part, as a way to pacify Meade's growing frustrations with Grant's direct control of the Army of the Potomac. "General Meade has more than met my most sanguine expectations," Grant wrote. "He and [William T.] Sherman are the fittest officers for large commands I have come in contact with. If their services can be rewarded by promotion to the ranks of major-generals in the regular army the honor would be worthily bestowed, and I would feel personally gratified."[28]

Grant's admiration for and close working relationship with Sherman has become Civil War legend. That makes Grant's dispatch all the more illuminating: Grant did not want Sherman's promotion to go forward unless Meade's promotion went forward with it. That suggests the high professional esteem Grant held for Meade at that moment. Unfortunately, their partnership would grow increasingly tense in the weeks and months ahead—moreso on Meade's part because he chaffed under the awkward command structure, a fact Grant seemed sympathetic to even if he did nothing to change it. As it happened, Meade's promotion got bogged down even as Sherman's went through—as did a subsequent piquesome promotion for Phil Sheridan to major general in the regular army. Not until November would Grant finally press the vexing matter to resolution.

Changes were taking place further down the army's chain of command, as well. Grant had issued a battlefield promotion to Horatio Wright to take John Sedgwick's place at the head of VI Corps; on May 13, he wrote to Washington to make the assignment permanent. Grant doled out a number of other stars and various other promotions, too, and also attended to some less-desirable business. Gone, for instance, was Gershom Mott's Fourth Division in the II Corps. According to Lyman, "Mott's division . . . behaved so badly it was broken up and put with Birney—a sad record for Hooker's fighting men!" Gone, as well, was Brig. Gen. J. Hobart Ward, brought up on charges of drunkenness.[29]

Also of concern was V Corps commander Gouverneur K. Warren, who had, in Grant's estimation, been increasingly demonstrating himself to be a problem. After sending Humphreys to Warren's front on May 12 with the order to relieve Warren if the V Corps didn't attack, Grant admitted disappointment. "I feel sorry to be obliged to send such an order in regard to Warren," he told a small group of his headquarters staff. "His quickness of perception, personal gallantry, and soldierly bearing pleased me, and a few days ago I should have been inclined to place him in

28 Meade, *Life and Letters,* 196.

29 Theodore Lyman, *With Grant & Meade: From Wilderness to Appomattox* (Lincoln, NE: University of Nebraska Press, 1994), 114.

command of the Army of the Potomac in case Meade had been killed; but I began to feel, after his want of vigor assaulting on the 8th, that he was not as efficient as I believed, and his delay in attacking and the feeble character of his assaults today [May 12] confirm me in my apprehensions."[30]

Some of the criticism against the V Corps commander was unwarranted. Warren had learned hard lessons during his days of assaults across Spindle Field, while Grant and Meade seemed to miss those lessons entirely. The Confederate position had proven—repeatedly—to be unassailable, yet Grant and Meade urged him onward, over and over, to everyone's increased frustration and Grant's diminished confidence in Warren.[31]

Warren's share of the blame rest in his inability to exert any kind of creative problem-solving to his situation. For being a man who often considered himself the smartest guy in the room, he did not apply his intelligence in any way helpful to himself. Meade sustained Warren for now, but whether Warren could redeem himself remained to be seen.[32]

As Grant mulled the situation, he attended to other shuffling. The Army of the Potomac and the attached IX Corps had lost more than 36,000 men since fighting began in the Wilderness. Some of those losses included veterans whose three-year enlistments had expired. Grant replaced them by calling up a number of heavy artillery units from Washington, who had, for years, manned the defenses around the capital. They had seen more action in the city's bars and brothels than on the field of battle.

Also arriving were new units of varying quality made up of volunteers and conscripts who, over the next few days and weeks, would see the elephant for the first time. Some 9,500 men would join the army as it continued its campaign around Spotsylvania, with more still to come.[33]

Initial conversations also began to circulate for addressing another aspect of the army's manpower problem: shirkers and skulkers. "Many officers as well as men, unequal to the long physical strain, from time to time gave evidence of demoralization, dropping back from their commands as opportunity offered,

30 Porter, 108.

31 "I don't know of any other battlefield where major attacks were made over the same ground on three different days," historian Greg Mertz has pointed out. "Isn't it said that one definition of crazy is doing the exact same things over and over with the expectation of different results?" Mertz to author, email, 23 April 2024.

32 For more on that, see notes about Meade's conversation with John Rawlins on 21 June 1864, *Papers of Ulysses S. Grant*, Vol. 11, 104–6. It's a little amazing Warren survived in command all the way until the end of March 1865.

33 Mark Boatner, *The Civil War Dictionary* (New York: Random House, 1991), 788.

Lieutenant Colonel Thomas Chamberlain of the 150th Pennsylvania reported that the regiment started at Spotsylvania with 276 but, by May 14, had dwindled to 93. "[D]eath and wounds were the main factors," he explained. The addition of Company Q served as a much-needed manpower boost even if the men at first seemed of questionable merit. *Emerging Civil War*

and trying by various pretexts to get into the hospitals," recounted Thomas Chamberlain of the 150th Pennsylvania. The provost guard "relentlessly gathered up" such men and typically returned them to their own regiments for punishment, but the 150th unexpectedly found itself playing host to an especially "unique squad of men" that became known as "Company Q."

"[S]everal line-officers from other organizations, whose valor had been badly shaken by repeated conflicts, were sent, stripped of the insignia of their rank . . . and provided with the arms and accoutrements of private soldiers, to share the fortunes of the regiment," Chamberlain explained. By serving "in the fore-front of battle," the officers could "redeem, if possible, their clouded reputations." Depending on their performance and conduct, the officers would either be dismissed from the army or restored to their former positions. "It is a pleasure to state," Chamberlain concluded, "that in subsequent engagements all of these delinquents acquitted themselves so creditably that they were eventually permitted to return to their old commands."[34]

As Grant and Meade oversaw the various structural changes necessary for the army, Meade also kept his eye on preparations for the shift of troops from the Federal right to its left. The previous day's fighting had oddly instilled confidence in the "Old Snapping Turtle," who wrote his wife, Margaretta, about the army's "decided victory over the enemy, he having abandoned last night the position he so tenaciously held yesterday."

34 Thomas Chamberlain, *History of the One Hundred and Fiftieth Regiment, Pennsylvania Volunteers, Second Regiment, Bucktail Brigade* (Philadelphia: F. McManus, Jr. & Co., 1905), 240.

"Our work is not over," Meade concluded, "but we have the prestige of success, which is everything, and I trust our final success will be assured."[35]

Even the weather tried to strike a cheerful tone despite the day's recurring gloom. "'May showers' still; first bright, hot sunshine; then a heavy, black rain," recorded Lyman. "The roads a slush of gray sand and water."[36]

By nightfall, Warren had completed his preparations and was ready to march. It was, a Massachusetts officer noted, "pitch dark, raining like fury and the mud knee deep. . . . The suffering of the men is almost indescribable."[37]

Troops had to cut trees and corduroy the road for part of the way just so they could get through. "It was rainy and foggy and black dark, and the roads were beaten into sloughs," recounted Abner Small of the 16th Maine. "Here and there to mark the way were log fires, flaring and hissing in the rain, and lonely and miserable guides huddling up to the smoky blaze. The going was slow. There was much straggling."[38]

The first leg of the trip took the men past Willis Landrum's farm, then being used as a hospital following the fighting at the nearby Mule Shoe—hardly an inspiring sight for a corps preparing for battle. Then the men moved north, fording the Ny River. "They had to wade the river, and the ground, without a road, was mostly unknown," pointed out Alanson A. Haines of the 15th New Jersey, who described it as a night "of constant alarms." "We passed a man sitting upon a stone, presenting a horrible appearance," he recounted. "His arms had been torn off, and his whole face was hanging in a bloody mass in front of him."[39]

The corps marched past the Stevens house, then past the Harris farm, and then linked up with the Fredericksburg Road, where they could finally turn south toward Spotsylvania Court House. The column moved accordion-like through the pitch. "On the slightest break in the column those in advance would disappear entirely" wrote a member of the 118th Pennsylvania, "and what was left behind would be compelled to halt until somebody found them or by some accident they made connection with the advance."[40]

35 Meade, *Life and Letters,* 195.

36 Lyman, *Meade's Army*, 157.

37 George Bernard, letter, 14 May 1864, George M. Bernard Papers, P376, Reel 17, Massachusetts Historical Society, FSNMP BV 248.

38 Grant, *Memoirs*, 451; Small, 141.

39 Haines, 182.

40 Survivors' Association, 424.

And so it went until morning, according to Massachusetts officer George Bernard:

> [T]he men falling over at every step as our road took us by the woods filled with uncared for wounded, howling for help. As they heard us groping along while I saw men in the ranks so utterly wretched that they threw themselves in the middle of the road wallowing in the mud under the horses feet, howling and crying like mad-men. I never knew such a horrible night; all mud, rain, darkness, and misery.[41]

"It was the hardest nights march we ever endured as it was hot-muggy, rained, dark," wrote Capt. George Hugunin of the 147th New York. "The pioneers had cut a road through the brushy woods and the stubs would trip, as the mud was deep and we found 2 streams, this was one of our movements and headquarters got to their position about daylight. . . . I wished I was a private so I could quietly drop beside the road and sleep without anyone saying anything."[42]

For those privates, though, their exhaustion went to the bone. "We stood sorely in need of both quiet and rest, having been continually on the march and fight since the night of the third of May," wrote John Haley of the 17th Maine. "My endurance has been so outrageously taxed that I sometimes envy those who have laid down their lives; they sweetly sleep while we toil on."[43] It was as close to dead tired as the living could get.

The 12th day of the campaign was, even then, trying to push through the gray clouds.

41 Bernard.

42 George Hugunin, diary, 14 May 1864, 23-24, FSNMP BV 358.

43 Haley, 158.

# May 10
# May 11
# May 12
# May 13
# May 14

Shift left and attack at dawn: Grant's quick-strike plan. He hoped to catch a weak spot in Lee's line before Lee had the chance to react to the shift.

But Grant had still not yet learned one of the most important lessons of the campaign: the Army of the Potomac did not handle with the same road performance as his smaller, more flexible armies in the West. It did not move with alacrity, lacking, in the words of a Federal staff officer, "springy formation, and audacious, self-reliant initiative."[1]

And so dawn, such as it was, broke on May 14 with the VI Corps and most of the V Corps still in motion. Fewer than 2,500 of Warren's 14,000 or so men were ready to attack, the rest of the column still strung out in the mud. "[T]he troops, wearied and scattered by their night march, were in no condition to do anything beyond establishing a line," admitted Abner Small of the 16th Maine.[2]

Warren, under scrutiny from headquarters because of his spotty performance thus far, had a lot riding on a successful maneuver, but he was flummoxed. "I have spared no effort, but my men could not be gotten up . . ." he lamented to Meade. "I have not more with me than would make a good skirmish line for the corps."

How "good" the skirmish line could have been is debatable: Warren reported those men as "excessively weary."[3] Wright's corps, meanwhile, had to wait for Warren's strung-out column to clear out of the way before they—equally weary and strung-out—could even get into position.

1 Schaff, 201.

2 Small, 141.

3 David Jordan, *"Happiness Is Not My Companion": The Life of General G.K. Warren* (Bloomington, IN: Indiana University Press, 2001), 153.

At 6:30 a.m., Warren admitted defeat. "The understanding I had was to attempt to carry the enemy's line by surprise at dawn this morning," he wrote to headquarters. "My inability to get my men here prevented this. My men are gradually coming in, but a large portion will be all day, and are exhausted with fatigue. I do not think they are in condition to fight to advantage."[4]

The entire maneuver was a failure.

Not that speed would have mattered. "The enemy was found in front ubiquitous as ever, and leisurely engaged in strengthening his works which was understood to be of long standing and very formidable," wrote a New York newspaper correspondent. A dejected Warren reported as early as 4:00 a.m.: "The enemy is here in some force."[5]

Even as Warren's men trudged along sloppy roads to get into position, Confederate Third Corps commander Jubal Early had realized something was happening. He sent word to Lee that the Federals were on the move, and although he had no details, he readied for a possible engagement. Early's corps held a strong line northwest of the Fredericksburg Road. His fortified men had clear fields of fire; beyond, rivers, streams, and marshes provided natural obstructions to bog down any advances against them. The fresh rainfall had made the terrain especially difficult to cross, leaving some parts of Early's line nearly impossible to strike.

To the east of the road, though, Early's line was not as strong, and the Third Corps's flank essentially hung in the air, although Federals would not discover this until later in the morning, after the VI Corps settled in on that sector of the battlefield.

Meanwhile, the V Corps settled into positions near the Fredericksburg Road. Some men filled works left empty by Burnside's shift toward the East Angle and Heth's Salient; others extended the Federal line farther to the southeast. Many simply filed into place and crashed.

As the morning wore on, the weather broke and a breeze kicked up. "The land was all aglow with sunlight," wrote a member of the 118th Pennsylvania, the Corn Exchange Regiment, "all the heavy somber clouds had disappeared, the pelting rain had ceased to fall, every blade and spear of grass danced and glistened in the radiance of a noon-day sun." Behind the Federal line, "The sluggish Ny traced a devious course over fallow and meadow and through the wood, until it lost itself in the greater streams beyond."[6]

4 *O.R.* 36:2:756.

5 Anonymous, "The Grand Campaign: A Pause in the Struggle," Albany *Atlas & Argus*, 18 May 1864, FSNMP BV 401; *O.R.* 36:2:755.

6 Survivors' Association, 426

"We laid around all day drying out and brushing off, cleaning up, making rifle pits," wrote Capt. George Hugunin of the 147th New York. "[T]he ground was muddy and springy so we could not dig much as we would have to stand and lay in the mud and water."[7]

But the New York newspaper correspondent recorded observations differently. "The advance forces of both armies were quietly digging within four hundred yards of each other, exposing their bodies in full view without firing a shot…" he wrote. "[T]he troops on both sides were too worn out by hard fighting and marching to waste their strength in the useless animosities of the picket line."[8]

Warren made his headquarters at Whig Hill, the home of Francis C. Beverly just off the south edge of the Fredericksburg Road. Meade and Grant, meanwhile, made their headquarters on the Anderson farm, a half-mile east. Meade had arrived on the eastern sector of the battlefield shortly after dawn, peevish because of Warren's failure, and settled in at the Anderson house to help direct Wright into line. "It was a quite large place, built with a nest of out-houses in the southern style," wrote Theodore Lyman.

> They have a queer way of building on one thing after another, the great point being to have a separate shed or out-house for every purpose, and then a lot more sheds and outhouses for the negroes. You will find a carpenter's shop, tool-room, coach-shed, pig-house, stable, out-kitchen, two or three barns, and half-a-dozen negro huts, besides the main house, where the family lives. Of the larger houses, perhaps a quarter are of brick, the rest of wood. They are plain, rarely with any ornament; in fact, these "mansions" are only farmhouses of a better class.[9]

Although Warren could not make a major assault on May 14, he had spied a moderate prominence to his southwest known as Bleak Hill, "a bold, round hill on the south bank of the Ny, upon which was a well-appointed farmer's dwelling." The home belonged to John Henry and Mary Elizabeth Myer, who had just purchased the 400-acre farmstead a year earlier. John had since been conscripted into the 40th Virginia Infantry—on May 14, he was hunkered down in Heth's Salient, in the shadow of his hilltop homestead—and Mary and their three small children had left the house to a caretaker named Jett.

7 Ibid.

8 Anonymous, "The Grand Campaign."

9 Lyman, *Meade's Headquarters*, 115–16.

John Henry Myer, photographed here as a young man, bought his Spotsylvania farm to get away from war-torn Fredericksburg. He had owned a home and a shop in the heart of downtown, where he worked first as a saddler then as a baker and confectioneer. *Fredericksburg Area Museum*

The Myer house sat on a plateau at about 300 feet up the hill, though the ground rose beyond as high as 330 feet, making it an ideal spot for Confederate observers to spy on the Federal army—but if held by the Federals, it would allow them to spy on Lee's army, in turn, and perhaps allow them to threaten Lee's right flank. The hill seemed only lightly defended. "There was a rebel cavalry regiment there," Lyman noted, "and we plainly could see them with our glasses, walking about and taking it easy."[10]

Warren ordered Romeyn Ayres to take the position.[11] Ayres sent the 140th New York and 91st Pennsylvania up the hill—the same units that had opened the Overland Campaign in Saunders Field in the Wilderness on May 5. The 140th, bedecked in their flamboyant Zouave uniforms with baggy pantaloons and red fezzes, had been whittled down to 210 men after starting the campaign with 529. The 140th's Lt. Col. Elwell S. Otis led the task force. "It was like witnessing a puppet-show!" said Lyman, still watching through his spyglass. "Our men suddenly came out from the woods and ran, as hard as they could, at the house."[12]

Partway up the hill, the two regiments encountered troopers from the 9th Virginia Cavalry, part of Brig. Gen. John Chambliss's Brigade. Many of the cavalrymen were local men from the town and surrounding countryside. Home field advantage or not, Ayres's infantrymen made short work of the horsemen and captured the hill. The caretaker of the Myer house, Jett, took shots at the Federals from the house before thinking better of it and followed Chambliss's example.

10 Lyman, *Meade's Army*, 158.

11 Survivors Association, 426–27.

12 Quoted in John F. Cummings III, "The Struggle for and Tragedy of Myer's Hill," *On the Front Line*, Winter 2019, 7. The author wishes to acknowledge the yeoman's work Cummings has done over decades to advocate for the preservation of Myer's Hill and the stories of the men who fought there.

Mary Elizabeth Myer (left) and three of the Myer children (right). John and Mary also lost three children, all under the age of two, to illness. *Fredericksburg Area Museum*

---

Chambliss was not set to give up so easily, though. He rallied the two other regiments of his brigade and, together, the three surrounded Otis's suddenly beleaguered force, pinning them around the buildings of the Myer's homestead.

Ayres had not been the only Federal with his eyes on the hill, however. Colonel Emory Upton, marching at the head of the VI Corps column, saw another opportunity for himself and his four undersized regiments, some 800 men in all—about half as many as Upton had started with. Upton nonetheless felt confident he had enough strength to capture the hill, and he rode directly to Grant and Meade to say so. The commanders, at their headquarters at the Anderson fouse, were watching the unfolding action on Myer's Hill. "I can take that hill with my brigade," Upton proclaimed. "I hope you will let me try it; I'm certain I can make it."[13]

Meade gave the okay, and Upton and his brigade arrived on the hilltop at 10:00 a.m., just in time to scatter Chambliss's men for good. "The position was occupied easily," declared Isaac Best. Otis, relieved, got word from Meade that his men could retire. Upton's men, meanwhile, began constructing fortifications using fence rails near some of the Myer farm's slave cabins, "making protection of the rails as best we could."[14]

13 Porter, 118.

14 Best, *History*, 149; Ibid., 149-51.

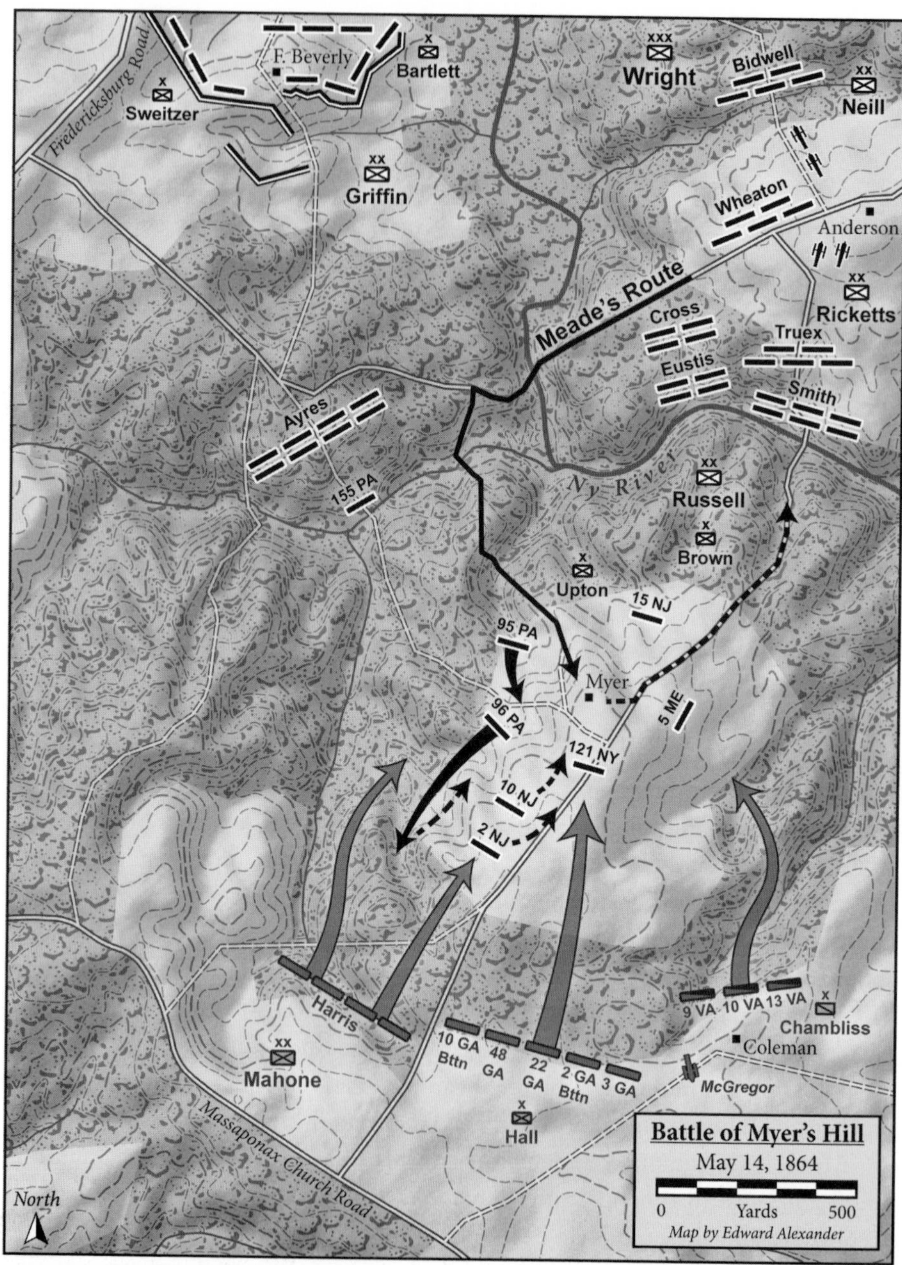


**Battle of Myer's Hill**—Upton's brigade occupied Myer's Hill following its capture by the 140th New York and the 91st Pennsylvania. Meade rode to the hilltop for a look at the ground and nearly ended up a prisoner when Confederates counterattacked, sweeping Federals from the hill. Meade then ordered a counter-counterattack, which reclaimed the hill even as Confederates withdrew under orders.

"[R]ather gruff with a sense of humor . . . [Jubal] Early was ambitious, critical, and outspoken to the point of insubordination," says historian Donald C. Pfanz of "Old Jube." "Under certain circumstances he could be devious and malevolent." *Library of Congress*

"We rapidly got into our rail barricades, and swallowing what we could of our food in a hurry at the same time, we watched for the Rebs to appear," recounted Col. Clinton Beckwith of the 121st New York. "We knew we would be the first to be attacked because a piece of woods in our front reached to within 600 feet of our position, and the rail fence running along it would conceal and shelter the advancing force until they came up to it."[15]

Lookouts climbed to the roof of the Myer house. From there, they could see the town and Early's corps to the northwest. Lee's right flank, which extended past the village along the Massaponax Church Road, essentially hung in the air. Chambliss's cavalry had been the anchor—and the Myer's Hill task force had driven them off.

Upton knew Early would want his hill back, so he called for reinforcements. They came in the form of two more battered regiments, the 2nd and 10th New Jersey. That gave Upton six regiments atop Myer's Hill, totaling perhaps 1,200 effectives. The two Garden State regiments filed in as backstop support behind a semi-circle of Upton's brigade: the 96th and 95th Pennsylvania, the 121st New York, and the 5th Maine, from right to left.[16]

And, indeed, Early did want his hill back. Lee had been slow to recognize the growing threat on his right, and had Grant been able to launch a major attack against that sector of the line, an opportunity might have presented itself. As it was, Lee's "Bad Old Man" acted vigilantly enough for himself and his commander. Early dispatched Brig. Gen. Ambrose "Rans" Wright's five Georgia regiments and battalions, and Nathaniel Harris's four small Mississippi regiments. Harris's men

15 Ibid., 150.

16 William Matter, *If It Takes All Summer: The Battle of Spotsylvania* (Chapel Hill, NC: UNC Press, 1988), 285.

had been brutalized a few days earlier at the Bloody Angle, while Wright's men had seen comparatively less action in the campaign thus far. A state senator from Georgia, Wright was one of the countless politicians who doubled as officers, although he and his men had earned a solid reputation as hard fighters. Chambliss's troopers, who had initially held the hill, rode on their right flank as support.[17]

The Southerners advanced up the hill from the south, emerging from the woods and across an open field. The Federal lookouts atop the Myer house spotted them, giving Upton the chance to send the 96th Pennsylvania and two companies of the 2nd New Jersey to intercept. Henry Keiser of the 96th said they "had not gone far when a short distance ahead, I seen a Rebel hat lying on the edge of a gully washed out along the edge of the woods. I says to . . . the man to my right, 'There is a Rebel hat, and the Rebel is not far off.' I soon seen the top of a Reb's head, who was sitting down in the gully." It turned out to be a lone officer, a major in Wright's brigade, "but not one minute after he was taken to the rear, we ran into two full lines of Rebs, and I tell you, we were not slow in getting back, each one for himself."[18]

The Federal skirmishers "had scarcely disappeared in the woods when they met the enemy, and immediately the battle broke out," Best, watching from the semicircle of defensive works, would write.[19]

As Pennsylvanians and New Jerseyans fell back, the rest of Upton's men, from behind the safety of their hilltop fortifications, opened fire—but onward the Georgians still came. "Their alignment was perfect, their steps regular and unwavering," praised one of Chambliss's watching horsemen, "and when cannon shots or bullets made gaps in their line, they were promptly filled up, and when a color-bearer was shot down, another man at once seized the flag."[20]

Chambliss's troopers, meanwhile, hit the 5th Maine on the Mainers' left flank, and the New Englanders crumbled. The 2nd New Jersey, just behind them, took the brunt of the attack. Their colonel, Charles Wiebecke, "raised himself from behind the protection of a few rails, whence his men were firing, to reconnoiter the advancing foe. While doing so, he was struck by a bullet, which entered at the

17 Harry Pfanz, *Gettysburg: The Second* Day (Chapel Hill, NC: UNC Press, 1987), 388-89. For instance, Wright's men advanced father than any other Confederates at the battle of Gettysburg. On July 2, they reached deeper into the Federal center than Pickett's men did on July 3. Wright even claimed that he eyed a small white house on the far side of Cemetery Ridge. If this is true, he was either looking at the Jacob Hummelbaugh house and some its outbuildings—the site of the death of William Barksdale July 3—or he was looking at Lydia Leister's farm, which was Meade's headquarters.

18 Henry Keiser, diary, 112, FSNMP BV 41.

19 Best, *History*, 150.

20 George William Beale, *A Lieutenant of Cavalry in Lee's Army* (Boston: The Gorham Press, 1918), 143.

right eye, penetrated to his brain, causing instant death. His men were compelled to fall back immediately, leaving his body for a few hours with the rebels." Confederates plundered Wiebecke's corpse for his watch, money, and much of his clothing. Comrades would later bury him "in a beautiful spot" along the Ny.[21]

Colonel Charles Wiebecke, initially buried on the battlefield, now rests in Fredericksburg National Cemetery. *Library of Congress*

Lieutenant Sheldon Redway of the 121st New York attempted to prevent a Federal rout. As he gathered a few men around him, an artillery shell crashed in and threw the men into further disarray.[22]

"We gave the yell and they commenced skedaddling," wrote Charlie Booher of the 2nd Battalion of Georgia Infantry. The Federals fell back through the complex of buildings around the Myer house, through an orchard, and down the face of the hill. "[W]e drove them across the river 'pell mell' throwing away guns, knapsacks, etc.," recalled Alfred Zachry of the 3rd Georgia.[23]

The Ny River, "dark and silent," waited at the bottom of the hill as a final obstacle. Thinking they would run across, men simply plunged in, not realizing the narrow rivulet ran a deceptive course. "[T]he water was too deep and they were fished out, wetter and wiser men," said one soldier. Pennsylvanian Henry Keiser got over the Ny on a submerged log, but not everyone was so lucky. "A poor excited soldier jumped into the stream right below me, with his knapsack still on his back," Keiser acknowledged, "and all that could be seen after were a few bubbles."[24]

It was "run for sweet life," said Daniel Holt, the 121st New York's surgeon. "[W]e come flying back in all sorts of a hurry. Every man for himself. . . . Plenty of

21 Cummings, 8.

22 Best, *History*, 150.

23 Charlie Booher, letter, June 12, 1864, FSNMP BV 378; Alfred Zachry, "Four Shots for the Cause," *Civil War Times Illustrated*, Nov./Dec. 1994, 103.

24 Best, 150; Keiser, diary.

grape and canister, minie balls and shot help us over the ground. Their arguments are useless. We will get away just as fast as we can without them." The affair christened the Ny with a new nickname, he said: "From the fact that we ran *so well* and after the command to *advance*, it is henceforth to be known as 'Upton's Run!'"[25]

Upton did his best to rally his men. Atop his mount, he appeared along the south bank of the river, trying to bring order to the chaos. He ordered his men to cross to the north side and then rally on the colors in an adjacent field.[26]

Early's men pursued a couple hundred yards but were largely content to hold the hilltop and settle in. "We killed, wounded and captured over 200, suffering a loss of 100 ourselves . . ." said Peach Tree State soldier Charlie Booher. "We got a fine lot of Yankee plunder such as knapsacks, haversacks filled with crackers, meat, sugar and coffee, rubber clothes, tents, etc."[27]

According to Federal artillerist Charles Wainwright, Upton was lucky Early had not scooped up the entire band: "A strong force of rebs pounced upon him so suddenly that they were within an ace of making all prisoners."[28]

* * *

Luckiest of all, perhaps, was George Meade.

Once Upton had first secured the Myers' farmstead, Meade decided to ride to the top of the hill and see for himself what vantage point the position offered. What might he learn about Lee's lines? What might he learn about his own? What might he have prevented Lee from seeing by denying Lee the hill?

Accompanied by VI Corps commander Horatio Wright, Meade and his staff forded the Ny along a farm lane from the Anderson house. They circled from the north up to the crest of the hill, where they saw Upton's busy men fortifying. At some point, the skies opened, and with "the shower at its height," the gaggle of generals and staffers "rode up to this house, entered it and sat down for a light conference."[29]

Not long after, the rattle of musketry outside startled them. An instant later, another volley, nearer. Yells and shouts. Bullets began hitting the house. Everyone tumbled out of the home to see Upton's men falling back around them. The

25 Holt, 189.

26 Ibid, 150–51

27 Booher, letter.

28 Wainwright, 371–72.

29 Quotes here and next paragraph from Anonymous, "The Grand Campaign."

Alfred Waud sketched "Narrow escape of Genl. Meade 1864": "Some cavalry dashing out of the woods suddenly upon the genl. and his attendants came very near cutting off their retreat and making a capture of the party. Prominent near the genl., Col. Michler on a rough track or farm road that wound along the foot of a tree covered knoll out from which came the rebs to cut them off." *Library of Congress*

generals mounted their horses when, said an observer, "the enemy came down upon the house and the troops around it like wolves."

"Gen. Meade had to gallop for it," Lyman recalled, "and, not being familiar with the paths came quite near enough being cut off!"[30] Engineer Nathaniel Michler, who had earlier scouted the area as part of a mapmaking project for Meade, knew the way to a ford. The Confederates "were close on Genl. M's heels," recalled Maj. James C. Biddle of Meade's staff. "[T]hey cut him off." As the party neared the

30 Lyman, *Meade's Headquarters,* 159.

river, seven troopers from the 13th Virginia Cavalry swooped in on Meade's flank. With Federal infantry also swarming to the river, Meade's party took advantage of the confusion and turned the tables on the Virginians, taking them all prisoner.[31]

Meade was not quite out of the woods yet, though. The refugees dislodged from the top of the hill continued to create a tangle. Colonel Clark Edwards of the 5th Maine had a servant named Jimmy "who was leading my pack-horse covered with kettle, coffee-pots, etc., behind my second horse." As Meade rode by, "his stirrup accidentally caught in some trappings and the General, narrowly escaped being thrown into the river."[32]

* * *

As Meade recouped from his misadventure on the hill, Grant took the time to catch up on administrative matters. He had an entire war to run, after all, and Myer's Hill was but a tiny blip on this full canvass.

To catch up on his correspondence, he looked for a temporary office, settling on the Gayle house. Wounded men filled the porch, the rooms—all "in accordance with the usual custom of wounded men to seek a house," Porter recounted. "It seems to be a natural instinct, as a house conveys the idea of shelter and of home."[33]

Porter looked for a dry spot where Grant might be able to lay out his maps and write his letters. In the back room, they found a single chair occupied by a Confederate corporal—a W. R. Thraxton of Georgia, as it turned out, recently wounded in the fight at the top of the hill. "[He] had been shot in the right cheek just under the eye, the ball coming out near the left ear," Porter saw. "A mass of coagulated blood covered his face and neck, and he presented a shocking appearance."

Lyman, who had seen Thraxton earlier, described him as "positively facetious! His face was black and swelled and he talked thickly, but seemed otherwise vigorous. . . . He saw & heard perfectly."[34]

The corporal certainly saw Grant and stood the moment he and Porter entered. Thraxton smiled, bowing. "Here," he said, "take my chair, sir."

31 James C. Biddle, letter, May 16, 1864, James C. Biddle Papers at the Historical Society of Pennsylvania, Philadelphia, Pennsylvania, FSNMP 404; Third Pennsylvania Cavalry Association, 426–27.

32 Clark Edwards, "War Reminiscences of the Bethel Company, Company I, Fifth Maine Regiment. No. 20," 17, FSNMP BV 316.

33 This full story comes from Porter, 119. Porter later reported, "Thirty-three years afterwards I discovered . . . that he was in excellent health and living in Macon."

34 Lyman, *Meade's Headquarters,* 158.

"Ah, you need that chair much more than I," Grant replied, "Keep your seat. I see you are badly hurt."

"If you folks let me go back to our lines, I think I ought to be able to get a leave to go home and see my girl," the corporal said good-naturedly. "But I reckon she wouldn't know me now."

"I will see that one of our surgeons does all in his power for you," Grant promised. He sent in a surgeon to tend to Thraxton and found another place to do his work.

* * *

If luck rode with Meade on May 14, it had also spent the day with Lee at his Zion Church headquarters on the edge of Spotsylvania Court House. Lee still had not awakened to the potential seriousness of the situation on his right. Had Grant forged ahead with any large-scale attack against that flank during the day, the Army of Northern Virginia would have been hard-pressed to mount a credible defense.

A midafternoon dispatch from First Corps commander Richard Anderson finally snapped Lee from his sluggishness. "The enemy have disappeared from opposite our extreme left," Anderson reported at 3:30 p.m. "Their pickets and sharpshooters have just retired, and there are no troops in the breast-works. I have not yet ascertained the full extent of the movement, but am inclined to believe that it includes the entire right of the enemy's line."[35]

Lee urged Second Corps commander Richard Ewell to find out if he still had any Yankees in his front—he did—and now Early's reports about the Federals along the Ny began to take on a much different, and more ominous, shape. Lee quickly ordered Anderson to shift troops from his extreme left to the army's right. Extending his line would leave Early's small force atop Myer's Hill isolated, so he informed his Bad Old Man that he did not need to hold his position there.

That was just as well for Early, because at that moment, Meade's temper was up. Infuriated that his men had lost Myer's Hill—and probably just as angry, or angrier, that he had nearly been captured—"Old Peppery" was going on the offensive. He ordered Horatio Wright to retake the hill, authorizing him to use two of his VI Corps divisions and a division from the V Corps, as well.

Two batteries bombarded the hill in preparation for the assault, which was again led by Ayers's V Corps men. "[W]hen all was ready the bugle sounded the charge and we broke from cover like quarter horses and with a volley of cheers mounted the hill," said a member of the 12th U.S. Infantry.

35 Anderson to Lee, May 14, 1864, *O.R.* 51:2:929.

> The rebs were lying on the other side to avoid our shells which were hissing and exploding around the crest and when they heard our cheers supposed a mighty force was coming and so they ran like the devil. When we got on to the top of the hill we saw the last of them going on the double about half a mile beyond. It was now dusk and our artillery men could not see us on the hill and so continued their fire. We had to get behind the hill to get out of our own fire, several men were killed before we could let them know their mistake. . . . The prisoners said that Gen. Lee and staff were on the hill an hour before we took it. We left it about 9 p.m. in charge of Pa. troops who will work all night throwing up entrenchments.[36]

Early had slipped away under Lee's orders even as Ayres—and then the two VI Corps divisions—converged on the hilltop. Myer's Hill was securely in Federal hands.

On the porch of the Myer house, the Federals found one of their own sitting in a rocking chair, shot dead during Early's attack, his rifle still in his hands. The Myers' family dog lay on the ground nearby, also shot dead. Inside, they found "six rebs who had got down [in the] cellar to get out of the way of the shells & found a number of our men who had been wounded in the other charge—the dead bodies of the volunteers who were killed were stripped naked by the rebs." Such treatment prompted a newspaper correspondent to report, "[T]he enemy behaved toward our dead and wounded with remarkable barbarity."[37]

The Federals would return the favor. The next day, May 15, they torched the Myer house in retaliation for the potshots caretaker Jett had taken at them on May 14. "It was a good building," Holt wrote, "and its destruction helped to pay for that shot."[38]

John Henry Myer, hunkered in the trenches of Heth's Salient as a conscripted member of the 40th Virginia, no doubt saw the column of smoke billowing from the hilltop.

36 C. Bowen, diary, May 14, 1864.

37 Beale, 144; Bowen, diary; Anonymous, "The Grand Campaign."

38 Holt, 189.

# May 11 May 12 May 13 May 14 May 15–17

May 15 brought more rain. "The whole country is a sea of mud," wrote a Federal artillerist. The weather meant more delay for Grant. "The very heavy rains of the past three days have rendered the roads so impassable that but little will be done until there is a change of weather, unless the enemy should attack, which they have exhibited little inclination to do for the last week," the general wrote in a dispatch to Washington.[1]

Indeed, Lee was still trying to discern the nature of Grant's recent movements. Unsure if all Federal troops had shifted from the Brock Road sector to the Fredericksburg Road sector, the Confederate commander sent out a mixed reconnaissance force to gain intelligence. Up the Brock Road went Brig. Gen. Thomas Rosser's Laurel Brigade of cavalry and Joseph Kershaw's infantry division from Anderson's First Corps.

Kershaw's men soon found deserted works, abandoned arms, and some aide stations and hospitals. Eventually they came upon troops of Hancock's II Corps, which now stood as the Federal army's right flank. The II Corps had been ordered overnight to prepare for a morning march that would reposition them behind the IX Corps—an attempt by Meade to reunite the Army of Potomac since Burnside still operated independently of, although in conjunction with, Meade's forces.

When Kershaw's men appeared on their reconnaissance mission, Hancock's men took up positions near the Landrum farm on the same ground they had made their assault across on May 12. Kershaw, not knowing the exact size of the Federal force, tested the line, held by David Birney's division. Birney's men had been the last II Corps

1 Wainwright, 372; Grant to Halleck, May 15, 1864, *O.R.* 36:2:781.

soldiers in place and represented the Federal army's extreme right flank. Kershaw attacked them aggressively. John Brown Gordon of the Confederate Second Corps sent a small force to aid Kershaw's men with a sustained artillery barrage. "[T]he enemy administered a vigorous shelling," wrote Francis A. Walker of the II Corps.[2]

Although battered, Birney's men managed to hold their own, allowing the bulk of the II Corps to finish its movement. By 1:00 p.m., Kershaw withdrew. Had Lee thrown his entire First Corps at Birney instead of just Kershaw's Division, the Army of Northern Virginia could have destroyed one of Hancock's finest divisions. Such opportunities for Lee would be few and far between, yet Anderson and Kershaw, still inexperienced in their new positions, let this one slip by. Birney rejoined the II Corps, which eventually went into bivouac around the Harris farm along the Fredericksburg Road, where it could support both Warren and Wright as well as Burnside.[3]

* * *

Aside from Kershaw's reconnaissance, Lee also sent a cavalry detachment under Thomas Rosser on an intelligence-gathering mission later that afternoon.

The 27-year-old Rosser had attended West Point, where he roomed with future Federal cavalry luminary George Armstrong Custer. Two weeks before graduation, Rosser left West Point because of the outbreak of the Civil War. A resident of east Texas and a native of Virginia, he chose to cast his lot with the Confederacy.

Rosser started the war as an artillerist, leading the famed Washington Artillery of New Orleans. By midsummer 1862, he was promoted to command the 5th Virginia Cavalry. Following the battle of Gettysburg in July 1863, he was promoted to command of the Laurel Brigade as a brigadier general. Known "as a daring and successful soldier" with "a reputation for courage and dash," Rosser was popular with his men. The brigade historian described him as "Tall, broad-shouldered and muscular, with black hair and moustache, dark brown eyes, strong jaw, and a countenance denoting self-confidence, a good horseman and always superbly mounted."[4]

Rosser had already been out the day before and had caused trouble for a Federal field hospital near the Brown farm, where Hancock's men had assembled prior to their May 12 attack. More than 600 wounded men, not yet able to transfer to better hospital accommodations in Fredericksburg, spread across the

2 Walker, 482.

3 Gordon, *Reminiscences*, 288-92.

4 William Naylor McDonald, *A History of the Laurel Brigade* (Baltimore, MD: Sun Job Printing Office, 1907), 196.

Brigadier General Thomas Rosser—called "Tex" by his friend George Armstrong Custer—seemed ubiquitous at Spotsylvania, which only helped to underscore the absence of Federal cavalry. *Library of Congress*

yard of a home owned by 64-year-old Elizabeth Couse, a former New Yorker with strong Union sympathies. Mrs. Couse also housed a number of refugees from local farms and homes that had been overrun by the armies. Rosser's men swooped in, drove away Hancock's pickets, stole as much as they could, liberated 80 wounded Confederates at the hospital, and kidnapped several Federal medical attendants. Hancock got word of the raid and sent the 12th New Jersey to the hospital, but Rosser's men vanished before the Garden State men arrived.

Now on May 15, Rosser's Brigade moved north again, even farther into the Federal right rear—a maneuver that left him dangerously isolated. He was far from reinforcements, and the roads his men traversed were muddy. Continuing thunderstorms throughout the day only worsened travel conditions.

Rosser and his men set off from Todd's Tavern on the Brock Road, then turned northeast along the Catharpin Road in an effort to gain the Orange Plank Road. Grant's supply train was reportedly lined up along that road in the vicinity of the former Chancellorsville battlefield, and Rosser wanted to see what he might be able to do to throw it into turmoil. "Some of the boys said he only took the brigade down to hold the usual Sunday morning service, as the General had recently joined the Episcopal Church," one trooper joked, "but others remarked that he made a mistake in the prayer book, as Colt's was not generally used in that Church."[5]

Ironically, one Federal soldier Rosser was about to sermonize would describe the feeling in his camp as if "[e]very person felt nearly as secure as though at church at home." Just after passing Piney Branch Church, the horsemen found the

5 Frank M. Myers, *The Comanches: A History of White's Battalion, Virginia Cavalry* (Baltimore, MD: Kelly, Piet & Co., Publishers, 1871), 281.

2nd Ohio Cavalry, encamped along the Catharpin Road. The Ohioans were one of four cavalry regiments assigned to the IX Corps—the only troopers left with Grant's forces after Sheridan had ridden away with all of the Army of the Potomac's cavalry. Assigned to protect supply lines and move prisoners to the rear, the veteran Ohio regiment was unprepared to receive the enemy. Except for pickets on the south bank of a tributary of the Ny River, most of the men were on the north bank, dismounted with their horses unsaddled.[6]

"The bottom of the creek was a regular mire hole," recalled Pvt. William James Smith of the 2nd Ohio Cavalry. "The only place it could be crossed was at the road, where there had been a ford made by filling it up with stone. As soon as the pickets were fired on, the [company] that was saddled up dashed across to help those on the other side hold them back, and the five companies left in camp divided, half grabbing their guns and running to the creek to help them back over, while the rest saddled up."[7]

Smith had run into Rosser's horsemen once already that morning. He and two other troopers had been sent to check on the field hospital at the Couse House when a contingent of Rosser's men rode up, looking to pick a fight with the 12th New Jersey, which had departed hours earlier with a few hundred wounded who were able to travel. Smith made a lucky getaway. "I had a good horse, and used my spurs, and after about a four mile spurt got away," he recounted. "Oh no, I didn't run from them. That might be called cowardly. I just FLEW." The other two troopers in his detail "landed in Andersonville," he added. Smith had just returned to his regiment's base and reported his incident to his commanding officer when Rosser's main force appeared on the Piney Branch Road.

With a roar, Rosser's men fell on them. "If the fool Johnnies had only kept their throats closed, they would have bagged the regiment almost entire," said one Ohio trooper.[8]

Regimental commander Maj. A. Bayard Nettleton immediately sent word rearward for reinforcements. He knew Federal infantry guarded the wagon train; if he could hold the Confederates off long enough, that infantry might be able to rescue his troopers, which were outnumbered more than 2-to-1.

But rather than merely wait for the infantry to come up, Nettleton ordered his men to fall back toward those reinforcements, thus shortening the gap the infantry

6 Gordon C. Rhea, *To the North Anna River: Grant and Lee, May 13-25, 1864* (Baton Rouge, LA: Louisiana State University Press, 2000)103.

7 William James Smith, "Just a Little Bit of the Civil War, as Seen by W. J. Smith, Company M, 2nd O.V. Cavalry—Part I," Robert W. Hatton, ed., *Ohio History Journal*, 84 (1975), 114.

8 Rhea, *To the North Anna River,* 103.

would have to travel. "The road from where we were to the plank road was through an almost impenetrable woods, and very crooked, and the crooks helped us out," Smith said. "At a bend in the road we would form, three or four deep across the road, and as the Rebs would come around the next corner, we would empty our seven-shooters, then fall back, when they got to the next corner, another volley awaited them." By the time they got to the Alrich farm, though, at the intersection of the Catharpin Road and the Plank Road, "we were out on open ground, and surely needed help."[9]

The 35th Virginia Battalion of Cavalry led the chase. Known as "White's Comanches," the unit held the distinction of being the first Confederate unit to enter the town of Gettysburg 10 months earlier, tangling with Pennsylvania militia. Today, they drove the Ohioans back, although they were about to find a more formidable foe ahead.

Several miles to the north, Edward Ferrero's division in the IX Corps protected the Federal wagon train. A former New York City dance instructor, Ferrero had earned a reputation as a proven combat leader. At Antietam, Ferrero's men took the Rohrbach Bridge after severe fighting. Now he commanded a division of USCT. Assigned to protect the rear of Grant's forces, Ferrero's men had never seen combat. "We have not had any engagement as yet though we have been drawn up in line of battle a number of times . . ." wrote Lt. Charles F. Stinson of the 19th USCT. "I think Gen Grant don't intend to put us in the fight unless he is short of men. Our Div. is guarding wagon trains or on picket all the time where it would take white troops, so we are of service."[10]

As it turned out, guard duty gave the USCT their first glimpses of the Army of Northern Virginia—and, for the Confederates, their first glimpses of black soldiers. Rebels captured during the May 12 fighting and sent to the rear found themselves marching past the wagon train. The USCT were "camped as if there were no enemy within twenty miles," a member of the 33rd Virginia said scornfully; "the men camping & dawdling about & the officers lounging and smoking in their tents & within sound of the frightful musketry at Spotsylvania C.H. where the fate of an empire seemed to tremble in the balance."[11]

The African-American soldiers, willing and able to fight, wanted the chance to help tip that trembling balance, as any of them would attest. The problem was that most Federal commanders had no idea how to employ them. The USCT

9 Smith, 114.

10 Charles F. Stinson, letter, May 19, 1864, L. Leigh Collection, USMHI, FSNMP BV 106.

11 Anonymous, Hotchkiss Papers, LOC, FSNMP BV 55. The soldier's screed only went downhill from there, tainted by his racism and his bitterness at being captured.

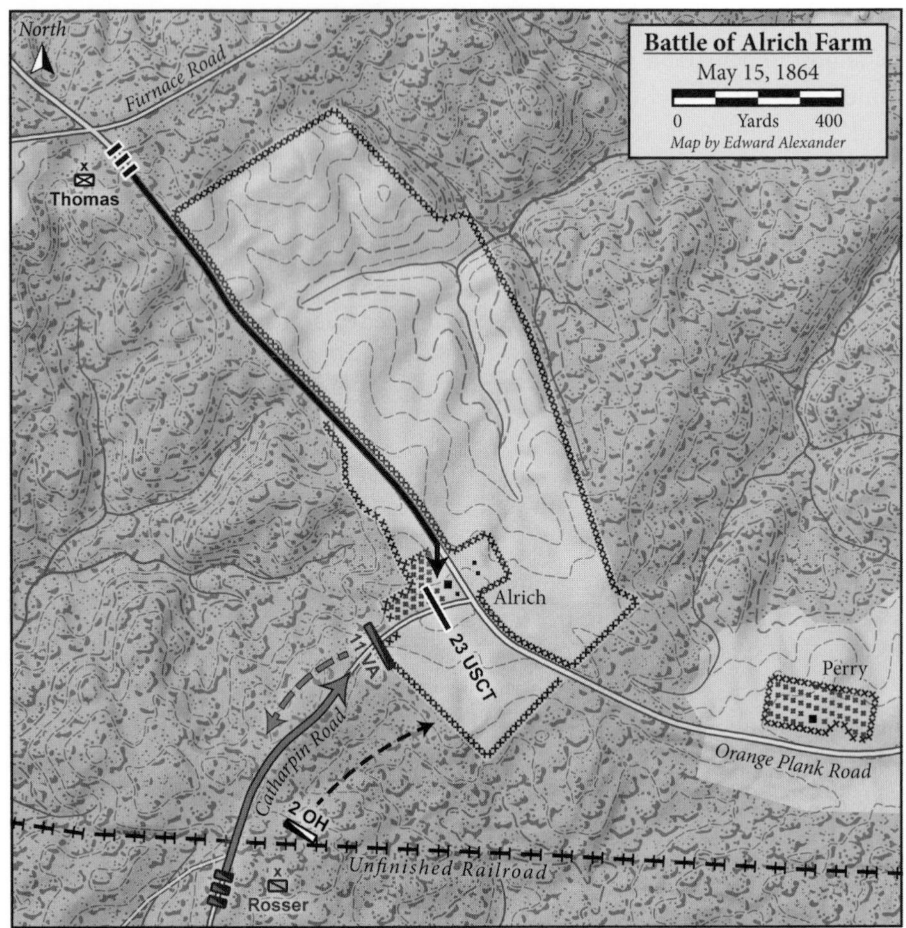


**Battle of Alrich Farm**—First contact between the Army of Northern Virginia and the United States Colored Troops resulted in a decisive defeat for Thomas Rosser's Confederate cavalry. After chasing the 2nd Ohio Cavalry northward, Rosser's troopers ran into the 23rd USCT, which deployed in the open field of the Alrich farm.

soldiers struggled under the stigma that, in a battle, they would simply run away, although many officers were convinced the men of the USCT would fight like demons. Other officers, including Meade, worried that throwing them into battle, no matter the circumstance, would be perceived as using the men for cannon fodder. Still others did not want to use them because it was an election year, and politicos spun scenarios that suggested black troops would help or would hurt the administration's chances for reelection. The entire situation was fraught—and for the black soldiers itching to fight for their own freedom, frustrating.

On May 15, Ferrero's men would see action whether their superiors liked it or not.[12]

Word arrived at Ferrero's headquarters along the Orange Turnpike that the Ohioans needed help. "When the Gen. got the word, he had the long roll sounded, and told his men that the bull dogs . . . were in trouble, and must have help soon or all be butchered . . . " a Buckeye later recounted. "[T]hey did not wait to form ranks, but all grabbed their guns and cartridge boxes and started, and came . . . on a run."

An unidentified trooper from the 2nd Ohio Cavalry. One of the frustrating aspects of the battle of Alrich farm is that so many components of it have been downplayed and undocumented: Confederates, embarrassed to be defeated by USCT, didn't report their presence; many members of the 23rd USCT, as former slaves, weren't literate enough to leave written contemporaneous accounts; and the Ohioans get overlooked because popular assumption holds that Sheridan took all the Federal cavalry (and because the IX Corps in general remains overlooked and underrated). *Library of Congress*

Ferrero deployed the 23rd USCT down the Plank Road toward its intersection with the Catharpin Road. "It did us good to see the long line of glittering bayonets approach, although those who bore them were Blacks," wrote one of the Ohioans who had fled to the Alrich farm for safety, "and as they came nearer they were greeted by loud cheers."[13]

Ferrero immediately recognized the cavalrymen's precarious situation. "I found the Second Ohio driven across the road, and the enemy occupying the cross-roads,"

12 Augustus Woodbury, *Major General Ambrose Burnside and the Ninth Army Corps: A Narrative of the Campaigns in North Carolina, Maryland, Virginia, Ohio, Kentucky, Mississippi, and Tennessee, During the War for the Preservation of the Republic* (Providence, RI: Sidney S. Rider & Brother, 1867), 376–79.

13 Rhea, *To the North Anna River,* 106.

Ferrero reported. The 23rd swung off the road and into battle formation, sending out a thick line of skirmishers in advance.[14]

Rosser's men hit the open fields around the Alrich farm and quickly dismounted. Rosser commanded some of the best fighting cavalry in the Army of Northern Virginia, but even against green infantry they stood little chance. The 23rd USCT fired into the Southern cavalry at a few hundred yards. While the volley produced few casualties, it was enough to convince Rosser's horsemen to withdraw. They were engaging an unknown force behind enemy lines, with bad roads their only means of escape and thunderstorms looming in the sky. Rosser made the prudent call to pull out. "The Rebs didn't wait to say goodby, but got a move on them," said Ohioan William Smith. Ferrero proudly—and justifiably—crowed that his men "drove the enemy in perfect rout."[15]

"Our boys got behind the wagons and done good work for green boys," declared William Baird of the 23rd. "They fired three or four rounds and captured quite a number of saddles which the Confederates left."[16]

The Ohioans pulled themselves back together and gave chase as far as Piney Branch Church but seemed content to let the numerically superior Confederates go. The Buckeyes reoccupied their former position.

Still, Rosser wasn't through with his recon. Following a network of muddy roads, his cavalrymen gained the rear of the main Federal army near the burned-out Stevens farm, about one mile northwest of the Federal headquarters at the Harris farm. The 7th and 11th Virginia Cavalry engaged the pickets of Birney's division, who were having a long day themselves, fresh off their scuffle with Kershaw. The incident, though brief, gave the Federal high command a scare.

* * *

Lee set out from his headquarters near Zion Church to inspect the line as it adjusted to the new Federal configuration. Rosser's mission, combined with Kershaw's foray earlier in the day, gave him valuable intelligence. He now knew where the main body of the Federal army was—and it seemed like the Federals in that sector weren't going anywhere.

But he was hungry for as much information as he could get, and he could not resist a chance to take a look for himself. From the high ground in the interior

14 Edward Ferrero, report, *O.R.* 36:1:986; Woodbury, 377–78.

15 Ferrero, 986.

16 William Baird, letter, Michigan Historical Collection, Bentley Historical Library, University of Michigan, FSNMP BV 35.

of Heth's Salient, he could look out over portions of Burnside's current positions as well as a portion of Warren's. Lieutenant Colonel William Thomas Poague—whose guns had staved off Confederate annihilation on the morning of May 6 in the Wilderness—had positioned his batteries in a small redan on the eastern edge of Heth's Salient, with Henry H. Walker's brigade posted around them as support. Walker had been wounded on May 10, and Robert M. Mayo now commanded the brigade.

Someone somewhere in the Federal line must have been watching Lee watching them, Poague guessed. "[T]he enemy's batteries opened suddenly and furiously on my position while General Lee, on foot, was examining their positions in front, as if they had discovered his presence. And perhaps with a powerful glass they had seen a prominent officer inspecting their lines," the artillerists later wrote. "A great strapping fellow of ours actually almost dragged General Lee down into a gunpit, so anxious was he for the safety of our beloved commander."[17]

As it happened, Grant had been on the front that day, as well. A private in the 16th Michigan saw Grant "taking a survey of the Confederacy."[18]

While the two commanders puzzled and their armies prodded, the rain continued to fall. Overnight it rained, too, and into the next day. The trench lines snaking through the rolling countryside filled with water stained orange by the Virginia clay, which trapped the rain and offered no drainage. "The roads have now become so impassable that ambulances with wounded men can no longer run between here and Fredericksburg," Grant wrote to Halleck on May 16.

"An ordinary rain, lasting for a day or two, does not embarrass troops," lamented Horace Porter. "But when the storm continues for a week it becomes one of the most serious obstacles in a campaign.

> The men can secure no proper shelter and no comfortable rest; their clothing has no chance to dry; and a tramp of a few miles through tenacious mud requires as much exertion as an ordinary day's march. Tents become saturated and weighted with water, and draft animals have increased loads and heavier roads over which to haul them. Dry wood cannot be found; cooking becomes difficult; the men's spirits are affected by the gloom, and even the most buoyant natures become disheartened.[19]

17 William Thomas Poague, *A Gunner With Stonewall,* Monroe F. Cockrell, ed. (Jackson, TN: McCowat-Mercer Press, 1957), 93.

18 Alfred Apted, diary, May 15, 1864, FSNMP BV 195.

19 Porter, 121.

Grant, from his top perch at army headquarters, saw a different view, perhaps willfully so. "The army is in the best of spirits," he wrote Halleck in that same May 16 letter, "and feel the greatest confidence of ultimate success." He assured Washington that "the elements alone have suspended hostilities, and that it is in no manner due to weakness or exhaustion on our part."[20]

Grant had the opportunity to make that point in person with a sympathetic audience who would surely return to Washington and share his impressions: Senator John Sherman of Ohio, brother of Grant's trusted right-hand commander in the West. Lyman described Sherman as "very tall, as flat as a pancake, and ornamented with a long linen 'duster' that made him look 12 feet high. He plainly is a very superior man, as becomes the brother of the General." Senator William Sprague of Rhode Island joined Sherman and "rode fearlessly about in a straw hat."[21]

During their stay with the army, which lasted a couple rainy days, the senators made a special effort to visit Meade. They were "highly complimentary," Meade later wrote his wife.[22]

*In Washington, it's well understood these are your battles*, the senators told the general.

"Such is not the case," Meade replied. "At first I had maneuvered the army, but gradually, and from the very nature of things, Grant has taken the control." Meade did not seem to begrudge the situation—at least not then—and admitted, "It would be injurious to the army to have two heads."

Meade cited a newspaperman who wrote, "Grant does the grand strategy, and I the grand tactics." But he thought another reporter had articulated an even better description: "the army of the Potomac, directed by Grant, commanded by Meade, and led by Hancock, Sedgwick, and Warren."

"A quite good distinction," Meade summarized, "and about hits the nail on the head." Meade's stoic acceptance of the situation would sour considerably over the next couple weeks, though.

Indeed, Grant had become the *de facto* hands-on general he had initially promised Meade he wouldn't be. He used the respite of these rainy days to refine plans for a new assault against the southern end of the Confederate line. Rather than strike down the Fredericksburg Road, as he had originally planned, he would concentrate the attack along the Massaponnax Church Road another mile and a half to the south. Hancock's II Corps would lead the attack; Wright's VI Corps

20 Grant to Halleck, *O.R.* 36:2:810.

21 Lyman, *Meade's Headquarters,* 161.

22 The following account comes from Meade, *Life and Letters,* 197–98.

would support; Burnside's IX Corps would exploit the breakthrough; and Warren's V Corps would stand in reserve. Preparations, said Army of the Potomac Chief of Staff Andrew Humphreys, kept the V and VI Corps busy, even in the rain. They "advanced their intrenched lines, established batteries, opened roads, examined the country and roads leading southward, and . . . prepared an intrenchment."[23]

Grant also used the lull in action to check on the reinforcements he had ordered from Washington. Chief of Staff Maj. Gen. Henry Halleck had stripped the city's defenses and sent 30,000 fresh troops toward the front. The first of those soldiers, the 1st Vermont Heavy Artillery under Colonel James M. Warner, arrived on May 15 and attached to Col. Lewis Grant's Vermont Brigade, nearly bled out two weeks earlier at the Wilderness. With 1,500 men in the ranks, organized into 12 companies of 125 men each, the new regiment had "a larger number than was now left of the other five regiments put together," said the Vermonters' regimental historian. "It was finely equipped, ably officered, and in all respects a splendid body of soldiers."[24]

Lee did not have the luxury of immediate reinforcement, although prospects were improving. In the Shenandoah Valley, Confederate Maj. Gen. John C. Breckinridge, a former vice president of the United States, defeated the inept Franz Sigel at New Market. Lee wired his congratulations to Breckinridge and suggested he chase Sigel all the way to the Mason-Dixon Line: "If you can follow Sigel into Maryland, you will do more good than by joining us." But, if he couldn't, "you can be of great service to this army."[25]

Word also arrived on May 17 that Benjamin Butler's Federal army had been bottled up at Bermuda Hundred, Virginia, freeing up Confederate troops—Maj. Gen. George Pickett's Division—from around the Richmond and Petersburg areas. "The army received with joy the news of General [P. G. T.] Beauregard's success south of James River, as reported in the papers of to-day," Lee wrote to Secretary of War James Seddon.[26]

Still, it would be days before Lee would see reinforcements from either sector.[27]

Commanders of both armies used the rain delay to attend to a myriad of other details. Lee, for instance, denied a request for Maj. Gen. Lafayette McLaws to return to the Army of Northern Virginia. McLaws had fallen afoul of his former

23 Humphreys, 109.

24 Benedict, 451.

25 Lee, *Wartime Papers*, 732.

26 Ibid.

27 James McPherson, *Ordeal by Fire: The Civil War and Reconstruction* (Boston: McGraw Hill, 2001), 452–58.

As the artillery reserve got shuffled, it concentrated along the Fredericksburg Road. This photo was taken from Whig Hill looking west. The artillery's horses are assembled on the far hillside. *Library of Congress*

corps commander, James Longstreet, following operations outside Nashville the previous winter. In deference to his Old Warhorse, Lee did not want to invite McLaws back.

On the Federal side, Grant received word from Secretary of War Edwin Stanton that, "If you deem it expedient to promote any officer on the field for gallant conduct, you are authorized to do so provisionally." (Stanton had reminded him two days earlier that "brevets can be given without limit.") A flurry of names circulated: Horatio Wright, John Gibbon, Samuel Carroll, William McCandless, Emory Upton, Simon Griffin, John Hartranft.[28]

Gershom Mott's division—"which has behaved badly, thus far," according to Lyman—was incorporated into Birney's division, and the Army of the Potomac's Artillery Reserve was broken up. Brigadier General Robert O. Tyler, commander of the Artillery Reserve, was converted to an infantry commander and put in charge of the first reinforcements even then marching to join the army.[29]

Artillerist Charles Wainwright complained about the breakup of the Artillery Reserve, but considering the condition of the artillery's horses, perhaps it was for the best. "My poor horses are suffering terribly under this hard work," Wainwright had complained on May 15. Teams were on half rations—five pounds of grain a day and nothing else. Not that there was "hardly a sack of grain in my whole command," he winced. It was "barely enough to keep life in a horse provided he had nothing to do."

28 Stanton to Grant, May 15, 1864 (received May 16), *O.R.* 36:2:781, 746.

29 Lyman, *Meade's Headquarters,* 161.

**FOLLOWING PAGES: SPOTSYLVANIA, MAY 8–15, 1864**—One of the enduring myths about Ulysses S. Grant born during the Overland Campaign is that "Grant the Butcher" uncreatively relied on direct assaults to the exclusion of other tools. A look at the changing alignment of the Federal positions at Spotsylvania clearly undercuts that criticism because Grant's willingness to maneuver for advantage becomes evident. Confederates chose the initial position, based on advantageous topography; Federals chose their positions in reaction. As Grant maneuvered for an opening, Lee was then forced to realign his position in reaction. See also the maps on pages 254 and 276 for additional reconfigurations over time.

---

Wainwright tried to secure more forage and food, but his quartermaster's wagons kept getting commandeered to transport wounded men to the rear.[30]

Newspaperman Charles Carleton Coffin took a lull in the fighting to follow that train of wounded to Fredericksburg. "The city is a vast hospital," he reported; "churches, public buildings, private dwellings, stores, chambers, attics, basements, all full. There are thousands upon the sidewalk. All day long the ambulances have been arriving from the field."[31]

This was of particular concern to Brig. Gen. Montgomery Meigs, quartermaster general of the U.S. Army, who was conducting a personal inspection of Fredericksburg. "There are many badly wounded here, for whose transportation the opening of the Rappahannock is very desirable," he wrote to Stanton from Fredericksburg. Thousands of POWs needed to be shipped northward, too. Per instructions from Grant, Meigs ordered the repair of the railroads around Fredericksburg, northward toward the supply base on Aquia Creek and southward toward Hamilton's Crossing—a signal of Grant's intentions to possibly move in that direction.[32] The general in chief had not yet hinted at any such movement, but he wanted to keep his options open.

On May 17, the sun finally made its first real appearance in days. The day turned out warm and sunny, but that offered little consolation to Grant. "The condition of the roads was such that nothing was done on the 17th," he wrote.[33]

The condition of the men, too, was worrisome. In a letter to his wife, Meade wrote: "To-morrow we shall begin fighting again, with, I trust, some decided result, for it is hardly natural to expect men to maintain without limit the exhaustion of such a protracted struggle as we have been carrying on."[34]

30 Wainwright, 372–73.

31 Coffin, 326.

32 M. C. Meigs to E. M. Stanton, May 17, 1864, *O.R.* 36:2:854.

33 Grant, *Memoirs*, 318.

34 Meade, *Life and Letters,* 196.

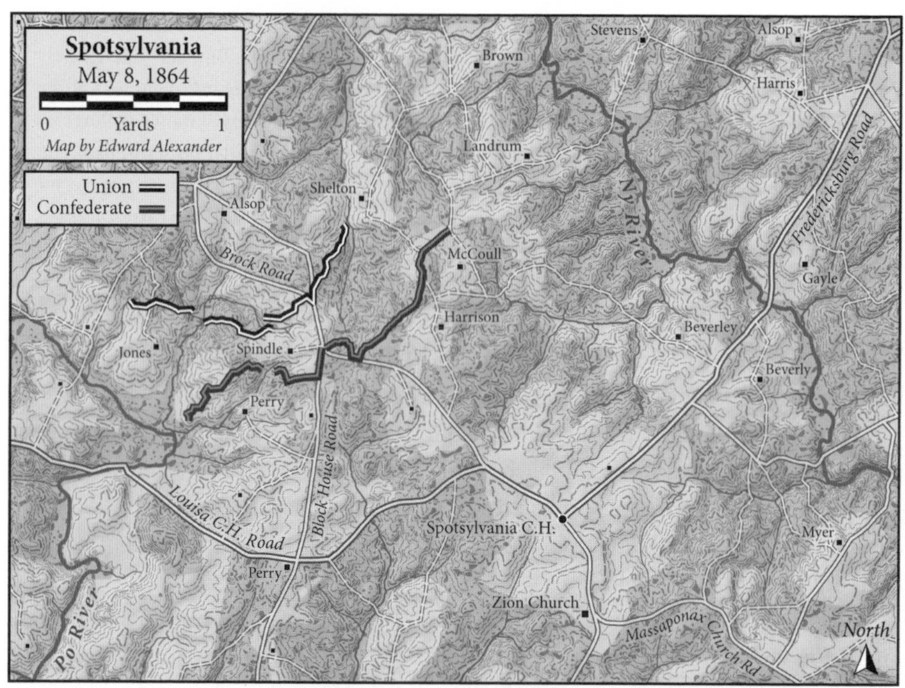
Spotsylvania
May 8, 1864
0 Yards 1
Map by Edward Alexander
Union
Confederate
Stevens
Alsop
Brown
Harris
Fredericksburg Road
Landrum
Ny River
Shelton
Alsop
Brock Road
McCoull
Gayle
Harrison
Beverley
Jones
Spindle
Beverly
Perry
Block House Road
Louisa C.H. Road
Spotsylvania C.H.
Myer
Perry
Zion Church
Po River
Massaponax Church Rd
North

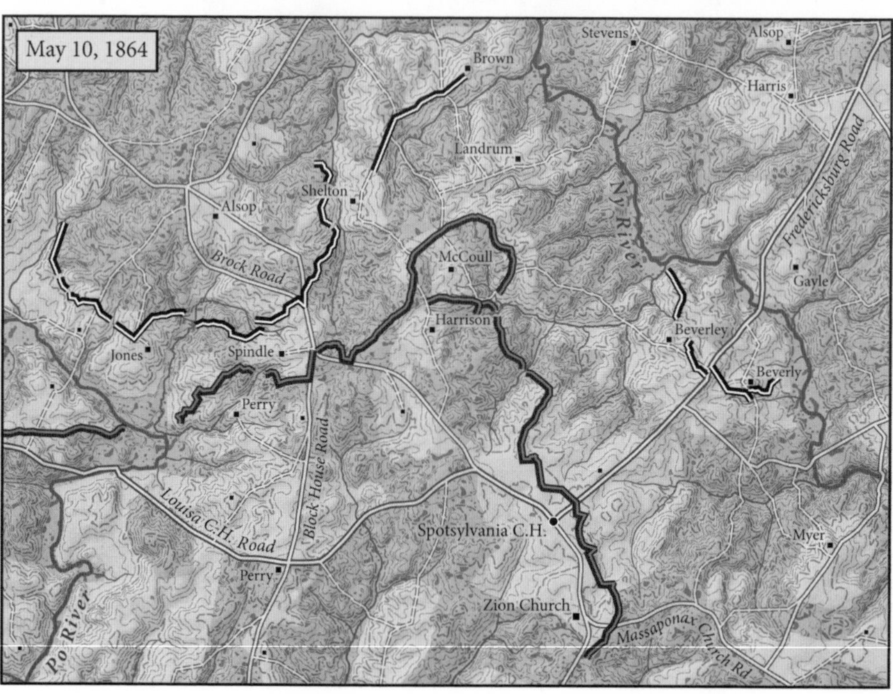
May 10, 1864
Stevens
Alsop
Brown
Harris
Fredericksburg Road
Landrum
Ny River
Shelton
Alsop
Brock Road
McCoull
Gayle
Harrison
Beverley
Jones
Spindle
Beverly
Perry
Block House Road
Louisa C.H. Road
Spotsylvania C.H.
Myer
Perry
Zion Church
Po River
Massaponax Church Rd

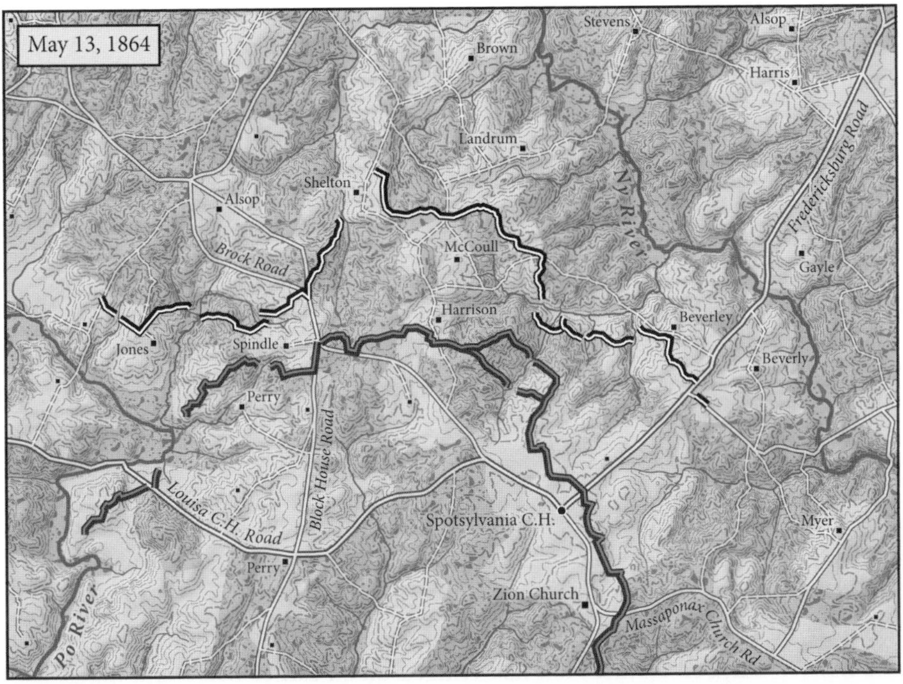

May 13, 1864
Stevens
Alsop
Brown
Harris
Landrum
Shelton
Alsop
Ny River
Fredericksburg Road
McCoull
Gayle
Brock Road
Harrison
Beverley
Jones
Spindle
Beverly
Perry
Block House Road
Louisa C.H. Road
Spotsylvania C.H.
Myer
Perry
Zion Church
Po River
Massaponax Church Rd

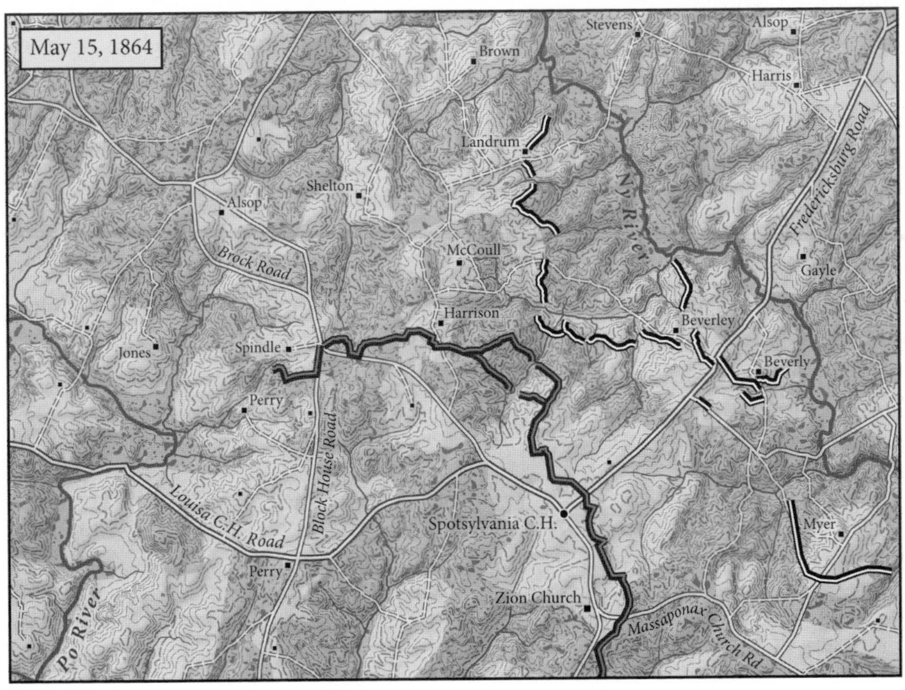
May 15, 1864
Stevens
Alsop
Brown
Harris
Landrum
Shelton
Alsop
Ny River
Fredericksburg Road
McCoull
Gayle
Brock Road
Harrison
Beverley
Jones
Spindle
Beverly
Perry
Block House Road
Louisa C.H. Road
Spotsylvania C.H.
Myer
Perry
Zion Church
Po River
Massaponax Church Rd

# May 14
# May 15
# May 16
# May 17
# May 18

It might have felt like déjà vu except for all the bodies. The grisly landscape Hancock's men surveyed on the morning of May 18 was the same landscape they had crossed on May 12. It was the same landscape so many of their comrades had died on. "The atmosphere is perfectly pestilential from decaying bodies of men and horses," surgeon Daniel Holt had cringed on an earlier visit—and things had only gotten worse.[1]

Rain had soaked the ground for five and a half days, and the stench rising from the gore-tinged Virginia mud "was so sickening and terrible that many of the men and officers became deathly sick from it," said William Mitchell, a II Corps staff officer. Hastily buried corpses, exhumed by the rain from their shallow graves, lay exposed in the mud. "[B]lack bloated bodies were sitting up and reaching out from the earth," a horrified Pennsylvanian noted.[2]

No one was resting in peace.

Thus far, Hancock's battered corps had been Grant's hammer of choice, and Grant intended to swing it again across the bloody landscape to strike a Confederate position he believed too weak to resist. Robert E. Lee, meanwhile, needed to remain the unmovable object—an ironic task considering his army's superior maneuverability over most of its previous career.

This had not been the plan Grant had conceived on May 16. That plan had called for Hancock's corps to join Wright's in an attack down the Massaponax Church Road toward Lee's line. Grant had hoped to find a weak spot south of Spotsylvania Court House and launch a successful assault that would split Lee's

1 Holt, 187.

2 Hancock, report, *O.R.* 36:1:361; Bolton, 206.

army in two and make the Confederate position untenable while, at the same time, driving a wedge between Lee and his supply base in Richmond.

But the area below Spotsylvania was an unexplored part of the battlefield and, of course, the army lacked cavalry to carry out the necessary exploration. Instead, Wright had to send a pair of infantry regiments—the 3rd Vermont and the 10th Massachusetts—on a reconnaissance. The New Englanders pushed out along the Massaponax Road and soon bumped into Confederate cavalry videttes, which they drove for about five miles. Then the driving stopped. "[W]e came upon the infantry, strongly posted in a dense wood, and about two miles from the Court House," a Massachusetts soldier wrote.[3]

"[T]ired and hungry," the reconnaissance party reported to Wright that the Confederates were too well positioned. According to another observer, "the country there badly wooded and unfavorable for attack." Wright passed word to Chief of Staff Andrew Humphreys; Humphreys passed word to Meade, who passed word to Grant. Grant, who had also probably looked over the ground himself at some point, accepted their judgment.[4]

With the Massaponax Road no longer a viable option, the general in chief looked back to the old battlefield of May 10 and 12. If Lee's right and center were strong, he reasoned, Lee must have stripped his line somewhere. He targeted the Confederate left, anchored on ground where the base of the Mule Shoe Salient had been. The remains of Ewell's Second Corps occupied the area, and Grant suspected those men would be easier to dislodge because they had taken such a beating in those earlier fights.

Grant cut orders to shift the II and VI Corps from the extreme Federal left and center back to the army's extreme right. Complicating matters, part of Hancock's artillery had already shifted to a position originally assigned for the May 16 attack, putting them farther out of position for the new attack. The artillery had to double back, creating the first of what would turn out to be several delays.

To help cover the sounds of the movement, some of Burnside's men played music from behind the lines. A battle of the bands erupted. "We had quite a musical contest this evening," noted a member of the 58th Virginia, posted in Heth's Salient opposite Burnside. "Our Bands were playing some Southern airs and the Yankees playing an opposition."[5]

Once more, the men of the II and VI corps endured a weary all-night march over muddy roads and across swollen streams, still expected to launch another

3 Alfred Roe, *The Tenth Regiment Massachusetts Volunteer Infantry 1861–1864: A Western Massachusetts Regiment* (Springfield, MA: Tenth Regiment Veteran Association, 1909), 270.

4 Ibid; Lyman, *Meade's Army*, 162.

5 W. H. Wingfield, diary, 56, FSNMP BV 167.

4:30 a.m. assault. "The Second and Sixth Corps are to return to the old ground on the right and pitch in there," wrote one Federal diarist. "[G]reat things are hoped from it by Grant. I fear he will not find Lee asleep."[6]

Not just "not asleep," but well rested. When Ewell's men had fallen back from the Mule Shoe in the predawn hours of May 13, they had taken a new position south of Edgar Harrison's homestead. Their new line, which sealed off the base of the former salient, ran across the top of a ridge that overlooked ravines and open fields. Because Grant had not exerted any pressure on that segment of the line since then—for five full days—Ewell's reorganized Second Corps, consisting of two stalwart divisions of veterans, had been gifted plenty of time to reorganize, refit, and, most important, catch up on their rest.

Robert Rodes's Division held the left of the new line; newly minted Maj. Gen. John Brown Gordon the right. Both division commanders had earned reputations as tough fighters on both offense and defense, although at the moment, their reputations were greater than the actual strength in their ranks. These once-strong divisions now totaled roughly 8,000 men, supported by 29 guns of Brig. Gen. Armistead Long, a practiced hand with a good eye.

They had settled into their new position with a kind of mad zeal. They cut logs to hold up the earthen walls of their trenches and provide themselves extra protection. They dug traverses that provided additional cover and, if necessary, defensive positions in the event of a breakthrough. The Confederate position at the Mule Shoe had likewise contained traverses, but there had not been enough of them, nor had they been placed at proper intervals. In the new position, Confederate engineers made sure to correct their earlier errors.

Sharpshooters even built small towers from which to shoot, each like a wooden camp chimney with "a little loop hole in front," an incredulous Theodore Lyman later recalled. "I never saw any like them."[7]

In front of their position, the Confederates cleared unobstructed fields of fire all the way to the plateau of the McCoull farm, a half-mile in front of them. Between the McCoull farm and the Confederate line, an open landscape rolled with small swales and knolls before eventually dropping into a marshy lowland. From there, "[t]he ground rose to a lofty cleared ridge, on with the most conspicuous object was a large white house," a Federal soldier later observed, referring to Edgar Harrison's house. "The ridge was the enemy's stronghold." Confederates had littered the open ground with piles of slashings and abatis to slow any Federal advance."

6 Wainwright, 375.

7 Lyman, postwar journal, April 15, 1866, Lyman Family Papers, Microfilm P374, Reels 15 and 28, Massachusetts Historical Society, Boston, FSNMP BV 405.

Unknown to Grant, the new Confederate line represented the strongest field fortifications yet seen in the Eastern Theater—exactly where he planned to attack.[8]

* * *

The VI Corps, which had started its march into place just after dark on May 17, was ordered to deploy on the far right, along the western side of the former Mule Shoe, stacking its divisions in massive assault columns similar to the tactic Emory Upton had used a week earlier. Brigadier David Russell would be on the far right, Brig. Gen. James Ricketts would be in the center, and Brig. Gen. Thomas Neill on the left.

Hancock would line up his II Corps divisions in traditional lines of battle on Wright's immediate left, across from Doles's Salient and up to the area already known as "the Bloody Angle." Brigadier General John Gibbon would be on the right of the formation, linking with Neill; Brig. Gen. Francis Barlow's division would be on the left. Brigadier General Robert Tyler's division of fresh reinforcements—heavy artillery regiments newly arrived the day before—would advance to protect the left flank, while Brig. Gen. David Birney's division would hang back as the reserve near and on the Landrum farm, acting as a link between the VI and II Corps and Burnside's IX Corps farther east.

There on the eastern front, across from Heth's Salient, Grant deployed the IX Corps to hold Early's Third Corps in position while the other two Federal corps launched the main attack. Leaning less on the V Corps following Warren's disappointing performance thus far in the campaign, Grant ordered Warren's artillery to support the attack and be ready as general reserves.

The plan fell apart almost from the start. The VI Corps took too long to get into position, which subsequently slowed the movement of II Corps. By the time the VI Corps reached its launch point, the men were so strung out that Wright was able only to bring Neill's full division online for the assault. As Neill got into place, Ricketts didn't show. Neither did Russell. Both divisions had been swallowed by the darkness and mud. Eventually, one brigade of Ricketts's division arrived, though too late to participate in the assault.

A graduate of West Point's Class of 1847, Neill had grown into division command after a rough spot on May 9.[9] Emulating tactics used on May 10 and again on May 12, he assembled his division in brigade battle front—four brigades

8 Galwey, 218.

9 Warner, *Generals in Blue,* 342–43.

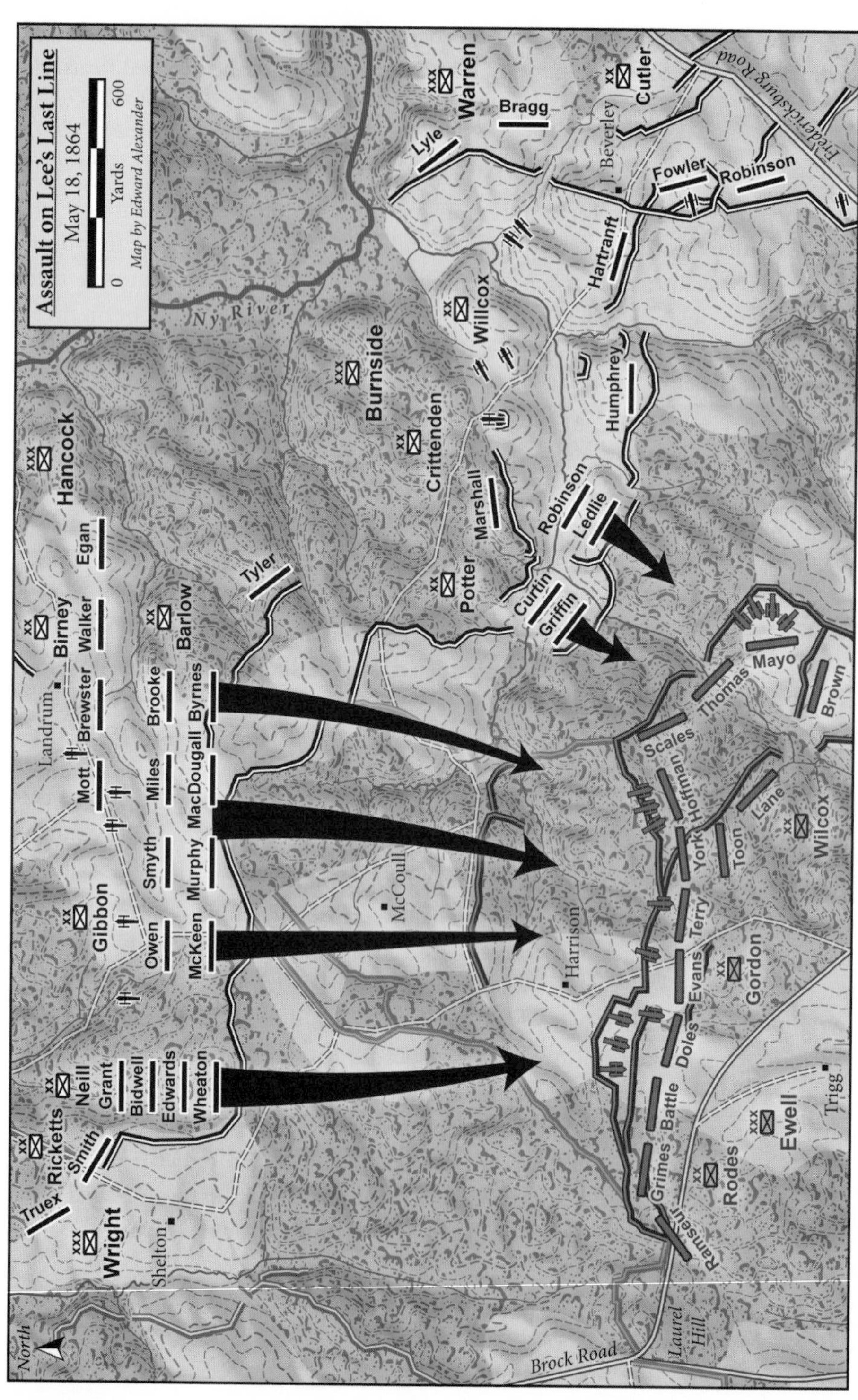
Assault on Lee's Last Line
May 18, 1864
0
Yards
600
Map by Edward Alexander
North
Ny River
Hancock
Birney
Gibbon
Egan
Walker
Brewster
Mott
Landrum
Smyth
Owen
Barlow
Brooke
Miles
Murphy
McKeen
Byrnes
MacDougall
Tyler
Wright
Ricketts
Neill
Truex
Smith
Grant
Bidwell
Edwards
Wheaton
Shelton
Burnside
Crittenden
Potter
Willcox
Marshall
Robinson
Ledlie
Curtin
Griffin
Humphrey
Hartranft
Warren
Lyle
Bragg
Cutler
J. Beverley
Fowler
Robinson
Fredericksburg Road
McCoull
Harrison
Scales
Thomas
Mayo
Brown
Hoffman
Lane
York
Toon
Wilcox
Terry
Evans
Gordon
Doles
Battle
Grimes
Ramseur
Rodes
Ewell
Trigg
Laurel Hill
Brock Road

**Assault on Lee's Last Line**—Conceived as an attack every bit as large as the one on May 12, the May 18 attack got off to a diminished start because of two missing divisions. The three divisions that did assault did so across the remains of the former Mule Shoe Salient against the strongest Confederate fortifications yet built in the Eastern Theater. Confederate artillery dominated the field, casting doubt on whether the two missing Federal divisions would have made any difference. A simultaneous Federal attack against the new Confederate center met with similar grief.

---

stacked one behind the other, with Brig. Gen. Frank Wheaton's mixed New York and Pennsylvania brigade in the van, followed by the brigades of Colonel Oliver Edwards, Colonel Daniel Bidwell, and Brig. Gen. Lewis Grant. Their formation represented most of the Northeastern states.

To Neill's left, Gibbon's and Barlow's divisions each aligned two brigades wide and two brigades deep. Gibbon's front line consisted of Col. Boyd McKeen's brigade and Col. Matthew Murphy's newly christened "Irish Legion."[10] The second line consisted of Brig. Gen. Joshua Owen's "Philadelphia Brigade" and Col. Thomas Smyth's brigade. Barlow lined up the brigade of newly promoted Col. Clinton MacDougall to the right of Col. Richard Byrne's famed Irish Brigade, both in the front line, followed by the battered ranks of Colonels Nelson Miles and John Brooke's brigades. Most of the brigades were still reeling from the hammerings they both gave and received on May 12 at the Bloody Angle.

Hancock had received some eight thousand reinforcements in the five days since that bloody fight, "enough to make good, numerically, the losses of the corps in the campaign thus far," noted II Corps historian Francis Walker. But Walker added an important caveat:

> Yet all this could not make good the losses which the corps had sustained in the first fortnight of the campaign. Those who had fallen were men inured to camp life, to hardship, exposure, and fatigue; in bivouac they knew how to make themselves almost comfortable with the narrowest means; how to cover themselves in rain and storm; how to make fires out of green wood, find water in dry ground, and cook their rations to the best advantage. On the march they had learned to cover the greatest distance with the least wear and tear; on picket and skirmish they had learned a score of tricks by which they at once protected themselves

10 The regiments had formerly been known as the "Corcoran Legion," named after former commander Brig. Gen. Michael Corcoran, killed in December 1863 in a noncombat horseback riding accident.

"Gibbon—in Position, May 18, 1864" by Alfred Waud. *Library of Congress*

> and became more formidable to the enemy. In battle, officers and men had become veterans through a score of fierce encounters; no form of danger could be a surprise to them. With a high price bought they this knowledge! Thousands had died that these regiments might know how to advance and how to retire as occasion should demand; how to cover themselves most completely through long hours of waiting and how to throw themselves, body and soul, into one tremendous blow, on the vital spot, at the critical instant.[11]

Hancock's men were positioned to cross ground they had crossed only six days earlier, nearly to the hour. "The Second Corps, starting from the works gained by it on the 12th, was to advance inward through the salient, and attack the intrenchments built by the enemy to cut off that portion of their line," Walker explained.[12]

11 Walker, 483–84.

12 Walker, 485.

"The troops were in position before day light," Brig. Gen. Regis De Trobriand reported of the II Corps. "It was hoped to surprise the enemy sleeping; but he had his eyes open, and was protected by acres of impenetrable *abatis*."[13]

To make matters worse, the ground the Federals needed to negotiate was rolling, crisscrossed by lines of trenches filled with water, mud, and dead soldiers. Days of war had transformed the agrarian landscape into fields of devastation "strewn with clothing, knapsacks, canteens, muskets, dead horses and broken artillery caissons, and the trees were riddled with bullet, shot and shell," recalled a drummer boy of the 2nd New York Heavy Artillery, recently added to Hancock's corps from Washington's defenses.

The previous days of rain had washed away the dirt from the shallow graves, and black, bloated bodies were sitting up and reaching out from the earth. "The general appearance of the dead who had been exposed to the sun so long was horrible in the extreme as we marched past and over them," wrote William Mitchell, "a sight never to be forgotten by those who witnessed it."[14]

13 Regis De Trobriand, *Four Years With the Army of the Potomac* (Boston: Ticknor & Company, 1889), 581. De Trobriand was away on detail in New York City at the time of the battle, but he would return to the II Corps when the army reached Petersburg.

14 Hancock, report, *O.R.* 36:1:361.

* * *

Fog rose from the bottomlands, muffling sound and obscuring anything beyond the middle distance. At 4:00 a.m., off to the Federal left, the boom of artillery cut through the white, announcing the start of Burnside's diversionary attack. Hancock and Wright, however, dared not send their own men forward yet—not without Ricketts's and Russell's missing units, still mired in mud and darkness, lost in the fog.

For days, Burnside's men had gazed over a field of woe similar to the one the II Corps had discovered just that morning. "We could see many dead men lying in the ravine," wrote Lyman Jackman of the 6th New Hampshire, "and the stench, borne by the wind from that quarter, was almost unendurable, for the bodies had lain there five days in the sun and rain." Confederate sharpshooters made it hot work for rescue parties to retrieve wounded men mixed among the decomposing dead, although night offered some degree of cover.[15]

Now, on the morning of May 18, the IX Corps men "were roused from our uneasy slumber in the trenches" and sent into that landscape, under the cover of fog rather than darkness. "We felt that it was almost sure death to go down into and across the field before us and up the slope on the opposite side, but we were there to fight, and so when the order to advance came, the men leaped over the works," Jackman wrote.[16]

It was a doomed venture from the beginning. For starters, Burnside sent in only half his corps: Crittenden's and Potter's; Willcox's hung back in reserve, and the Ferrero's remained well to the rear with the wagon trains.

Crittenden commanded some strong units, but unfortunately, 32-year-old Brig. Gen. James Ledlie helmed his First Brigade at the front of the column. Like Crittenden, Ledlie was a political appointee and, by all accounts, had an overfondness for alcohol while on duty. Backstopping his men was Lt. Col. Gilbert Robinson's small brigade of three regiments; Robinson had recently replaced Daniel Leasure, knocked out of command by a head injury during the May 12 fighting.

Burnside's Second Division, under Potter, was in much better shape than Crittenden's. Potter, 34, "tall, with a full, phlegmatic black eye," had a Robert Shaw-as-Captain Quint look about him, although "particular about his dress" and of few words. A lawyer by trade, Potter had proven himself time and again on the battlefield. He had been the lieutenant colonel of the 51st New York and

15 Lyman Jackman, *History of the Sixth New Hampshire Regiment in the War for the Union* (Concord, NH: Repub. Press Association, 1891), 249.

16 Houston, 156; Jackman, 249.

had served with Burnside on the North Carolina Coast. He had helped secure Rohrbach's Bridge at Antietam and had commanded a division since March 1863. Potter stacked his two brigades with Brig. Gen. Simon Goodell Griffin's brigade in front, followed by Colonel John I. Curtain's.[17]

The 39-year-old Griffin, from Keene, New Hampshire, had earned promotion to brigadier just days earlier for gallantry during the fight against the Mule Shoe. He advanced his brigade side by side with Ledlie's—Ledlie on the left, Griffin on the right. Immediately behind them, Robinson advanced next to Curtain.

Facing Burnside inside the salient were the brigades of Brig. Gen. Alfred Scales and Brig. Gen. Joseph R. Davis of Cadmus Wilcox's and Henry Heth's Divisions, respectively. Following the collapse of the Mule Shoe and the reconfiguration of Ewell's line, Heth's Salient was now more vulnerable than ever. The position resembled a sideways "U" with its nose staved in. Where Ewell's line connected with Early's on the northern edge of the position, the works formed a sharp angle susceptible to enfilading fire from both Hancock's and Burnside's men. The two Federal corps brought 95 guns to bear on that sector of the Confederate line, an advantage Burnside noted in his after-action report. "This attack was well supported by the artillery, particularly by the batteries of General [Orlando] Willcox's division," he wrote, emphasizing the role of his gunners.[18]

Through the fog, Burnside's men "advanced gallantly over their works" and "moved up in admirable style," according to Griffin and Ledlie, both in the advance.[19] They crossed a small open field and down into the ravine, pushed across marshy lowlands, traversed rain-swollen streams, and finally "forced their way up the opposite side close to the enemy's lines,—intrenching themselves within fifty yards of their works," Griffin said. "But the proximity was too close and the fire too deadly."[20]

All the while, "the rebels opened upon us with shot, shell, and musketry," Jackman recounted. "They let go their big 'war dogs' from a fort [redan] hidden in the woods a little to our left, and the cold lead and iron was slung around us fearfully. . . . [T]he shot and shell came nearly as thick and fast as the Minié balls." Heavy ordnance "did sad havoc" as shells tore through the intervening heavy growth of timber.[21]

The corpses of fallen comrades, killed in previous fighting, made the crossing especially gruesome. "Here were the enemy's dead, both men and horses, of the

17 Lyman, 162.

18 Burnside, report, *O.R.* 36:1:911.

19 Simon Griffin, unpublished memoir, 119, author's collection; Ledlie, 917. The author thanks Ron Veen for providing a copy of Griffin's memoir.

20 Griffin, 119.

21 Jackman, 251.

battle of the 12th, lying thick in all directions, and loathsomely swollen and disfigured," Jackman recalled with revulsion. "They were rapidly decomposing, having lain here six days in the warm sun and rain. We were obliged to pass directly over them, and we did so as quickly as possible, for it was impossible to breathe in that locality. . . . [J]ust as we were passing the loathsome spot two or three shells struck and exploded among the dead bodies, and sent their fragments flying in all directions." The gore-splattered men pushed on.[22]

Potter's two brigades hit the Confederate line at a tangent that, in theory, would have allowed him to connect with Barlow's advance down from the old Mule Shoe and hit the Confederate line in tandem. Alas, Hancock had not yet advanced—still waiting for the two missing VI Corps divisions—which left Potter's right flank exposed. Confederate gunners went to work. "The rebels opened upon it with grape and canister and a volley of musketry, cutting the men down like grass before the mower's scythe," Jackman lamented.[23]

Being one of the regiments on the right, the 6th New Hampshire cringed leftward, bunching up with the 9th New Hampshire behind the 32nd Maine. "[C]onsequently, we could not fire a shot," Jackman discovered. "The colonel halted us, telling us to protect ourselves as best we could."[24]

Georgians from Edward Thomas's Brigade sensed an opportunity in the chaos—an opportunity that would not have been available had the II Corps been tying the Georgians down as planned. "The enemy sought to take advantage of this, and push a column into the gap, and thus strike us in flank and rear," recalled Henry Houston of the 32nd Maine.[25]

The 32nd was a newly arrived regiment of men who, weeks earlier, had been at home around York and Biddeford and Kittery in the state's southernmost counties. The Georgians poured "a rattling volley or two . . . at very short range" into the Mainers, who hastily tried to change front under the "storm of missiles." What they lacked in well-drilled smoothness, they made up for with vigor. "We were new to such work, and may have manifested some awkwardness in the delicate and dangerous manoeuvre [*sic*] of changing front under fire," Houston admitted.[26]

This maneuver further mixed the 32nd Maine with the 6th and 9th New Hampshire.[27]

22 Ibid.

23 Ibid., 252.

24 Ibid.

25 Houston, 157.

26 Ibid.

27 Jackman, 252.

Lacking cohesion, with "the screeching 'Johnnies' pouring volley after volley into them, the Pine Tree State soldiers began to break, and some of the White Mountain State solders rose to join them in their flight. "Steady, men!" cried a number of their officers. "Hold your ground!" This seemed to fortify the New Hampshire men, who then "all poured a volley into the rebels, checking them, and compelling them to retire within their works, which were in plain sight."[28]

Exhausted and entangled, Griffin's men "began at once to dig like beavers, rolling up old logs, cutting down small trees, adding brush and earth, and in less than an hour had breastworks three feet high to protect our heads from the rebel shot," Jackman said. "All this time the enemy's sharpshooters were busy picking off our men, as these became exposed."[29]

"I could hear their bullets strike the ground all around me . . . sounding 'Put, Put, Put,'" Griffin later marveled. "They were evidently taking aim at me and doing their best to kill me, and why they failed has always been a mystery to me."[30]

* * *

Ledlie's brigade—on Griffin's left—ran into similar grief. Snarled in abatis, they were completely unaware of a curve in the Confederate line that gave Brig. Gen. Joseph Davis's Mississippians and North Carolinians an open field of fire straight into the Ledlie's flank. Davis, a nephew of the Confederate president, gave the order to fire, catching the Federals off-guard. Ledlie's men melted. "[T]he limbs, and even trees, were cut down like grass, and the place was most decidedly uncomfortable," wrote Col. Stephen Weld of the 56th Massachusetts.[31]

Weld offered a glimpse of the chaos under Ledlie's so-called "leadership." "I sent the sergeant major to General Ledlie with the information that we could not take the works," Weld recorded. "He returned, but could get no instructions." Unable to get support from the 35th Massachusetts, which "ran away" instead—"for which I did not blame them," the colonel admitted—Weld ordered the regiment to fall back to the former Confederate skirmish line. But then they were "ordered into the

28 Ibid. Jackman's editor, in a footnote to the account, included here, identifies "the Excelsior Brigade of Hancock's Corps" as the troops who fled through Griffin's brigade. *The History of the Ninth Regiment, New Hampshire Volunteers* by Edward O. Lord lays the blame more generally at "a division of the Second Corps" (375); however, it is not clear that Hancock's advance had even started yet by this point, let along having made it to the Confederate works. The 32nd Maine, for its part, contended: "[W]e did not show any want of courage" (Houston, 157).

29 Jackman, 253.

30 Griffin, 119.

31 Weld, 194.

woods again" and told to lie down. Then they were ordered into the breastworks again. The rest of the brigade went in with them but got no farther.

When they finally returned to their original lines, a highly animated Ledlie greeted them personally. "Fall in, Thirty-Fifth! Steady, Thirty-Fifth!" the general said in a "rather excited manner."[32]

Despite Ledlie's Kewpie doll face and walrus moustache, the men of the regiment did not recognize the "natty-looking officer" because he had been so recently promoted to command. "Don't trouble yourself," one of the 35th's officers told him. "You attend to your business and we'll attend to ours!"

If Ledlie heard the comment, he made no reply. "[F]ortunately for all concerned," the regimental historian wrote later, "he probably did not."[33]

The confusion was but a harbinger of worse to come later in the campaign under Ledlie, and it reinforced Weld's regret at the death of his friend, division commander Thomas Greely Stevenson, days earlier. "He will be a sad loss to us all," Weld wrote prophetically at the time—a loss Ledlie was already making them feel all the more keenly.[34]

When Ledlie's men fell back, it uncovered Griffin's brigade to their right. Hunkered down behind their beaverish barricades, Griffin's men held tight, though the Confederates kept them pinned in place for hours. Burnside's entire advance had collapsed.

* * *

By 4:20 a.m., unable to wait any longer for fear of completely losing the element of surprise, Hancock and Wright finally sent their men forward.

"Early on the morning of Wednesday, May 18, the whizzing of shells announced that the second great battle of Spottsylvania [*sic*] Court House had been commenced," wrote VI Corps surgeon W. G. T. Morton. And with that, one Rhode Islander wrote, "another butchery had begun."[35]

According to Confederate Charles Minor Blackford, the artillery booming across the area was "second only to that of Gettysburg." In fact, with the guns

32 Weld, 294.

33 Committee of the Regimental Association, 233.

34 Ledlie would, against orders, lead the brigade into a disastrous attack at the North Anna River on May 24, be found drunk behind the lines at Cold Harbor, and send his unwary men to slaughter at the Crater on July 30 while he, again, hid behind the lines and drank.

35 W. T. G. Morton, "The First Use of Ether as an Anesthetics," *The Journal of the American Medical Association*, April 23, 1904, 1071, FSNMP bound manuscript collection.

of the II, V, and IX corps all roaring, it was the largest bombardment in the Eastern Theater since Pickett's Charge. II Corps artillerists ran their guns right up to the backs of Hancock's men, and from under the cover of that "tremendous artillery fire . . . firing over their heads, the devoted lines moved forward to the assault," said James Bowen of the 37th Massachusetts.[36]

In 1846, William T. G. Morton earned fame for being the first doctor to publicly demonstrate the use of ether for medical procedures. During the Civil War, he volunteered as a surgeon with the VI Corps and reportedly operated on more than two thousand soldiers during his tenure. He wrote one of the most harrowing accounts of the May 18 battle. *National Library of Medicine*

"Smoke and mist hung pale, heavy and motionless over the troops" as the infantry advanced, Morton said. Confederates watched the Federals materialize out of the fog. "All were astonished," said artillery major Wilfred Cutshaw, "and could not believe a serious attempt would be made to assail such a line as Ewell had, in open day, over such distance." Cutshaw knew the effect his cannons were about to have, even as outnumbered as his pieces were.[37]

The Federals chased away Confederate pickets as they moved across the no-man's land toward Ewell's fortifications. "Then," wrote Bowen, "as the Confederate skirmishers were swept back before the strong lines of blue, the restrained tempest broke forth, and with shriek and scream and hissing, poured its death blast in the faces of the Union soldiers."[38]

"The rebels were there," Morton noted, "armed and vigilant."[39]

36 Susan Leigh Blackford, Charles Minor Blackford, *Letters From Lee's Army or Memoirs of Life In and Out of the Army in Virginia During the War Between the States* (Lincoln, NE: University of Nebraska Press, 1998), 246; J. Bowen, "In the Wilderness," June 27, 1885, *Philadelphia Weekly Times*, FSNMP BV 141.

37 Morton, 1071; Wilfred E. Cutshaw, John Warwick Daniel Papers Univ. of Virgina, FSNMP BV 134.

38 J. Bowen, "In the Wilderness."

39 Morton, 1071.

Armistead Long's artillery opened fire when the Federals advanced within 300 yards of the Confederate works. At their Northern counterparts in the woods opposite, Southern artillerists unleashed solid shot, intending to rain iron and tree branches on the enemy to wound and disrupt unit cohesion; at the Northern soldiers advancing across the open fields, though, the artillerists unleashed canister and case shot. "The rebels allowed our column to advance within point blank range, and then let out their death volleys," an unnamed Rhode Islander later wrote. "Heads, arms and legs were blown off like leaves in a storm."[40]

"[T]heir Artillery cut our men down in heaps," wrote another Rhode Islander, Lt. Elisha Hunt Rhodes.[41]

"Who does not believe it seemed a lifetime to many of those men, who, with bent body and erect bayonet, won their perilous way, foot by foot, through whistling balls, bursting shells, gnawing grape," Morton wrote years later, only a little melodramatically.[42]

The attackers came within sight of the Confederate line and made a charge, but, according to Rhodes, "it was of no use. . . . We reached the glacis in front of the Rebel forts, and here we were obliged to lay exposed to their fire." A Confederate artillerist called the attempted charge "very feable [*sic*], the artillery having completely demoralized them before they got within musket range."[43]

On the left, Hancock's men pushed forward as far as they could through no-man's land, but *abatis* tangled them midway between the McCoull farm and the new Confederate position. In the front line, the newly arrived Fourth Brigade of Barlow's division ground to a halt as the green soldiers neared the obstructions. Barlow reported to Hancock that the abatis was impenetrable, "the most dense . . . he has ever seen," estimating it was 100 yards deep in places—and it had been pre-sighted by Confederate gunners.[44]

From that position, though, Barlow's men attempted several runs at the Confederate works, only to be blasted back. "Our troops were received by a fire of both artillery and musketry, which swept the approaches and made great havoc in the ranks," wrote a II Corps officer. "Nevertheless, they continued to advance to the edge of the abatis, which in connection with a deadly fire, stopped further

40 Douglas Southall Freeman, *Lee's Lieutenants Volume 3: Gettysburg to Appomattox* (New York: Charles Scribner's Sons, 1944), 436–38; Unsigned letter, "From the Rifle Pits, May 19, 1864, Providence (RI) *Daily Journal*, June 1, 1864.

41 Rhodes, 154.

42 Morton, 1071.

43 Rhodes, 153–54; George W. Zirkle, letter, May 20, 1864 (sic: May 19, 1864), FSNMP BV 207.

44 Hancock to Williams, May 18, 1864, *O.R.* 36:2:868.

progress. Many brilliant efforts were made to penetrate the enemy's lines, but without success."[45]

"General B[arlow] thinks doubtful if our men can penetrate it," Hancock wrote to headquarters an hour into the fight. "I have no option but to order them to continue, unless I hear from you to the contrary."[46]

Some reports tell of the Federal divisions coming to ground on a set of abandoned reserve works John Brown Gordon's men had assaulted from during the initial Confederate counterattacks on May 12. Some of Barlow's men reported hunkering down and reversing the works. "That is, with axe, spade, and shovel, we reversed them as well as we could to make them defensible from our side," explained Thomas Galwey of the 8th Ohio. "These works were merely a heavy breastwork of logs—a 'simple sap'—with the earth from the ditch thrown up against the outer face and rammed."[47]

The majority of firsthand accounts strongly suggest, however, such progress was not widespread. Instead, Federal soldiers stood in the open, firing away, "but were soon disperced [*sic*] by the iron hail hurled against their close ranks," wrote Virginian George W. Zirkle of the Salem Flying Artillery. "There was a great many killed in front of our Battery."[48]

As the battle raged, Gibbon discovered that one of his brigades had not moved out to support the assault. In fact, Owen's veteran "Philadelphia Brigade" had never even stepped off. Further embarrassing Gibbon was the fact that he had not even noticed the missing brigade until one of Hancock's staff officers called it to his attention. Infuriated, Gibbon ordered the absent brigade to go in—but to no avail. Brigadier General Joshua T. Owen refused to budge.[49]

"[I]nstead of moving forward as directed in support of the first line, [Owen's brigade] had fallen back into a line of works into its rear," an infuriated Gibbon

45 De Trobriand, 581.

46 Hancock to Humphreys, May 18, 1864, *O.R.* 36:2:867.

47 Galwey, 217.

48 Zirkle, letter.

49 Gibbon, report, *O.R.* 36:1:431; Bradley Gottfried, *Brigades of Gettysburg: The Union and Confederate Brigades at the Battle of Gettysburg* (Cambridge, MA: Da Capo Press, 2002), 143-51. Gibbon had a series of run-ins with the brigade. A year earlier during the Gettysburg Campaign, Owen was arrested and his brigade was placed under the commanded of Brig. Gen. Alexander Webb during the battle itself. When dispatched to Culp's Hill on the evening of July 2, one of the brigade's regiments fled the field after receiving a volley in the dark. On July 3, during Pickett's Charge, some of the men refused to budge and help repulse the Southern assault. At Spotsylvania, they did not go in on May 18, and again at Cold Harbor, Owen would fail to carry out orders on the field—and was again brought up on charges by Gibbon. Owen was never brought to trial, though; he was quietly discharged from the army in July 1864.

reported. "The brigade had not at all supported the attack." Owen's disobedience would eventually lead to charges that resulted in his dismissal from the army.[50]

New Federal arrivals tried to show their mettle to the veterans. Colonel Matthew Murphy's brigade of four New York regiments anchored the left of Gibbon's division. These recent additions, coupled with Tyler's heavy artillery regiments supporting the left of Barlow's division, increased the II Corps' strength by nearly 8,000 rifles. Despite the weight of the New Yorkers' numbers and bravado, they too came to grief assaulting Ewell's heavily fortified line. Murphy advanced toward the Bloody Angle, but his brigade became separated due to botched orders from Gibbon's staff. Two of his four regiments, the 155th and 164th New York, "advanced immediately without my being informed," Murphy later reported. By the time he found them to his right and rear, they had been engaged so long "their ammunition was very nearly expended."[51]

Meanwhile, Murphy led his other two regiments, the 170th and 182nd New York, to within a few hundred yards of the Confederate line, but withering small-arms fire—mainly from Clement Evans's all-Georgia Brigade and a few scattered Virginians—pinned them down. Confederate artillery positioned on the New Yorkers's right and left flank swept their position with a deadly crossfire. Murphy tried to reunite his divided command, but by the time he shuffled his two regiments to the right and rear where the other two regiments were located, those units had already fallen back. Before he could figure out a next move, a bullet to the arm took Murphy out. His replacement, Col. J. P. McIvor, had no idea what Gibbon intended. Hunkered down and directionless, all the New Yorkers could do was call for help.[52]

To Hancock's right, Wright's attack met similar results. Neill's VI Corps division had not stepped off in concert with Gibbon's men, nor had they caught up. They had perhaps the toughest task, ordered as they were to follow the western leg of the Mule Shoe, scarred with deep trenches that cut brigades and regiments in two, wrecking their formations. Frank Wheaton's brigade led the way. In slight disarray, they swept down into a swale that offered cover, but from which they could not advance. In the front line, the 102nd and 93rd Pennsylvania found themselves isolated from the rest of the brigade due to a patch of woods. They eventually found themselves stumbling directly across the Confederate line of fire

50 Gibbon, report, *O.R.* 36:1:431–2.

51 Matthew Murphy, report, *O.R.* 36:1:459.

52 The 182nd consisted of men from the 69th New York State Militia, and Murphy referred to the regiment as such in his official report.

and paid a heavy toll as a result, falling back in disarray and stalling the entire division's advance.[53]

Their predicament resulted in an unfortunate chain reaction. Oliver Edwards's brigade got backed up as a result, and that stacked up Daniel Bidwell's brigade. Behind Bidwell came Lewis Grant's Vermont Brigade arrayed in two lines of battle—the five original regiments in front, and the 1st Vermont Heavies, owing to its size, alone in the second. "The Vermont regiments moved through the woods, with hostile shells crashing and cracking through the branches over their heads," the regimental historian later reported. The Vermonters were supposed to bring up the rear, but the traffic jam forced them to the front. "[T]he brigade soon overtook the front line, and was kindly permitted to take the front," a survivor noted wryly. There, the "bursting shell and rattling musketry" pinned them down. "The rebel sharpshooters were also busy in the tree-tops in front," the historian noted. One sharpshooter clipped Col. James Warner of the Heavies through the neck—"which narrowly escaped being a mortal [wound]"—but Warner retained command.[54]

Two VI Corps officers, trying to sort out the cluster, had their mission disrupted by Confederate artillery. "Arthur McClellan's bay horse had a shell pass directly through him as I happened to be looking," recounted a shocked Thomas Hyde. "The distressing cry seemed to tear our ears, while the collapse of the beautiful animal was a picture of pain framed by the smoking forest." Isaac Best of the 121st New York, who likewise witnessed the event, said the shell had "[cut] the covering of his intestines, letting them run out. The poor brute stood for some little time looking pitifully around, until the officer, coming up looked at the wound, drew his revolver and killed him."[55]

As Neill's division wallowed and thrashed about, jammed up on itself and against enemy artillery, Confederates began slipping around the flank of the trapped brigades, triggering an unsteady retreat first by Edwards's men and then by Neill's entire division. "[T]roops to the right and left were breaking into fragments and scrambling to the rear as best they could." noted a discouraged James Bowen. Their retreat took them "through the tempest of fire," back to "the sheltering earthworks from which [the men] had come."[56]

53 Mark Penrose, *Red, White, and Blue Badge: Pennsylvania Veteran Volunteers A History of the 93rd Regiment, Known as the "Lebanon Infantry" and "One of the 300 Fighting Regiments" From September 12th, 1861 to June 27th, 1865* (Mark Penrose, 1911), 269-270.

54 Benedict, 453.

55 Hyde, 204; Best, 151.

56 J. Bowen, "In the Wilderness."

There, they found Ricketts's division finally in place at its intended jumping-off point—but watching the carnage on the field, they in no way intended to advance. Meanwhile, Russell never showed at all.

* * *

By 9:00 a.m., word had gone up the chain of command that the attack was fruitless, and word came back down for the men to pull out. Grant decided to call off the futile attacks. "[T]he attack is abandoned," Humphreys reported to Hancock, directing action on the front.[57]

"The task undertaken was too trying," one soldier summarized, "the slaughter would be too terribly certain, the prospect of success was too remote.[58]

Regiments began to extricate themselves as best they could. "We sent our men back to the woods a few at a time until all were out of the direct fire," wrote Rhode Islander Rhodes.[59]

"This morning," wrote Capt. George A. Bowen of the 12th New Jersey, "we advanced . . . over essentially the same ground we did on the 12th without accomplishing anything except to meet with very considerable loss." James Bowen of the 37th Massachusetts—no relation to George—put it even more bluntly: "No attempt ever more completely failed."[60]

The lopsidedness of the Federal casualties spoke to the strength of the Confederate position and the triumph of engineering over infantry. Northern losses exceeded 1,500; Southern losses topped just 250. "We went in, lost some men and came out again—that is all there was to it!" the Bay State Bowen said.[61]

For the second time in less than a week, the ground around the former Mule Shoe was saturated with blood and strewn with bodies. Corpses from the earlier battle lay comingled with a fresh crop of dead. "After the fight," wrote a Confederate artillerist, "the battle field presented a horrible spectacle, some having their heads and limbs torn away from their bodies." It was, said Maj. Wesley Brainerd of the 50th New York engineers, "an awfully grand spectacle, one often repeated around that ground which has been justly styled 'Bloody Spotsylvania.'"[62]

57 Humphreys to Hancock, *O.R.* 36:2:869.

58 J. Bowen, "In the Wilderness."

59 Rhodes, 153-55.

60 George Bowen, diary; J. Bowen, "In the Wilderness."

61 Ibid.

62 Zirkle, letter; Wesley Brainerd, *Bridge Building in Wartime: Colonel Wesley Brainerd's Memoir,* Ed Malles, ed., (Nashville, TN: University of Tennessee Press, 1997), 221.

In April 1866, Dr. Reed Bontecou of the Army's medical department visited Spotsylvania and the Wilderness with a photography crew. Their work documented some of the aftermath of the battle, including scarred landscapes, temporary graves, and human remains. *Library of Congress*

Theodore Lyman spent part of his afternoon that day at a field hospital, there to see a friend and fellow Bostonian, Capt. Arthur Russell Curtis of the 20th Massachusetts, struck in the shoulder by case shot. "Most wounds today are from artillery and very bad," he noticed.[63]

Curtis was about to be bustled off with other wounded men to Fredericksburg. "He exhibited great stoicism under the terrible trial of seeing most of his brother officers shot down within these few days . . ." Lyman observed, "but plainly he was depressed by it." The Harvard Regiment had lost nine officers of lieutenant rank or higher since the start of the campaign—and 266 men in all of the approximately 575 men it had started with.[64]

Another officer from the regiment slated for evacuation was Capt. John Kelliher. The 20th Massachusetts had advanced with Col. Boyd McKeen's brigade in the front ranks of Gibbon's attack. Regimental surgeon John G. Perry, following them into battle, saw a pair of boots sticking out from a clump of bushes and discovered the semi-conscious Kelliher. "He had been struck by a shell and fearfully mangled," recounted regimental historian George Bruce. A shell had torn Kelliher's arm and shoulder blade off, displaced three of his ribs, and broken his jaw. Arterial bleeding left him "in expectation that death would soon follow." Perry triaged the captain, then had him evacuated to the field hospital for surgery. By the time Perry and his

63 Lyman, 163.

64 Lyman, 163; Bruce, 352, 379–82.

team finished their grim work, the line of Kelliher's sutures "ran from the ear to an inch of the pelvis."

Kelliher was slated for evacuation to the rear, but Perry believed he would not survive the journey. *I'll take all the risks*, Kelliher insisted. *I am going to live*.

And he did. By November, Kelliher would be back with the army and later would, for a short time, even command the regiment. "His powerful will alone saved him," Bruce said.[65]

The sun went down red that night. Wrote W. G. T. Morton: "The smoke of the battle of more than two hundred thousand men destroying each other with villainous saltpeter through all the long hours of a long day, filled the valleys, and rested on the hills of all this wilderness, hung in lurid haze all around the horizon, and built a dense canopy overhead, beneath which this grand army of freedom was preparing to rest against the morrow."[66]

As Federal troops trudged back to their previous day's positions, May 18 ended with a sublime coda. "[D]efeated by the all-day's thunder of artillery, and weary and sore from the march and straggling of the day . . ." II Corps staff officer Robert Robertson said, "we witnessed a sight worth a day's battle and a midnight march to see. It was raining and shortly after midnight the moon shone through a rift in the clouds clearly outlining on the opposite clouds a beautiful rainbow."

The wearied and drooping soldiers looked upon it as "a bow of promise," Robertson said, "and greeted it with cheers that made the gloomy forests ring."[67]

Grant had ridden to the army's right to watch the morning attack unfold and so saw for himself the formidable display of Confederate artillery. Even as he called off the assaults, he began formulating his next move. *I can't get at Lee here*, he realized. He needed to change the field of battle. His time at Spotsylvania was over.

Riding back to headquarters, Grant and his staff passed a group of wounded men along the roadside. One, lying close to the road, caught Grant's eye. "The man's face was beardless," Horace Porter remembered; "he was evidently young; his countenance was strikingly handsome, and there was something in his appealing look which could not fail to engage attention." Blood flowed from a wound in the man's chest, and bloody froth covered his mouth. "[H]is wandering, staring eyes gave unmistakable evidence of approaching death," Porter concluded.

65 Bruce, 385.

66 Morton, 1071.

67 Robertson, "From the Wilderness to Spotsylvania."

A young staff officer bolted past at full gallop. His horse's hooves kicked up black mud from a puddle, splashing the wounded man's face. The soldier "gave a piteous look," Porter said. *Couldn't you let me die in peace and not add to my sufferings?*

Grant, distressed, started to get down from his horse, but Porter leapt down first. Kneeling, he wiped the man's face with his handkerchief and offered words of comfort. "[B]ut in a few minutes the unmistakable death-rattle was heard," Porter said. The soldier breathed his last.

"The poor fellow is dead," Porter announced.

Grant looked pained, and he remained silent for a long while after. "While always keenly sensitive to the sufferings of the wounded," Porter later said, "this pitiful sight seemed to affect him more than usual."[68]

"It was a depressing day!" Theodore Lyman declared, summing things up for everyone. "Ill news from all sides; and the enemy securely on guard." That ill news sprang on Grant all at once, as soon as he returned to headquarters: John Breckinridge had beaten Franz Sigel at New Market and now Sigel was retreating northward down the Shenandoah Valley; Benjamin Butler had been driven from Drewry's Bluff outside Richmond and now seemed bottled up at Bermuda Hundred; Nathaniel Banks had suffered defeat in Louisiana. No word came from Sherman, but otherwise, all the spokes of Grant's grand strategy were snapping—a complete turnaround from just days earlier when good news seemed abundant.[69]

"I thought the other day that they must feel pretty blue in Richmond over the reports of our victories," Grant mused. No more.

*This is no time for repining*, he told himself.

Grant sat down at his field desk and began to write out orders.[70]

* * *

Robert E. Lee was happier about recent Confederates successes than Grant realized.

Lee's scouts had brought news of the Federal reinforcements marching down the Fredericksburg Road to join Grant's army. "General Grant can, and if permitted will, repair the losses of the late battles, and be as strong as when he began operation," Lee worried.[71] Meanwhile, the Army of Northern Virginia had no corresponding

68 This tale comes from Porter, 124.

69 Lyman, *Meade's Army*, 163; Porter, 124.

70 Porter, 124; Grant, memoirs, 558.

71 Robert E. Lee, *Lee's Dispatches: Unpublished Letters of General Robert E. Lee, C.S.A., to Jefferson Davis and the War Department of the Confederate States of American, 1862–1864*, Douglas Southall Freeman and Grady McWiney, eds. (New York: Putnam's, 1957), 185.

reinforcements of its own. Thus, Lee had cast his hopeful eye on the Confederate forces freed up by those events that Lyman had characterized as "ill news."

"If the changed circumstances as around Richmond will permit," Lee asked Jefferson Davis, "I recommend that such troops as can be spared be sent to me at once." Otherwise, were those troops required to stay in Richmond, Lee worried his army would have to fall back to the capital in order to still have the strength to fight.[72]

In a longer missive to Davis later that evening, Lee explained that his diminished army was still in no condition to attack. "His position is strongly entrenched, and we cannot attack it with any prospect of success without great loss of men which I wish to avoid if possible," he wrote. Nor did Lee think he could force Grant into making a blunder that might, in turn, create some kind of opportunity. "[N]either the strength of our army nor the condition of our animals will admit, of any extensive movement with a view to draw the enemy from his position," he wrote.[73]

The opportunist in him, though, still sought a way to strike a blow that would at least slow Grant and force him to fight on terms favorable to Lee. "I shall continue to strike him whenever opportunity presents itself," the Confederate chieftain pledged.

Ironically, the opportunity Lee considered most likely was "to engage him when in motion." Men in the Federal II, V, and VI corps might have pointed out to Lee that their entire lives had felt "in motion" since the start of the campaign and, in particular, during all the back-and-forth night marches across the battlefield from May 13 onward. Lee had just had no way to get at them. "[N]othing at present indicates any purpose on his part to advance," Lee told Davis.

But even as the general wrote those words, reports kept coming in to his headquarters suggesting movement by the Federal army away from the northernmost sector of the battlefield, where fighting had taken place just that morning, toward the Fredericksburg Road. This was the return of the II and VI Corps to their previous day's positions. Lee had no way to know whether it was opportunity or danger, but he began to realize something was afoot.

"The importance of this campaign to the administration of Mr. Lincoln and to General Grant," he told Davis, "leaves no doubt that every effort and every sacrifice will be made to secure its success."[74]

* * *

72 Lee, *Wartime Papers*, 733.

73 Lee, *Dispatches*, 183-84.

74 Ibid., 185.

Hancock "the Superb" was Hancock the exhausted. As his corps shifted back to its position on the Federal left, Hancock paid a visit to army headquarters. Tired as he was, he sat with Lyman, lit a pipe, and "poured out a volume of energetic conversation." Then, just like that, he laid his big head on his arm and "went off like a babe."[75]

Lyman liked Hancock and considered him "a man of ability," but he worried that Hancock's old Gettysburg injury was troubling him more than he was letting on. "[H]is bone wound threatened to slough" is how John Gibbon had put it. The grueling pace of the campaign—unrelenting, unforgiving—was sapping even the strongest men, and Hancock's corps was being used especially hard.[76]

Hancock would need all the rest he could get. Grant again had his eye on the II Corps and intended to use it for more hard work—this time, as bait.

As Grant envisioned it, "Wright and Burnside should . . . force their way up as close to the enemy as they can get without a general engagement . . . and entrench" (or "with a general engagement if the enemy will come out of their works to fight," he added hopefully). With Confederates thus distracted, Hancock was to set out "with all his force and as much cavalry as can be given to him, to get as far toward Richmond on the line of the Fredericksburg railroad as he can make, fighting the enemy in whatever force he may find him." With any luck, Grant hoped Lee would pounce on the isolated Hancock, trusting his II Corps commander to hold on until reinforcements arrived. "If the enemy makes a general move to meet this," Grant explained, "they will be followed by the other three corps of the army, and attacked if possible before time is given to entrench."[77]

"Lee held upon Spottsylvania with a grip that no efforts of ours could unloosen," a VI Corps officer would later remark. "It had become a veritable woodland fortress." If Grant could not break Lee at Spotsylvania, as had been the case at the Wilderness, he would simply go around him—again—and flush Lee out that way. Hancock was to head to the southeast by 1:00 a.m. on May 20.[78]

Hancock's staff finally came to wake him. He jumped up—"awake as quickly as asleep," Lyman noted—and strode out of the tent. He did not know it yet, but he had a little more than 32 hours to rest his men and get organized for the move.

75 This tale comes from Lyman, *Meade's Army*, 163.

76 Ibid., 121–2, 118.

77 Grant to Meade, May 18, 1864, *O.R.* 36:2:865.

78 Hyde, 203.

# May 15
# May 16
# May 17
# May 18
# May 19

Thursday, May 19 opened quietly. "The day was beautiful almost beyond description, reminding me of . . . June days in New England," wrote Joseph W. Gardner of the newly arrived 1st Massachusetts Heavy Artillery. Along the lines, Federals and Confederates alike enjoyed the morning's respite and traded coffee, tobacco, and newspapers. "Nearly all fagged out and need rest," wrote Confederate brigade commander Bryan Grimes to his wife.[1]

Thomas Galwey and some of his comrades from the 8th Ohio took the opportunity about noon to go down to the banks of the Ny River and bathe. "I doffed my apparel and jumped in," Galwey said. "I was joined by others. As we had neither soap nor towels we dried in the sun."[2]

Federal artillerist Charles Wainwright, who had found time for a proper bath, shuddered at the thought of such rustic accommodations and wondered how infantrymen managed: "[A] fortnight without a change [of clothes] is something awful to contemplate."[3]

In the camp of the 4th New York Heavy Artillery, some of the men debated the fate of an ox slated for slaughter. "The ox had been driven around so many days that he had become quite a pet with the boys," wrote the regimental historian.

*Seems a pity to slaughter the old fellow*, one of them said.

1 Roe and Nutt, 153; Bryan Grimes, *Extracts of Letter of Major Gen'l Bryan Grimes to His Wife* (Raleigh: Edwards, Broughton & Co., 1883), 55.

2 Galwey, 218.

3 Wainwright, 374.

"Getting' tender-hearted, eh?" said the butcher. "I shouldn't wonder if you fellers would be a-killin' men afore night."

That somehow settled the matter. The ox was slaughtered, cooked, and eaten, and "the excellent beef allotted each man" duly satisfied any remaining "compunctions of sympathy."[4]

George Meade started the day by dashing off a letter to his wife, the first in days for the usually regular correspondent. "We did not have the big battle which I expected yesterday," he wrote, "as on advancing, we found the enemy so strongly entrenched that even Grant thought it useless to knock our heads against a brick wall, and directed a suspension of the attack. We shall now try to maneuver again, so as to draw the enemy out of his stronghold, and hope to have a fight with him before he can dig himself into an impregnable position."[5]

About 1:30 p.m., orders arrived at Hancock's headquarters for the move southeast, now set to commence at 2:00 a.m. He was to go as far as Milford Station, about 25 miles away. "Should you encounter the enemy, you will attack him vigorously," the order said.[6]

"There is an old adage that it is the willing horse that is worked to death," grumbled Charles Hale Morgan, the II Corps chief of staff, who proceeded to go off like a rocket, reciting the litany of the heavy fighting the corps had engaged in since the campaign's start. "And now," he growled indignantly, "on the third consecutive night, it was proposed to send it on a flank march, over twenty miles, to 'attack vigorously' in the morning."

Hancock, dutiful as ever, accepted the orders with more stoicism. "Under the circumstances it might be well for me to march earlier, so that I could get beyond Guiney's and well toward Bowling Green by daylight," he told headquarters. Meade responded with confidence in his corps commander: "Start at such hour as you deem best."[7]

As II Corps staff officer Francis Walker later noted, however, "Providence and the Confederates interfered to prevent the movement."[8]

* * *

4 Hyland Clare Kirk, *Heavy Guns and Light: A History of the 4th New York Heavy Artillery* (New York: C. T. Dillingham, 1890), 218.

5 Meade, *Life and Letters,* 196–97.

6 Humphreys to Hancock, *O.R.* 36:2:910.

7 Ibid.

8 Walker, 487.

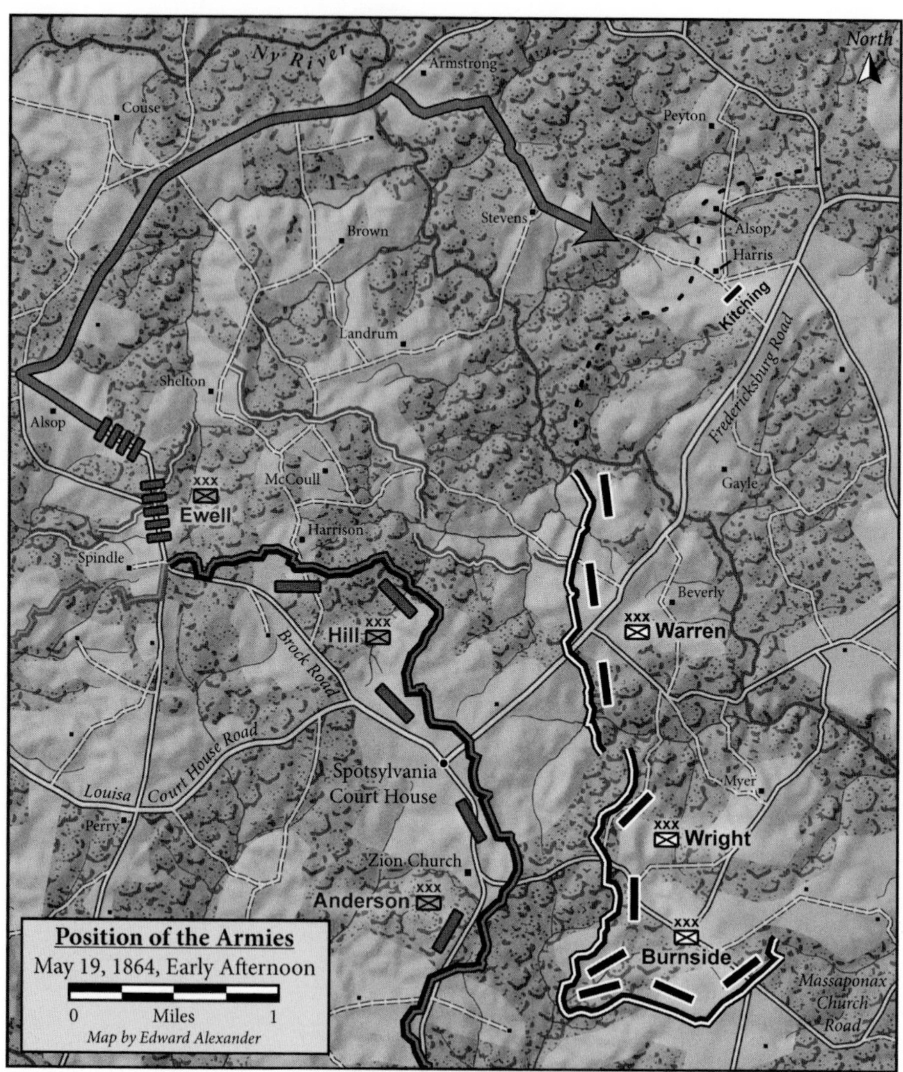


**Position of the Armies**—By the morning of May 19, 1864, the armies had sidled eastward across the Spotsylvania landscape. If the battle opened on May 8 at 10:30 on a clock face, eleven days later, the contending forces had moved to 2:00, with southernmost flanks stretching down beyond 3:00. Needing fresh intelligence, Lee sent his Second Corps on a flanking maneuver to probe the rear of Grant's army and look for an offensive opportunity.

---

May 19 was "do or die" day for Richard Ewell, although the lieutenant general did not know it. Perhaps Robert E. Lee didn't even recognize it as such, either, though he was certainly looking for just such an inflection point by then.

A member of West Point's Class of 1840, the 47-year-old Ewell had performed well early in the war as one of Stonewall Jackson's hardest-fighting subordinates. Major General Richard Taylor, who had served with Ewell during the Shenandoah Valley Campaign in the spring of 1862, praised Ewell's "fine tactical eye on the battle field," but said "he was never content with his own plan until he had secured the approval of another's judgment." [9]

After losing his left leg during the Second Manassas campaign in August 1862, Ewell returned to the army in the wake of Chancellorsville in time to be tapped as one of the fallen Jackson's successors. During his absence, he married his childhood sweetheart, a widowed cousin named Lizinka, whom he introduced to people by her married name, "Mrs. Brown."

John Brown Gordon described Ewell "as a compound of anomalies, the oddest, most eccentric genius in the Confederate Army":

> No man had a better heart nor a worse manner of showing it. He was in truth as tender and sympathetic as a woman, but, even under slight provocation, he became externally as rough as a polar bear, and the needles with which he pricked sensibilities were more numerous and keener than porcupine quills. His written orders were full, accurate, and lucid; but his verbal orders or directions, especially when under intense excitement, no man could comprehend. At such times his eyes would flash with a peculiar brilliancy, and his brain far outran his tongue.[10]

Taylor's smartly written memoir described Ewell's "[b]right, prominent eyes, a bomb-shaped, bald head, and a nose . . . [that] gave him a striking resemblance to a woodcock, and this was increased by a bird-like habit of putting his head on one side to utter his quaint speeches. He fancied that he had some mysterious malady. . . . His nervousness prevented him from taking regular sleep, and he passed the nights curled around a camp-stool, in positions to dislocate an ordinary person's joints."[11]

Things started well enough for Ewell, who scored a victory at Second Winchester early in the Gettysburg campaign, making a favorable impression on his men. "The more I see of [Ewell] the more I am pleased to be with him . . ." admitted Alexander "Sandie" Pendleton, who had served as the Second Corps' chief of staff under Stonewall Jackson and continued to do so under Ewell. "I

9 Richard Taylor, *Destruction and Reconstruction: Personal Experiences of the Late War* (New York: Appleton, 1879), 37.

10 Gordon, 38.

11 R. Taylor, 37.

Artillery officer John Cheves Haskell described Lt. Gen. Richard Ewell as "a queer character, very eccentric, but upright, brave and devoted. He had no very high talent but did all that a brave man of moderate capacity could do." *Library of Congress*

look for great things of him, and am glad to say that our troops have for him a good deal of the same feeling they had towards General Jackson."[12]

Pendleton's opinion would sour over time, however. "Gen. Ewell, tho' he has quick military perceptions & is a splendid executive officer, lacks decision, and is too irresolute for so large & independent a command as he has," he declared by mid-autumn.[13]

Lee's opinion of Ewell seems to have followed a similar trajectory, traceable all the way back to the first day at Gettysburg on July 1, 1863. That evening, malcontent Maj. Gen. Isaac R. Trimble—serving as a kind of factotum for the Second Corps because Lee had nothing else for him to do—had bad-mouthed Ewell for not taking his suggestion to attack East Cemetery Hill.[14] Ewell had actually made competent, well-reasoned decisions that day—still second-guessed more than a century and a half later—but Trimble, an insulted gadfly, had his dander up.[15] Lee faced various problems with his high command across the board, but Ewell came away from Gettysburg the most tarnished.

12 Quoted in Freeman, *Lee's Lieutenants: Cedar Mountain to Chancellorsville*, 713.

13 Quoted in Pfanz, 342.

14 Portrayed in the movie *Gettysburg*, with William Morgan Sheppard as Isaac Trimble, this encounter is one of the stand-out scenes of the movie. Alas, Sheppard's strong performance helped cement the one-sided argument against Ewell in the public's mind.

15 For more on this, see "Second-Guessing Richard Ewell" by Chris Mackowski and Kristopher D. White, *Civil War Times*, August 2010. Ewell's only real crime at Gettysburg was that he wasn't Stonewall Jackson, although virtually all of his actions mirror decisions Jackson would likely have made based on Jackson's own record.

Ewell also carried baggage from a missed opportunity at Bristoe Station, Virginia, in October 1863. Third Corps commander A. P. Hill had bungled an opportunity to defeat a portion of the Army of the Potomac there, even though Ewell's Corps had deployed in a position to perhaps salvage the battle. When the Federals escaped overnight, Lee blamed it in part on the Second Corps's slow arrival on the field the previous day, although Lee had overseen the corps' movement himself.

Ewell had opened the spring 1864 campaign on a strong note, performing well in the Wilderness—but Lee, on the far side of the battlefield, missed most of it. According to one account, Lee arrived on Ewell's front late on May 6 just in time to hear self-serving complaints from John Brown Gordon—in the petulant tradition of Isaac Trimble—that neither Ewell nor Early had taken his suggestions for an attack against the Federal right flank.[16]

As a result, says Ewell biographer Donald C. Pfanz, Lee looked at everything Ewell did at Spotsylvania with a poisoned eye. "Ewell had brought his troops to the battlefield in good time on 8 May and had successfully repulsed major Federal attacks on 10, 12, and 18 May, albeit at a high cost to his corps," Pfanz writes. "Yet Lee saw much to criticize in his lieutenant's conduct." Lee blamed Ewell for the "unfortunate advice" to hold the Mule Shoe Salient—a recommendation supported by Lee's artillerists and chief engineer and that Lee, as a trained engineer himself and as the final arbiter of all things under his command, had ultimately accepted. Lee blamed Ewell for Robert Rodes's "imperfect fortifications" on May 10 that allowed Upton's breakthrough. Finally, Lee was deeply offended by Ewell's "unprofessional conduct" as the Second Corps commander tried to rally "Alleghany" Johnson's men in the wake of the salient's collapse on May 12.[17]

Whether Ewell saw these events in the same light is unknown, but his aide—his stepson, Campbell Brown—cast them in favorable terms. "So far the Gen's. health is excellent," he wrote to his mother, "[and] he has done more work than any man in the Army I think, since commencement of this affair, over two weeks ago."[18]

Whether May 19 offered any opportunity for Ewell's redemption seems unlikely, considering how poisoned Lee's eye was by then, but the day certainly seemed ripe with the possibility for ruination.

Lee desperately needed intelligence. His cavalry, however, was still spread out and his most trusted cavalry leader dead. So, as in the days before Chancellorsville, the Confederate commander sent out his Second Corps on a reconnaissance-

16 Accounts disagree as to what exactly happened, making this one of the Wilderness's enduring controversies.

17 Pfanz, 402.

18 Brown, 258.

in-force. It could not have been an easy choice for Lee. Aside from his lack of confidence in Ewell himself, the corps had been mauled during the previous week and was thus dramatically understrength. Occupying the extreme Confederate left as it did, though, the Second Corps was perfectly situated for the task, and Lee's need for information was great.

"[H]e believed that Grant was about to move to our right," explained Lee's aide, Walter Taylor, "and he wished to force his hand and ascertain his purpose." *Demonstrate against the enemy in our front*, Lee told Ewell.

Ewell, however, expressed concern about the weakened state of his corps and questioned whether it was up to a stand-up fight outside its defensive works, so he instead suggested a movement toward and perhaps around the enemy's right. "General Lee approved," Taylor recorded.[19]

Ewell set out that afternoon with just more than 6,000 men and a six-gun battery from Lt. Col Carter Braxton's artillery battalion. He left the rest of his artillery behind because the roads were still too muddy to allow him to move quickly with the big guns. He also wanted to leave them behind as a way to help cover his understrength line, which would be held temporarily by Kershaw's Division, called in by Lee from its reserve position south of town. Lee later noticed the left-behind artillery—a mistake, in his mind, which he tried to correct by shifting some of Early's Third Corps guns. Ewell would compound the poor decision by eventually sending Braxton's artillery back, too, worried they would bog down in the ample mud.

"[W]e stole out from our lines very secretly and marched miles to the rear of the enemy's right," wrote one Confederate. With a cavalry screen from Thomas Rosser in the lead, the Second Corps' route took it up the Brock Road, then northeast along Gordon Road. A day earlier, this same area had been thick with Federals during Hancock's overnight movement to the Brown farm on May 12; now, the entire area seemed unprotected. Ideally, Federal cavalry would have patrolled the area to keep it safe but, again, Sheridan's folly continued to nag the army.[20]

The cross-country trek crept along. After traversing the Ny River, the army moved overland past the Armstrong and Stevens farms, through heavy woods, and finally to the rolling farmland near the Harris and Alsop farms west of the Fredericksburg Road.

* * *

19 Taylor, *General Lee: His Campaigns in Virginia*, 243.

20 William. W. Smith to John W. Daniel, letter, October 12, 1904, The Randolph-Macon System, College Park, Lynchburg, Virginia, FSNMP BV 50.

Members of the 1st Massachusetts Heavy Artillery were roused at 4:00 a.m. on May 19, and each man cooked coffee in his own cup and ate his hardtack. "The stillness and splendor of all nature was to me ominous," wrote Joseph Gardner, "and the thought struck me forcibly that any change in the surroundings and situation could not be for the better, but must be for worse."[21]

For better or worse, though, the artillerists-turned-infantrymen were finally on the cusp of battle. Heavy artillery units—or "Heavies," as they became known—had spent most of the war serving in the defenses around Washington. The regiments had as many 1,800 men in them, trained not only as artillerists for the forts' giant guns, but also trained to be the guns' built-in infantry support. Most Heavies enjoyed the comfort and safety of garrison duty in the nation's capital—cushy even by the standards of regular garrison duty—and most infantrymen derided Heavies as "band-box soldiers" for being neat and clean, unmuddied and unbloodied by field service.[22] At a point in the war when many 1,000-man regiments had been whittled down to a few hundred men, the undecimated Heavy Artillery regiments were sometimes mistaken as brigades or even divisions.[23]

By 1864, Washington was the most heavily fortified city in the world. Grant believed such strong fortifications didn't require that many men to defend them and thought those soldiers could be better used at the front. As he cast about for reinforcements to replace his mounting casualties, he stripped the Heavies from the Washington defenses and called them to central Virginia. "At last, after long months of garrison duty, days of waiting and impatience to the majority who wanted action, a share in the fighting and glory of achievement . . ." Gardner wrote. "[A]t last came the orders which brought the regiment into the midst of the bloodiest conflicts of the war."[24]

Other Heavy Artillery units, toiling under reputations for softness, felt the same. "The boys had been hoping to hear such news for a long time before it came, but it came at last," recalled a member of the 1st Maine Heavy Artillery. A newspaper from their home state reported, "The boys were highly gratified at the prospect of having a finger in the final grand struggle, and went forward with the greatest enthusiasm."[25]

21 Roe and Nutt, 153.

22 Other insults included "Abe's pets" and "paper collars."

23 For an example, see Augustus Cleveland Brown, *The Diary of a Line Officer* (New York: 1906), 11.

24 Roe and Nutt, 150. Gardner's comment comes in a regimental history written decades later, when veterans tended to put a more patriotic spin on their experiences, but contemporaneous accounts suggest the sentiment was true in the moment.

25 Gillman, 1; *Whig & Courier*, May 19, 1864, 2.

The Heavies "accepted the order to move with a grim joy that words will not reveal," Gardner said.[26]

The Bay State men arrived at Belle Plain on May 16 and, at 8:00 the next morning, began a 23-mile march to Spotsylvania. "On the road between Fredericksburg long lines of ambulances with ghastly loads were met," Gardner recounted. "The sight of all these bloody, suffering wounded men was enough to impress the stoutest heart."

Yet even wounded men often found strength enough to trash-talk the Heavies on their march to the battlefield. "Go it, Heavies," one of them called. "Old Grant'll soon cut you down to fighting weight." "How are you, Heavies? Is this work heavy enough for you?"

"The wounded seem to delight in making us as uncomfortable as possible," marveled a mystified Gardner.[27]

The 1st Maine Heavies had a similar experience on their march. "We did not know why they should sneer and scoff and insult us," one of them said. "But they did so, and it only made us more anxious to 'go in' and show them that we could fight."[28]

The Massachusetts men arrived at Spotsylvania late on May 17. "[T]heir new uniforms and bright muskets formed a striking contrast to the travel-stained clothing and dull-looking arms of the other regiments," noticed Horace Porter. They did not have long to rest, though, before they were directed into position for the fight on May 18. They saw no actual action, posted as they were in support of Federal artillery, but they saw and heard Confederate counterbattery fire overshoot their position. It was for them, for the first time, the sound of war.[29]

The 1st Massachusetts Heavies camped that night near the Anderson farm, hunkered down near several other Heavy Artillery units under Robert O. Tyler, a New York native and graduate of the West Point Class of 1853. A career artillerist, Tyler had earned a respected reputation for himself as an officer in the Artillery Reserve, but like the Heavies he now commanded, he had been converted to the infantry.[30]

Other Heavies—the 4th, 6th, and 15th New York—encamped along the rolling hills between the Ny and the Clement Harris farm in the Federal right-rear, tasked with protecting the supply route along the Fredericksburg Road. Grant had

26 Roe and Nutt, 153.

27 Roe and Nutt, 151; Porter, 128.

28 Augustus Buell, *The Cannoneer: Recollections of Service in the Army of the Potomac* (Washington, D.C.: *The National Tribune*, 1890), 169-70.

29 Porter, 128.

30 Jordan, 154–55.

Colonel J. Howard Kitching and Brigadier General Robert O. Tyler would both rise to the occasion in their new roles as infantry commanders. *Emerging Civil War Library of Congress*

placed them under the command of Col. J. Howard Kitching, a 25-year-old New Yorker who had been with the army since the Gettysburg campaign. Kitching had formerly served as colonel of the 6th New York Heavies before being transferred to the Artillery Reserve; like Tyler, he had recently been converted to an infantry officer as part of that week's artillery reorganization.

Kitching understood that he served as the Federal right flank, and he kept a nervous eye to the north and west. The task proved more difficult than he expected, though. "I have had some difficulty forming my line this morning," he admitted, "owning to the fact that my officers and men are entirely ignorant of picket duty." As he reported to Warren, "The cavalry with me are all new and not at all useful as scouts." Sheridan's absence continued to be a problem.[31]

Kitching eventually posted three companies of the 4th New York Heavy Artillery regiment—440 men—in a battalion-sized skirmish line that ran from the Harris farm northward through a patchwork of woodlots, meadows, and cornfields to the Alsop farm, where it then looped east to anchor on the Fredericksburg

31 Kitching to Marvin, May 19, 1864, *O.R.* 36:2:923; Kitching to Warren, May 19, 1864, *O.R.* 36:2:923.

Road. Between the two farmhouses, the ground dipped into a shallow swale with a streamlet at the bottom. Captain Augustus Cleveland Brown, tasked as the line officer of the day, described the formation as an upside-down fishhook.[32]

To their west, the hills descended to low, marshy ground bisected by one of the many small streams that fed into the Ny, and "a low miry swamp . . . filled thick with cat's-tails" extended toward the Federal right. A rail fence lined the hillside on the east side of the stream.[33]

Private Warren Works, a member of Company K, had settled comfortably into his picket post when a game of cards broke out with members of the next post over. Scarcely had the game gotten underway when "a squad of rebel cavalry came suddenly dashing out of the woods, and almost rode over us," Works wrote. "We were as much surprised as they were. We all fired at the same time, when they about-faced and galloped away, emptying their pistols as they wheeled."[34]

Such outbursts pestered Kitching all day. Rosser's cavalry, in its efforts to find the Federal flank, kept popping up. Kitching reported the ongoing harassment, although he assured Warren, "I am all right."[35]

* * *

While Rosser's troopers led the way for Ewell, they eventually split away as the infantry neared the Federal flank. The bulk of Rosser's men traveled northeast along the Gordon Road, cutting deeper into the Federal rear. Their route took them on a side road that ran north to the Plank Road, where they found themselves once more blundering into combat with the 2nd Ohio Cavalry and Edward Ferrero's USCT—their victorious foes from May 15. Most of the wagon train the Federals guarded had, by that point, moved safely east toward Salem Church, but Rosser managed to find the column's rear guard. "[T]he cavalry carbines began to crack at a furious rate," wrote Lt. Freeman S. Bowley of the 30th USCT, who heard the sounds in the distance.[36]

Ferrero ordered the 2nd Ohio Cavalry to engage until he could bring infantry support. The 30th was among those units sent on the run. Nearing the site of the cavalry fight some 300 yards away, the infantry deployed five or six paces apart and

32 Brown, *Diary of a Line Officer,* 49.

33 Kirk, 219.

34 Ibid.

35 Kitching to Warren, May 19, 1864, *O.R.* 36:2:923.

36 Bowley's account comes from Freeman S. Bowley, *A Boy Lieutenant* (Philadelphia: Henry Altemus Company, 1906), 68–70.

advanced. "Now just imagine you are hunting for coons and keep your eyes open," said the 30th's Maj. James C. Leake. "Skirmishers, forward!"[37]

"'Pears like 'twas de coons doin' de huntin' dis time," laughed one of the infantrymen as they advanced.[38]

For Lieutenant Bowley, this was his first march into battle. "Here was my chance," he wrote. "I would fire my first shot for the old flag and the Union." With great deliberation, he raised his Enfield to his shoulder and "took aim at a horseman who appeared to be an officer, and fired. The rifle . . . kicked spitefully, and gave me the impression that my shoulder had been almost dislocated. And the officer? He did not notice it at all, but rode down his line perfectly unconcerned."

Thomson's battery of horse artillery, part of Rosser's force, fired a pair of shots "to cool the ardor of the Yankee infantry and to acquaint them with the fact that we had something around there a little heavier than a common musket." Confederates soon fell back, though, and vanished into the gloaming.[39]

All told, the fight lasted about an hour. Confederate artillerist George Michael Neese described it as "a severe little battle," but Ferrero dismissed the late-day brush-up as nothing more than "a slight skirmish with the enemy."[40]

* * *

Meanwhile, Ewell positioned himself on the right-rear flank of the rest of the Federal army. Robert Rodes's Division led the Confederate advance. Rodes—who had aged into a fine division commander since his promotion to the position a year earlier—approached the Harris farm with caution, deploying his most trusted brigade under Stephen Ramseur, who commanded four Tar Heel regiments that numbered nearly 600 men. The North Carolina native was still recovering from a wound on May 12, the same day his men had been battered in the Mule Shoe, but they still had fight in them and so did he.

37 Ferrero to Richmond, May 26, 1864, *O.R.* 36:1:987.

38 Bowley, 68-70. Leake, whose name is sometimes spelled "Lake" in regimental records, had come to the 30th USCT from the 5th Ohio. He would die August 15 after being shot through the right lung at the battle of the Crater on July 30, 1864. He is buried in Cincinnati. Thanks to Ryan Quint for helping me run down the background on this story.

39 Neese, 272.

40 Neese, 272; Ferrero to Richmond, *O.R.* 36:1:987. For more on this action, see Noel Harrison, "The Mysterious, Second Combat-Action for USCT's in Spotsylvania County," 1 March 2012, *Mysteries & Conundrums*. https://npsfrsp.wordpress.com/2012/03/01/the-mysterious-second-combat-action-for-uscts-in-spotsylvania-county-2/. Based on Harrison's research, this fight likely took place across property that is now the Mackowski family's yard.

Remembered Captain Brown of the 4th New York Heavies:

> I saw a rebel picket line advancing across an open field in our front, and just behind it two lines of battle closely massed, with flags flying and officers on horseback, emerging from the woods in the rear of the field, but with their flanks so masked in woods on either side of the field that I could not see how far they extended. It was a magnificent sight, for the lines moved as steadily as if on parade, and if ever I longed for a battery of artillery with guns shot with grape and canister, and my own men behind those guns, it was then and there, for I do not think the lines were more than two or three hundred yards from where I stood.[41]

It did not take Ramseur long to find the New Yorkers, who, despite the size of their unit, were outclassed by Ramseur's battle-hardened veterans. The North Carolinians poured from the woods and opened fire on the green troops. "I did'nt [*sic*] believe there would be left ten of those greenies together in ten minutes after," wrote Tar Heel William Smith.[42]

Private Warren Work's picket vidette took cover in a nearby abandoned house and began firing out of the chinks and upstairs windows. The Confederates poured a volley at them. "It seemed to me that it tore away the whole side of the building," Works said. Another man marveled, "The balls came through as if the building were paper, and several men were struck." After exchanging a few more shots, Work and his comrades beat a retreat, but Work "was unfortunate enough to get mired in the slough, though pretty well concealed by the sedge. The flags and cat's-tails were cut about my head in a way that was anything but pleasant. Throwing away my blanket and also a large frying-pan, I gained the other side pretty well blown."[43]

Brown ordered "a slow and stubborn withdrawal of the line," worried that the hidden ends of Ramseur's lines extended beyond his own. "Their bulldog fighting, together with advantage of ground—as there was a swampy spot, which made it difficult for the enemy to cross in their front—was all that saved the plucky little battalion from entire destruction," wrote drummer boy James Lockwood.[44]

41 Brown, 48–9.

42 Wm. W. Smith to John W. Daniel, letter.

43 Kirk, 220.

44 Brown, 49; James Lockwood, *Life and Adventures of a Drummer Boy: or Seven Years a Soldier* (Albany, NY: 1893), 68.

Kitching promptly pled for help. "Our pickets are being driven in on the right," he scribbled to Warren. "Do not know the force, but it must be quite large as our picket was strong."[45]

Grant and Meade, at their Anderson farm headquarters a mile and a half to the southeast, heard the ruckus "behind us in just the last position at which we should have expected it," according to a member of headquarters staff. Meade authorized the movement of additional Heavy Artillery regiments to Kitching's assistance. The 1st Massachusetts Heavies were the first to mobilize, but additional reinforcements were soon on the move, too.[46]

Brigadier General Stephen Ramseur took a bullet on May 12 but was back on his feet by May 19. He had six months and a day left to live.

*Generals and Brevets*

Grant sent Porter to act as his eyes and ears. "Urge upon the commanders . . ." the general told his aide, "not only to check the advance of the enemy, but to take the offense and destroy them."[47]

* * *

After calling for aid, Kitching turned his attention to his men. "While the shells are flying over us, and the bullets whizzing past us, he is walking leisurely up and down the line," one of them noticed, "and if any of the boys should dodge, he will say with a smile, 'No ducking,—stand up!' His demeanor and example in battle has made heroes of the meanest cowards."[48]

As the bullets whizzed by in greater and greater numbers, "cutting the boughs, flags, and men promiscuously," a big yellow dog belonging to J. Lobdell of Company D appeared on the field. The dog began to snap and run after the *zzzips* made by passing bullets, "showing unmistakable signs of rage," said one observer. Another noted "his ears and tail up, and his whole appearance indicating the intensest interest in his pursuit of the imaginary birds." Suddenly, one of the

45 Kitching to Warren, May 19, 1864, *O.R.* 36:2:924.

46 Fielding H. Garrison, *John Shaw Billings: A Memoir* (New York: G. P. Putnam's Sons, 1915), 91.

47 Porter, 127.

48 Theodore Irving, *More Than Conqueror: Memorials of Col. J. Howard Kitching* (New York: Hurd and Houghton, 1873), 129.

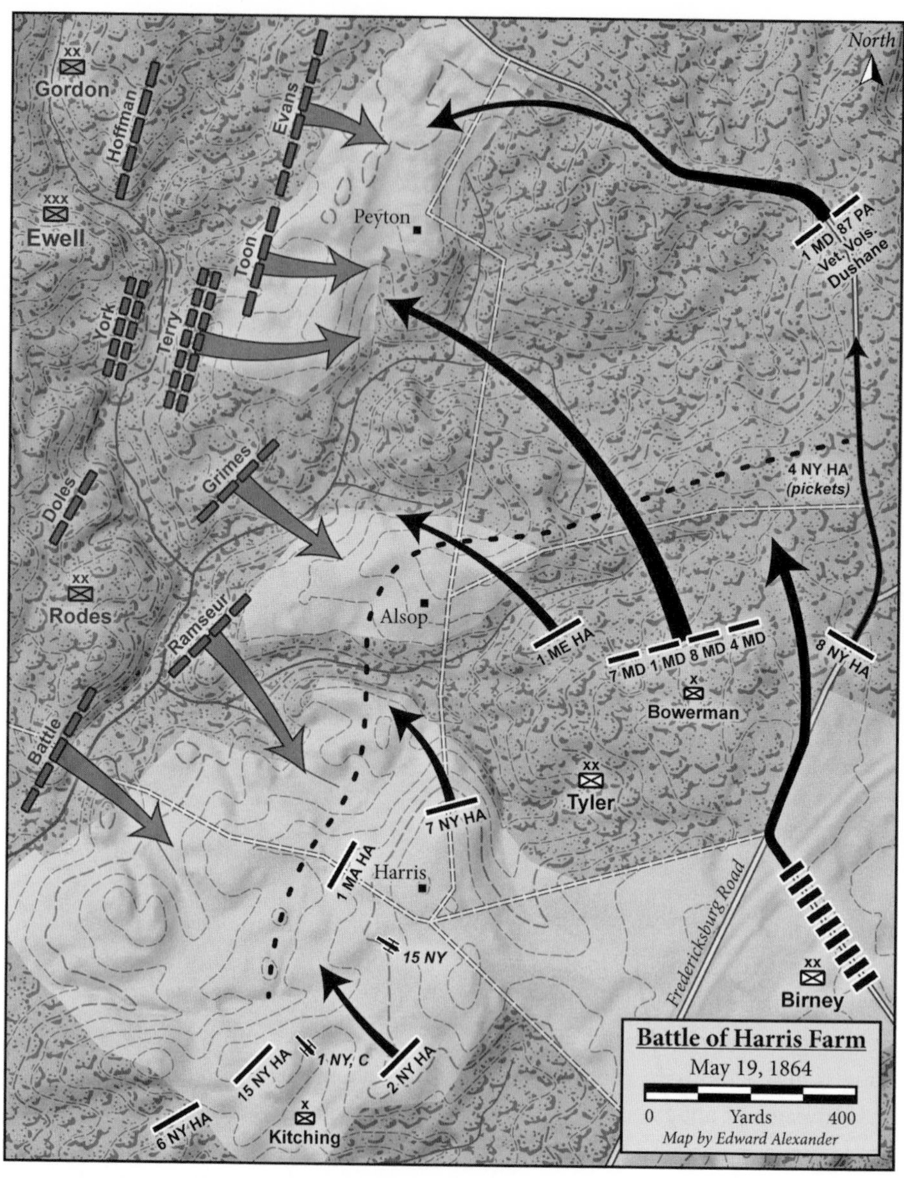


**Battle of Harris Farm**—The Second Corps' appearance in the Federal rear pitted battle-hardened Confederates against several inexperienced and mostly unprepared Federal heavy artillery units. The experience of the Confederates and the greater numbers of the Federals resulted in a back-and-forth fight as units came in from one side and then the other. Federals had more units to feed into the fight, and their weight of numbers began to tell. Confederates held on until dark and then slipped away.

"birds" took off the end of the dog's tail. "[D]own went his ears and the rest of his tail," the witness said, "and with intermittent but emphatic 'ki-yis,' he went to the rear like a yellow streak."[49]

As the New Yorkers stubbornly gave ground, the 1st Massachusetts Heavies arrived on the field, bringing just more than 1,600 men into the fray. Marching up the Fredericksburg Road from the south, they wheeled onto a farm lane and deployed past the Harris farmhouse. Two companies moved forward to join the New York pickets while the rest of the regiment shook itself out and prepared for battle. On the left, Maj. Frank A. Rolfe rode up and down his line, urging his men on. "I thought he was rash, for he was in uniform and a conspicuous target," admitted Pvt. N. P. Cutler.[50] On the right, Maj. Nathaniel Shatswell offered similar encouragement to his green men. A battery under Capt. Almont Barnes pulled up and deployed to the left of the farmhouse. In the farmhouse's garden, Thomas Harris, the oldest of the four Harris children, climbed a cherry tree to watch the action about to unfold.[51]

"We received orders not to fire until we saw something to fire at, and then to fire low," wrote Gardner, sharing a good reminder for green troops. "Now and then we could hear the crack of a rifle in the woods in our front and it was evident that the enemy were coming nearer. Still there was no idea that their force was formidable."[52]

Rolfe determined to find out. "Men, we want to see if there are Rebels in those woods," he said. "If there are, we must drive them out." *Fix bayonets!* he called. *Forward! March!*

And down they went, said Cutler. Rolfe led his Bay State battalion to meet the Tar Heels, while Shatswell held the hill as the reserve.

Ramseur's men saw the Heavies coming and, from the cover of woods, unleashed a concentrated volley. "So complete was the surprise and so deadly the effect," Gardner wrote, "that the battalion was demoralized. It was like a stroke of lightning from clear skies. In an instant the scene was transformed from peace and quiet to one of pain and horror."

The volley knocked Rolfe from his horse, "pierced by eleven Rebel bullets," dead by the time he hit the ground. Gardner estimated fully half of the 350 men were dead or disabled.

49 Kirk, 223; Brown, 50.

50 Roe and Nutt, 156.

51 Souvenir. *First regiment of heavy artillery, Massachusetts volunteers. Dedication of monument, May 19, 1901*, 12.

52 Details in the account in the four three paragraphs come from Roe and Nutt, 154, 152, 156, 153.

Taking advantage of the confusion, the North Carolinians charged. "With the most terrific yells on came Ramseur's brigade, crashing through us, firing as they came and wounding and killing our men at short range," Gardner recalled. "The powder stains on the bodies we buried later told the story of this fight hand-to-hand."[53]

Events seemed almost as chaotic from the Confederate perspective, as recounted in a colorful sequence by one of Ramseur's men:

> We could hear the commands and then the tramp, tramp, of the line advancing. When we thought them near enough we let loose a volley and then pandemonium broke loose! Halt! halt! What are you running for? Back in line! stop! &c. &c.' Then a pause. 'Now men, don't' you fire until I give the order. Forward! charge!' Then after a few minutes of silence, Rrrrrrrrrrng, rrrrrng, rrrrng from our lines and a wild volley at the skies from theirs, and again the cries of the exasperated officers trying to rally their flying forces.[54]

Rolfe's men fell back to the top of the ridge, compelling young Thomas Harris to scramble out of his cherry-tree perch, taking refuge with his mother, sister, and two brothers in the farmhouse basement as the fight closed in.[55] To the north, widowed Susan Alsop, just 24 or 25, likewise hid in her basement with her only child.[56]

Shatswell helped rally the Bay State men even as the 2nd New York Heavy Artillery came up on their left as support. A bullet clipped Shatswell in the scalp, but the Massachusetts Heavies held. The New Yorkers connected with the 15th New York Heavy Artillery, already positioned with Kitching's old regiment, the 6th New York Heavy Artillery, to the left. "The brigade took position in a wood," wrote Lt. Col. Michael Wiedrich of the 15th Heavies, "and although unprotected by any kind of works, and without the assistance of artillery, several attacks made with all the energy of desperation were repulsed."[57]

With the addition of the 2nd New York Heavies, the far superior Federal numbers put Ramseur's men in a tight spot, despite their experience. "I advanced and drove the enemy rapidly and with severe loss until my flanks were both partially enveloped," the general would later write. Rodes sent the rest of his division in to help. Ramseur linked up with both Cullen Battle's Alabama Brigade and Grimes's

53 Roe, 154.

54 Wm. W. Smith to John W. Daniel, letter.

55 Souvenir, *First regiment of heavy artillery,* 12.

56 James A. Alsop died in December 1860, but Susan reportedly got along just fine after her husband's death with ten enslaved workers and a white farmhand.

57 Michael Wiedrich, report, *O.R.* 36:1:609.

LEFT: On May 16, days before he was killed, Maj. Frank Rolfe wrote to his wife, "I am well. Write to mother. From Frank." Originally buried on the Harris farm, he was reinterred at Fredericksburg National Cemetery; his wife was eventually buried there with him. *MOLLUS Collection, U.S. Army Heritage and Education Center*

RIGHT: Major Nathaniel Shatswell survived his head wound and the war. He was, said the regimental history, "devoted to the interests of the regiment after the war and never missed a reunion, when he could possibly attend . . . and his speeches were always charged with feeling, patriotism and sterling common sense." *MOLLUS Collection, U.S. Army Heritage and Education Center*

---

North Carolinians. May 19 marked Grimes's first official day as a brigadier general; he had recently taken over command of the five North Carolina regiments after the mortal wounding of Brig. Gen. Junius Daniel at the Bloody Angle on May 12. "The bullets fell thick and heavy around me and amid it all my life has again been spared," he later marveled in a letter to his wife.[58]

North of Rodes, Ewell sent Gordon's division in, which began to extend beyond Kitching's right flank. At least some of Gordon's men made it as far as the Fredericksburg Road, where they intercepted a wagon train laden with supplies—which they promptly plundered, stalling their momentum.[59]

58 Stephen D. Ramseur, report, *O.R.* 36:1:1083; Cullen Battle, *Third Alabama! The Civil War Memoir of Brigadier General Cullen Andrews Battle, CSA,* Brandon Beck, ed. (Tuscaloosa, Al: University of Alabama Press, 2000), 116-17; Grimes, 56.

59 Gordon, who never seemed to miss a chance in his memoirs to toot his own horn about any of his achievements, ended his account of Spotsylvania after a brief recounting of the May 18 fighting. Surprisingly, he skipped the fight at Harris Farm—and his role in it—entirely.

But even then, the men of the 1st Maine Heavy Artillery arrived on the field from the south. May 19, said one Pine Tree Stater, would be "a day long to be remembered by the 1st Maine Heavy, as it was on this day that we received our baptism of fire and learned the stern duties of a soldier." Right behind them marched the 7th and 8th New York Heaves.[60]

The Mainers, at the head of the column, passed behind the rear of the 2nd New York Heavies, who had gone to the assistance of their Massachusetts comrades. The Mainers swung off the road through the fields and forests of the Alsop farm, northeast of the Harris farm, bringing 1,800 men onto the battlefield. "[W]e charged at double quick . . . and pressed on for half or three quarters of a mile beyond," recalled Lt. Frederick C. Low. Low's fellow lieutenant, George W. Grant, waved his men on with his sword. "Boys, this is what we came out here for!" he called—before falling mortally wounded.[61]

Confederate resistance stiffened, recalled Pvt. George Coffin. "[W]hen we came out into the open we fetched up against a rebel line of battle about forty yards off," he wrote. "They gave us a terrible volley and we returned the fire, and for over one hour we stood up there and blazed away. After a volley or two it was all smoke and confusion and we could see nothing to fire at."[62]

Some men waited for the smoke to clear so they could find a target before firing. The Confederates, in contrast, hunkered down behind any cover they could find, blazing away into the cloud of smoke, knowing the Heavies were standing in the open.

Colonel Daniel Chaplin did his best to encourage his Mainers: "Steady! Steady, men! Fire low!" he called. It was, said Lieutenant Low, the crucible of battle: "We kept our line under a murderous fire for an hour or two without supports, our men falling and dying, while many wounded were carried to the rear. We held our line until ordered back for more ammunition. We lost some noble men."[63]

Fellow Mainer John Haley—who would arrive on the battlefield shortly as part of General Birney's reinforcements—said the 1st Maine Heavies, "much larger than any brigade of ours," presented a splendid front to the foe:

> [B]ut this was their first experience on the battlefield and they didn't understand how to take advantage of the situation. Being novices in the

60 George H. Coffin, *Three Years in the Army*. The full manuscript, courtesy of Clarence Woodcock, can be found at http://www.cwoodcock.com/firstmaine/3years/index.html.

61 *Whig & Courier*, May 30, 1864, 3.

62 G. Coffin, *Three Years*.

63 *Whig & Courier*, May 30, 1864, 2, 3.

> art of war, they thought it cowardly to lie down, so the Johnnies were mowing them flat. Had our arrival been delayed only a short time, they would have been nearly annihilated. . . . Being simple and cowardly enough to lie down and take advantage of the situation, we lost but two men in the time the other regiment had lost over 200. We not only took advantage of our trees and hillocks, but we dug trenches with our tin plates and bayonets.[64]

The veterans did enjoy one grotesque windfall from the courageous naivete of the Heavies. "They were particularly anxious to get hold of the new arms of the fresh troops," recounted Porter, "and when a man was shot down a veteran would promptly seize his gun in exchange for his own, which had become much the worse for wear in the last week's rain-storms."[65]

The Heavies just didn't know any better than to stand there, a sympathetic Lyman later explained. "They had no idea of covering themselves and even shot each other in the excitement of battle. All of which illustrates that drill is but part of the soldier; for they are the best drilled troops in the army." Yet some of the Heavies saw this as an advantage, even as they tried to duke it out from their exposed position. "I wish to say that this body of troops were fully versed in the manual of arms," one of them proudly noted; "firing by Company, front and rear rank was executed with as much precision as though we were engaged in practice firing on our old drill grounds near fortifications for the school of the soldier." Their "greenness" cost them, although most of the Heavies didn't realize it in the moment.[66]

The Confederates marveled at the sight of the enemy troops standing tall, unprotected in the open, even as they shot the Heavies down. "You seemed then to me the biggest men I had ever seen," Cyrus B. Watson of the 45th North Carolina told the 1st Massachusetts Heavies years later. "You were so near that I noticed that you all wore clean shirts. There was the most perfect discipline and indifference to danger I ever saw. It was the talk of our men."[67]

* * *

64 Haley, 160.

65 Porter, 128.

66 Lyman, *Meade's Army*, 164; Wilbur Russell Dunn, *Full Measure of Devotion: The Eighth New York Volunteer Heavy Artillery* (Kearney, NE: Morris Publications, 1997), 286.

67 Souvenir, *First regiment of heavy artillery*, 16.

The 7th New York Heavies fell in on the left of the Mainers and the right of the Massachusetts men, plugging a gap. The 1st Massachusetts Heavies had hunkered down around the Harris farm, holding on against repeated assaults from Rodes's entire division. Major Shatswell had returned to the front after getting his head wound patched. "He was," wrote Gardner, "an inspiration": "Tall and grand, with a voice like the roar of a lion, hatless, blood trickling from beneath the bandage down his cheek till his coat was saturated with it."[68]

Opposite Shatswell, Col. Samuel Hill Boyd of the 45th North Carolina had likewise been wounded early in the engagement but had returned. Boyd had been restored to command of the regiment just two days earlier, May 17, after a months-long stint as a POW following the battle of Gettysburg. A tall man—6'4"—he wore a bright new uniform, "which made him a shining mark for the enemy's riflemen," said Cyrus B. Watson, the regiment's historian. A few minutes before ordering a charge, Boyd took a gunshot wound in the arm. "He had his arm bandaged with his handkerchief to stop the flow of blood, refused to leave the field, and was killed a few moments later," Watson wrote.[69]

Several men of the 1st Massachusetts Heavies, including Pvt. Thomas A. Stevens, took refuge—such as it was—behind a rail fence. "The bullets striking the fence and pine trees about us came like hailstones, scattering splinters and the perfume of pine," he wrote. Recalled Pvt. Charles A. Lewis: "At times, the smoke was so thick we could not see ten feet away; we could not see the Rebs but we knew they were there, for the bullets came thicker."[70]

As the slugfest continued, the Fredericksburg Road continued to serve as a pipeline for more Federal reinforcements, some of whom had already been on the march from Fredericksburg to join the army. Down the road came a demi-brigade under Col. Nathan Dushane—the 1st Maryland and the 87th Pennsylvania Veteran Volunteers—escorting wagons of supplies. The Veteran Volunteers consisted of soldiers "who had served in the field for two years" and, offered "strong inducements," reenlisted for the duration of the war. About 340 members of the original 1st Maryland had taken up the government's offer and had gone home on furlough. May 19 marked the day of their return. As it happened, the terms of the men who had not re-upped expired on May 19, and they were ordered home to be mustered out.[71]

68 Roe and Nutt, 154. I want to give a shout out to Frederick William Unger of the 7th New York Heavies, ancestor of Spotsylvania-area historian John Cummings. John has done much to encourage preservation of the Spotsylvania battlefield. Unger was wounded during the May 19 fight at Harris Farm.

69 Watson, "Forty-Fifth Regiment."

70 Roe and Nutt, 160, 157.

71 *History and Roster of Maryland Volunteers, War of 1861–5*, Volume 1, Archives of Maryland Online, Vol. 367, 13. < https://msa.maryland.gov/>

The veterans showed up just as some of Gordon's men tried to outflank the Maine Heavies on the right. Without orders, Dushane threw his men into Gordon's—a move that proved decisive. "This unexpected appearance of old fighters from a quarter which Gordon had been informed was free from troops served to check his advance," Gardner wrote. "The steadiness of these veterans caused the Rebels to believe that we had been reinforced from the main army."[72]

Still, Clement Evans's Georgians and Thomas Toon's North Carolinians significantly outnumbered the two Veteran Volunteer regiments, which had to fall back—but then up the road from the south came the 8th New York Heavy Artillery. "Col. [Peter A.] Porter passed along the line cheering his men and urging them to be firm," recalled Capt. James Maginnis of the 8th New York Heavies. "Soon he gave the order to charge the woods. Up sprang the boys and forward they went with a deafening yell into the woods." Another member of the 8th, Marshall Norton Cook, remembered the regiment "sweaping [*sic*] everything rebelliously inclined before it." Added Maginnis: "We drove the rebels like sheep, and many of them were left dead on the field as we found their bodies thickly strewn upon the field."[73]

Dushane, who had his horse shot out from under him in the fight, was "severely strained" by the fall but survived. "Dushane lost his horse, but won his star in this brilliant fight," Gardner concluded.[74]

The weight of the 8th New York Heavies added to Dushane's force checked the two Confederate brigades for good. Any time the Confederates made any headway, the pipeline fed more Federals into the fight.

Next up the road marched Col. Richard N. Bowerman's Maryland Brigade—the 4th, 7th, 1st, and 8th Maryland—which came online to the right of the 1st Maine Heavies and the left of the Dushane's Maryland veterans. Bowerman had taken over the brigade from Andrew Denison, felled during the opening engagement at Spindle Field on May 8. "The brigade became hotly engaged at once, firing very brisk," Bowerman reported.[75]

And the Federals kept coming. As fighting began to swirl around the Peyton farmstead, up the road marched Birney's division, deploying on the Marylanders' right flank. Birney's men looked to drive Gordon from the field and, at first, found success, but Gordon was able to stave off defeat by deploying Col. John Hoffman's all-Virginia brigade.

72 Ibid., 155.

73 James Maginnis *Lockport Daily Journal and Courier*, June 29, 1864; Dunn, 287.

74 Roe and Nutt, 155.

75 Bowerman, report, *O.R.* 36:1:605.

Federal staff officer Francis Walker later reflected on the scene that greeted the II Corps' arrival. "The 'Heavies' were found fiercely engaged in their first battle against some of the most redoubtable troops of the Confederate army," he wrote. "[T]hey received without panic a sudden attack, which was intended to be another Chancellorsville surprise; faced the dread music of battle for the first time without flinching."[76]

* * *

Horace Porter arrived on the scene as Grant's emissary to find Robert Tyler, an old army friend, "making every possible disposition to check the enemy's advance." Grant would be pleased, Porter knew. "Tyler, you are in luck to-day," he said. "It isn't everyone who has a chance to make such a debut on joining an army. You are certain to knock a brevet out of this day's fight."

Tyler was pleased to hear it—as pleased as he was with the performance of his troops. "As you see," he replied, "my men are raw hands at this sort of work, but they are behaving like veterans."[77]

Though most of the Heavies did perform well, others did more harm than good to their own men. "Most laughable accounts are given of this fight," wrote Charles Wainwright, who was not laughing:

> To nearly all of Tyler's command it was the first for both officers and men; they consequently went in very much jumbled up, and doubtless did fire at our own men in some few cases, but not nearly to the extent talked of. Our loss was probably double what it would have been had the officers seen more service. The best account of it is given by one of the quartermasters, who claims to have seen it as follows: 'First there was Kitching's brigade firing at the enemy; then Tyler's men fired into his; up came Birney's division and fired into Tyler's; while the artillery fired at the whole d-----d lot.[78]

To add to the afternoon's confusion, the clouds opened, soaking the already-soaked landscape with more rain.

By this point, Ewell was fighting not to gain ground or disrupt the Federals' supply line or loot their wagon train but to stave off destruction. To withdraw now

76 Walker, 488.

77 Porter, 127.

78 Wainwright, 379.

would invite a rout with so many Federals pressing in on his outnumbered men. Alternatively, if he kept up the pressure, it would hold the Federals at bay until, he hoped, he could finally disengage under the cover of darkness and escape. If he could not, he risked losing his entire corps. As he tried to respond to the crisis, he had his horse shot out from under him, though escaping injury.

Lee feared the same destruction when he became aware of Ewell's situation. He quickly ordered Jubal Early to advance parts of his Third Corps north from the Court House to link up with Ewell. Early had little hope of success, though. Alfred Scales and Edward Thomas pushed their brigades forward but immediately bumped into Lysander Cutler's division of the Federal V Corps. "Our skirmishers advanced upon the Federal skirmish line, cheering and firing," wrote J. F. J. Caldwell of McGowan's Brigade, sent as support.

Cutler's skirmishers fell back into their breastworks, shouting defiantly at the Confederates, who soon discovered, "The prospect was rather serious." The Federals, it turned out, had works "even superior to our own, and their artillery could rake us in front and on the flank, as we moved on them."

"Charge your charge!" Cutler's men cried, feeling perfectly secure behind their works.

"The 'charge' was not 'charged,'" Caldwell deadpanned.

The three Confederate brigades kept up small-arms fire for show, and the Federals threw a few shells in response, but the Confederates advanced no farther.[79]

Around the Harris farm, both sides continued to slug it out with far more purpose, even as darkness thickened around them. Although many of the Federal soldiers were new and in the open, they stood shoulder to shoulder, blasting away at Lee's hunkered-down veterans, who "threw up some little breastworks with our bayonets" within speaking distance of the Federals. Ewell did not have enough power to throw his opponents back. Instead, it was all his men could do to hold on until dark. "We lay there . . . in mud and water, behind our little mounds of earth thrown up with our bayonets and hands," said a member of Ramseur's brigade.[80]

Ewell later suggested that he was, in fact, already in the process of withdrawing when the counterattacks pinned him in place. "[The enemy's] position being developed and my object attained, I was about to retire, when he attacked me," he reported. By the time of that writing, though, Ewell must have known his "do or die" day had not "done" for him at all, regardless of how he spun events.[81]

79 Caldwell, 151.

80 Battle, 25 May 1864, letters.

81 Ewell, report, *O.R.* 36:1:1073. Ewell authored his report on 20 March 1865, with the benefit of nearly a year of hindsight and the soreness of a deeply bruised ego. Lee had, by then, exiled Ewell to command of the Richmond defenses, well away from the Army of Northern Virginia. He was "done," all right.

Dark finally came—early, because of the rain—finally giving Ewell the protection he needed to disengage. In ones and two, his men slipped away and made their way back to their former entrenchments in the main Confederate line. "We had a stiff fight . . ." a North Carolinian noted. "Some of our men were so badly hurt that we had to leave them."[82]

"[W]e were ordered to fall back as quietly as possible," added Walter Battle of the 4th North Carolina. "Such a command at such a time puts a strange feeling on a person, a relief to the mind which I can't describe, nor any one realize, but those who have once been placed in that situation." Rosser's cavalry arrived to provide some degree of escort and direction, but the men strung out and straggled, disorganized and demoralized. "Only one thing was plain, and that was dreadfully plain," said a member of McGowan's Brigade, who watched Ewell's men return, "the flank movement had failed."[83]

Ewell recorded his losses in the engagement at about 900, although they most likely broke 1,000—more than 15 percent of his men, lost on in a fruitless reconnaissance mission. "[W]e certainly accomplished very little, whilst we lost some good men," complained a bitter soldier from Ramseur's brigade.[84]

Federal forces paid an even higher price for holding the field: 1,500 killed, wounded, and missing. The majority of the losses came from the heavy artillery units who stood in the field trading volleys with Southern riflemen. The three companies of 4th New York Heavies, for instance, had fielded 440 men and lost 82, a casualty rate of nearly 19 percent. The 1st Massachusetts Heavies lost 394 men killed, wounded, or missing, a 24 percent casualty rate. The 1st Maine Heavies suffered 524 casualties—nearly one man in three.[85]

"We had a terrible battle last night, and our regiment behaved splendidly, although we were dreadfully cut up," Frederick Low wrote to his father back in Maine. Corporal Walter S. Gilman agreed, though he adopted a stoic air about it. "The boys all felt very bad when they saw how many of their comrades had fallen a victim to the Reb's bullets," he wrote, "but this is the fortune of war."[86]

Grant gave high praise to the "band box" regiments for making their stand. "Tyler received the attack with his raw troops," Grant wrote, "and they maintained their position, until reinforced, in a manner worthy of veterans."[87]

82 Venner, 178;

83 Battle, 25 May 1864, letters; Caldwell, 152.

84 Scott, *O.R.* 36:2:1070-75; Venner, 179–80.

85 Kirk, 225; Roe and Nutt, 155; Chris Mackowski, "'Baptism of Fire': The First Maine Heavy Artillery at Harris Farm," *Blue & Gray*, Vol. 26:6, 2011.

86 *Whig & Courier*, May 30, 1864, 3; Gillman, 2.

87 Grant, *Memoirs*, 319.

# May 16
# May 17
# May 18
# May 19
# May 20–21

Photographer Timothy O'Sullivan had been with the Federal army for weeks, although he'd not had many opportunities to take many pictures. On May 4, he captured images of the army crossing the Rapidan River, but once the tempest of battle erupted the next day, followed by the constant on-the-move nature of the campaign, he had not been able to take any additional photos. Even after the armies had settled in—relatively speaking—around Spotsylvania Court House, he could not get close enough to the action without finding himself in harm's way. Unlike sketch artists like Alfred Waud, who could inspect a landscape after the fact and, based on witness accounts, re-create a scene, O'Sullivan depended on real-time opportunities.

The weather had not helped, either. Once the rain started on May 11, atmospheric conditions did not lend themselves to field photography—not just because of the rain but because of the lack of sunlight to illuminate scenes.

The 24-year-old O'Sullivan had already demonstrated himself one of the most important photographers of the Civil War. Despite the remarkable documentary record he left not only during the war but also of postwar explorations of the new American West, little is known of O'Sullivan himself. He was either born in Ireland or shortly after his parents had emigrated from there to New York. He may or may not have been enrolled in the U.S. Army in the early months of the war—he claimed he had been a first lieutenant, but searches for his enlistment records have turned up nothing.

By September 1862, he was working for Mathew Brady's photography studio in Washington, D.C. He accompanied Alexander Gardner to the battlefield outside Sharpsburg, Maryland, where they created a series of 70 post-battle images often credited as the birth of American photojournalism. When Gardner left Brady's studio to set up shop on his own, O'Sullivan went with him. Their subsequent work together on the Gettysburg battlefield became an iconic chronicle of the battle's aftermath.

O'Sullivan was one of several photographers to descend on the Fredericksburg area once the 1864 spring campaign rumbled to life, but for reasons unknown, the other photographers did not join the army as it moved across the Rapidan and into the Wilderness. The other crews would create remarkable photographic chronicles of the campaign's wounded as they transformed Fredericksburg into a city of hospitals, but O'Sullivan would capture something wholly unique and remarkable.[1]

On the afternoon of Thursday, May 19, 1864, the photographer made his headquarters with the Army of the Potomac's V Corps at Whig Hill, the home owned by Francis Beverly. Finally, circumstances conspired to give O'Sullivan the opportunity to break out his photography equipment. "[T]he location was a reasonably safe distance behind the front lines; there was no fighting going on in the immediate vicinity; and the sun was shining brightly," says photographic historian William Frassanito. O'Sullivan grabbed a pair of shots that day about midday: one of the house itself including, apparently, O'Sullivan's mobile photography studio parked out front, the other of the V Corps' artillery reserve.[2]

From Whig Hill, O'Sullivan could clearly hear battle erupt in the army's rear when Ewell's infantry made first contact with Kitching's brigade at the Harris farm. The photographer could not rush to the scene without putting himself in harm's way, though, so he tried to wait out the action, only to have darkness fall before the action quieted.

And so it was, the next morning, May 20, that O'Sullivan steered his wagon northward to document what he could of the previous evening's fight. The wagon crossed the Ny then ascended the gentle north slope of the river valley, passing the Gayle house on the right until he reached the dirt lane to the Harris farm on the left.

The 1st Massachusetts Heavies, which had fought at the Harris farm and had spent the night there, had been detailed that morning to bury the dead. "The ground was strewn with dead and wounded, and it was a sad sight that greeted us with the dawn of the next day," Corp. J. W. Whipple of Company L wrote to the *Danvers* (Mass.) *Mirror.* As a precaution against a repeat of the previous night's surprise, the men threw up a line of rifle pits as they worked.[3]

1 William A. Frassanito, *Grant and Lee: The Virginia Campaigns, 1864–1865* (New York: Macmillan Pub. Co, 1986), 99.

2 Frassanito, 101.

3 Roe and Nutt, 158. Whipple's letter appeared in the newspaper in February 1894.

The 1st Massachusetts Heavies engaged in some of their emotionally heaviest work yet: gathering the dead around the Alsop farm for burial. *Library of Congress*

Augustus Brown described that work:

> Trenches were dug in the light soil some six feet wide and two or three feet deep, and the dead were laid side by side with no winding sheets but overcoats or blankets, though occasionally an empty box which had contained Springfield rifles did duty as a coffin. Care was taken to cover the faces of the dead with the capes of their overcoats or with blankets, and where the name, company, regiment, division or corps could be ascertained, the information was written in pencil on a board or smoothly whittled piece of wood, which was driven into the earth at the man's head, and the grounds about the Harris House presented the appearance of a cemetery.[4]

4 Brown, 52–3.

"A little wooden cross was placed at the head of each, with name and regiment, if known," added Whipple, "and then the earth was quietly replaced, with no noise, no speech, no ceremony whatever. Many a brave fellow we laid away that day.[5]

By the time O'Sullivan arrived at the Harris farm, the Heavies may have already completed their work there because, rather than capturing any images on the property, he steered his wagon north along the farm lane that connected the Harris farm to the Alsop farm. There, he finally set up his equipment, and over the course of his work, he captured six shots. In the words of Frassanito, they comprise "one of the most timely and tragically memorable series of photographs ever to be recorded during the entire four-year conflict. It was the kind of series that most battlefield cameramen probably dreamed of but that few were ever afforded the opportunity of actually securing."[6]

Although never identified, the dead were most likely North Carolinians in Bryan Grimes's brigade. The Heavies had repulsed initial attacks by Ramseur's North Carolinians closer to the Harris farm, three quarters of a mile south, and Grimes's men had come online as support, extending the Confederate line northward. At the Alsop farm, the 1st Maine Heavies had pushed in on the Massachusetts men's right, extending the Federal line in response.

Two of O'Sullivan's photographs capture a burial detail on the Alsop farm—men of the 1st Massachusetts Heavies engaged in their grim work collecting and burying the dead—and individual bodies in those photos are seen in other images in the series. In another image, collected corpses have been lined up in a neat row, each awaiting his turn for more permanent rest.

In the others: A Confederate nestled in the crook of a snake-rail fence. Another with his hands, rigor mortis-frozen, held up next to his chest, his hat, cartridge box, canteen tumbled out beside him. In both pictures, O'Sullivan laid a rifle across each man as a prop to heighten dramatic effect—the images, after all, needed to have commercial value. That's why the photographer was there in the first place.

Captain Augustus Brown made note of one young Carolinian he interred:

> [He was] a handsome boy of perhaps eighteen years, who, though clad in the dirty butternut-colored uniform of a private, showed every indication of gentle birth and refined home surroundings. His hands and feet were small and delicately moulded; his skin white and soft as a woman's, and his lair, where not matted by the blood from a cruel

5 Roe and Nutt, 158.

6 Frassanito, 108. Thanks to Garry Adelman for answering questions about the set-up of cameras in the field.

Photographer Timothy O'Sullivan added the rifle as a prop to make the image more interesting—and thus, more commercially lucrative. *Library of Congress*

---

wound in the forehead, was fair and wavy as silk, and as I thought of the desolate home somewhere in the South, thus robbed of its pride and its joy, and of the loving mother who would never know where her darling was laid, tears actually came to my eyes, and I turned away leaving the poor boy to find a resting place at the hands of a burial party of a not ungenerous foe.[7]

Ulysses S. Grant overslept on the morning of May 20. The previous evening, he had waited for the action at the Harris farm to quiet down, still holding out hope that perhaps Hancock's move south might still get underway overnight.

7 Brown, 52–3.

But with Birney's and Tyler's divisions both involved in the fight along the Fredericksburg Road—and thus out of position for the planned march—Hancock needed time to reconcentrate the II Corps before he could march away with it. The late night on May 19 snoozed into a later-than-usual morning on May 20.

Grant dressed "as quick as a lightning-change actor in a variety theater," according to Porter, and he soon had himself together and at the mess table, ready for the day. He was up early enough, though, to see Birney's division marching past headquarters as the regiments returned to their position beyond the Anderson farm. Hancock soon received a corrective dispatch from army headquarters: Birney's men were in full view of the enemy. "They should be directed to pass through the woods to the rear of these headquarters, out of view of the enemy," the dispatch read.[8]

Hancock responded with an explanation and blamed an intervening fog, which had apparently foiled Hancock's messenger to Birney but which had burned off by the time Birney moved. It was probably just as well. The sight of Hancock's movement was the first of several pieces of puzzling information that threw Lee off his game that morning. By that point, Lee was getting as little as three hours of sleep per night and was beginning to feel the first rumblings of what would become a debilitating case of dysentery. It is little wonder he may have felt bleary-eyed and unsure about the tea leaves he was trying to read.

"The enemy has continued quiet to-day," he wrote to Secretary of War Seddon early in the day; "he is taking ground toward our right and entrenching, but whether for attack or defense is not apparent." On that end of the line, Charles Field of Anderson's Corps—which had rested quietly for days on the army's right flank—reported a skirmish line still in his front but could not tell if it was "supported by any respectable force."[9]

Then reports came in of a Federal cavalry force, backed by infantry, along the Telegraph Road where it crossed the Ny River. The main route between Fredericksburg and Richmond, the Telegraph Road ran east of the armies' position at Spotsylvania. Was Grant shifting even farther to Lee's right than Lee realized? If so, where were those Federals coming from?

The action was actually a quick strike by a 1,900-man Federal cavalry force under Brig. Gen. Alfred Torbert, newly returned to the army from sick leave and placed in command of the cobbled-together horsemen. Lee did not know Torbert's

8 Porter, 129. Humphreys to Hancock, May 20, 1864, *O.R.* 36:3:7-8.

9 Lee to Seddon, May 20, 1864, *O.R.* 36:3:800; Field to Sorrel, May 20, 1864, *O.R.* 36:3:800.

force even existed. Instead, he wondered whether Grant was stripping troops from the Army of the Potomac's right and moving them around Lee's right.

Lee asked Ewell, on the Army of Northern Virginia's left, "whether you discover any movement of the enemy in your front, and whether his rear is weak enough for you to strike at?" One can only imagine Ewell's reaction to such a note. Justy the previous evening, he had learned a hard lesson about whether the Federal rear was weak enough to strike at.[10]

Ewell, however, made the mistake of not answering Lee—or not answering quickly enough. Or, if he did answer, his reply got lost along the way and has remained lost to time. At 8:30 p.m., Charles Venable of Lee's staff sent Ewell a telegram tinged with venom. "[The commanding general] has heard nothing from you of the enemy in your front," Venable complained. "He desires you to have your troops in readiness to move at daybreak tomorrow to take position on the right." Ewell was not to wait for further orders before executing the move, although Venable did stress that Lee "desires to hear from you."[11]

Again, it is unknown whether Ewell responded, but he certainly proved responsive enough to Lee's order to move. At 1:30 a.m. on May 21, bugle calls woke his men for a 3:00 a.m. march to Mudd Tavern, nine miles away. If Ewell could capture the intersection there, he could secure the Telegraph Road for Lee's army and the inside track to Richmond. By that point, Lee remained unsure of Grant's intentions or even his exact position, but possession of the Mudd Tavern crossroad seemed like good insurance. He could block a direct move south by Grant, protect the Confederate capital, and secure his own escape route from Spotsylvania all at once.

Although possession of the intersection would prove vital for Lee as the campaign shifted to its next phase, the II Corps was not aiming for Mudd Tavern. "Major-General Hancock: The orders given you yesterday will be repeated to-night," headquarters informed him on May 20. By 1:00 a.m. on May 21, the vaunted II Corps, diminished by more than two weeks of hard fighting, stepped off, heading east along the Massaponax Church Road in a wide sweeping movement around Lee's flank toward Guiney Station and, eventually, to Bowling Green. Being alone in the open country of Caroline County might serve as bait to draw Lee from the works around Spotsylvania so Grant could get at him.[12]

Their route took the soldiers into a part of Virginia that had not yet been touched by war's hard hand—a contrast made starker considering the blighted landscape the

10 Marshall to Ewell, May 20, 1864, *O.R.* 36:3:801.

11 Venable to Ewell, May 20, 1864, *O.R.* 36:3:801.

12 Meade to Hancock, May 20, 1864, *O.R.* 36:3:8.

The Federal army crossed the Ny River on its withdrawal from Spotsylvania Court House.
*Harper's Weekly*

men had created around Spotsylvania. "Trees are perfectly riddled with bullets . . ." complained one New York doctor. "Every tree is like a brush broom!" Yet in Caroline County, "Forests were standing untouched, farm lands were protected by fences, crops were green and untrampled, birds were singing, flowers blooming—Eden everywhere. Even my horse seemed to feel the change from the crowded roads, the deadly lines, the dust, the dirt, the mud, the blood, the horror," wrote a Confederate who would pass through the unspoiled country on a parallel path.[13]

The mazework of empty trenches and massive field fortifications behind them around Spotsylvania Court House represented a forerunner of things to come. Every time the two armies had stopped during the first weeks of the campaign, they had entrenched. "It is a rule that, when the Rebels halt, the first day gives them a good rifle-pit; the second, a regular infantry parapet with artillery in position; and the third a parapet with an abattis [*sic*] in front and entrenched batteries behind," a Federal soldier commented. "Sometimes they put this three days' work into the first twenty-four hours." The resulting wasteland of mud and carnage would presage the stark no-man's-land battlefields of World War I.[14]

13 Holt, 190; Stiles, 268.

14 Ernest B. Fergerson. *Not War but Murder: Cold Harbor 1864* (New York, NY: Vintage Books, 2001), 86.

As the campaign continued to Richmond and beyond, and soldiers of both sides gained more experience in building works and had easier access to better entrenching equipment, fortifications became even more formidable and elaborate.

"I never saw more digging," wrote George Mardon of the 1st U.S. Sharpshooters. "Every advance is made as sure as logs and dirt can make it. Every step is clinched with roots and *abbattis*. At the same time, [Grant] is continually pushing here a little and there a little and all the time gaining a little. The rebels evidently see this. Their old dash has failed them. Since the first day they have assumed the defensive and kept it."[15]

Hancock's maneuver made Lee's defensive position in Spotsylvania untenable because it threatened to put Grant's army between Lee and Lee's supply base in Richmond. In a best-case scenario for Grant, Lee would try to pounce on the dangling II Corps and Grant would pounce on Lee in turn; in a worst-case scenario for Lee, Grant could beat him to the North Anna River, entrench, and force an engagement. Lee would have to attack because, if he didn't, Grant could strike at Richmond, and the fall of the Confederate capital would surely boost Lincoln's reelection chances.[16]

Lee would not take the II Corps' bait, however. "By some telepathic process this purpose of [Grant's] seems to have been made known to General Lee . . ." wrote Lee's aide de camp, Walter Taylor. Instead, Lee did what he so often did during the war and flipped the script. He slipped past Grant, keeping the inside track to Richmond, and with a direct, forced march, he reached the North Anna River first. As his army settled into a strong defensive position on the south bank, much-needed reinforcements arrived from Richmond and the Valley. "Grant found Lee always in his front whenever and wherever he turned," Charles Venable exulted.[17]

Indeed, one of Lee's greatest gifts as a commander was his ability to read his opponent, at least prior to 1864. This "superpower" became enshrined in the Lee myth. John Brown Gordon, who benefitted greatly from Lee's patronage over the course of the war, articulated it best:

> As Lee divined Grant's movement to Spottsylvania almost at the very instant the movement was taking shape in Grant's brain, so on each succeeding field he read the mind of the Union commander, and developed his own plans accordingly. There was no mental telepathy

15 Marden, journal.

16 While Lee would be on Grant's supply lines from Fredericksburg in such a scenario, Grant could instead draw supplies from the river system east of Richmond, which he ultimately did.

17 Taylor, *General Lee*, 243; Venable, 14.

> in all this. Lee's native and tutored genius enabled him to place himself in Grant's position, to reason out his antagonist's mental processes, to trace with accuracy the lines of his marches, and to mark on the map the points of future conflict which were to become the blood-lettered mile-posts marking Grant's compulsory halts and turnings in his zigzag route to Richmond.[18]

But Gordon gave Lee too much credit in this regard, even if postwar Confederates held it dear as a matter of faith. In truth, Lee had terribly misread Grant on several occasions:

- Prior to the start of the campaign, Lee had no idea in which direction Grant would move and therefore had to wait for the Federals to show their hand, thus surrendering the campaign's initiative to Grant from the get-go.

- On the night of May 5 in the Wilderness, Lee gambled that Grant would not make a morning attack the next day, and that misjudgment nearly led to the destruction of the Army of Northern Virginia. Only the last-minute arrival of Longstreet on the battlefield saved the Confederates.

- On May 11, Lee again misinterpreted Grant's intentions and, as a result, nearly had his army split in two on May 12. Once again, only the serendipitous arrival of reinforcements prevented complete collapse.

- On May 14, Lee underestimated the threat to his right flank when Grant shifted toward the Fredericksburg Road and Myer's Hill. Muddy roads alone saved Lee from what would have otherwise been a massive morning attack for which he was unprepared.

Even when Lee initially moved to Spotsylvania, it wasn't because he had telepathically discerned Grant's march there. Spotsylvania seemed a good place to react to the three mostly likely movements Grant might make: down the Brock Road to Spotsylvania; east to Fredericksburg to refit; or east toward Fredericksburg to the Telegraph Road continuing the movement toward Richmond. Only Anderson's decision to march then bivouac, rather than bivouac then march, saved Lee's army at the gates of the village.

18 Gordon, 297.

On May 21, when Hancock pulled out of Spotsylvania in the wee hours, with Warren following just after daybreak, Lee again could not discern Grant's motives. His inability to read Grant would lead to several more near-misses of potentially catastrophic proportion as the armies shifted to the North Anna River. That third "epoch" of the campaign, as the soldiers would refer to it, would starkly highlight the impact of Grant's war of attrition on the commanders themselves, even as Spotsylvania highlighted its impact on the individual soldiers.

"If [the Yankees] would retire beyond the river and give us a breathing spell, it would be decidedly advantageous," wished exhausted Confederate brigade commander Bryan Grimes. But that was just the point: Grant did not want Confederates to catch their breath, not even a little.[19]

The Army of Northern Virginia had entered the Wilderness with 66,000 men; by the time it left that dark, close wood along Pendleton's makeshift road, the army was down to 55,000 men. After thirteen days at Spotsylvania, the army had lost another 12,687 killed, wounded, or missing. Lee would march to the North Anna River with slightly more than 42,300 men.

Toughest to replace would be the losses to the army's leadership. At the corps level, Lee had lost his First Corps commander James Longstreet in the Wilderness, and the next day, he temporarily lost Third Corps commander A. P. Hill to illness. Most mournful of all to Lee, personally, was the permanent loss of cavalryman and protégé Jeb Stuart. Meanwhile Second Corps commander Richard Ewell had, in Lee's eyes, cracked under pressure. His career with the Army of Northern Virginia was virtually over. Ewell would soon take sick leave—debilitated by the same dysentery now besetting Lee—and the army commander would take the opportunity to replace him. Ewell pleaded to return, but his pleas fell on deaf ears, and it would not be until the retreat from Petersburg, in the fateful days before Appomattox, that he would rejoin the army—just in time to be captured at Sailor's Creek on April 6, 1865.[20]

Meanwhile, the army's casualties at the division and brigade levels meant a diminished talent pool to promote upward as vacancies occurred. Johnson and Steuart had been marched off the field after the capture of the Mule Shoe. Abner Perrin was dead and Junius Daniel mortally wounded. James Walker, Robert Johnston, Stephen Ramseur, and Samuel McGowan had all suffered wounds.

19 Grimes, 55.

20 Longstreet would return in October; A. P. Hill on May 22, although events on May 23 at North Anna probably made him wish he hadn't. Ironically, the underperforming Hill likewise committed major mistakes and took countless days of sick leave, yet he met with no repercussions from Lee. Not Ewell.

These losses would all take a serious toll on the Army of Northern Virginia as the campaign continued.

Lee had uncertain success with the men he tapped for advancement. Richard Anderson had performed ably in his first few days of command, but once the First Corps dug in, it had little to do but repulse assault after assault. It likewise had little to do for the entire second week at Spotsylvania, which meant Anderson remained largely untested. John Brown Gordon rose to the occasion as a temporary division commander in the Second Corps, filling in for Jubal Early as Early filled in for Hill. Early continued to impress Lee, who had been giving him increasing responsibilities for months. Lee would soon tap Early to lead the Second Corps in the wake of Ewell's removal and then send him on a crucial independent mission to the Shenandoah Valley. Gordon, too, would eventually get a chance at corps command.

More and more starkly, Lee stood as the Army of Northern Virginia's indispensable man—indeed, as the Confederacy's indispensable man. He adapted well to adversity, but he had few subordinates to lean on. Unable to fill leadership voids faster than they occurred, he himself filled the roles of army, wing, corps, and division commander at various times during the campaign. He even acted as a brigade commander, showing an unprecedented willingness—on multiple occasions—to put himself in harm's way to lead men into battle, but that only underscored the gravity of the situations, as well as the depth of Lee's concerns.

Overall, though, the morale of Lee's army remained high. Soldiers believe they had checked Grant at every turn, even if sometimes at high cost. Operating on the defense, they did not feel the same bone-depth exhaustion that Grant's men felt from their incessant marching, maneuvering, and charging. Used to perpetual supply shortages, Confederates were also more accustomed to going without full bellies and adequate clothes than their Federal counterparts, who had enjoyed plentitude while in winter camps but now faced deprivations while on the march as they often outpaced their own mud-bogged supply trains. The march-fight-march pace often left Federals without time for even a cup of coffee for days at a stretch.

"Our army is in excellent condition," wrote Walter Taylor; "its morale as good as when we met Grant—two weeks since—for the first time."

> Our list of casualties is a sad one to contemplate, but does not compare with [Grant's] terrible record of killed and wounded: he does not pretend to bury his dead, leaves his wounded without proper attendance, and seems entirely reckless as regards the lives of his men. This, and his remarkable pertinacity, constitute his sole claim to superiority over his predecessors. He certainly holds on longer than any of them. He alone, of all, would have remained this side of the Rapidan after the battles of the Wilderness.

"He will feel us again before he reaches his prize," Taylor proclaimed.[21] Hidden beneath that bravado, though, was an implied admission that Grant was likely to indeed reach "his prize." The pertinacious general was not turning back.

What might Taylor have thought to know Abraham Lincoln agreed with him? "I believe if any other general had been at the Head of that army it would now be on this side of the Rapidan," the president told his secretary, John Hay. "It is the dogged pertinacity of Grant that wins." He told another confident, "The great thing about Grant is his perfect cool-headedness and persistency of purpose."[22]

Confederates gritted their teeth in the face of that persistency. "We have found Grant a tough old customer but have no idea of letting him whip us," boasted Confederate artillerist George Zirkle. "It is reported that he is being rapidly reinforced but we can kill them as fast as they come."[23]

And Grant would, indeed, keep coming and coming and coming, determined as he was to fight it out along that line if it took all summer. He understood the grim mathematics of the war. If Lee received reinforcements, the Confederate respite would be only temporary, whereas Grant had more men and material on which he could draw up to—and hopefully through—the fall election.

"Perhaps we, being so much better able to recruit our army, can wear the rebels out by this sort of fighting, which amounts to about the same kind of thing as giving two or three men for one," infantryman Charles Bowen wrote, "but I tell you that we old soldiers can't see what good it will do us for we are the ones to be killed off first, & it don't give us a fair chance for our lives. We expect to run risks & are willing to encounter dangers where anything is to be gained[,] but we don't like the idea of exchanging three of our lives for one rebel, & this seems about the way things are working now."[24]

With a kind of peverse irony, the grand strategy of attrition Grant had adopted to win the war was, in the short term, having the opposite effect on Lincoln's prospects for winning the upcoming election, which would in turn undermine Grant's ability to win the war. "[T]he feeling downtown today is despondent and bad," rued New York diarist George Templeton Strong on May 19. Expectations for Grant's campaign had been so high at the outset that the lack of immediate, clear victory "disappointed, disgusted" people—and the long casualty lists were only just beginning to crowd Northern newspaper columns and wounded soldiers

21 Taylor, *Four Years With Lee*, 133.

22 John Hay, "9 May 1864," *Letters of John Hay and Extracts from Diary*, Vol. 1 (New York: Gordian Press, 1969), 191; F. B. Carpenter, *The Inner Life of Abraham Lincoln: Six Months at the White House* (New York: Hurd and Houghton, 1874), 283.

23 Zirkle, letter.

24 Charles T. Bowen, letter, May 17, 1864, BV 209.

just beginning to crowd hospitals. Morale would sink even further as the campaign continued. "Lincoln's concern changed from one of dampening excessive Northern optimism in May to one of stemming the deep decline of morale . . ." notes historian James B. McPherson.[25]

"Grant is a fighter and bound to win," predicted soldier Elisha Hunt Rhodes, speaking for the majority of soldiers, who wanted Lincoln to see the thing through. "May God help him to end the war. We hope to see Richmond soon and humble the pride of the men who brought on this wicked war."[26]

A *fighter*, yes—but Grant had learned some hard combat lessons during the campaign thus far. "Grant has admitted the quality of Lee's fighting," a satisfied Meade told Lyman. "He told me that, after such an engagement as the Wilderness, Bragg or [Joe] Johnston would have *retreated*!" Everyone in the Army of the Potomac—from army commander Meade all the way down to the lowliest of privates—had wondered how the Victor of the West would stack up against "Bobby Lee." Meade would have simultaneously felt pleased with the army's success thus far even as he felt vindicated that Grant had found Lee every bit as challenging as Meade had found him.[27]

But Lee had not been Grant's only challenge—or perhaps even his biggest challenge. The Army of the Potomac—from army commander Meade all the way down to the lowliest of privates—had proven itself a puzzle to the Westerner. Grant had promised Meade a hands-off approach, and that agreement had lasted all of just a few days. By the end of the second day in the Wilderness, Grant had effectively assumed tactical command. Over the course of the army's time in Spotsylvania, Grant's tactical direction only intensified, and Meade's marginalization only increased. "If there was any honorable way of retiring from my present false position, I should undoubtedly adopt it," Meade finally wrote his wife on May 19, "but there is none and all I can do is patiently submit and bear with resignation the humiliation."[28]

Meade was not without fault in his handling of the situation, though. The more active Grant's hand became, the more hands off Meade became, in turn forcing Grant to become even more hands on. An analogy might be Grant as a

25 George Templeton Strong, *The Diary of George Templeton Strong*, Allan Nevins and Milton Halsey Thomas, eds. (New York: The Macmillan Company, 1952), 447; James B. McPherson, *Tried by War: Abraham Lincoln as Commander in Chief* (New York: Penguin, 2008), 221.

26 Rhodes, 153.

27 Lyman, 164–65.

28 Meade to wife, letter, 19 May 1864, George G. Meade Collection, Historical Society of Pennsylvania. Tellingly, editor George Meade, Jr., left this letter out of the curated *Life and Letters of George Gordon Meade*.

backseat driver, peppering Old Peppery with instructions as the car sped down the highway until, fed up, Meade took his hands off the steering wheel in a shrug, as if to say, "If you don't like the way, I'm driving, you do it," forcing Grant to reach forward from the backseat and drive from an awkward position.

With only three corps under his direct control—rather than the seven he commanded at Gettysburg—Meade had ample opportunity to work more closely with his corps commanders and exercise more direct control. Closer oversight might also have allowed him to demonstrate more of the sort of initiative the active-minded Grant expected. However, the army commander may just have been too temperamentally unsuited for that kind of adaptability: Even as one of the best combat officers in the Army of the Potomac, Meade was still a product of McClellan's early culture of caution.

In his memoirs, Grant admitted the situation with Meade was "embarrassing." By the time he wrote that, time and good manners had softened Grant's recollections. He had professed great satisfaction with Meade in his May 11 note to the war department, but when Meade's promotion did not initially go through, Grant's satisfaction with Meade had already waned to the point that Grant did not push the matter. Awkward pestering by Meade eventually spurred Grant to action, but the promotion did not go through until February 1865, back-dated to August 18, 1864. The growing tension between them during the first half of the Overland Campaign would lead to significant problems by the morning of June 3 at Cold Harbor and again on June 15 at the gates of Petersburg.[29]

The roots of that tension may have first taken hold on May 8 when Grant backed Sheridan over Meade in the argument over the army's cavalry. It was one of Grant's worst moments of the campaign, undercutting Meade's authority in the chain of command by backing a crony. Personal loyalty was always of monumental importance to Grant, and while it served as one of his greatest strengths, it would also, over and over, prove one of his biggest vulnerabilities. In this case, depriving the Army of the Potomac of its eyes and ears for two and a half weeks arguably cost of thousands of Federal lives because Meade had to grope his way across the Spotsylvania and Caroline county landscapes.[30]

The poison from that incident would likewise linger between Sheridan and Warren, leading eventually to Warren's ruination. On April 1, 1865, Sheridan would unjustly fire Warren at the battle of Five Forks, in part to cover Sheridan's

29 Grant, *Memoirs*, 2:117.

30 See the 1884 collapse of Grant & Ward for the most extreme example of Grant's loyalty as a "fatal flaw": Chris Mackowski, *Grant's Last Battle: The Story Behind the Personal Memoirs of Ulysses S. Grant* (El Dorado Hills, CA: Savas Beatie, 2015).

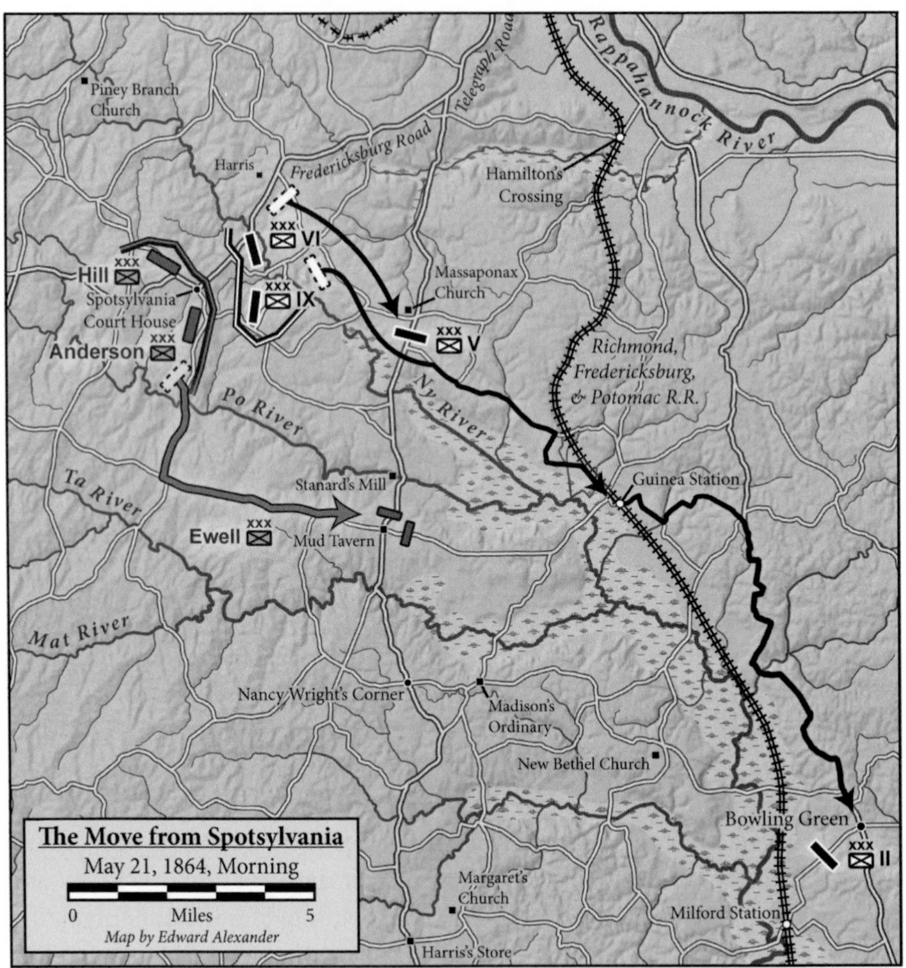


THE MOVE FROM SPOTSYLVANIA—Leading the Federal withdrawal from Spotsylvania Court House on the night of May 20–21, 1864, the II Corps marched east and south toward Bowling Green and then Milford Station. The V Corps followed. Grant hoped the maneuver would draw Lee out of his entrenchments and tempt him into an attack on the isolated II Corps. Lee did not take the bait, however, and instead secured the Mudd Tavern intersection and a direct route south to a highly defensible position along the North Anna River.

own bungling at the battle. It would take decades for Warren to clear his name, though the report doing so would not come out until after Warren's death in 1882.

Ambrose Burnside's independent IX Corps represented yet another awkward command situation for both Grant and Meade. Communication delays and poor coordination proved the biggest issues. Grant would finally solve the problem on May 24 by formally folding the corps into the Army of the Potomac, in violation of the protocol usually demanded by seniority. Burnside, to his credit, recognized it as a military necessity and accepted what was essentially a demotion with poise (and on the day after his 40th birthday, no less).

The Army of the Potomac's other corps also presented a challenge for Grant. Commanders performed less than admirably: Burnside's case of the slows, Warren's lack of enthusiasm, and Wright's newness to corps command. Even "Hancock the Superb" performed less than superbly by not thinking through the follow-up for his May 12 assault. Hancock's Gettysburg wound still plagued him, too, and he spent much of his time during the campaign riding in a carriage rather than on horseback. He would eventually leave active field service in November 1864.

In the ranks, attitudes about Grant were mixed. The good will and enthusiasm he had generated on the night of May 7 by moving forward from the Wilderness soon wilted under the strain of constant marching on dusty (and then muddy) roads, grinding combat, poor weather, and little rest. "The terrible losses sustained, and the continual checks we met, combined with the effects of this marching and counter-marching, from right to left, and left to right again, produced a feeling of listlessness and discouragement, which extended throughout the army," complained Alanson Haines of the 15th New Jersey. "The men felt that they were doomed to slaughter."[31]

Men also often felt frustrated and confused, and more than one doubted Grant's abilities or good sense. Maine soldier John Haley complained of "Grant's hammering generalship," which consisted of "sheer brute force": "No strategy, just hammer, hammer, hammer, until the enemy is flattened."[32]

Grant is frequently (and often intentionally) mischaracterized as someone who *only* hammered, but he demonstrated a remarkable versatility at Spotsylvania. He launched frontal assaults, but he also probed flanks, employed maneuver (often to the exhausted consternation of his marching men), marched at night (further depriving men of sleep in exchange for the element of surprise), and embraced innovation. Unfortunately, he often expected more of his army than its cumbersome size and risk-averse culture could deliver, and the more he pushed it, the more exhausted it became and the less effectively it could perform. "The boys are pretty tired and worn out; how much longer we can stand it is a question with some," admitted Austin Stearns of the 13th Massachusetts. Grant would not adequately begin to conquer those problems until after the army settled into its siege of Petersburg in mid-June.[33]

31 Haines, 183.

32 Haley, 148, 158.

33 Stearns, 267.

Despite the naysayers, the greater balance of men remained committed to the mission. "We have accomplished a good deal but more must be done," wrote Edward Wade of the 14th Connecticut. "Grant has done nobly and no mistake, and everybody talks in highest praise of him." Agreed sharpshooter George Mardon: "One thing we have and that is confidence in Grant. This has grown immensely on this campaign." P. A. Jewitt of the 1st Connecticut Heavies summed up the chorus: "[E]very man is of the same opinion as to our General, Grant, that he is the best & greatest Genl. in the world[.] [W]e almost worship him."[34]

Grant had begun the campaign with just less than 118,000 men. The fight in the Wilderness had cost him 17,666; Spotsylvania had cost him another 18,399; and Sheridan's cavalry raid against Stuart had also temporarily siphoned off some 12,000 more. Expiring enlistments, illness, and detachments to guard the supply line deprived him of even more. On the other hand, heavy artillery units and new draftees injected approximately 17,250 reinforcements into the army. By the time Grant reached the North Anna River, he had a force of roughly 68,000 men, many of them green.

At that moment, John Breckinridge's victorious force from New Market was moving toward Hanover Junction to join Lee's army. George Pickett's Division and Hoke's Brigade, both part of the victorious forces that recently defended Drewry's Bluff against Butler's Army of the James, were likewise converging for a junction with Lee, as was a mobile detachment under Col. Bradley Johnson known as the Maryland Line. All told, Lee would get an infusion of troops—all battle-hardened veterans coming off victories—that would bring him to more than 54,000 effectives along the banks of the North Anna. Compared to Grant's 68,000 men, the two armies would be as evenly matched along the North Anna River as they would ever be at any time during the Overland Campaign—indeed, during the entire war.

Daniel Morse Holt, the 44-year-old surgeon of the 121st New York, was up by half-past three on the morning of May 21. "I am more dead than alive," he had told his wife a few days earlier. From Herkimer County in upstate, the New Yorker had volunteered for service to "do his duty." He wrote to his wife frequently and kept a journal that chronicled his daily shock and deepening exhaustion. "Strange it is *how* we live at all," he would marvel.[35]

34 Edward H. Wade, letter, May 15, 1864, FSNMP BV 36; Marden, journal; P. A. Jewett, letter, May 20, 1864, Mss 2J5565b, Virginia Historical Society, Richmond, Virginia, FSNMP BV 353.

35 Holt, 188.

Warren's V Corps pulled out of Spotsylvania shortly after dawn that morning, with Grant and Meade accompanying them. The VI Corps, to which the 121st New York belonged, shifted position as Wright expanded his line to fill the vacuum created by Warren's departure. Burnside remained, too, to help keep Lee pinned in place. By the afternoon, Grant's army was perilously divided over a 30-mile arc, but Lee was too off-balance to take advantage and had no clear picture of his enemy. Were the Federals even still in Spotsylvania?

To find out, Lee ordered his Third Corps to make a late-day sortie against the VI Corps line. Wright quickly slapped it back. "[R]ebs charge upon our lines," Holt wrote, "and for *once* in their lives, get a belly so full as to cause *puking* and *purging* at the same time—a perfect *emeto-cathartic*!"

By then, the IX Corps had slipped away, and the VI Corps soon followed. "We marched all night with our usual snail-like rapidity," snarked Vermonter Wilbur Fisk. But he wrote of his departure from Spotsylvania in a serious tone, too. "I turned away from that place, glad to escape."[36]

Lee responded to the moves almost immediately, sending Anderson's First Corps to Mudd Tavern in the wake of Ewell's Second; the Third Corps withdrew along a different, parallel route to the west. All three made hurried marches southward in the hopes of winning the race to the North Anna.

Neither army could quite believe what they had gone through already that May. Between the Wilderness and Spotsylvania, the two armies had suffered casualties that exceeded 60,000 killed, wounded, and missing—and still, there was no end in sight. "One thing is certain of this campaign thus far," Holt had written in his diary on May 12, "and that is that more blood has been shed, more lives lost, and more human suffering undergone, than ever before in a season."[37]

And the season would drag on. The suffering would continue.

The North Anna River and Cold Harbor awaited.

"I have sometimes hoped, that if I must die while I am a soldier, I should prefer to die on the battle-field," Fisk would write. But, he added, after the sights of Spotsylvania, "one cannot help turning away and saying, Any death but that."[38]

36 Fisk, 225, 221.

37 Holt, 188, 187, 192, 187.

38 Fisk, 221.

# Order of Battle

**UNITED STATES ARMY**
Lt. Gen. Ulysses S. Grant

**ARMY OF THE POTOMAC**
Maj. Gen. George G. Meade

**Provost Guard** Brig. Gen. Marsena R. Patrick
*1st Massachusetts Cavalry, Companies C and D · 80th New York Infantry (20th Militia)*
*3rd Pennsylvania Cavalry · 68th Pennsylvania Infantry · 114th Pennsylvania Infantry*

**Volunteer Engineerr Brigade** Brig. Gen. Henry W. Benham
*15th New York Engineers · 50th New York Engineers · Battalion U.S. Engineers*

**Guards and Orderlies** *Independent Company Oneida (New York) Cavalry*

**SECOND ARMY CORPS** Maj. Gen. Winfield Scott Hancock
**Escort** *1st Vermont Cavalry, Company M*

**First Division** Brig. Gen. Francis C. Barlow
**First Brigade** Col. Nelson A. Miles
*26th Michigan · 61st New York · 81st Pennsylvania · 140th Pennsylvania · 183rd Pennsylvania*

**Second Brigade** Col. Thomas A. Smyth; Col. Richard Byrnes
*28th Massachusetts · 63rd New York · 69th New York · 88th New York · 116th Pennsylvania*

**Third Brigade** Col. Paul Frank; Col. Hiram R. Brown
*39th New York · 52nd New York · 57th New York · 111th New York · 125th New York*
*126th New York*

**Fourth Brigade** Col. John R. Brooke
*2nd Delaware · 64th New York · 66th New York · 53rd Pennsylvania · 145th Pennsylvania*
*148th Pennsylvania*

**SECOND DIVISION** Brig. Gen. John Gibbon
**Provost Guard** *2nd Company Minnesota Sharpshooters*

**First Brigade** Brig. Gen. Alexander S. Webb; Col. H. Boyd McKeen
*19th Maine · 1st Company Andrew (Massachusetts) Sharpshooters · 15th Massachusetts 19th Massachusetts · 20th Massachusetts · 7th Michigan · 42nd New York · 59th New York 82nd New York (2nd Militia)*

**Second Brigade** Brig. Gen. Joshua T. Owen
*152nd New York · 69th Pennsylvania · 71st Pennsylvania · 72nd Pennsylvania 106th Pennsylvania*

**Third Brigade** Col. Samuel S. Carroll; Col. Thomas A. Smyth
*14th Connecticut · 1st Delaware · 14th Indiana · 12th New Jersey · 10th New York Battalion 108th New York · 4th Ohio · 8th Ohio · 7th West Virginia*

**Fourth Brigade** Col. Matthew Murphy; Col. James McIvor
*155th New York · 164th New York · 170th New York · 182nd New York*

**THIRD DIVISION** Maj. Gen. David B. Birney
**First Brigade** Brig. Gen. J. H. Hobart Ward; Col. Thomas W. Egan
*20th Indiana · 3rd Maine · 40th New York · 86th New York · 124th New York 99th Pennsylvania · 110th Pennsylvania · 141st Pennsylvania · 2nd U.S. Sharpshooters*

**Second Brigade** Col. John S. Crocker; Col. Elijah Walker
*4th Maine · 17th Maine · 3rd Michigan · 5th Michigan · 93rd New York 57th Pennsylvania · 63rd Pennsylvania · 105th Pennsylvania · 1st U.S. Sharpshooters*

**FOURTH DIVISION** Brig. Gen. Gershom Mott[1]
**First Brigade** Col. Robert McAllister
*1st Massachusetts · 16th Massachusetts · 5th New Jersey · 6th New Jersey · 7th New Jersey 8th New Jersey · 11th New Jersey · 26th Pennsylvania · 115th Pennsylvania*

**Second Brigade** Col. William R. Brewster
*11th Massachusetts · 70th New York · 71st New York · 72nd New York · 73rd New York 74th New York · 120th New York · 84th Pennsylvania*

**Fourth Division** Brig. Gen. Robert O. Tyler[2]
*1st Maine Heavy Artillery · 1st Massachusetts Heavy Artillery · 2nd New York Heavy Artillery 7th New York Heavy Artillery · 8th New York Heavy Artillery*

**Artillery Brigade** Col. John C. Tidball
*Maine Light, 6th Battery (F) · Massachusetts Light, 10th Battery · New Hamsphire Light, 1st Battery 1st New Jersey Light, Battery B*[3] *· 1st New York Light, Battery G · 4th New York Heavy, 3d Battalion New York Light, 11th Battery*[3] *· New York Light, 12th Battery*[3] *· 1st Pennsylvania Light, Battery F 1st Rhode Island Light, Battery A · 1st Rhode Island Light, Battery B · 4th United States, Battery K 5th United States, Batteries C and I*

**FIFTH ARMY CORPS** Maj. Gen. Gouverneur K. Warren
**Provost Guard** *12th New York Battalion*

**First Division** Brig. Gen. Charles Griffin
**First Brigade** Brig. Gen. Romeyn Ayres
*140th New York · 146th New York · 91st Pennsylvania · 155th Pennsylvania*
*2nd United States, Companies B, C, F, H, I, and K*
*11th United States, Companies B, C, D, E, F, and G, First Battalion*
*12th United States, Companies A, B, C, D, and G, 1st Battalion*
*12th United States, Companies A, C, D, F, and H, 2d Battalion*
*14th United States, 1st Battalion · 17th United States, Companies A, C, D, G, and H, 1st Battalion*
*17th United States, Companies A, B, and C, 2d Battalion*

**Second Brigade** Col. Jacob Sweitzer
*9th Massachusetts · 22nd Massachusetts · 32nd Massachusetts · 4th Michigan · 62nd Pennsylvania*

**Third Brigade** Brig. Gen. Joseph J. Bartlett
*20th Maine · 18th Massachusetts · 1st Michigan · 16th Michigan · 44th New York*
*83rd Pennsylvania · 118th Pennsylvania*

**Second Division**[4] Brig. Gen. John C. Robinson
**First Brigade**[5] Col. Peter Lyle
*16th Maine · 13th Massachusetts · 39th Massachusetts · 104th New York · 90th Pennsylvania*
*107th Pennsylvania*

**Second Brigade**[6] Brig. Gen. Henry Baxter; Col. Richard Coulter; Col. James L. Bates
*12th Massachusetts · 83rd New York (9th Militia) · 97th New York · 11th Pennsylvania*
*88th Pennsylvania · 90th Pennsylvania*

**Third Brigade**[5] Col. Andrew W. Denison; Col. Charles E. Phelps Jr.;
Col. Richard N. Bowerman
*1st Maryland · 4th Maryland · 7th Maryland · 8th Maryland*

**Third Division** Brig. Gen. Samuel W. Crawford
**First Brigade** Col. William McCandless; Col. Wellington N. Ent
*1st Pennsylvania Reserves · 2nd Pennsylvania Reserves · 6th Pennsylvania Reserves*
*7th Pennsylvania Reserves · 11th Pennsylvania Reserves · 13th Pennsylvania Reserves (1st Rifles)*

**Third Brigade** Col. Joseph W. Fisher
*5th Pennsylvania Reserves · 8th Pennsylvania Reserves · 10th Pennsylvania Reserves*
*12th Pennsylvania Reserves*

**Fourth Division** Brig. Gen. Lysander Cutler
**First Brigade** Brig. Gen. William W. Robinson
*7th Indiana · 19th Indiana · 24th Michigan · 1st New York Battalion Sharpshooters*
*2nd Wisconsin · 6th Wisconsin · 7th Wisconsin*

**Second Brigade** Brig. Gen. James C. Rice; Col. Edward B. Fowler; Col. William J. Hoffman
*76th New York · 84th New York (14th Militia) · 95th New York · 147th New York*
*56th Pennsylvania*

**Third Brigade** Col. Edward S. Bragg
*121st Pennsylvania · 142rd Pennsylvania · 143rd Pennsylvania · 149th Pennsylvania*
*150th Pennsylvania*

**Heavy Artillery Brigade**
*6th New York Heavy Artillery · 15th New York Heavy Artillery (2 Battalions)*
*4th New York Heavy Artillery (2 Battalions)*

**Artillery Brigade** Col. Charles S. Wainwright
*Massachusetts Light, Battery C · Massachusetts Light, Battery E · Massachusetts Light, 9th Battery*[3]
*1st New York Light, Battery B*[3] *· 1st New York Light, Battery C*[3] *· 1st New York Light, Battery D*
*1st New York Light, Batteries E and L · 1st New York Light, Battery H · New York Light, 5th Battery*[3]
*New York Light, 15th Battery*[3] *· 4th New York Heavy, 2nd Battalion*
*1st Pennsylvania Light, Battery B · 4th United States, Battery B · 5th United States, Battery D*

**SIXTH ARMY CORPS** Maj. Gen. John Sedgwick; Brig. Gen. Horatio G. Wright
**Escort** *8th Pennsylvania Cavalry, Company A*

**First Division** Brig. Gen. Horatio G. Wright; Brig. Gen. David A. Russell
**First Brigade** Col. Henry W. Brown
*1st New Jersey · 2nd New Jersey · 3rd New Jersey · 4th New Jersey · 10th New Jersey*
*15th New Jersey*

**Second Brigade** Col. Emory Upton
*5th Maine · 121st New York · 95th Pennsylvania · 96th Pennsylvania*
*2nd Connecticut Heavy Artillery*[7]

**Third Brigade** Brig. Gen. David A. Russell; Col. Oliver Edwards
*6th Maine · 49th Pennsylvania · 119th Pennsylvania · 5th Wisconsin*

**Fourth Brigade** Brig. Gen. Alexander Shaler; Col. Nelson Cross
*65th New York · 67th New York · 122nd New York · 82nd Pennsylvania*

**Second Division** Brig. Gen. Thomas H. Neill
**First Brigade** Brig. Gen. Frank Wheaton
*62nd New York · 93rd Pennsylvania · 98th Pennsylvania · 102nd Pennsylvania*
*139th Pennsylvania*

**Second Brigade** Col. Lewis A. Grant
*2nd Vermont · 3rd Vermont · 4th Vermont · 5th Vermont · 6th Vermont*
*1st Vermont Heavy Artillery*[8]

**Third Brigade** Col. Daniel D. Bidwell
*7th Maine · 43rd New York · 49th New York · 77th New York · 61st Pennsylvania*

**Fourth Brigade** Brig. Gen. Henry L. Eustis
*7th Massachusetts · 10th Massachusetts · 37th Massachusetts · 2nd Rhode Island*

**Third Division** Brig. Gen. James B. Ricketts
**First Brigade** Brig. Gen. William H. Morris; Col. John W. Schall
*14th New Jersey · 106th New York · 151st New York · 87th Pennsylvania · 10th Vermont*

**Second Brigade** Col. Benjamin F. Smith
*6th Maryland · 110th Ohio · 122nd Ohio · 126th Ohio · 67th Pennsylvania · 138th Pennsylvania*

**Artillery Brigade** Col. Charles H. Tompkins
*Maine Light, 4th Battery (D) · Maine Light, Battery E*[3] *· Massachusetts Light, 1st Battery (A)*
*1st New Jersey Light, Battery A*[3] *· New York Light, 1st Battery · New York Light, 3rd Battery*
*4th New York Heavy, 1st Battalion · 1st Ohio Light, Battery H*[3] *· 1st Rhode Island Light. Battery C*
*1st Rhode Island Light, Battery E · 1st Rhode Island Light, Battery G · 5th United States, Battery E*[3]
*5th United States, Battery M*

**CAVALRY CORPS** Maj. Gen. Philip H. Sheridan
**Escort** *6th United States*

**First Division** Brig. Gen. Wesley Merritt
**First Brigade** Brig. Gen. George A. Custer
*1st Michigan · 5th Michigan · 6th Michigan · 7th Michigan*

**Second Brigade** Col. Thomas C. Devin
*4th New York · 6th New York · 9th New York · 17th Pennsylvania*

**Reserve Brigade** Col. Alfred Gibbs
*19th New York (1st Dragoons) · 6th Pennsylvania · 1st United States · 2nd United States*
*5th United States*

**Second Division** Brig. Gen. David McM. Gregg
**First Brigade** Brig. Gen. Henry E. Davies Jr.
*1st Massachusetts · 1st New Jersey · 6th Ohio · 1st Pennsylvania*

**Second Brigade** Col. J. Irvin Gregg
*1st Maine · 10th New York · 2nd Pennsylvania · 4th Pennsylvania · 8th Pennsylvania*
*16th Pennsylvania*

**Third Division** Brig. Gen. James H. Wilson
**Escort** 8th Illinois (detachment)

**First Brigade** Col. John B. McIntosh
*1st Connecticut · 2nd New York · 5th New York · 18th Pennsylvania*

**Second Brigade** Col. George H. Chapman
*3rd Indiana · 8th New York · 1st Vermont*

**ARTILLERY** Brig. Gen. Henry J. Hunt
**Artillery Reserve** Col. Henry S. Burton
**First Brigade** Col. J. Howard Kitching
*6th New York Heavy · 15th New York Heavy*

**Second Brigade** Maj. John A. Tompkins
*Maine Light, 5th Battery (E) · 1st New Jersey Light, Battery A · 1st New Jersey Light, Battery B New York Light, 5th Battery · New York Light, 12th Battery · 1st New York Light, Battery B*

**Third Brigade** Maj. Robert H. Fitzhugh
*Massachusetts Light, 9th Battery · New York Light, 15th Battery · 1st New York Light, Battery C New York Light, 11th Battery · 1st Ohio Light, Battery H · 5th United States, Battery E*

**Horse Artillery**
**First Brigade** Capt. James M. Robertson
*New York Light, 6th Battery · 2nd United States, Batteries B and L · 2nd United States, Battery D 2nd United States, Battery M 4th United States, Battery A · 4th United States, Batteries C and E*

**Second Brigade** Capt. Dunbar R. Ransom
*1st United States, Batteries E and G · 1st United States, Batteries H and I 1st United States, Battery K · 2nd United States, Battery A · 2nd United States, Battery G 3rd United States, Batteries C, F, and K*

**UNATTACHED**

**NINTH ARMY CORPS** Maj. Gen. Ambrose E. Burnside
**Provost Guard** *8th U.S. Infantry*
**First Division** Brig. Gen. Thomas G. Stevenson; Col. Daniel Leasure; Brig. Gen. Thomas Crittenden
**First Brigade** Lt. Col. Stephen M. Welsh Jr.; Brig. Gen. James H. Ledlie
*35th Massachusetts · 56th Massachusetts · 57th Massachusetts · 59th Massachusetts 4th United States · 10th United States*

**Second Brigade** Col. Daniel Leasure; Col. Joseph M. Sudsburg
*3rd Maryland · 21st Massachusetts · 100th Pennsylvania*

**Artillery**
*Maine Light, 2nd Battery (B) · Massachusetts Light, 14th Battery*

**Second Division** Brig. Gen. Robert B. Potter
**First Brigade** Col. Zenas R. Bliss; Col. John I. Curtain
*36th Massachusetts · 58th Massachusetts · 51st New York · 45th Pennsylvania · 48th Pennsylvania 7th Rhode Island*

**Second Brigade** Col. Simon G. Griffin
*31st Maine · 32nd Maine · 6th New Hampshire · 9th New Hampshire · 11th New Hampshire 17th Vermont*

**Artillery**
*Massachusetts Light, 11th Battery · New York Light, 19th Battery*

**Third Division** Brig. Gen. Orlando B. Willcox
**First Brigade** Col. John F. Hartranft
*2nd Michigan · 8th Michigan · 17th Michigan · 27th Michigan · 109th New York*
*51st Pennsylvania*

**Second Brigade** Col. Benjamin C. Christ; Col. William Humphrey
*1st Michigan Sharpshooters · 20th Michigan · 70th New York · 60th Ohio · 50th Pennsylvania*

**Artillery**
*Maine Light, 7th Battery (G) · New York Light. 34th Battery*

**Fourth Division** Brig. Gen. Edward Ferrero
**First Brigade** Col. Joshua K. Sigfried
*27th U.S. Colored Troops · 30th U.S. Colored Troops · 39th U.S. Colored Troops*
*43rd U.S. Colored Troops*

**Second Brigade** Col. Henry G. Thomas
*30th Connecticut (colored), detachment · 19th U.S. Colored Troops · 23rd U.S. Colored Troops*

**Artillery**
*Pennsylvania Light, Battery D · Vermont Light, 3d Battery*

**Cavalry**
*3rd New Jersey · 22nd New York · 2nd Ohio · 13th Pennsylvania*

**Reserve Artillery** Capt. John Edwards Jr.
*New York Light. 27th Battery · 1st Rhode Island Light, Battery D · 1st Rhode Island Light, Battery H*
*2nd United States, Battery E · 3rd United States. Battery G · 3rd United States, Batteries L and M*

**Provisional Brigade** Col. Elisha G. Marshall
*24th New York Cavalry (dismounted) · 14th New York Heavy Artillery*
*2nd Pennsylvania Provisional Heavy Artillery*

* * *

*1 Division disbanded on May 13.*
*2 Division arrived on May 18.*
*3 Transferred from artillery Reserve on May 16.*
*4 Division disbanded on May 9.*
*5 Transferred to 4th Division.*
*6 Transferred to 2nd Division.*
*7 Attached May 21.*
*8 Attached May 14.*

**ARMY OF NORTHERN VIRGINIA**
Gen. Robert E. Lee

**FIRST ARMY CORPS** Maj. Gen. Richard H. Anderson
**Kershaw's Division** Brig. Gen. Joseph B. Kershaw
**Kershaw's Brigade** Col. John W. Henagan
*2nd South Carolina · 3rd South Carolina · 7th South Carolina · 8th South Carolina*
*15th South Carolina · 3rd South Carolina Battalion*

**Wofford's Brigade** Brig. Gen. William T. Wofford
*16th Georgia · 18th Georgia · 24th Georgia · Cobb's (Georgia) Legion*
*Phillips (Georgia) Legion · 3rd Georgia Battalion Sharpshooters*

**Humphreys's Brigade** Brig. Gen. Benjamin Humphreys
*13th Mississippi · 17th Mississippi · 18th Mississippi · 21st Mississippi*

**Bryan's Brigade** Brig. Gen. Goode Bryan
*10th Georgia · 50th Georgia · 51st Georgia · 53rd Georgia*

**Field's Division** Maj. Gen. Charles W. Field
**Jenkins's Brigade** Col. John Bratton
*1st South Carolina · 2nd South Carolina (Rifles) · 5th South Carolina · 6th South Carolina*
*Palmetto (South Carolina) Sharpshooters*

**Law's Brigade** Col. William F. Perry; Brig. Gen. Evander McIver Law
*4th Alabama · 15th Alabama · 44th Alabama · 47th Alabama · 48th Alabama*

**Anderson's Brigade** Brig. Gen. George T. Anderson
*7th Georgia · 8th Georgia · 9th Georgia · 11th Georgia · 59th Georgia*

**Gregg's Brigade** Brig. Gen. John Gregg
*3rd Arkansas · 1st Texas · 4th Texas · 5th Texas*

**Benning's Brigade** Col. Dudley M. Dubose
*2nd Georgia · 15th Georgia · 17th Georgia · 20th Georgia*

**Artillery** Brig. Gen. Edward Porter Alexander

**Huger's Battalion** Lt. Col. Frank Huger
*Fickling's (South Carolina) battery · Moody's (Louisiana) battery · Parker's (Virginia) battery*
*Smith's, J. D. (Virginia), battery · Taylor's (Virginia) battery · Woolfolk's (Virginia) battery*

**Haskell's Battalion** Maj. John C. Haskell
*Flanner's (North Carolina) battery · Garden's (South Carolina) battery*
*Lamkin's (Virginia) battery (unequipped) · Ramsay's (North Carolina) battery*

**Cabell's Battalion** Col. Henry C. Cabell
*Callaway's (Georgia) battery · Carlton's (Georgia) battery · McCarthy's (Virginia) battery*
*Manly's (North Carolina) battery*

**SECOND ARMY CORPS** Lt. Gen. Richard S. Ewell
**Early's Division** Maj. Gen. Jubal A. Early; Brig. Gen. John B. Gordon
**Pegram's Brigade** Brig. Gen. John Pegram
*13th Virginia · 31st Virginia · 49th Virginia · 52nd Virginia · 58th Virginia*

**Gordon's Brigade** Col. Clement Evans
*13th Georgia · 26th Georgia · 31st Georgia · 38th Georgia · 60th Georgia · 61st Georgia*

**Johnston's Brigade**[1] Brig. Gen. Robert D. Johnston; Col. Thomas F. Toon
*5th North Carolina · 12th North Carolina · 20th North Carolina · 23rd North Carolina*

**Johnson's Division**[2] Maj. Gen. Edward "Alleghany" Johnson
**Stonewall Brigade**[3] Brig. Gen. James A. Walker
*2nd Virginia · 4th Virginia · 5th Virginia · 27th Virginia · 33rd Virginia*

**Jones's Brigade**[3] Brig. Gen. John M. Jones
*21st Virginia · 25th Virginia · 42nd Virginia · 44th Virginia · 48th Virginia · 50th Virginia*

**Steuart's Brigade**[4] Brig. Gen. George H. "Maryland" Steuart
*1st North Carolina · 3rd North Carolina · 10th Virginia · 23rd Virginia · 37th Virginia*

**Stafford's Brigade** Brig. Gen. Harry Hays; Col. Zebulon York
*5th Louisiana · 6th Louisiana · 7th Louisiana · 8th Louisiana · 9th Louisiana · 1st Louisiana*
*2nd Louisiana · 10th Louisiana · 14th Louisiana · 15th Louisiana*

**Rodes's Division** Maj. Gen. Robert E. Rodes
**Daniel's Brigade** Brig. Gen. Junius Daniel
*32nd North Carolina · 43rd North Carolina · 45th North Carolina · 53d North Carolina*
*2nd North Carolina Battalion*

**Doles's Brigade** Brig. Gen. George Doles
*4th Georgia · 12th Georgia · 44th Georgia*

**Ramseur's Brigade** Brig. Gen. Stephen D. Ramseur
*2nd North Carolina · 4th North Carolina · 14th North Carolina · 30th North Carolina*

**Battle's Brigade** Brig. Gen. Cullen A. Battle
*3rd Alabama · 5th Alabama · 6th Alabama · 12th Alabama · 26th Alabama*

**Artillery** Brig. Gen. Armistead L. Long
**Hardaway's Battalion** Lt. Col. Robert A. Hardaway
*Dance's (Virginia) battery · Graham's (Virginia) battery · C. B. Griffin's (Virginia), battery*
*Jones's (Virginia) battery · B. H. Smith's (Virginia), battery*

**Braxton's Battalion** Lt. Col. Carter M. Braxton
*Carpenter's (Virginia) battery · Cooper's (Virginia) battery · Hardwicke's (Virginia) battery*

**Nelson's Battalion** Lt. Col. William Nelson
*Kirkpatrick's (Virginia) battery · Massie's (Virginia) battery · Milledge's (Georgia) battery*

**Cutshaw's Battalion** Maj. Wilfred E. Cutshaw
*Carrington's (Virginia) battery · Garber's, A. W. (Virginia), battery · Tanner's (Virginia) battery*

**Page's Battalion** Maj. Richard C. M. Page
*Carter's, W. P. (Virginia), battery · Fry's (Virginia) battery · Page's (Virginia) battery*
*Reese's (Alabama) battery*

**THIRD ARMY CORPS** Lt. Gen. A. P. Hill; Maj. Gen. Jubal A. Early
**Anderson's Division** Brig. Gen. William Mahone
**Perrin's Brigade** Brig. Gen. Abner Perrin; Col. John C. C. Sanders
*8th Alabama · 9th Alabama · 10th Alabama · 11th Alabama · 14th Alabama*

**Harris's Brigade** Brig. Gen. Nathaniel H. Harris
*12th Mississippi · 16th Mississippi · 19th Mississippi · 48th Mississippi*

**Mahone's Brigade** Col. David A. Weisiger
*6th Virginia · 12th Virginia · 16th Virginia · 41st Virginia · 61st Virginia*

**Wright's Brigade** Brig. Gen. Amrose R. Wright
*3rd Georgia · 22nd Georgia · 48th Georgia · 2nd Georgia Battalion*

**Perry's Brigade** Brig. Gen. Edward A. Perry
*2nd Florida · 5th Florida · 8th Florida*

**Heth's Division** Maj. Gen. Henry Heth
**Davis's Brigade** Brig. Gen. Joseph R. Davis
*2nd Mississippi · 11th Mississippi · 42nd Mississippi · 55th North Carolina*

**Cooke's Brigade** Brig. Gen. John R. Cooke
*15th North Carolina · 27th North Carolina · 46th North Carolina · 48th North Carolina*

**Kirkland's Brigade** Brig. Gen. William W. Kirkland
*11th North Carolina · 26th North Carolina · 44th North Carolina · 47th North Carolina*
*52nd North Carolina*

**Walker's Brigade** Brig. Gen. Henry H. Walker; Col. Robert M. Mayo
*40th Virginia · 47th Virginia · 55th Virginia · 22nd Virginia Battalion · 13th Alabama*
*1st Tennessee (Provisional Army) · 7th Tennessee · 14th Tennessee*

**Wilcox's Division** Maj. Gen. Cadmus M. Wilcox
**Lane's Brigade** Brig. Gen. James H. Lane
*7th North Carolina · 18th North Carolina · 28th North Carolina · 33rd North Carolina*
*37th North Carolina*

**Scales's Brigade** Brig. Gen. Alfred M. Scales
*13th North Carolina · 16th North Carolina · 22nd North Carolina · 34th North Carolina*
*38th North Carolina*

**McGowan's Brigade** Brig. Gen. Samuel McGowan; Col. Joseph N. Brown
*1st South Carolina (Provisional Army) · 12th South Carolina · 13th South Carolina*
*14th South Carolina · 1st South Carolina (Orr's Rifles)*

**Thomas's Brigade** Brig. Gen. Edward R. Thomas
*14th Georgia · 35th Georgia · 45th Georgia · 49th Georgia*

**Artillery** Col. R. Lindsay Walker
**Poague's Battalion** Lt. Col. William T. Poague
*Richards' (Mississippi) battery · Utterback's (Virginia) battery · Williams' (North Carolina) battery*
*Wyatt's (Virginia) battery*

**Pegram's Battalion** Lt. Col. William J. Pegram
*Brander's (Virginia) battery · Cayce's (Virginia) battery · Ellett's (Virginia) battery*
*Marye's (Virginia) battery · Zimmerman's (South Carolina) battery*

**McIntosh's Battalion** Lt. Col. David G. McIntosh
*Clutter's (Virginia) battery · Donald's (Virginia) battery · Hurt's (Alabama) battery*
*Price's (Virginia) battery*

**Cutts's Battalion** Col. Allen S. Cutts
*Patterson's (Georgia) battery · Ross's (Georgia) battery · Wingfield's (Georgia) battery*

**Richardson's Battalion** Lt. Col. Charles Richardson
*Grandy's (Virginia) battery · Landry's (Louisiana) battery · Moore's (Virginia) battery*
*Penick's (Virginia) battery*

**CAVALRY CORPS** Maj. Gen. James E. B. Stuart
**Hampton's Division** Maj. Gen. Wade Hampton
**Young's Brigade** Brig. Gen. Pierce M. B. Young
*7th Georgia · Cobb's (Georgia) Legion · Phillips (Georgia) Legion · 20th Georgia Battalion*
*Jeff. Davis (Mississippi) Legion*

**Rosser's Brigade** Brig. Gen. Thomas L. Rosser
*7th Virginia · 11th Virginia · 12th Virginia · 35th Virginia Battalion*

**Butler's Brigade** Brig. Gen. Matthew C. Butler
*4th South Carolina · 5th South Carolina · 6th South Carolina*

**Fitzhugh Lee's Division** Maj. Gen. Fitzhugh Lee
**Lomax's Brigade** Brig. Gen. Lunsford L. Lomax
*5th Virginia · 6th Virginia · 15th Virginia*

**Wickham's Brigade** Brig. Gen. Williams C. Wickham
*1st Virginia · 2nd Virginia · 3rd Virginia · 4th Virginia*

**William H. F. Lee's Division** Maj. Gen. William H. F. Lee
**Chambliss's Brigade** Brig. Gen. John R. Chambliss, Jr.
*9th Virginia · 10th Virginia · 13th Virginia*

**Gordon's Brigade** Brig. Gen. James B. Gordon; Col. Clinton M. Andrews
*1st North Carolina · 2nd North Carolina · 5th North Carolina*

**Horse Artillery** Maj. R. Preston Chew
**Breathed's Battalion** Maj. James Breathed
*Hart's (South Carolina) battery · Johnston's (Virginia) battery · McGregor's (Virginia) battery*
*Shoemaker's (Virginia) battery · Thomson's (Virginia) battery*

*1 Brigade trasnferred from Rode's division to Early's on May 8.*
*2 Division ceased to exist on May 13, units were formally parceled out to other brigades and divisions on May 21.*
*3 Formally consolidated into Brig. William Terry's brigade on May 21.*
*4 Formally consolidated into Brig. William Terry's and Brig. Gen. Stephen D. Ramseur's brigades on May 21.*

# Medal of Honor Recipients

### 1864

**James M. Cutts**, captain, 11th U.S. Infantry
Gallantry in actions. (Received for actions in the Battle of the Wilderness, Spotsylvania, and Petersburg, Virginia.)

**Samuel Nicholl Benjamin**, first lieutenant, 2nd U.S. Artillery
Particularly distinguished services as an artillery officer. (Received for actions between Bull Run to Spotsylvania, Virginia. July 1861–May 1864)

### May 8, 1864

**George N. Galloway**, private, Co. G, 95th Pennsylvania Infantry
The President of the United States of America, in the name of Congress, takes pleasure in presenting the Medal of Honor to Private George Norton Galloway, United States Army, for extraordinary heroism on 8 May 1864, while serving with Company G, 95th Pennsylvania Infantry, in action at Alsops Farm, Virginia. Private Galloway voluntarily held an important position under heavy fire.

**Lee Nutting**, captain, Co. C, 61st New York Infantry
Led the regiment in charge at a critical moment under a murderous fire until he fell desperately wounded.

**Charles E. Phelps**, colonel, 7th Maryland Infantry
Rode to the head of the assaulting column, then much broken by severe losses and faltering under the close fire of artillery, placed himself conspicuously in front of the troops, and gallantly rallied and led them to within a few feet of the enemy's works, where he was severely wounded and captured.

**Robert S. Robertson**, first lieutenant, Co. K, 93rd New York Infantry
"[F]or extraordinary heroism on 8 May 1864, while serving with Company K, 93d New York Infantry, in action at Corbins Bridge, Virginia. While acting as aide-de-camp to a general officer, seeing a regiment break to the rear, First Lieutenant Robertson seized its colors, rode with them to the front in the face of the advancing enemy, and rallied the retreating regiment."

**John Cleveland Robinson**, brigadier general, U.S. Volunteers
Placed himself at the head of the leading brigade in a charge upon the enemy's breastworks; was severely wounded.

## May 10, 1864

**Moses A. Luce**, sergeant, Co. E, 4th Michigan Infantry
Voluntarily returned in the face of the advancing enemy to the assistance of a wounded and helpless comrade, and carried him, at imminent peril, to a place of safety.

**Thomas O. Seaver**, colonel, 3rd Vermont Infantry
At the head of 3 regiments and under a most galling fire attacked and occupied the enemy's works.

## May 12, 1864

**Frederick Alber**, private, Co. A, 17th Michigan Infantry
Bravely rescued Lt. Charles H. Todd of his regiment who had been captured by a party of Confederates by shooting down one, knocking over another with the butt of his musket, and taking them both prisoners.

**Robert Wesley Ammerman**, private, Co. B, 148th Pennsylvania Infantry
Capture of battle flag of 8th North Carolina (C.S.A.), being one of the foremost in the assault.

**Nathaniel C. Barker,** sergeant, Co. E, 11th New Hampshire Infantry
Six color bearers of the regiment having been killed, he voluntarily took both flags of the regiment and carried them through the remainder of the battle.

**John P. Beech**, sergeant, Co. B, 4th New Jersey Infantry
Voluntarily assisted in working the guns of a battery, all the members of which had been killed or wounded.

**Francis A. Bishop**, private, Co. C, 57th Pennsylvania Infantry
Capture of flag

**E. Michael Burk**, private, Co. D, 125th New York Infantry
Capture of flag, seizing it as his regiment advanced over the enemy's works. He received a bullet wound in the chest while capturing flag.

**Dayton P. Clarke**, captain, Co. F, 2nd Vermon Infantry
Distinguished conduct in a desperate hand-to-hand fight while commanding the regiment.

**Charles H. Clausen**, first lieutenant, Co. H, 61st Pennsylvania Infantry
Although severely wounded, he led the regiment against the enemy, under a terrific fire, and saved a battery from capture.

**Charles S. Fall**, sergeant, Co. E, 26th Michigan Infantry
Was one of the first to mount the Confederate works, where he bayoneted two of the enemy and captured a Confederate flag, but threw it away to continue the pursuit of the enemy.

**Charles H. Fasnacht**, sergeant, Co. A, 99th Pennsylvania Infantry
Capture of flag of 2nd Louisiana Tigers (C.S.A.) in a hand-to-hand contest.

**Archibald Freeman**, private, Co. E, 124th New York Infantry
Capture of flag of 17th Louisiana (C.S.A.).

**George W. Harris**, private, Co. B, 148th Pennsylvania Infantry
Capture of flag, wresting it from the color bearer and shooting an officer who attempted to regain it.

**William Jones**, first sergeant, Co. A, 73rd New York Infantry
Capture of flag of 65th Virginia Infantry (C.S.A.).[1]

**John M. Kindig**, corporal, Co. A, 63rd Pennsylvania
Capture of flag of 28th North Carolina Infantry. (C.S.A.).

**Albert Marsh**, sergeant, Co. B, 64th New York Infantry
Captured the enemy flag.

**Charles McAnally**, lieutenant, Co. D, 69th Pennsylvania Infantry
In a hand-to-hand encounter with the enemy captured a flag, was wounded in the act, but continued on duty until he received a second wound.

**Daniel McFall**, sergeant, Co. E, 17th Michigan Infantry
Captured Col. Barker, commanding the Confederate brigade that charged the Union batteries; on the same day rescued Lt. George W. Harmon of his regiment from the enemy.

1 Jones's is an interesting case because there was no 65th Virginia Infantry in the Army of Northern Virginia (or anywhere, for that matter, although there was a 65th Virginia militia unit, based in Southampton, no where near the battlefield). No records or accounts are currently known that explain which flag Jones actually captured. His Medal of Honor was awarded postumously—rare during the war itself—on December 1, 1864. He is buried in Fredericksburg National Cemetery.

**Alexander U. McHale**, corporal, Co. H, 26th Michigan
Captured a Confederate color in a charge, threw the flag over in front of the works, and continued in the charge upon the enemy.

**Alexander H. Mitchell**, first lieutenant, Co. A, 105th Pennsylvania Infantry
Capture of flag of 18th North Carolina Infantry (C.S.A.), in a personal encounter with the color bearer.

**Lewis Morgan**, private, Co. I, 4th Ohio Infantry
Capture of flag from the enemy's works.

**Benjamin Morse**, private, Co. C, 3rd Michigan Infantry
Capture of colors of 4th Georgia Battery (C.S.A.)

**Conrad Noll,** sergeant, Co. D, 20th Michigan Infantry
Seized the colors, the color bearer having been shot down, and gallantly fought his way out with them, though the enemy were on the left flank and rear.

**William W. Noyes**, private, Co. F, 2nd Vermont Infantry
Standing upon the top of the breastworks, deliberately took aim and fired no less than 15 shots into the enemy's lines, but a few yards away.

**Augustus I. Robbins**, second lieutenant, Co. B, 2nd Vermont Infantry
While voluntarily serving as a staff officer successfully withdrew a regiment across and around a severely exposed position to the rest of the command; was severely wounded.

**Thomas Robinson**, private, Co. H, 81st Pennsylvania Infantry
Capture of flag in hand-to-hand conflict.

**Valentine Rossbach**, sergeant, 34th New York Battery
Encouraged his cannoneers to hold a very dangerous position, and when all depended on several good shots it was from his piece that the most effective were delivered, causing the enemy's fire to cease and thereby relieving the critical position of the Federal troops.

**Lewis A. Rounds**, private, Co. D, 8th Ohio Infantry
Capture of flag.

**Charles L. Russell**, corporal, Co. H, 93rd New York Infantry
Capture of flag of 42d Virginia Infantry (C.S.A.).

**Philipp Schlachter**, private, Co. F, 73rd New York Infantry
Capture of flag of 15th Louisiana Infantry (C.S.A.).

**Charles A. Thompson**, sergeant, Co. D, 17th Michigan Infantry
After the regiment was surrounded and all resistance seemed useless, fought single-handed for the colors and refused to give them up until he had appealed to his superior officers.

**Charles H. Tracy**, sergeant, Co. A, 37th Massachusetts
At the risk of his own life, at Spotsylvania, 12 May 1864, assisted in carrying to a place of safety a wounded and helpless officer. On 2 April 1865, advanced with the pioneers, and, under heavy fire, assisted in removing two lines of chevaux-de-frise; was twice wounded but advanced to the third line, where he was again severely wounded, losing a leg.

**John H. Weeks**, private, Co. H, 152nd New York Infantry
Capture of flag and color bearer using an empty cocked rifle while outnumbered 5 or 6.

**William Westerhold**, sergeant, Co. G, 52nd New York Infantry
Capture of flag of 23d Virginia Infantry (C.S.A.).

**William H. Wilcox**, sergeant, Co. G, 9th New Hampshire Infantry
Took command of his company, deployed as skirmishers, after the officers in command of the skirmish line had both been wounded, conducting himself gallantly; afterwards, becoming separated from command, he asked and obtained permission to fight in another company.

**Christopher W. Wilson**, private, Co. E, 73rd New York Infantry
Took the flag from the wounded color bearer and carried it in the charge over the Confederate works, in which charge he also captured the colors of the 56th Virginia (C.S.A.) bringing off both flags in safety.

**Lewis S. Wisner**, first lieutenant, Co. K, 124th New York Infantry
While serving as an engineer officer, voluntarily exposed himself to the enemy's fire.

## May 18, 1864

**Richard Beddows**, private, 34th New York Battery
Brought his guidon off in safety under a heavy fire of musketry after he had lost it by his horse becoming furious from the bursting of a shell.

**John Kinsey**, corporal, Co. B, 45th Pennsylvania Infantry
Seized the colors, the color bearer having been shot, and with great gallantry succeeded in saving them from capture.

**Frank M. Whitman**, private, Co. G, 35th Massachusetts Infantry
Was among the last to leave the field at Antietam and was instrumental in saving the lives of several of his comrades at the imminent risk of his own. At Spotsylvania was foremost in line in the assault, where he lost a leg. Received for actions in the Battle of Antietam, Maryland (Sept. 17, 1862), and Battle of Spotsylvania Court House, Virginia (May 18, 1864).

# The Cover Photograph

*John F. Cummings III*

In April 1866, Union Surgeon, Dr. Reed Brockway Bontecou, traveling with a photographic entourage, produced 121 stereoviews of the battlefields around Fredericksburg. The cover image for this volume, taken on the farm of Neil McCoull, is part of that series. It shows the graves of members of the 16th Mississippi Infantry.

The summer before the expedition, a Federal burial party had returned to the silent battlefields to properly inter remains that had been left untended, exposed to the elements and potential maltreatment. Although focused on the remains of Federal soldiers, in rare instances, as with the graves seen here, the burial crew provided adequate marking for scattered Confederates.

The uncropped image shows eleven wood markers: eight legible, two masked by others, and one too blurred to decipher.

The 16th was part of Harris's Mississippi Brigade, which had been rushed forward on May 12, 1864, to expel the early morning Federal assault sweeping over the north face of the Mule Shoe Salient. Advancing, at General Lee's urging, they halted briefly at a secondary trench line, also visible in this photo, lightly masked by a belt of trees. It was here that the 16th took their first casualties of the action before pressing on to the main trench 175 yards to the right oblique. Initially buried where they fell by comrades in arms, makeshift markings were replaced by uniformly prepared wood markers provided by the Federal burial team.

The legible names are as follows, from left to right, and as complete as records will provide: Telford Kelly Currie, Silas Andrew Shirley, Albion Melanchton Swittenberg, Samuel C. Baskins, T. White, John B. Summer, Stephen W. Dampeer, and likely, but uncertain, A. Toner.

All men in their twenties, mostly farmers, one merchant, some with no documenting evidence at all. Lives cut short, their potential unrealized.

In time, they were disinterred and collected in a Confederate Cemetery close to Spotsylvania Courthouse where they rest together, still: the bivouac of the dead.

# Acknowledgments

In 2009, John Hennessy, then the chief historian and chief of interpretation at FredSpot, connected me and longtime collaborator Kris White with Dave Roth at the legendary *Blue & Gray* magazine. That connection led to the first magazine article we ever wrote about Spotsy. I am grateful to Dave for the opportunity and especially grateful to John for opening that door in the first place.

That same year, Greg Mertz, supervisory historian at FredSpot, allowed Kris and me to do five of the park's six programs for Spotsy's 145th anniversary. (Greg did the sixth, a tour of Spindle Field, which he had written about for *Blue & Gray*.) I have been doing battlefield tours of Spotsy ever since, most recently as historian in residence at Stevenson Ridge. It is a battlefield I have spent an immense amount of time on over the subsequent decade and a half. I'm grateful to Greg for that anniversary opportunity. I'm also grateful for the time he took to review this manuscript and offer comments on its development. Greg has been one of my most important mentors in my development as a historian, and I will forever be indebted to him.

Gordon Rhea, the dean of Overland Campaign scholars, has likewise been generous with his time and expertise over the years, as his foreword for this book demonstrates. Gordon exemplifies the idea of a gentleman and scholar. If John opened the door, Gordon showed me the way, setting the example of excellent Overland scholarship. His book *To the North Anna River* remains my favorite microtactical study of the Civil War. That book taught me how to run down sources.

The next key moment in my relationship with the Spotsy battlefield came in 2011 when I met my now-wife, Jennifer. Jenny's mother and stepfather, Debbie and Dan Spear, own nearly 90 acres on the battlefield's eastern front, and the three of them operate their business, Stevenson Ridge, on the property. I basically married into my own battlefield! I thank Dan, Debbie, and Jennifer for giving me free reign to explore, interpret, and share their family's historically important piece of ground. It has given me a vital familiarity with the larger story of Spotsy I never would have expected.

My involvement with the Central Virginia Battlefields Trust coincided with their opportunity to purchase historically important land at Myer's Hill. Because that property was not contiguous with the National Park Service's holdings, the NPS had twice passed up opportunities to purchase it. However, preserving that land has opened the story of the second week of the battle in important ways. Because the NPS did not hold much property related to that second week of the battle, that part of the battle has been under-interpreted for nearly a century. As the NPS told the story of Spotsy, the battle sort of ended on May 12 after the Bloody Angle (with a single sign explaining the May 18 fighting). CVBT has preserved land at Harris Farm, along the Po River, and, more recently, at Myer's Hill. I am grateful to CVBT and its president, Tom Van Winkle, for the organization's ongoing work to expand the story of Spotsy all the way through to the armies' exit.

For the final step in my Spotsy journey, I have to thank historian Jeff Wert, author of *The Heart of Hell: The Soldiers' Struggle for Spotsylvania's Bloody Angle.* Jeff doesn't realize it, but he gave me the kick in the pants I needed to finally pull this book together. When *The Heart of Hell* came out, I thought, "The dude has come into my own back yard and written a fantastic book. I need to get my butt in gear." And so I did. Jeff is an excellent storyteller, and his Spotsy book is fantastic—a worthy addition to his own oeuvre and a nice contribution to the literature of the battle.

* * *

At the core of this book sit a pair of articles Kris White and I wrote for *Blue & Gray.* The first, focusing on the May 12 fight at the Mule Shoe, appeared in early 2009 (vol. 26, issue #1); the second, outlining the fighting from May 13 until the armies withdrew from Spotsylvania Court House, appeared in late 2011 (vol. 27, issue #6). Dave Roth, editor of *Blue & Gray,* was gracious enough to allow me to use the text from those issues for this publication.

In December 2015, Kris and I revisited the oft-overlooked May 18 fight in greater detail for *Civil War Times*. In the winter of 2017, we collaborated on a pair of articles for the American Battlefield Trust's *Hallowed Ground*: one on Upton's May 10 attack and another on the May 12 attack at the Mule Shoe.

With Kris's permission, I have borrowed text from all of those articles. I have also borrowed from some of my work in *Traces of the Bloody Struggle: The Civil War at Stevenson's Ridge, Spotsylvania Court House,* a booklet in the Emerging Civil War Series that focuses on action that occurred on property owned by my in-laws on the eastern front of the battlefield.

With the bones of those previous pieces as my skeleton, I proceeded to "fill in the blanks" on the parts of the battle I had not written about before. I also significantly added to and revised the text from those previous publications. Passages still exist here and there, but the vast majority of that original material has been significantly rewritten. Nonetheless, Kris White's fingerprints exist all over the background of this manuscript, and I am grateful for those contributions.

For many years, I have been extremely fortunate to have at my disposal the incredible research library amassed by the Fredericksburg and Spotsylvania National Military Park. Most of the items in the bound manuscript volumes have come from other collections, and I have tried to list the original repositories where I'm able, but this project—indeed, my knowledge of the battle of Spotsylvania—will ever be indebted to "the BVs" at FredSpot. It is just one of several ways I have benefitted from the intellectual tradition cultivated by the legendary Bob Krick, who first worked to amass, curate, and make available for researchers this remarkable collection.

I feel like Edward Alexander has become my secret weapon in any project I do. He was "raised" on the same FredSpot battlefields I was, and so he knows the ground as well (or better) than I do. He not only serves as a double-check on my research but, as a cartographer, he knows how to illuminate my work to its best advantage. I'm not sure he realizes how much of a privilege I consider it to work with him. I hope his series of excellent maps helps add to the overall literature of the battle of Spotsylvania Court House.

Speaking of double-checks, Ryan Quint not only looked over parts of the manuscript but also helped run down several especially esoteric pieces of information along the way. Likewise, Noel Harrison, Eric Mink, and Garry Adelman all answered questions for me at various points. Pete Maugle provided additional assistance. John Cummings, a champion of preservation on the eastern front, likewise answered questions and provided information on the cover photo.

Doug Litts of Archives and Special Collections at the United States Military Academy helped me track down the cover image. Kylie Thomson of the Fredericksburg Area Museum helped me with the photos of the John Myer family. Brian Swartz shared his photo of John Haley from the Sacco Library. Kris White shared his photo of the plaque on John Sedgwick's grave. Kevin Levin helped me grab the photo of Thomas Greely Stevenson's memorial in the Massachusetts State House. Ron Veen shared the unpublished memoir of Brig. Gen. Simon Griffin. Chris Kolakowski and Jon-Erik Gilot both sent newly discovered accounts my way. Each contribution added to the richness and depth of this manuscript, and I am grateful.

Late in this process, I had the good fortune of being able to work with editor Chris Howland, former editor at *America's Civil War* magazine. Chris is someone whose work I respect immensely, and I was pleased to discover Ted had assigned him as my copyeditor. As a professor, I urge my students to challenge every sentence, every phrase, and every word; Chris did that for me with this text. We have slightly different approaches to how to deploy language as a tool for not only conveying information but as a means of expression, and what I appreciate about Chris so much is that we can have *those sorts* of conversations about a sentence. It was wonderful! (I suspect everything I just said would put most readers to sleep, but craftspeople *love* that kind of stuff.)

Theodore P. Savas made sure this book made it to bookshelves. I thank him and his stalwart staff at Savas Beatie World Headquarters for all they do to promote my work and the work of my colleagues at Emerging Civil War. Thank you, Veronica, Lisa, Sarah K., Sarah C., Donna, and Angela! Veronica did a lot of heavy lifting on this project, and I am lucky to have a production manager I trust so implicitly.

At St. Bonaventure, my dean, Aaron Chimbel, continues to give me tremendous flexibility to write. I am grateful for his ongoing, unqualified support of my work. My colleagues in the Office of Marketing and Communications—Tom Donahue, Beth Eberth, and Tom Missel—continue to be good to me, and I am grateful. Thanks, too, to my colleagues in the Jandoli School of Communication, particularly Pauline Hoffmann and Denny Wilkins.

Last but not least, I would like to thank my family: my daughter and son-in-law, Steph and Thomas, and my beautiful granddaughters, Sophie (the Pip) and Gracie; my sons, Jackson and Maxwell; and my wife, Jennifer. These are the people on whom my sun rises and sets. Jenny, in particular, tolerated my particularly intense work schedule on this book. She is a lovely woman, and I appreciate her patience and grace. To borrow from one New York soldier, "It was plainly a question of bravery and endurance. . . ."

My first visit to the Spotsylvania Court House battlefield came on May 25, 1998, at the tail end of Memorial Day weekend. My daughter, Stephanie, then four and a half, had recently discovered the Civil War and had begun asking to visit battlefields (her idea, not mine!). Traveling home to northwest Pennsylvania from the Outer Banks, we made what was supposed to be a brief stop at Fredericksburg and Spotsylvania National Military Park so she could, for the first time, see the spot at Chancellorsville where Stonewall Jackson had been mortally wounded.

While at the park, Steph heard there was a place at one of the battlefields called "the Bloody Angle." She insisted we take a look. She wanted to see if there was still any blood. Ironically, the dirt path that led from the parking area to the head of the hiking trail consisted primarily of red clay, which can look blood-tinged enough for a four-year-old's imagination. Although the Angle itself no longer ran red with blood, the large battle painting there by Sidney King made it perfectly clear that the name "Bloody Angle" was, unfortunately, all too appropriate.

We couldn't stay long to explore, but on August 19, we returned. It was evening, the crepuscular hour, and we took our time strolling along the walking path, surrounded by tall grass, scrubby oak seedlings, leafy sumac. Deer poked their heads above the foliage. Here and there, a monument invited visitors to pay their respects. Steph hitched a ride on my shoulders for much of the way until a bat fluttered by, sending her to ground.

Once she found her courage again, she ran ahead down the path, then back to me, then ahead again. Footsteps on the earth. The hum of insects. Laughter.

The gloaming thickened, and we headed back toward the parking lot, holding hands.

# Bibliography


## Collections

FSNMP Bound Manuscript Volumes.

Museum of the Confederacy Collection.

Wisconsin Historical Society Archives.

*Collected Works of Abraham Lincoln*, Volume 7 [Nov. 5, 1863–Sept. 12, 1864] (New Brunswick, NJ: Rutgers University Press, 1953).

Histories of the Several Regiments and Battalions from North Carolina in the Great War, 1861-65, Walter Clark, ed., 5 volumes (Raleigh, NC: State of North Carolina, 1901).

*The Papers of Ulysses S. Grant*, Volume 09: July 7–December 31, 1863, John Y. Simon, editor, (Carbondale, IL: Southern Illinois University Press, 1982).

*The War of the Rebellion: A Compilation of the Official Records of the Union and Confederate Armies*, Robert N. Scott, ed. (Wilmington, NC: Broadfoot Publishing Company, 1985).

## Primary Sources

John Gregory Bishop Adams, *Reminiscences of the Nineteenth Massachusetts Regiment* (Boston: Wright & Potter printing company, 1899).

Allen D. Albert, ed., *History of the Forty-Fifth Regiment, Pennsylvania Veteran Volunteer Infantry, 1861–1865*. (Williamsport, PA: Grit Publishing Company, 1912).

E. Porter Alexander, *Fighting for the Confederacy: The Personal Recollections of General Edward Porter Alexander*, Gary W. Gallagher, ed. (Chapel Hill, NC: The University of North Carolina Press, 1989).

E. Porter Alexander, *Military Memoirs of a Confederate*. (New York, 1907).

John Anderson, *The Fifty-Seventh Regiment of Massachusetts Volunteers in the War of the Rebellion: Army of the Potomac* (Boston: E. B. Stillings & Company, printers, 1896).

Charles H. Banes, *History of the Philadelphia Brigade: Sixty-Ninth, Seventy-First, Seventy-Second, and One Hundred and Sixth Pennsylvania Volunteers* (Philadelphia: J. B. Lippincott & Co., 1876).

Cullen Battle, *Third Alabama! The Civil War Memoir of Brigadier General Cullen Andrews Battle, CSA*, Brandon Beck, ed. (Tuscaloosa, AL: University of Alabama Press, 2000).

George William Beale, *A Lieutenant of Cavalry in Lee's Army* (Boston: The Gorham Press, 1918).

George Grenville Benedict, *Vermont in the Civil War: A History of the Part Taken by the Vermont Soldiers and Sailors in the War for the Union, 1861-5*, Vol. 1 (Burlington, VT: Free Press Association, 1886).

Isaac Oliver Best, *History of the 121st New York State Infantry* (Chicago: Jas. H. Smith, 1921).

John D. Black, "Reminiscences of the Bloody Angle," *Glimpses of the Nation's Struggle* (St. Paul, MN: H. L. Collins Co., 1898).

Susan Leigh Blackford, Charles Minor Blackford, *Letters From Lee's Army or Memoirs of Life In and Out of the Army in Virginia During the War Between the States* (Lincoln, NE: University of Nebraska Press, 1998).

J. D. Bloodgood, *Personal Reminiscences of the War* (New York: Hunt & Eaton; Cincinnati, OH: Cranstons & Curts, 1893).

William J. Bolton, *The Civil War Journal of Colonel William J. Bolton, 51st Pennsylvania, April 20, 1861–August 2, 1865*. Richard A. Sauers, ed. (Conshohocken, PA: Combined Publishing, 2000).

James N. Bosang, *Memoirs of a Pulaski Veteran of the Stonewall Brigade* (Pulaksi, VA: 1912).

Freeman S. Bowley, *A Boy Lieutenant* (Philadelphia: Henry Altemus Company, 1906).

Gordon Bradwell, *Under the Southern Cross: Soldier Life With Gordon Bradwell and the Army of Northern Virginia*, Pharris Deloach Johnson, ed. (Macon, GA: Mercer University Press, 1999).

Wesley Brainerd, *Bridge Building in Wartime: Colonel Wesley Brainerd's Memoir*, Ed Malles, ed., (Nashville, TN: University of Tennessee Press, 1997).

Charles Brewster, *When This Cruel War Is Over: The Civil War Letters of Charles Harvey Brewster*, David W. Blight, ed. (Amherst, MA: University of Massachusetts Press, 1992).

Augustus Cleveland Brown, *The Diary of a Line Officer* (New York: 1906).

Campbell Brown, *Campbell Brown's Civil War With Ewell and the Army of Northern Virginia*, Terry L. Jones, ed. (Baton Rouge, LA: Louisiana State University Press, 2001).

George A. Bruce, *The Twentieth Regiment of Massachusetts Volunteer Infantry 1861–1865* (Boston, 1906).

Augustus Buell, *The Cannoneer: Recollections of Service in the Army of the Potomac* (Washington, DC: The National Tribune, 1890).

J. F. J. Caldwell, *The History of a Brigade of South Carolinians* (Philadelphia: King & Baird, 1866).

F. B. Carpenter, *The Inner Life of Abraham Lincoln: Six Months at the White House* (New York: Hurd and Houghton, 1874)

Robert Goldthwaite Carter, *Four Brothers in Blue: A Story of the Great Civil War From Bull Run to Appomattox* (Washington, DC: Press of Gibson Bros., Inc., 1913).

Thomas Carter, "The Bloody Angle," *Southern Historical Society Papers*, Vol. 21.

John O. Casler, *Four Years in the Stonewall Brigade* (Guthrie, OK: State Capital Printing Company, 1893).

Thomas Chamberlain, *History of the One Hundred and Fiftieth Regiment, Pennsylvania Volunteers, Second Regiment, Bucktail Brigade* (Philadelphia: F. McManus, Jr. & Co., 1905).

Charles Carleton Coffin, *Four Years of Fighting: A Volume of Personal Observations With the Army and Navy, From the First Battle of Bull Run to the Fall of Richmond* (Boston: Ticknor and Fields, 1866).

George H. Coffin, *Three Years in the Army* (1976), Maine History Documents, 267. https://digitalcommons.library.umaine.edu/mainehistory/267

Committee of the Regimental Association, eds. *History of the Thirty-Fifth Regiment Massachusetts Volunteers, 1862–1865* (Boston: Mills, Knight & Company, 1884).

Cyrus B. Comstock, *The Diary of Cyrus B. Comstock*, Merlin E. Sumner, ed. (Dayton, OH: Morningside, 1987).

John Coxe, "Last Struggles and Successes of Lee," *Confederate Veteran*, Vol. 22.

David Craft, *History of the One Hundred Forty-first Regiment* (Towanda, PA: Reporter-Journal Printing Company, 1885).

Lewis Crater, *History of the Fiftieth Regiment, Penna. Vet. Vols., 1861-65* (Reading, PA: Coleman Printing House, 1884).

Simon Burdick Cummins, *Give God the Glory: Memoirs of a Civil War Solider,* Melvin Jones, ed. (Paris Press, 1979).

Byron M. Cutcheon, *The Story of the Twentieth Michigan infantry, July 15th, 1862, to May 30th, 1865* (Lansing, MI: R. Smith Printing Co., 1904).

William Meade Dame, *From the Rapidan to Richmond and the Spotsylvania Campaign* (Baltimore: Green-Lucas Company, 1920).

Charles Davis, *Three Years in the Army. The Story of the Thirteenth Massachusetts Volunteers from July 16, 1861, to August 1, 1864* (Boston: Estes and Lauriat, 1894).

Rufus Dawes, *Service With the Sixth Wisconsin Volunteers*, (Marietta, OH: E.R. Alderman & Sons, 1890).

Regis De Trobriand, *Four Years With the Army of the Potomac* (Boston: Ticknor & Company, 1889).

John E. Devine, *35th Virginia Battalion Virginia Cavalry* (Lynchburg, VA: H.E. Howard, Inc., 1985).

Augustus Dickert, *Kershaw's Brigade, with complete roll of companies, biographical sketches, incidents, anecdotes, etc.* (Newberry, SC: E. H. Aull Company, 1899.

William S. Dunlop, *Lee's Sharpshooters; or, The Forefront of Battle: A Story of Southern Valor That Never Has Been Told* (Little Rock, AR, 1899).

Jubal Anderson Early, *Lieutenant General Jubal Anderson Early, C.S.A.: Autobiographical Sketch and Narrative of the War Between the States* (Philadelphia: J. B. Lippincott Company, 1912).

Porter Farley, *An Unvarnished Tale: The Public and Private Civil War of Porter Farley 140th N.Y.V.I.*, ed. Brian A. Bennett (Wheatland, NY: Triphammer Publishing, 2007).

Josiah Marshall Favill, *The Diary of a Young Officer Serving With the Armies of the United States During the War of the Rebellion* (Chicago: R. R. Donnelley & Sons, 1909).

*First Regiment of Heavy Artillery, Massachusetts Volunteers. Dedication of Monument, May 19, 1901,* Souvenir booklet.

Wilbur Fisk, *Hard Marching Every Day: The Civil War Letters of Private Wilbur Fisk, 1861–1865*, Emil and Ruth Rosenblatt, eds. (Lawrence, KS: University of Kansas Press, 1992).

Theodore Stanford Garnett, *Riding with Stuart: Reminiscences of an Aide-de-Camp* (Shippensburg, PA: White Mane, 1994).

Fielding H. Garrison, *John Shaw Billings: A Memoir* (New York: G. P. Putnam's Sons, 1915).

William Gilfillan Gavin, *Campaigning With the Roundheads: The History of the Hundredth Pennsylvania Veteran Volunteer Infantry Regiment in the American Civil War 1861–1865: The Roundhead Regiment* (Dayton, OH: Morningside, 1989).

John Brown Gordon, *Reminiscences of the Civil War* (New York, 1903).

Ulysses S. Grant, *The Personal Memoirs of Ulysses S. Grant,* 2 Vols. (Hartford, CT: Charles Webster & Co., 1885).

Bryan Grimes, *Extracts of Letter of Major Gen'l Bryan Grimes to His Wife* (Raleigh, NC: Edwards, Broughton & Co., 1883).

B. J. Haden, *Reminiscences of J. E. B. Stuart's Cavalry* (Charlottesville, VA: Progress Publishing Co., undated).

Alanson A. Haines, *History of the Fifteenth Regiment New Jersey Volunteers* (New York: Jenkins & Thomas, 1883).

John Haley, *The Rebel Yell and the Yankee Hurrah*, Ruth L. Silliker, ed. (Camden, ME: Down East, 1985).

John Hay, *Letters of John Hay and Extracts from Diary*, Vol. 1 (New York: Gordian Press, 1969).

Daniel Holt, *A Surgeon's Civil War: The Letters and Diary of Daniel M. Holt, M.D.* James M. Greiner, Janet L. Coryell, and James R. Smither, eds. (Kent, OH: Kent State University Press, 1991).

David Holt, *A Mississippi Rebel in the Army of Northern Virginia*, Thomas D. Cockrell and Michael B. Ballad, eds. (Baton Rouge, LA: Louisiana State University Press, 2001).

Jedediah Hotchkiss, *Make Me a Map of the Valley*, Archie P. McDonald, ed. (Dallas, TX: Southern Methodist University Press, 1973).

Henry C. Houston, *The Thirty-Second Maine Regiment of Infantry Volunteers: An Historical Sketch* (Portland, ME: Press of Southworth Brothers, 1903).

McHenry Howard, *Recollections of a Maryland Confederate Soldier and Staff Officer Under Johnston, Jackson, and Lee*, (Baltimore, 1914).

Andrew Humphreys, *The Virginia Campaign of '64 and '65: The Army of the Potomac and The Army of the James* (New York: Charles Scribner's Sons, 1883).

Robert Hunter, "Major Hunter's Story," *Southern Historical Society Papers*, Vol. 33.

Thomas Hyde, *Following the Greek Cross, or, Memories of the Sixth Army Corps*, (Columbia, SC: University of South Carolina Press, 2005).

Theodore Irving, *More Than Conqueror: Memorials of Col. J. Howard Kitching* (New York: Hurd and Houghton, 1873).

Lyman Jackman, *History of the Sixth New Hampshire Regiment in the War for the Union* (Concord, NH: Repub. Press Association, 1891).

Hyland Clare Kirk, *Heavy Guns and Light: A History of the 4th New York Heavy Artillery* (New York: C. T. Dillingham, 1890).

Robert E. Lee, *Lee's Dispatches: Unpublished Letters of General Robert E. Lee, C.S.A., to Jefferson Davis and the War Department of the Confederate States of American, 1862–1864*, Douglas Southall Freeman and Grady McWiney, eds. (New York: Putnam's, 1957).

Robert E. Lee, *The Wartime Papers of Robert E. Lee*, Clifford Dowdey and Louis H. Manarin, eds. (New York: Da Capo, 1961).

Abraham Lincoln, *Collected Works of Abraham Lincoln*, 8 Vols. (New Brunswick, NJ: Rutgers University Press, 1953).

William Henry Locke, *The Story of the Regiment* (Philadelphia: J. B. Lippincott & Co., 1868).

James Lockwood, *Life and Adventures of a Drummer Boy: or Seven Years a Soldier* (Albany, NY: 1893).

Andrew D. Long, *Stonewall's "Foot Cavalryman"* (Austin, TX: Walter Long, 1965).

Armistead L. Long, *Memoirs of Robert E. Lee, his military and personal history; together with incidents relating to his private life, also a large amount of historical information hitherto unpublished* (London: Sampson, Low, Marston, Searle, and Rivington, 1886).

Theodore Lyman, *Meade's Army: The Private Notebooks of Lt. Col. Theodore Lyman*, David W. Lowe, ed. (Kent, OH: Kent State University Press, 2007).

Theodore Lyman, *Meade's Headquarters, 1863–1865: Letters of Colonel Theodore Lyman From the Wilderness to Appomattox*, George R. Agassiz, ed. (Freeport, NY: Books for Libraries Press, 1922).

Theodore Lyman, *With Grant & Meade: From Wilderness to Appomattox* (Lincoln, NE: University of Nebraska Press, 1994).

Edwin C. Mason, *Through the Wilderness to the Bloody Angle at Spotsylvania Court House: Glimpses of the Nation's Struggle, 4th Series* (St. Paul, MN: H.L. Collins Co., 1893).

Robert McAllister, *The Civil War Letters of General Robert McAllister*, James I. Robertson, Jr., ed. (New Brunswick, NJ: Rutgers University Press, 1965).

William Naylor McDonald, *A History of the Laurel Brigade* (Baltimore: Sun Job Printing Office, 1907).

Martin T. McMahon, "The Death of General John Sedgwick," *Battles & Leaders of the Civil War*, vol. 4, (New York: The Century Co., 1884).

George Gordon Meade, *The Life and Letters of George Gordon Meade*, 2 Vols. (New York: Charles Scribner's Sons, 1913).

Holman S. Melcher, *With a Flash of His Sword: The Writings of Major Holman S. Melcher 20th Maine Infantry*, William B. Styple, ed. (Kearny, NJ.: Belle Grove Publishing Co., 1994).

W. T. G. Morton, "The First Use of Ether as an Anesthetics," *The Journal of the American Medical Association*, April 23, 1904.

J. W. Muffly, *The Story of Our Regiment: A History of the 148th Pennsylvania Volunteers* (Des Moines, IA: The Kenyon Printing & MFG. Co., 1904).

St. Claire Augustine Mulholland, *The Story of the 116th Pennsylvania Volunteers in the War of the Rebellion: The Record of a Gallant Command*, (Philadelphia, 1899).

Ephraim E. Myers, "Three Years' and Five Months' Experience of an Orange Recruit," *History of the Forty-Fifth Regiment, Pennsylvania Veteran Volunteer Infantry, 1861–1865*, Allen D. Albert, ed. (Williamsport, PA: Grit Publishing Company, 1912).

Frank M. Myers, *The Comanches: A History of White's Battalion, Virginia Cavalry* (Baltimore: Kelly, Piet & Co., Publishers, 1871).

George Michael Neese, *Three Years in the Confederate Horse Artillery* (New York: The Neale Publishing Company, 1911).

Charles L. Peirson, "The Operations of the Army of the Potomac May 7–11, 1864," *The Wilderness Campaign*, Papers of the Military Historical Society of Massachusetts, Vol. IV (Boston: The Military Historical Society of Massachusetts, 1905).

Mark Penrose, *Red, White, and Blue Badge: Pennsylvania Veteran Volunteers A History of the 93rd Regiment, Known as the "Lebanon Infantry" and "One of the 300 Fighting Regiments" From September 12th, 1861 to June 27th, 1865* (Mark Penrose, 1911).

William Thomas Poague, *A Gunner With Stonewall*, Monroe F. Cockrell, ed. (Jackson, TN: McCowat-Mercer Press, 1957).

Horace Porter, *Campaigning With Grant* (New York: Mallard Press, 1991).

Benjamin F. Powelson and Aleck Sweeney, *The History of Company K of the 140th Regiment Pennsylvania Volunteers (1862–'65)* (Steubenville, OH: The Carnahan Printing Company, 1906).

Stephen Dodson Ramseur, *The Bravest of the Brave: The Correspondence of Stephen Dodson Ramseur*, George C. Kundahl, ed. (Chapel Hill, NC: The University of North Carolina Press, 2010).

William Brooke Rawle, *History of the Third Pennsylvania Cavalry*, (Philadelphia: Franklin Printing Company, 1905).

Thomas B. Reed, *A Private in Gray* (Camden, AR: T.B. Reed, 1905).

Robert Robertson, "From the Wilderness to Spotsylvania," *Sketches of War History 1861–1865: Papers Read Before the Ohio Commander of the Military Order of the Loyal Legion of the United States, 1883–1886 Volume I*, (Cincinnati, OH: Robert Clarke & Co., 1888).

Elisha H. Rhodes, *All for the Union* (New York: Orion Books, 1985).

Alfred Seelye Roe and Charles Nutt, *History of the First Regiment of Heavy Artillery, Massachusetts Volunteers, formerly the Fourteenth Regiment of Infantry, 1861–1865* (Boston: Regimental Association, 1917).

Alfred Roe, *The Tenth Regiment Massachusetts Volunteer Infantry 1861–1864: A Western Massachusetts Regiment* (Springfield, MA: Tenth Regiment Veteran Association, 1909).

Morris Schaff, *The Battle of the Wilderness* (Boston: Houghton Mifflin Co., 1910).

Kate M. Scott, *History of the One Hundred and Fifth Regiment of Pennsylvania Volunteers: A Complete History of the Organization, Marches, Battles, Toils, and Dangers participated in by the regiment from the beginning to the close of the war, 1861–1865* (Philadelphia: New-World Publishing Company, 1877).

Abner Small, *The Road to Richmond: The Civil War Letters of Major Abner Small of the 16th Maine Volunteers*, Harold Adams Small, ed. (New York: Fordham University Press, 2000).

John Day Smith, *The History of the Nineteenth Regiment of Maine Volunteer Infantry, 1862–1865* (Minneapolis, Great Western printing company, 1909).

William James Smith, "Just a Little Bit of the Civil War, as Seen by W. J. Smith, Company M, 2nd O.V. Cavalry—Part I," Robert W. Hatton, ed., *Ohio History Journal*, 84 (1975).

G. Moxley Sorrel, *Recollections of a Confederate Staff Officer* (New York: Neale Publishing Company, 1917).

George T. Stevens, *Three Years in the Sixth Corps* (New York: D. Van Nostrand, 1870).

Joshua Thomas Stevenson, *Memorial of Thomas Greely Stevenson, 1836–1864* (Boston: Welch, Bigelow, & Company, 1864).

Robert Stewart, *History of the One Hundred and Fortieth Regiment Pennsylvania Volunteers* (Regimental Association, 1912).

Robert Stiles, *Four Years Under Marse Robert*, (New York, 1903).

George Templeton Strong, *The Diary of George Templeton Strong*, Allan Nevins and Milton Halsey Thomas, eds. (New York: The Macmillan Company, 1952)

Survivors Association, *History of the 118th Pennsylvania Volunteers: The Corn Exchange Regiment* (Philadelphia: J. L. Smith, 1905).

William Swinton, *Campaigns of the Army of the Potomac; a critical history of operations in Virginia, Maryland and Pennsylvania, from the commencement to the close of the war, 1861-5* (New York: C. B. Richardson,1882).

Richard Taylor, *Destruction and Reconstruction: Personal Experiences of the Late War* (New York: Appleton, 1879).

Walter H. Taylor, *Four Years With General Lee*, James I. Robertson, Jr., ed. (Indianapolis: Indiana University Press, 1996).

Walter H. Taylor, *General Lee: His Campaigns in Virginia, 1861–1865* (Lincoln, NE: University of Nebraska Press, 1994).

Third Pennsylvania Cavalry Association, *History of the Third Pennsylvania Cavalry* (Philadelphia: Franklin Printing Co., 1905).

Henry W. Thomas, *History of the Doles-Cook Brigade of Northern Virginia* (Atlanta: The Franklin Printing and Publishing Company, 1903).

O. R. Howard Thompson, *History of the "Bucktails,"* (Philadelphia: Electric Printing Co., 1906).

William Todd, *The Seventy-Ninth Highlanders, New York Volunteers in the War of Rebel-lion, 1861-1865* (Albany, NY: Brandow, Barton & Co.)

Charles Wainwright, *A Diary of Battle*, Allan Nevins, ed. (New York: Da Capo, 1998).

Jane W. Wait, *History of the Wofford Family* (Spartanburg, SC: Band & White Printers, 1928).

Earnest Linden Waitt, *History of the Nineteenth Regiment, Massachusetts Volunteer Infantry, 1861–1865* (Salem, MA: Salem Press, 1906).

Charles Folsom Walcott, *History of the Twenty-first Regiment, Massachusetts Volunteers, in the War for the Preservation of the Union, 1861–1865: With Statistics of the War and of Rebel Prisons* (Boston: Houghton, Mifflin and Company, 1882).

Francis A. Walker, *History of the Second Army Corps in the Army of the Potomac* (New York: C. Scribner's Sons, 1886).

Cyrus B. Watson, "Forty-Fifth Regiment." *Histories of the Several Regiments and Battalions From North Carolina in the Great War, 1861–65,* Walter Clark, ed., Vol. I (Raleigh, NC: State of North Carolina, 1901), 35-61.

Stephen Minot Weld, *War Diary and Letters of Stephen Minot Weld, 1861–1865* (Boston: Massachusetts Historical Society, 1979).

Robert S. Westbrook, *History of the 49th Pennsylvania Volunteers* (Altoona, PA: Altoona Times Print., 1898).

Charles H. Weygant, *History of the One Hundred and Twenty-Fourth Regiment, N.Y.S.V.* (Newburgh, NY: Journal Printing House, 1877).

George F. Williams, *Bullet and Shell* (New York: Forbes, Howard & Hulbert, 1884).

James Harrison Wilson, *Under the Old Flag; Recollections of Military Operations in the War for the Union, the Spanish War, the Boxer Rebellion* (New York: D. Appleton, 1912).

L. A. Wolmer, *History and Roster of Maryland Volunteers, War 1861–1865,* (Baltimore: Guggenheimer, Weil and Col, 1880).

Augustus Woodbury, *Major General Ambrose Burnside and the Ninth Army Corps: A Narrative of the Campaigns in North Carolina Maryland Virginia Ohio Kentucky Mississippi and Tennessee, During the War for the Preservation of the Republic* (Providence, RI: Sidney S. Rider & Brother, 1867).

John H. Worsham, *One of Jackson's Foot Cavalry* (New York: The Neale Publishing Company, 1912).

## Secondary Sources

Edward A. Altemos, *From the Wilderness to Appomattox: The Fifteenth New York Heavy Artillery* (Kent, OH: The Kent State University Press, 2023).

Stephen Ambrose, *Upton and the Army* (Baton Rouge, LA: Louisiana State University Press, 1964).

Mark Boatner, *The Civil War Dictionary* (New York: Random House, 1991).

Gregg S. Clemmer, *Old Alleghany: The Life and Wars of General Ed Johnson* (Staunton, VA: Hearthside Publishing Company, 2004).

Joseph H. Crute, Jr., *Lee's Intrepid Army: A Guide to the Units of the Army of Northern Virginia* (Madison, GA: Southern Lion Books, Inc., 2005).

John F. Cummings III, "The Struggle for and Tragedy of Myer's Hill," *On the Front Line,* Winter 2019.

Wilbur Russell Dunn, *Full Measure of Devotion: The Eighth New York Volunteer Heavy Artillery* (Kearney, NE: Morris Publications, 1997).

Ernest B. Fergerson. *Not War but Murder: Cold Harbor 1864* (New York: Vintage Books, 2001).

David J. Fitzpatrick, *Emory Upton: Misunderstood Reformer* (Norman, OK: University of Oklahoma Press, 2017).

Shelby Foote, *The Civil War: A Narrative, Vol. 1: Fort Sumter to Perryville* (New York: Random House, 1958).

William A. Frassanito, *Grant and Lee: The Virginia Campaigns, 1864–1865* (New York: Macmillan Pub. Co, 1986).

Douglas Southall Freeman, *Lee's Lieutenants, Vol. 1: Manassas to Malvern Hill* (New York: Scribners and Sons, 1970).

Douglas Southall Freeman, *Lee's Lieutenants, Vol. 2: Cedar Mountain to Chancellorsville* (New York: Scribners and Sons, 1970).

Douglas Southall Freeman, *Lee's Lieutenants Volume 3: Gettysburg to Appomattox* (New York: Charles Scribner's Sons, 1970).

Gary W. Gallagher, "Two Generals Who Resist Each Other: Perceptions of Grant and Lee in the Summer of 1864," *Cold Harbor to the Crater: The End of the Overland Campaign* (Chapel Hill: The University of North Carolina Press, 2015).

Bradley Gottfried, *Brigades of Gettysburg: The Union and Confederate Brigades at the Battle of Gettysburg* (Cambridge, MA: Da Capo Press, 2002).

Noel Harrison, *Gazetteer of Historic Sites Related to Fredericksburg and Spotsylvania National Military Park*, Vol. 1 (Fredericksburg and Spotsylvania National Military Park, 1986).

Raymond Herek, *These Men Have Seen Hard Service: The First Michigan Sharpshooters in the Civil War* (Detroit: Wayne State University Press, 1998).

David Jordan, *"Happiness Is Not My Companion": The Life of General G.K. Warren* (Bloomington, IN: Indiana University Press, 2001).

Robert K. Krick, *Lee's Colonels: A Biographical Roster of the Field Officers of the Army of Northern Virginia* (Dayton, OH: Morningside, 1992).

Chris Mackowski, "'Baptism of Fire': The First Maine Heavy Artillery at Harris Farm," *Blue & Gray*, Vol. 26:6, 2011.

Chris Mackowski, *The Great Battle Never Fought: The Mine Run Campaign, November 26–December 2, 1863* (El Dorado Hills, CA: Savas Beatie, 2018).

Chris Mackowski, *Hell Itself: The Battle of the Wilderness, May 5-7, 1864* (El Dorado Hills, CA: Savas Beatie, 2016).

Chris Mackowski and Kristopher D. White, "Second-Guessing Richard Ewell," *Civil War Times*, August 2010.

William Matter, *If It Takes All Summer: The Battle of Spotsylvania* (Chapel Hill, NC: The University of North Carolina Press, 1988).

James McPherson, *Ordeal by Fire: The Civil War and Reconstruction* (Boston: McGraw Hill, 2001).

James B. McPherson, *Tried by War*: Abraham Lincoln as Commander in Chief (New York: Penguin, 2008).

Gregory A. Mertz, "Upton's Attack and the Defense of Doles Salient," *Blue & Gray Magazine*, August 2001.

Gregory A. Mertz, "General Gouverneur K. Warren and the Fighting at Laurel Hill During the Battle of Spotsylvania Court House, May 1864," *Blue & Gray Magazine*, Summer 2004.

Roy Morris, Jr., *Sheridan: The Life and Wars of General Phil Sheridan* (New York: Crown Publishing, 1992).

Donald C. Pfanz, *Richard S. Ewell: A Soldier's Life*, (Chapel Hill: The University of North Carolina Press, 1998).

Harry Pfanz, *Gettysburg: The Second* Day (Chapel Hill, NC: The University of North Carolina Press, 1987).

Carol Reardon, "A Hard Road to Travel: The Impact of Continuous Operations on the Army of the Potomac and the Army of Northern Virginia in May 1864," *The Spotsylvania Campaign*, Gary W. Gallagher, ed. (Chapel Hill, NC: The University of North Carolina Press, 1998).

Gordon C. Rhea, *Carrying the Flag: The Story of Private Charles Whilden, The Confederacy's Most Unlikely Hero* (Basic Books, 2003).

Gordon C. Rhea, *The Battles for Spotsylvania Court House and the Road to Yellow Tavern, May 7–12, 1864* (Baton Rouge, LA: Louisiana State University Press, 1997).

Gordon C. Rhea, *To the North Anna River: Grant and Lee, May 13-25, 1864* (Baton Rouge, LA: Louisiana State University Press, 2000).

James I. Robertson, Jr., *Stonewall Jackson: The Man, The Soldier, The Legend.* (New York: Macmillan, 1997).

Kevin Conley Ruffner, *Maryland's Blue & Gray: A Border State's Union and Confederate Junior Officer Corps* (Baton Rouge, LA: Louisiana State University Press, 1997).

Brooks Simpson, "Lincoln and Grant," *Abraham Lincoln: His Speeches and Writings*, Roy Basler and Carl Sandburg, eds., (New York: Da Capo Press, 2008).

Ernest D. Spisak, *Pittsburgh's Forgotten Civil War Regiment: A History of the 62nd Pennsylvania Volunteer Infantry & The Men Who Served With Distinction* (Tarentum, PA: Word Association Publishers, 2020).

William Thomas Venner, *The 30th North Carolina Infantry in the Civil War: A History and Roster* (Jefferson, NC: McFarland & Company, Inc., 2018).

Ezra J. Warner, *Generals in Blue: Lives of the Union Commanders* (Baton Rouge, LA: Louisiana State University Press, 1964).

Ezra J. Warner, *Generals in Gray: Lives of the Confederate Commanders* (Baton Rouge, LA: Louisiana State University Press, 1959).

Jeffry D. Wert, *Cavalryman of the Lost Cause: A Biography of J.E.B. Stuart* (New York: Simon & Schuster, 2008).

Jeffry D. Wert, *General James Longstreet: The Confederacy's Most Controversial Soldier* (New York: Simon & Schuster, 1993).

Jeffry D. Wert, *The Heart of Hell: The Soldiers' Struggle for Spotsylvania's Bloody Angle* (Chapel Hill: The University of North Carolina Press, 2022).

Alfred Zachry, "Four Shots for the Cause," *Civil War Times Illustrated*, Nov./Dec. 1994.

**Newspapers**

*Albany* (NY) *Atlas & Argus*
*Apollo* (PA) *Sentinel*
*Baltimore* (MD) *Sun*
*Charleston* (SC) *Daily Courier*
*Confederate Veteran*
*Lockport* (NY) *Daily Journal and Courier*
*Montgomery* (AL) *Daily Advertiser*
*National Tribune*
*New York Times*
*Philadelphia* (PA) *Weekly Times*
*Providence* (RI) *Daily Journal*
*Raleigh* (NC) *Weekly Confederate*
*Richmond* (VA) *Sentinel*
*Richmond* (VA) *Times-Dispatch*
Xenia (OH) *Torch-Light*

**Websites**

Archives of Maryland Online: https://msa.maryland.gov
Congressional Medal of Honor Society: www.cmohs.org
Emerging Civil War: www.emergingcivilwar.com
Library of Congress: www.loc.gov
Piney Branch Baptist Church: pineybranchbc.org/about/
U.S. Army Military History Institute: www.carlisel.army.mil/ahec

# Index

# About the Author

Chris Mackowski, Ph.D., is the editor-in-chief and co-founder of Emerging Civil War and the series editor of the award-winning Emerging Civil War Series, published by Savas Beatie. Chris is a writing professor in the Jandoli School of Communication at St. Bonaventure University in Allegany, NY, where he also serves as associate dean for undergraduate programs. He is also historian-in-residence at Stevenson Ridge, a historic property on the Spotsylvania battlefield in central Virginia. He has worked as a historian for the National Park Service at Fredericksburg & Spotsylvania National Military Park, where he gives tours at four major Civil War battlefields (Fredericksburg, Chancellorsville, Wilderness, and Spotsylvania), as well as at the building where Stonewall Jackson died.

Chris has authored or co-authored more than two dozen books and edited a dozen essay collections on the Civil War, and his articles have appeared in all the major Civil War magazines. In 2023, he was honored with the Houston Civil War Round Table's Frank Vandiver Award and also selected as a Copie Hill Fellow at the American Battlefield Trust.